Embodiment

⌠ OXFORD **PHILOSOPHICAL** CONCEPTS ⌡

OXFORD PHILOSOPHICAL CONCEPTS

Christia Mercer, Columbia University
Series Editor

PUBLISHED IN THE OXFORD PHILOSOPHICAL CONCEPTS

Efficient Causation
Edited by Tad Schmaltz

Sympathy
Edited by Eric Schliesser

The Faculties
Edited by Dominik Perler

Memory
Edited by Dmitri Nikulin

Moral Motivation
Edited by Iakovos Vasiliou

Eternity
Edited by Yitzhak Melamed

Self-Knowledge
Edited by Ursula Renz

Embodiment
Edited by Justin E. H. Smith

Dignity
Edited by Remy Debes

FORTHCOMING IN THE OXFORD PHILOSOPHICAL CONCEPTS

Animals
Edited by G. Fay Edwards and Peter Adamson

Evil
Edited by Andrew Chignell

Health
Edited by Peter Adamson

Pleasure
Edited by Lisa Shapiro

Persons
Edited by Antonia LoLordo

Space
Edited by Andrew Janiak

OXFORD PHILOSOPHICAL CONCEPTS

Embodiment

A HISTORY

Edited by Justin E. H. Smith

OXFORD
UNIVERSITY PRESS

OXFORD
UNIVERSITY PRESS

Oxford University Press is a department of the University of Oxford. It furthers
the University's objective of excellence in research, scholarship, and education
by publishing worldwide. Oxford is a registered trade mark of Oxford University
Press in the UK and certain other countries.

Published in the United States of America by Oxford University Press
198 Madison Avenue, New York, NY 10016, United States of America.

© Oxford University Press 2017

All rights reserved. No part of this publication may be reproduced, stored in
a retrieval system, or transmitted, in any form or by any means, without the
prior permission in writing of Oxford University Press, or as expressly permitted
by law, by license, or under terms agreed with the appropriate reproduction
rights organization. Inquiries concerning reproduction outside the scope of the
above should be sent to the Rights Department, Oxford University Press, at the
address above.

You must not circulate this work in any other form
and you must impose this same condition on any acquirer.

Library of Congress Cataloging-in-Publication Data
Names: Smith, Justin E. H., editor.
Title: Embodiment / edited by Justin Smith.
Description: New York : Oxford University Press, 2017. |
Series: Oxford philosophical concepts series | Includes bibliographical references and index.
Identifiers: LCCN 2016033659 (print) | LCCN 2017006030 (ebook) |
ISBN 9780190490454 (pbk. : alk. paper) | ISBN 9780190490447 (cloth : alk. paper) |
ISBN 9780190490478 (online course) | ISBN 9780190490461 (pdf)
Subjects: LCSH: Human body (Philosophy)
Classification: LCC B105.G64 E43 2017 (print) | LCC B105.G64 (ebook) |
DDC 128/.6—dc23
LC record available at https://lccn.loc.gov/2016033659

1 3 5 7 9 8 6 4 2

Paperback printed by Webcom, Inc., Canada
Hardback printed by Bridgeport National Bindery, Inc., United States of America

This book is dedicated to the memory of Helen Lang (1947–2016).

Contents

SERIES EDITOR'S FOREWORD IX
CONTRIBUTORS XI

Introduction 1
JUSTIN E. H. SMITH

1 The Body of Western Embodiment: Classical Antiquity and the Early History of a Problem 17
BROOKE HOLMES

2 Embodied or Ensouled: Aristotle on the Relation of Soul and Body 51
HELEN LANG

3 Beautiful Bodies and Shameful Embodiment in Plotinus's *Enneads* 69
LESLEY-ANNE DYER WILLIAMS

4 Augustinian Puzzles about Body, Soul, Flesh, and Death 87
SARAH CATHERINE BYERS

5 Medieval Jewish Philosophers and the Human Body 109
YOAV MEYRAV

6 Scholastic Philosophers on the Role of the Body in Knowledge 143
RAFAEL NÁJERA

7 Hobbes's Embodied God 171
GEOFFREY GORHAM

8 Leibniz's View of Living Beings: Embodied or Nested Individuals 189
OHAD NACHTOMY

9 Descartes and Spinoza: Two Approaches to Embodiment 215
ALISON PETERMAN

10 Man-Machines and Embodiment: From Cartesian Physiology to Claude Bernard's "Living Machine" 241
PHILIPPE HUNEMAN AND CHARLES T. WOLFE

11 The Embodiment of Virtue: Toward a Cross-Cultural Cognitive Science 277
JAKE H. DAVIS

Reflections

The Devil in the Flesh: On Witchcraft and Possession 299
VÉRONIQUE DECAIX

Phantom Limbs 307
STEPHEN GAUKROGER

Embodied Geometry in Early Modern Theatre 311
YELDA NASIFOGLU

Ghosts in the Celestial Machine: A Reflection on Late Renaissance Embodiment 317
JONATHAN REGIER

The Genotype/Phenotype Distinction 325
EMILY HERRING

BIBLIOGRAPHY 331

INDEX 357

Series Editor's Foreword

Oxford Philosophical Concepts (OPC) offers an innovative approach to philosophy's past and its relation to other disciplines. As a series, it is unique in exploring the transformations of central philosophical concepts from their ancient sources to their modern use.

OPC has several goals: to make it easier for historians to contextualize key concepts in the history of philosophy, to render that history accessible to a wide audience, and to enliven contemporary discussions by displaying the rich and varied sources of philosophical concepts still in use today. The means to these goals are simple enough: eminent scholars come together to rethink a central concept in philosophy's past. The point of this rethinking is not to offer a broad overview, but to identify problems the concept was originally supposed to solve and investigate how approaches to them shifted over time, sometimes radically. Recent scholarship has made evident the benefits of reexamining the standard narratives about western philosophy. OPC's editors look beyond the canon and explore their concepts over a wide philosophical landscape. Each volume traces a notion from its inception as a solution to specific problems through its historical transformations to its modern use, all the while acknowledging its historical context. Each OPC volume is a history of its concept in that it tells a story about changing solutions to its well-defined problem. Many editors have found it appropriate to include long-ignored writings drawn from the Islamic and Jewish traditions and the philosophical contributions of women. Volumes also explore ideas drawn from Buddhist, Chinese, Indian, and other philosophical cultures when doing so adds an especially helpful new perspective. By combining scholarly innovation with focused and astute analysis, OPC encourages a deeper understanding of our philosophical past and present.

One of the most innovative features of Oxford Philosophical Concepts is its recognition that philosophy bears a rich relation to art, music, literature, religion, science, and other cultural practices. The series speaks to the need for informed interdisciplinary exchanges. Its editors assume that the most difficult and profound philosophical ideas can be made comprehensible to a large audience and that materials not strictly philosophical often bear a significant relevance to philosophy. To this end, each OPC volume includes Reflections. These are short stand-alone essays written by specialists in art, music, literature, theology, science, or cultural studies that reflect on the concept from their own disciplinary perspectives. The goal of these essays is to enliven, enrich, and exemplify the volume's concept and reconsider the boundary between philosophical and extraphilosophical materials. OPC's Reflections display the benefits of using philosophical concepts and distinctions in areas that are not strictly philosophical, and encourage philosophers to move beyond the borders of their discipline as presently conceived.

The volumes of OPC arrive at an auspicious moment. Many philosophers are keen to invigorate the discipline. OPC aims to provoke philosophical imaginations by uncovering the brilliant twists and unforeseen turns of philosophy's past.

Christia Mercer
Gustave M. Berne Professor of Philosophy
Columbia University in the City of New York
June 2015

Contributors

SARAH CATHERINE BYERS is an associate professor in the philosophy department at Boston College. She is the author of the monograph *Perception, Sensibility, and Moral Motivation in Augustine: A Stoic-Platonic Synthesis* (Cambridge University Press, UK: 2013) and of articles in, for example, the *Journal of the History of Philosophy*, the *Cambridge History of Moral Philosophy*, the *Routledge Handbook of the Stoic Tradition*, *A Companion to Augustine* (Wiley-Blackwell), and *Augustine's City of God: A Critical Guide* (Cambridge Critical Guides).

JAKE H. DAVIS is a visiting assistant professor at Brown University and Research Associate at New York University. He holds a PhD in Philosophy from CUNY Graduate Center, with an Interdisciplinary Concentration in Cognitive Science, as well as a Master's in Philosophy from the University of Hawai'i. He has authored and coauthored articles at the intersection of Buddhist philosophy, moral philosophy, and cognitive science, and is editor of the forthcoming volume, *"A Mirror is For Reflection": Understanding Buddhist Ethics* (Oxford: OUP).

VÉRONIQUE DECAIX is Associate Professor of Philosophy at the University Paris 1 Panthéon-Sorbonne. She specialized in medieval philosophy. Her research interests are mainly focused on intentionality, the mind-body problem, and the theory of knowledge in the middle Ages. She has also published on ontology and metaphysics. She is currently writing a book on "intentionality as constitutive function of the human mind."

STEPHEN GAUKROGER is Emeritus Professor of History of Philosophy and History of Science at the University of Sydney. His books include *Explanatory Structures* (1978), *Cartesian Logic* (1989), *Descartes: An Intellectual Biography* (1995), *Francis Bacon and the Transformation of Early-Modern Philosophy* (2001), *Descartes' System of Natural Philosophy* (2002), *Le Monde en Images* (2015), and three volumes of a tetralogy: *The Emergence of a Scientific Culture: Science and the Shaping of Modernity, 1210–1685* (2006), *The Collapse of Mechanism and the Rise of Sensibility: Science and the Shaping of Modernity, 1680–1760* (2010), and *The Natural and the Human: Science and the Shaping of Modernity, 1739–1841* (2016).

GEOFFREY GORHAM is Professor and Chair of Philosophy at Macalester College and Resident Fellow at the Minnesota Center for Philosophy of Science, University of Minnesota. He is co-editor of *The Language of Nature: Reassessing the Mathematization of Natural Philosophy in the Seventeenth Century* (University of Minnesota, 2016), and author of *Philosophy of Science: A Beginner's Guide* (One World, 2009) as well as numerous articles on the philosophy and science of Descartes, Hobbes, Newton, and Locke.

EMILY HERRING is a PhD candidate in the School of Philosophy, Religion, and History of Science at the University of Leeds. Her research concerns 20th century evolutionary theories in France and the English-speaking world—in particular, the reception of Henri Bergson's metaphysical take on evolution in biological communities.

BROOKE HOLMES is Robert F. Goheen Professor of the Humanities in the Department of Classics at Princeton University, where she also directs the Interdisciplinary Doctoral Program in the Humanities (IHUM). She is the author of *The Symptom and the Subject: The Emergence of the Physical Body in Ancient Greece* (2010) and *Gender: Antiquity and Its Legacy* (2012), as well as numerous articles on the history of philosophy, the history of medicine, and Greek literature. She has also edited *Aelius Aristides: Between Greece, Rome, and the Gods* (2008), *Dynamic Reading: Studies in the Reception of Epicureanism* (2012), and *The Frontiers of Ancient Science: Essays in Honor of Heinrich von Staden* (2015). She is currently at work on *The Tissue of the World: Sympathy and the Concept of Nature in Greco-Roman Antiquity*; a multiauthored book entitled *Postclassicism*; and two edited projects, *Antiquities beyond Humanism* and *Liquid Antiquity*.

PHILIPPE HUNEMAN is a researcher (*Directeur de recherche*) at the Institut d'Histoire et de Philosophie des Sciences et des Techniques, CNRS/Université Paris I Panthéon Sorbonne. After having worked and published on the constitution of the concept of organism and Kantian metaphysics (including many papers and the book *Métaphysique et biologie* [Paris: 2008]), he currently investigates philosophical issues in evolutionary theory and ecology, such as the emergence of individuality, the relations between variation and natural selection in evolutionary theory, the role of the concept of organism, and the varieties of explanations in ecology. He also wrote several papers on the emergence of modern psychiatry, especially in eighteenth-century France. He was a visiting professor at the University of Chicago (2005) and is affiliated professor to the University of Toronto. His research has been published in *Erkenntnis, Synthese, Philosophy of Science, Biology and Philosophy*, etc. As editor he published *Functions: Selection And Mechanisms* (Synthese Library, Springer, 2012), *From Groups to Individuals. Evolution and Emerging Individuality* (MIT Press, 2013, with Frédéric Bouchard), *Handbook of Evolutionary Thinking in the Sciences* (Springer, 2015 with T. Heams, G. Lecointre, M. Silberstein), and *Challenges to the Modern Synthesis: Development, Inheritance and Adaptation* (Oxford UP, 2016, with D. Walsh) He belongs to the editorial board of the European Journal for Philosophy of Science and is the series coeditor of History, Philosophy and Theory in the Life Sciences (Springer, with T. Reydon and C. Wolfe).

Until her death in 2016, HELEN LANG was a professor of philosophy at Villanova University. She was a specialist in ancient and medieval philosophy and in the history of science, and the author, notably, of *The Order of Nature in Aristotle's Physics: Place and the Elements* (Cambridge, 1998), and *Aristotle's Physics and its Medieval Varieties* (SUNY Press, 1992). She also published, with A. D. Macro, a critical edition and translation of Proclus's *De Aeternitate Mundi* (University of California Press, 2001).

YOAV MEYRAV is a junior faculty member of the Department of Philosophy at Tel Aviv University. He is interested in the transfer of Greek philosophy to the medieval Arabic and Hebrew worlds, Hebrew philosophical terminology, and philosophy of religion. He is currently working on a new critical edition of the complete medieval Hebrew translation and Arabic fragments of Themistius' "Paraphrase of Aristotle's *Metaphysics* 12," lost in Greek. An English translation of Themistius's paraphrase (co-authored with Carlos Fraenkel) is also in preparation.

OHAD NACHTOMY is Associate Professor and head of the philosophy department at Bar-Ilan University, Israel. He works on early modern philosophy, philosophy and history of biology, Wittgenstein's philosophy, and multicultural theory (especially in the Israeli context). His publications include some forty articles and the following books: *Possibility, Agency, and Individuality in Leibniz's Metaphysics* (Springer, 2007); *The Life Sciences in Early Modern Philosophy* (Oxford University Press, 2014) coedited with Justin E. H. Smith; *Machines of Nature and Corporeal Substances in Leibniz* (Springer, 2010), coedited with Justin E. H. Smith; *The Multicultural Challenge in Israel* (Academic Studies Press, 2009) coedited with Avi Sagi; and *Examining Multiculturalism in Israel* (in Hebrew, Magnes Press, 2003).

RAFAEL NÁJERA is a research fellow at the Thomas Institute (University of Cologne). Previously he was a postdoctoral fellow at the Cogut Center for the Humanities and the Department of Philosophy at Brown University, and a visiting scholar at the University of Alberta. He received his PhD from McGill University in 2012. His research focuses on notions of science in the medieval period, both in the Latin and Arabic traditions.

YELDA NASIFOGLU is a research associate at the History Faculty, University of Oxford. With a background in architecture and the history of science, she is interested in the development of the idea of *praxis* in early modern mathematics and architecture. She is currently engaged in research into the dissemination and interpretation of geometry with the AHRC-funded project "Reading Euclid: Euclid's *Elements of Geometry* in Early Modern Britain."

ALISON PETERMAN is Assistant Professor of Philosophy at the University of Rochester. She is especially interested in natural philosophy, metaphysics, and philosophy of mind in the early modern period, and has written articles on the natural philosophy of Spinoza, Leibniz, Descartes, Newton, and Margaret Cavendish.

JONATHAN REGIER is a postdoctoral fellow at the Institute for Advanced Study, The Hong Kong University of Science and Technology. He is a *chercheur associé* with the HPS Laboratory SPHERE (UMR 7219) at France's Centre National de la Recherche Scientifique (CNRS). He did his graduate work at Université Paris Diderot. His thesis and recent publications have focused on natural philosophy and the mathematization of nature in the sixteenth and seventeenth centuries. He is co-editor, with Koen Vermeir, of *Boundaries, Extents and Circulations: Space and Spatiality in Early Modern Natural Philosophy* (2016). He is also pursuing research on the social integration and diffusion of new technologies.

LESLEY-ANNE DYER WILLIAMS received her PhD in Medieval Studies from the University of Notre Dame and is an assistant professor of English at LeTourneau University. She also holds an MPhil in Theology from the University of Cambridge and BA from Baylor University. She specializes in the history of the Platonic tradition in the Middle Ages. Her publications include articles on the works of Anselm of Canterbury, John Wyclif, Peter Abelard, Hilary of Poitiers, and Richard of St. Victor. She is currently finishing the edits on her book, *Eternity and the Summum Bonum in the Twelfth Century,* for the Pontifical Institute of Medieval Studies Press in Toronto.

CHARLES T. WOLFE is a research fellow in the Department of Philosophy and Moral Sciences, Ghent University. He works primarily in history and philosophy of the early modern life sciences, with a focus on materialism and vitalism. He is the author of *Materialism: A Historico-Philosophical Introduction* (2016), and has edited volumes including *Monsters and Philosophy* (2005); *The Body as Object and Instrument of Knowledge* (2010, with O. Gal); *Vitalism and the Scientific Image* (2013, with S. Normandin); and *Brain Theory* (2014). His current project is a monograph on the conceptual foundations of Enlightenment vitalism. He is also the co-editor of the Springer series in History, Philosophy and Theory of the Life Sciences.

Introduction

Justin E. H. Smith

Embodiment—having, being in, or being associated with a body—is a feature of the existence of many entities, perhaps even of all entities. Why entities should find themselves in this condition has often been held to be a philosophical problem. This problem is often seen as including, but also going beyond, the philosophical problem of body—that is, what the essence of a body is, and how, if at all, it differs from matter—but also includes much else besides. On some understandings there may exist bodies, such as stones or asteroids, that are not the bodies of any particular subjects. To speak of embodiment by contrast is always to speak of a subject that finds itself variously inhabiting, or captaining, or being coextensive with, or even being imprisoned in, a body. The subject may in the end be identical to, or an emergent product of, the body—that is, a materialist account of embodied subjects may be the correct one. But insofar as there is a philosophical problem of embodiment, the identity of the embodied subject with the body stands in need of an argument and cannot simply be assumed. The reasons, nature, and consequences of the embodiment of subjects as conceived in the long history of philosophy in Europe as well as in the broader Mediterranean region and in South and East Asia—with forays into religion, art, medicine, and other domains of culture—will be the focus of this volume.

More precisely, the contributors to this volume will seek to shine a light on a number of questions that have animated reflection on embodiment throughout the history of philosophy. What is the historical and conceptual relationship between the idea of embodiment and the idea of subjecthood? Am I who I am principally in virtue of the fact that I have the body I have? Relatedly, what is the relationship of embodiment to being and to individuality? Is embodiment a necessary condition of being? Of being an individual? What are the theological dimensions of embodiment? To what extent has the concept of embodiment been deployed in the history of philosophy to contrast the created world with the state of existence enjoyed by God? What are the normative dimensions of theories of embodiment? To what extent is the problem of embodiment a distinctly western preoccupation? Is it the result of a particular local and contingent history, or does it impose itself as a universal problem, wherever and whenever human beings begin to reflect on the conditions of their existence? Finally, to what extent can natural science help us to resolve philosophical questions about embodiment, many of which are vastly older than the particular scientific research programs we now believe to hold the greatest promise for revealing to us the bodily basis, or the ultimate physical causes, of who we really are?

Many philosophers and theologians have held that embodiment is the consequence of some sort of fall from an originally superior state of either pure mental existence or of a more rarefied, ethereal, or "pneumatic" bodily existence. Sometimes this fall is accounted for in strictly mythological terms. At other times, as in certain tendencies in the

Platonic tradition, the religious background commitment to the inferiority of bodily existence is given a sophisticated elaboration within a metaphysical scheme that assigns differing degrees of reality to different varieties of being in view of their degree of bodiliness—that is, in view of the relative extent to which the body of a being determines its nature or capacities. Often the degree of bodiliness of a being is accounted for in more or less overtly moral terms as the consequence of some sort of failure, transgression, or lapse. Thus the first-century Church Father Origen tells of how, at the beginning of time, the angels circled around God in a completely immaterial state. They were entirely focused on him, but at some point they became distracted, and they began to fall away from him; and as they fell they grew heavier and heavier, and fell faster and faster. To be a bodily thing, and to mistake the world for a world of bodily things, is to be a thing that is distracted from the divine. As Origen explains in his treatise *On First Principles*: "Material substance of this world, possessing a nature admitting of all possible transformations, is, when dragged down to beings of a lower order, moulded into the crasser and more solid condition of a body."[1] Later, the 17th-century Cambridge Platonist Anne Conway would describe bodies as nothing more than "lazy" and "sluggish" spirit.[2]

There is considerable disagreement throughout the history of philosophy as to the extent to which the embodied condition is necessary to a being's existence: are bodily creatures entirely dependent on their bodies? Or is the fact that they are embodied a contingent feature of them? If embodiment is deemed necessary to a creature's existence, moreover, then there arises a related question as to whether the particular conformation of that creature's body determines what that creature itself is, or whether instead there is some identity that endures

---

1 Origen, "On First Principles," in *An Exhortation to Martyrdom, Prayer, and Selected Works*, ed. and tr. Rowan A. Greer (New York: Paulist Press, 1979), 2.2.2.
2 Anne Conway, *Principles of the Most Ancient and Modern Philosophy*, ed. and. tr. Taylor Corse, and Allison P. Coudert (Cambridge, UK: Cambridge University Press, 1996), 29.

beneath all possible bodily transformations. Thus in the seventeenth century there was a lively debate as to whether "monsters"—that is, offspring with serious birth defects, or traits atypical to a species—may nonetheless be said to belong to the same species as their parents. Similarly, there was significant debate about other ways in which bodily conformation—the arrangement of the organs, the shape of the skeleton, but also more evidently superficial features such as the distribution of the hair or the color of the skin—might be the underlying cause of a given being's nature and capacities. Thus the seventeenth-century English anatomist Thomas Willis supposed that the depth of the fissures on the surface of an animal's brain were a direct measure of the complexity of its volitions and actions: a cat's brain is smooth, and correspondingly its nature is relatively simple and its actions relatively predictable, but a human being's brain reveals, in the depth of its fissures, the complexity of human decision-making. Thus Willis writes: "Those Gyrations or Turnings about in [the brains of] four footed beasts are fewer, and in some, as in a Cat, they are found to certain figure and order: wherefore this Brute thinks on, or remembers scarce any thing but what the instincts and needs of Nature suggest."[3]

In a rather more politically charged domain of debate, from the eighteenth century into the middle of the twentieth century many European authors and public figures sought to link human racial inequality to particular physiological differences. In retrospect this was all along little more than an *a posteriori* rationalization of already existing social inequalities, but the belief that it is the body that gives rise to the person, a central commitment of modern naturalism, helped in important ways to make this rationalization appear as a model of sound scientific reasoning. Throughout the history of antiracist thinking in Europe, in turn, we find the view that no physiological feature, such as skin color, could ever serve as a criterion for separating those

---

3 Thomas Willis, *De anima brutorum* (1672), in *Opera omnia* (Geneva: Samuel de Tournes, 1676), 76.

who participate fully in human nature from those who do not. Thus we find in the 1789 memoirs of the freed slave Olaudah Equiano (also known as Gustavus Vassa): "Are there not causes enough to which the apparent inferiority of an African may be ascribed, without limiting the goodness of God, and supposing he forbore to stamp understanding on certainly his own image, because 'carved in ebony'?"[4]

No serious member of the global scientific or philosophical community today takes seriously the possibility of essential racial differences within the human species. But in other ways there is still lively interest in the nature and degree of the connection between forms of embodiment and the variety of human identities. In recent years, perhaps the most important question emerging from reflection on embodiment concerns the extent to which subjectivity is determined by embodiment—that is, the extent to which one's own subjective experience of the world is forged or inflected by the particular sort of body one has. This question arises both in the most abstract philosophical speculation about what it would be like to be equipped with the sort of body no philosopher will ever have—the body of a bat, with its unique sensory apparatus, for example—as well as in more concrete reflection on the way differences within the human species with respect to race, gender, and physical and cognitive ability have an impact upon the way different people navigate through and make sense of the world.

In important respects, newer iterations of the problem share a continuous history with the most ancient ones. Then as now, the fact that human existence and subjective experience require a body, and the fact that the condition of the body largely determines the sort of experiences each of us will have, seem to be in tension with other convictions we have about ourselves—for example that our moral character and cognitive abilities, perhaps even our beauty, should not be dependent

---

4 Olaudah Equiano, *The Interesting Narrative of the Life of Olaudah Equiano, or Gustavus Vassa, The African, Written by Himself*, ed. Werner Sollors (New York: Norton, 2001 [1789]), 31.

upon our mortal and precarious bodies. Much of the history of philosophy may be seen as an attempt to resolve this tension.

So far, we have been paying attention to what might be called the "core" philosophical problems that have animated the discussion of embodiment in the philosophical tradition extending from ancient Greece, through the Christian and Islamic worlds, and into the more secular period of modern European philosophy. There are also several important questions of a contextual and historical nature. To what extent is "the" problem of embodiment in fact only the product of one particular culture's, or historical legacy's, attempt to account for the bodily dimension of human existence? In other words, is embodiment experienced everywhere as a problem, let alone as a philosophical problem? Or are there cultures in which it is not perceived to be of a problematic nature, either because it is simply taken for granted, or indeed because it is not even recognized as a condition of human existence at all? In the rigorous textual traditions of South and East Asian philosophy, we find as much diversity on the topic of embodiment, depending on the school of thought and the historical period in question, as we find in European philosophy: there are materialists who deny that the self is anything apart from the physical body (as in the "unorthodox" Indian school of Carvaka), and there are others who maintain that the body is a fleeting illusion while the true and immaterial self is eternal (as in the "orthodox" Indian school of Samkhya). Beyond the fairly parallel diversity of views that we find in the developed schools of philosophy in Europe and in Asia, as we move further out across the globe we find many examples of cultures that do not seem to take embodiment as a defining feature of human existence, or at least do not conceptualize embodiment in ways that can be easily put into comparison with any of the familiar positions of the Eurasian philosophical traditions.

Unfortunately, the cultural-historical contingency of the problem of embodiment has not been part of the standard approach among philosophers, including historians of philosophy, to the problems that interest us. The situation is rather different in other areas of intellectual history. Thus Sheldon Pollock, writing of the history of Sanskrit literature, pays considerable attention to the parallel history of European Latinity. "There is a natural tendency," Pollock explains, "exhibited even (or especially) in social and cultural theory, to generalize forms of life and experience as universal tendencies and common sense." The way out of this intellectual dead-end is comparison, which "offers an antidote . . . by demonstrating the actual particularity of these apparent universalisms."[5] As to the question that interests us, a comparative approach reveals that embodiment is the product of a mostly local, particular history, with a particular starting point and a possible future end.

Bruno Snell has compellingly shown that Greeks in the age of Homer still lacked a conception of the body (see Brooke Holmes's chapter in the present volume for a critical engagement with Snell's argument), and that such a conception would only appear at the moment the complementary notion of spirit took shape. On this view, in order to think of oneself as being embodied, one must first come to think of oneself as some sort of immaterial, or at least pneumatic, subject capable of being embodied. Yet many thinkers and traditions of thought have also imagined subjects without bodies—that is, the idea of spirit does not always lead to an idea of embodied spirit. This much is particularly clear from what is often called "dualism," a doctrine associated with a number of modern European philosophers, and above all with Descartes. The ability to conceptualize spirit independently of body has often been taken to be a singular attainment of abstract reflection, as a thinking away from the givens of perceptual experience. Notwithstanding Snell's thesis, it has generally been supposed in and of the western philosophical tradition

---

5 Sheldon Pollock, *The Language of the Gods in the World of Men: Sanskrit, Culture, and Power in Premodern India* (Berkeley: University of California Press, 2006), 259.

that we *start* with the obviousness of the body, and we *discover* the secret of the spirit through great effort (and perhaps some assistance from divine sources).

This may be a case of hasty self-congratulation. Sometime in the 1920s, the French Catholic missionary and ethnographer Maurice Leenhardt found himself in conversation with a Melanesian acquaintance named Boesoou. Leenhardt suggested that as a result of contact with Europeans, the Kanaks of Melanesia had been introduced in their thinking to the notion of spirit. Boesoou protested: "Spirit? Bah! You didn't bring us spirit. We already knew about the existence of spirit. We always acted in accordance with spirit. What you brought is the body."[6] Why, now, does Boesoou's observation strike us as counterintuitive? We seem to suppose that, whereas our mental faculties are something that need to be discovered through a process of reflection, undertaken only by adults, or by the learned, or by members of certain "advanced" cultures, our embodiment is something immediate, certain, and obvious to any sentient creature, even those presumed to be incapable of reflection.

It may be that the order of obviousness here is not simply dictated by our primary experience, but rather is conditioned by what we might identify as a historical ontology: the history of the way people talk about the basic elements of reality. But what, we may ask in turn, would it be like to be born into a different ontological legacy, such as the Melanesian, in which, if Boesoou is to be believed, the notion of one's own embodiment does not arise? Could it really be that under these circumstances one would not even notice one's own embodiment? Now of course there are Melanesian words for "hand" and "foot" and "torso," and no one wants to say that until the missionaries came the Kanaks never noticed that they were be-torsoed, be-footed, etc. The suggestion seems to be rather that it was an imported European idea,

---

6 Maurice Leenhardt, *Do kamo. la personne et le mythe dans le monde mélanésien* (Paris: Gallimard, 1947), 212.

whatever the evangelists may have wanted to teach about the immortal and saveable soul, that beings are as it were made up out of body parts integrated into a whole, physical self.

The evidence from the Americas is particularly compelling. From the very earliest encounters between two broad philosophical world views—the Spanish Christian-Aristotelian and the Native American—we see a reciprocal confusion about the basic ontological commitments held by the people on the other side. Thus Claude Lévi-Strauss tells in his *Race and History* of 1952 of the Indigenous peoples of the Caribbean, who in the 16th century "were busy drowning white prisoners in order to determine, through extended observation, whether their cadaver was or was not subject to putrefaction."[7] The common gloss on this by now well-documented reciprocal misunderstanding has it that while the Europeans often suspected the Native Americans of being animals, the Americans in turn took the Europeans for gods, and therefore had trouble believing that the Europeans' bodies were in fact bodies in the normal, biological sense. This is a partially adequate characterization, but of course in it we are constrained to understand "god" in terms that flatter the Europeans.

It would be somewhat more accurate to say, following Eduardo Viveiros de Castro, that the encounter was a clash of two different forms of ethnocentrism, or, to put it differently, of two different "ontological regimes."[8] In the European regime, the soul is the "marked dimension," the element that must be there in order for some being that is held up for candidacy in the human species to qualify as a human being. But for the Europeans the bodiliness of any such candidate-being is never in question: the body is the part that is certain. For the Native Americans

---

[7] Claude Lévi-Strauss, "Race et histoire," in *Anthropologie structurale deux* (Paris: Plon, 1973 [1952]), 384.
[8] Eduardo Viveiros de Castro, *Métaphysiques cannibales. Lignes d'anthropologie post-structurale*, tr. Oiara Bonilla (Paris: Presses Universitaires de France, 2009), 16.

by contrast there is never any doubt that the Europeans have souls, and yet this in itself does not qualify them as human beings—it must also be determined whether their apparent bodies are real bodies.

We all have the reflex, now, of denouncing as absurd the Spanish conquistador's doubt as to the full humanity of the Native Americans he was in the course of conquering. In retrospect, we are able to see that this doubt arose from rather provincial ontological commitments, or, to put this another way, we are easily able to unmask the ontology as mere ethnocentrism. But the overwhelming nature of the conquest has occluded from our view the fact that there was also a Native perspective on the Europeans—that the Native Americans asked themselves questions about the nature of the Europeans, questions that were in their own way motivated by nonuniversal ontological commitments. To the extent that these commitments can be recovered, what we find when we study them is that the European philosophical model of the human being as essentially a soul that is embodied within a corporeal home or prison, and that is wrapped up with it in varying degrees of intimacy but never identical with it, is not a universal tendency, nor simple common sense. It is the product of a particular, local history, which just happens to be the local history that would overflow its traditional boundaries, conquer the world by force, and, in time, impose its own philosophy curriculum.

These brief considerations of the broader global context of our topic will be the furthest we will stray from the more familiar, and more explicitly and self-consciously philosophical, traditions of Europe, the Mediterranean, and Asia. Yet however brief, they are nonetheless important to bear in mind, as they confirm for us that indeed there is no single, context-independent problem of embodiment, but rather only different cultural responses to the bodily dimensions of human existence.

There is one approach to embodiment that might inspire hope of moving beyond the contingencies of local tradition, and arriving at a clearer understanding of those dimensions of it that are relevant in all places and times. This approach, namely, is the scientific approach. Whatever one's ontological commitments about the relationship between the self and the body, it seems undeniable that laboratory studies on, say, the perception of phantom limbs, or on so-called out-of-body experiences, or the connection between electrical stimulation to the brain and experience of the bodily presence of strictly non-present beings, might all help us to gain a better understanding of the problem of embodiment in a context-neutral way. We tend to suppose that the sort of understanding scientific research yields is relevant for all of humanity, no matter what the beliefs of the people being studied might be. If an MRI scan shows that a person having an extracorporeal experience undergoes, among other things, a severe deactivation of the visual cortex, we may be confident that such a change of brain state is part of the context-independent, universally true account of what an extracorporeal experience is. But it remains the case that different culturally informed philosophical commitments will cause different people who have such experiences to interpret them differently, no matter what the MRI technicians have to say. For this reason, we must suppose that neuroscience can be part of the philosophical study of a topic like embodiment, but must never set itself up as offering the definitive answer to the philosophical questions that caused us to take an interest in neuroscience in the first place. Thus some of the most interesting philosophical investigations of embodiment in recent years, such as Jake Davis's contribution to the present volume, consider it precisely at the point of intersection between contemporary experimental science and the varieties of cultural interpretation offered for the phenomena that are of interest to experimental science.

The concept of embodiment, as we have begun to see, is deeply rooted in history and extends through all the major periods of philosophy in both Europe and Asia. In this volume we cover most of this vast history, from Homer in deepest antiquity to the physiological studies of Claude Bernard and others in the nineteenth century and on to some of the most recent issues at the boundary between philosophy and neuroscience. Throughout we see an abiding interest among philosophers in the relationship between body and self, and in those fundamental questions that run like a leitmotif throughout so much of the history of philosophical reflection: Do I have a body? If so, what is this "I" that is distinct from the body? Am I essentially or only contingently a bodily thing? And so on.

In the early period of philosophical reflection, these questions were not yet given articulate expression. A number of historical and conceptual preconditions needed first to take shape. In particular, as Brooke Holmes contends in the initial chapter of the volume, "in order for the problem to arise, a concept of the body as material and physical and, so, in some sense other to the embodied person—is required." Holmes argues that there is good reason to believe that these preconditions emerged in Greece in the fifth and fourth centuries BCE, and her contribution helps us to see precisely what was at stake in that context, and in turn how this chapter of the history of the concept would help to shape the entire subsequent debate in the millennia to follow.

As becomes very clear in the contributions from Helen Lang, by the third century BCE the concept of body had come to the center of the most profound philosophical debates concerning the nature of substance and so also the nature of natural beings in general. Within the context of Aristotle's hylomorphic metaphysics, a key question became that of determining whether it is more accurate to speak of the form as being embodied, or rather of the matter of the body as being informed or ensouled. If there is in fact no priority at all that can be found here, then how can we speak of embodiment as if it were a process? As we see in the contributions of Lesley-Anne Dyer Williams and Sarah Byers, in turn, in later philosophy influenced by Plato as well as in the Christianized Aristotelianism of Augustine, the concept of bodiliness becomes increasingly associated with the degraded state of earthly beings, and most significantly of human beings: a state that will be conceptualized in Christian philosophy in terms of sin. In the later Middle Ages, in turn, as Rafael Nájera adeptly shows, angels become centrally implicated in philosophical reflections on the precise nature of the embodied condition—this both for theological reasons, but also, following an insight of Dominik Perler, because angelology had become a fertile domain for the testing of thought experiments on hypothetical beings, experiments that admit of no empirical refutation and that may thus be freely developed according only to the exigencies of conceptual possibility.[9] In medieval Jewish philosophy, meanwhile, as Yoav Meyrav shows, discussions of the human body were often focused on day-to-day regulation of conduct, and thus often seemed to go off in very different directions than the Greco-Arabic-Christian traditions. And yet the doctrinal pressures on philosophical discussion also yielded up innovative ways of attempting to reduce the apparent ontological distance between body and mind.

In the early modern period, with angels now largely withdrawn from the center of philosophical attention, God will in turn emerge at the center of debates about bodiliness. As Geoffrey Gorham discusses in his contribution, if one believes, as Thomas Hobbes does, that everything that is is a body, then how can one remain committed to the existence of a Supreme Being who is supposed, by definition, to be beyond all bodily existence? Does Hobbes's commitment not compel him to accept atheism? As Gorham shows, in fact Hobbes is able to access a long tradition of somewhat unorthodox, yet not completely heretical or marginal, theological thinking in order to make sound philosophical sense of his belief in God's embodiment, a belief that will in turn continue to echo in much later theology, not least that of the American Mormons.

Another feature of much early modern discussion of embodiment, as seen for example in Spinoza and in Leibniz, is the widespread view that what we think of as "being in a body" can in fact be analyzed,

---

[9] See Dominik Perler, "Thought Experiments: The Methodological Function of Angels in Late Medieval Epistemology," in *Angels in Medieval Philosophical Inquiry: Their Function and Significance*, eds. Isabel Iribarren and Martin Lenz (Aldershot, UK: Ashgate, 2008), 143–154.

in metaphysical rigor, as a certain mode of perception of the world. That is, bodiliness is the perception of the world through a body, and it just is the nature of what we think of as bodily beings, or, which is the same thing, of corporeal substances, to perceive the world in this way. But a number of philosophical puzzles arise from this basic view. As Alison Peterman discusses, there appear to be some deep tensions between Spinoza's central belief that "the mind is the idea of the body," on the one hand, and his view, for example, that mind and body are one and the same thing. Peterman argues in fact that Descartes and Spinoza each approach the embodiment question from two different directions: one approach starts with some metaphysical commitments about the kinds of entities, properties, and interactions there are in the world, and the other starts by attending to the experience of an embodied subject. These problems continue in the philosophy of Leibniz, but are in turn rendered vastly more complex, as Ohad Nachtomy shows, in view of Leibniz's theory of the infinite hierarchical nestedness of substances implicated in the bodies of natural beings.

Leibniz's metaphysics of corporeal substance anticipates, in surprising ways, the monistic and vitalistic materialism of the eighteenth and nineteenth centuries, which will be the focus of the next chapter. Here, as Charles Wolfe and Philippe Huneman show, the insight that all parts of a living being appear to contain the principle that explains and makes possible the organization of all other parts, tends to lead, willy-nilly, to a view of living beings simply as masses of living stuff, as quantities of vital matter that may be separated and recombined in new ways, without any underlying principles of unity of the sort Leibniz had defended until the end of his career. This vitalistic monism, Wolfe and Huneman show, would prove to be a very useful theoretical supposition for the advancement of physiological research, yet it left many philosophical questions about the nature of embodiment unresolved.

The volume concludes with Jake H. Davis's discussion, already mentioned, of some of the recent scientific study of the cognitive basis of embodied ethics, while also contextualizing this research against the broad historical and cross-cultural background of ethical theory in the Aristotelian, Confucian, and Buddhist traditions. The volume also features several shorter contributions, "Reflections," on topics in the history of thinking about embodiment that approach it from domains of culture somewhat outside of, though still connected to, philosophy in the strict sense. Thus Véronique Decaix tells us about the special problems of the embodiment of witches in early modern Europe, while Stephen Gaukroger discusses the medical and phenomenological problem of phantom limbs. Yelda Nasifoglu treats the history of theatre, uncovering a peculiar forgotten play in which the main characters are geometrical shapes. Jonathan Regier discusses the question of the embodiment of celestical bodies in Renaissance cosmology, while Emily Herring treats the history of the genotype/phenotype distinction in biology as a case study in thinking about the relationship between outer bodily expression and inner code or program.

The history of the concept of embodiment, as spelled out here, begins with what we might call naive moral philosophy (i.e., "What sort of thing am I?") and weaves from there through metaphysics, theology, angelology, back through metaphysics, and finally into the science of physiology. What is remarkable is that the problem can enter into so many apparently very different domains while still appearing recognizably as the same problem. This is what is perhaps the most valuable aspect of a concept such as embodiment, which makes its longue durée historical study so important: that it unites disciplines that subsequent historiography strives to keep separate, and brings back into view the occluded connections between them.

CHAPTER ONE

The Body of Western Embodiment

CLASSICAL ANTIQUITY AND THE EARLY HISTORY OF A PROBLEM

Brooke Holmes

1. Introduction

The state of being embodied requires, first, a body to be in. How one interprets the logistics of "in" is a question I set aside for now in order to focus on the more basic belief that a person is not synonymous with his or her body but, instead, *has* a body. The idea that we all have bodies is deeply ingrained in European traditions of thought. As Bernard Williams writes in a study of early Greek notions of the self, "we do indeed have a concept of a body, and we agree that each of us has a body."[1] The "we" in question need not in fact be restricted to "we Westerners." The anthropologist Philippe Descola has claimed that all human cultures recognize a duality between "interiority" and

---

1 Bernard Williams, *Shame and Necessity* (Berkeley: University of California Press, 1993), 26.

"physicality," where the former corresponds to something like mind (intentionality, subjectivity, reflexivity, feelings, ability to express oneself and dream) and the latter not just to external form or material being but "the whole set of visible and tangible expressions of the dispositions peculiar to a particular entity when those dispositions are reputed to result from morphological and physiological characteristics that are intrinsic to it."[2] Developmental psychologists have argued that dualist intuitions are innate to all human beings.[3] It is admittedly hard to shake the worry that the dualisms being ascribed to cultures and children by these researchers remain caught within the terms of a peculiarly western dualism. Nevertheless, the experience of consciousness makes it equally hard to doubt that some perception of difference between what we sense of ourselves and what we see of ourselves as actors in the world is part of being human.

When we speak of the body, however, we mean something more specific and narrow than Descola's "physicality." In one important sense, we mean an object of specialized scientific knowledge—biological, medical, neurological, and so on—that is not immediately available to the understanding and unmediated control of the person to whom this body belongs. If bodies are objects it is because they are governed by the same kinds of principles or laws that govern other physical objects, and not the codes of behavior proper to the social sphere or, at least transparently, the logic of thought. The discontinuities between the body understood in these terms and a mind, soul, or self give rise to a broad but coherent set of problems that are at once aesthetic, metaphysical,

---

[2] Philippe Descola, *Beyond Nature and Culture*, trans. Janet Lloyd (Chicago: University of Chicago Press, 2013), 116. See also Michael Lambek, "Body and Mind in Mind, Body and Mind in Body: Some Anthropological Interventions in a Long Conversation," in *Bodies and Persons: Comparative Perspectives from Africa and Melanesia*, eds. M. Lambek and A. Strathern (Cambridge, UK: Cambridge University Press, 1998), 103–123.

[3] Paul Bloom, *Descartes' Baby: How the Science of Child Development Explains What Makes Us Human* (New York: Basic Books, 2004); R. A. Richert and P. L. Harris, "The Ghost in My Body: Children's Developing Concept of the Soul," *Journal of Cognition and Culture* 6.3–4 (2006): 409–427.

religious, epistemological, and ethical problems around the [relation]ship of these two parts of the person to one another; substant[ial dif]ferences; the difficulties of knowing the body in all its aspects; and [the] potentially problematic influence of the body on the mind or soul (less frequently, vice versa).

Many of these problems first take shape with the conceptualization of the physical or biological body and its relationship to the person or "true self" in classical (fifth- and fourth-century BCE) Greece and, more specifically, in the Hippocratic medical texts and the writings of Plato. That is not to say that all the philosophical problems we associate with the body appear like Athena from the head of Zeus in the fifth century BCE, as the other essays in this volume make clear.[4] It is only in Aristotle, for example, that the question starts to gain traction of how body and soul or body and mind relate. Socrates' claims about the corporeality of the soul in Plato's *Phaedo* are more ethical than ontological.[5] Still it is easy to lose sight of the forest for the trees. We are often so focused on locating the origins of the "modern" body (e.g., in Descartes or the clinic) or tracing points of similarity or difference

---

4 See Wallace I. Matson, "Why Isn't the Mind-Body Problem Ancient?" in *Mind, Matter, and Method: Essays in Philosophy and Science in Honor of Herbert Feigl*, eds. Paul K. Feyerabend and Grover Maxwell (Minneapolis: University of Minnesota Press, 1968), 92–102. Matson argues for the absence in Greek philosophy of what goes by the name of the "mind-body" problem in modern philosophy, although he arrives at his position by defining that problem fairly narrowly. Framed as a larger question of causal interaction, the mind-body problem takes off with Aristotle and his Hellenistic successors. See also Christof Rapp, "Interaction of Body and Soul: What the Hellenistic Philosophers Saw and Aristotle Avoided," in *Common to Body and Soul: Philosophical Approaches to Explaining Living Behaviour in Greco-Roman Antiquity*, ed. R. A. H. King (Berlin: Walter de Gruyter, 2006), 187–208.

5 On questions of causal interaction between body and soul in Aristotle's psychology, see Stephen Menn, "Aristotle's Definition of the Soul and the Programme of the *De anima*," *Oxford Studies in Ancient Philosophy* 22 (2002): 82–139. For a comparison of Plato and Descartes that touches on the difference between ethical and ontological concerns, see Sarah Broadie, "Soul and Body in Plato and Descartes," *Proceedings of the Aristotelian Society* 101 (2001): 295–308, esp. 299–300; see also G. R. Carone, "Mind and Body in Late Plato," *Archiv für Geschichte der Philosophie* 87 (2005): 227–269. While questions about the soul's substance and corporeality are murky in Plato, they become important questions to the ancient philosophical tradition, especially after claims about the corporeality of soul become more precise in the Stoics and Epicureans.

in the formulation of the mind-body problem that we take the category of the physical body itself for granted, forgetting that it, too, has a genealogy. We are still too much under the sway of Descartes and his understanding of body in terms of *res extensa* to appreciate that the physical body is not a three-dimensional object always already there. It is better understood as what I have elsewhere called a "conceptual object," by which I mean an object inferred through signs as much as it is encountered phenomenologically and so an object embedded in frameworks of interpretation and the dynamics of history.[6] The physical body is not timeless. It crystallizes as an object of thought and praxis in ancient Greece. The philosophical puzzles that have clustered around embodiment therefore have deep roots in Greek medicine and philosophy.

In this essay, I want to sketch the emergence of the physical body (*sōma*) as a conceptual object in fifth- and fourth-century BCE medical writing and the Platonic dialogues on the grounds that a better understanding of this story can shed light on how the problem of embodiment developed in later ancient and European philosophy.[7] I also suggest that the conceptualization of the body helps motivate the conceptualization of the soul as the locus of the person, which is defined in an important way as *not*-body. My approach to "embodiment" thus analyzes the idea of "body" as a locus for a self or person seen as not entirely coincident with the body but also as a dynamic force-field that produces and disrupts conscious experience.[8] In the texts I examine

---

[6] The equation of body with extension occurs already in antiquity but it is not the dominant meaning and in some contexts it is entirely misplaced—as, for example, in readings of *asōmatos* at Melissus Fr. 9 (Diels-Kranz) (see Brooke Holmes, *The Symptom and the Subject: The Emergence of the Physical Body in Ancient Greece* [Princeton, NJ: Princeton University Press, 2010], 101–108; on the phrase "conceptual object," see 9–19). See also Helen Lang, "Plato on Divine Art and the Production of Body," in *The Frontiers of Ancient Science: Essays in Honor of Heinrich von Staden*, eds. B. Holmes and K.-D. Fischer (Berlin: Walter de Gruyter, 2015), 307–338.

[7] I have defended these claims at greater length in Holmes, *The Symptom and the Subject*.

[8] In other words, I have tried to use the historical category of body that I examine here to construct the idea of embodiment, rather than adopt a definition of embodiment developed for

here all too briefly, embodiment represents a new way of being in the world compared to what we can determine of archaic Greek concepts of personhood and physicality. To the extent that it represents a way of being that entails new risks, embodiment also calls for new techniques of control.

To home in on classical Greece as a point of origin for the dualisms that come to shape European philosophy is by no means an unpracticed move. But most scholars do not see the body as a concept that had to be theorized. Williams claims that we all have a concept of the body in order to draw a contrast with the history of the soul: "We do not, *pace* Plato, Descartes, Christianity, and Snell, all agree that we each have a soul. Soul is, in a sense, a much more speculative or theoretical conception than body."[9] That the soul is something requiring conceptual effort and so subject to historical discovery is a position that Williams shares with Bruno Snell, who articulates a story of the soul's discovery in archaic and classical Greece in his classic but controversial *Discovery of the Mind*.[10] But Williams and Snell also disagree on an important point. Whereas Williams takes the body as always given, Snell argues that Homer, taken as metonymic of early Greek thought, lacks not only a concept of the soul but also a concept of the body. This is because for Snell, there can be no concept of body without a concept of soul.

I begin this chapter by briefly reconsidering the merits of Snell's claims about the absence of body in Homer. I try to deepen these claims by sketching the model of the person that we do find in

---

etic application to a wide range of historical periods and cultures. For such a definition, see, for example, T. Csordas, "Somatic Modes of Attention," *Cultural Anthropology* 8.2 (1993): 135–156, 135 (embodiment is "an indeterminate methodological field defined by perceptual experience and the mode of presence and engagement in the world" against the body understood as "a biological, material entity"); see also Lambek, "Body and Mind in Mind, Body and Mind in Body."

9 Williams, *Shame and Necessity*, 26.

10 Bruno Snell, *The Discovery of the Mind*, trans. T. Rosenmeyer (Oxford: Blackwell, 1953).

Homer. I turn in the next section to the corpus of approximately sixty medical texts ascribed to Hippocrates since the Hellenistic period as a resource for examining the formation of a concept of a body defined as having a nature (*physis*). These texts range from formal taxonomies of disease to more theoretical works on human nature, embryology, and environmental determinism, with many texts combining theoretical and practical elements.[11] They nonetheless share an understanding of the physical body as nonconscious and harboring a wide range of impersonal forces (*dynameis*) that are invested with causal power over mental states, character, and ethical judgment while largely resisting control from the mind or soul. The control of the body is instead mediated by the interpretation of symptoms and technical interventions in the mixture of the body's constituent stuffs, ideally supervised by physicians.

It is in fact misleading to suggest that the physical body is an object that preexists the interpretation of symptoms and practical interventions. More accurately, it is through inferences based on signs that the physical body, imagined as a concealed interior populated by impersonal forces, comes into visibility—hence its status as a conceptual object. In the same way, a body defined by its nature is realized through the practices designed to act on that nature. For this reason, the body's nature has to be seen within a dynamic field of action and reaction.[12]

The reliance of physicians on interpretation and praxis is one reason why medical texts are so important to a philosophical history of bodies

---

[11] For a general introduction to the Hippocratic Corpus, see Jacques Jouanna, *Hippocrates*, trans. M. DeBevoise (Baltimore: The Johns Hopkins University Press, 1999); Elizabeth Craik, *The "Hippocratic" Corpus: Content and Context* (London: Rouledge, 2014).

[12] The remarks of Annemarie Mol on a "praxiographic ontology," developed in relationship to a study of atherosclerosis in a modern Dutch hospital, are useful here. See Annemarie Mol, *The Body Multiple: Ontology in Medical Practice* (Durham, NC: Duke University Press, 2002). On the praxis-focus in ancient medicine, see S. De Hart, "Hippocratic Medicine and the Greek Body Image," *Perspectives on Science* 7 (1999): 349–382.

and embodiment.[13] For they show the physical body emerging not as an abstract or isolated object of analysis but as a dynamic, layered, and vulnerable object located between two subjects, one who is inside the body but does not coincide with it (that is, the patient), and one who sees and affects the body from outside of it (that is, the physician).[14] These perspectives are not given equal weight in our texts. The physician has reasons for minimizing the epistemic value of embodied experience even as he appropriates subjective symptoms for expert analysis. The patient only regains control over his body, almost invariably figured as unstable or potentially unstable in the medical writings, by adopting the knowing position of the physician vis-à-vis his own body.[15] These self-reflexive techniques of mastery have a significant impact on the tradition of philosophical ethics and its techniques of caring for the soul.[16] The impact is especially visible in the medical analogy in philosophical ethics, which formalizes the body as the model object

---

13 They are also important simply because we lack so much Presocratic biological writing. That the discussions of the body and disease that we see in the extant medical texts exist on a continuum with discussions by those who would have defined their expertise as concerning nature more generally is confirmed by the list of theories (attributed largely to named figures who would now be classified as sophists and philosophers) in the Peripatetic medical doxography *Anonymus Londinensis*. Still, we must be careful about turning to the medical texts simply to plug the hole in our more philosophical sources, thereby losing sight of the importance of a praxis-oriented perspective to the conceptualization of the physical body.

14 I am here arguing that the importance of a medical context to the crystallization of the physical body plays an important role in its later fate in the philosophical and ethical tradition, as well as the learned medical tradition, but I would not want to imply that there are not other ways of imagining the body or being embodied that coexist with these in the ancient world. Barbara Duden has shown how the assumed schemas by which bodies are lived are slow to change, especially outside elite circles. See Duden, *The Woman Beneath the Skin*, trans. T. Dunlap (Cambridge, MA: Harvard University Press, 1991), esp. 37, 179–184. De Hart makes stronger claims on behalf of medicine's impact on lived body images in classical Greece. See De Hart, "Hippocratic Medicine and the Greek Body Image."

15 The "his" is not generic here. Male patients are the primary subjects of self-care in the corpus: see Lesley Dean-Jones, "The Politics of Pleasure: Female Sexual Appetite in the Hippocratic Corpus," *Helios* 19 (1992): 72–91.

16 On medical analogy in the classical period and Plato, see Brooke Holmes, "Body, Soul, and the Medical Analogy in Plato," in *When Worlds Elide: Classics, Politics, Culture*, eds. J. Peter Euben and Karen Bassi (Lanham, MD: Lexington, 2010), 345–385 and Holmes, *The Symptom and the Subject: The Emergence of the Physical Body in Ancient Greece*, ch. 5. For Aristotle and the Hellenistic period,

of care even as it marks the limits of the body—and, by extension, medicine—with regard to the person and establishes the soul as a more valuable object of attention, as we will see in the third section. In short, the strong role of medicine in defining what it means to be located in a physical body and what it means to control that body no doubt contributes significantly to the body's status in the later tradition as an opaque, alien, and unstable object requiring practices of care known first and foremost to experts.

The importance of expert knowledge brings us back to the idea that a body can be known and manipulated, even in its hidden recesses, precisely because it has a nature. Indeed, a number of Hippocratic texts suggest that the whole of human nature might be understood through the study of the physical body. Their ambitions draw attention to some of the insufficiencies within an explanatory apparatus populated exclusively by material stuffs and their capacities. It is in part by recognizing these limits that subsequent philosophers may have been moved to speculate about what is, if not incorporeal, at least *other* than body in human nature, soul or mind—that is, to carve out a psychology within the domain of physiology mapped by the medical writers and others working in the "inquiry into nature" tradition. In a famous passage from Plato's *Phaedo*, Socrates complains about explanations of human behavior in terms of "ridiculous" things like hot, cold, wet, and dry. I would not be sitting here in jail if it were up to my sinews and joints, he says. Rather, I am here because the Athenians have deemed it best to condemn me, and I deem it best to undergo whatever penalty they order.[17] Socrates' demand comes out

---

see Martha Nussbaum, *The Therapy of Desire* (Princeton, NJ: Princeton University Press, 1993). On ancient philosophy and "the care of the self," see Pierre Hadot, *Exercices spirituels et philosophie antique*, 2nd ed. (Paris: Études Augustiniennes, 1987), partially translated in Pierre Hadot, *Philosophy as a Way of Life: Spiritual Exercises from Socrates to Foucault*, trans. M. Chase (Cambridge, MA: Wiley-Blackwell, 1995); see also Michel Foucault, *The History of Sexuality, Volume II: The Use of Pleasure*, trans. R. Hurley (New York: Pantheon, 1985); and Michel Foucault, *The History of Sexuality, Volume III: The Care of the Self*, trans. R. Hurley (New York: Pantheon, 1986).

17 Plato, *Phaedo* 98e1ff.

of his frustration with what we would call a reductively materialist (here Anaxagorean) model. What he wants is an account that takes mind and ultimately the Good as an independent causal factor rather than as a product of conditions in the body or a physical stuff (e.g., blood, air).

Socrates' complaint hints again at weaknesses in the standard narrative that starts with the "discovery" of the soul or mind and either neglects the body altogether or radically subordinates its history to that of the soul. The evidence is not as abundant as one would like. But it seems more likely that the converse is true: medico-philosophical attempts to explain human nature via the body—and their limits—end up driving speculation about soul and mind as alternative sites of the "true" self. The problem is that, in developing models of soul and mind that are relatively autonomous vis-à-vis the body, philosophers face the difficulties of reestablishing continuities between body and soul (and body and mind). Plato rightly occupies a seminal place in the tradition of embodiment because of the very strong opposition that he develops between soul and body. Yet Plato, like thinkers before him, also leaves open the question of the "common ground" (*koinōnia*) between soul and body, as Aristotle complains in the *De anima*.[18] Aristotelian hylomorphism may or may not solve the problem in the eyes of contemporary philosophers. It is, at any rate, historically an unstable solution—hence the tenacious problem of bodies and souls and bodies and minds in western philosophy.[19] It is not the task of this chapter to track these difficulties. In the last section, however, I turn to Plato as the first major philosopher to grapple with the stakes of embodiment after the emergence of the physical body.

---

18 Aristotle, *De anima* 407b13-26. On Plato's reticence about the *koinōnia* of body and soul see Brian Dillon, "How Does the Soul Direct the Body, After All? Traces of a Dispute on Mind-Body Relations in the Old Academy," in *Body and Soul in Ancient Philosophy*, eds. Dorothea Frede and Burkhard Reis (Berlin: Walter de Gruyter, 2009), 349–356.

19 On Aristotelian hylomorphism, see Lang in this volume.

2. The *Sōma* in Homer

Snell begins *The Discovery of the Mind* by making a philological argument with far-reaching consequences. Each of the eight instances of *sōma* in the two Homeric epics, he establishes, refers to a dead body.[20] In the absence of another word that could be translated as "body," Snell argues that Homer lacked a word to designate a unified, living body and, therefore, he concludes, in Sapir-Whorf fashion, that he lacked the concept of the unified, living body.

Snell's argument has been attacked from a number of different angles—philological, linguistic, philosophical. Much of the resistance is driven by the difficulty of imagining a person without a body. Some of the critiques are more incisive. But while Snell's argument has real shortcomings, as we will see in a moment, he does pick up on something important in the Homeric poems. When we speak about the body, we imply that there is something of the person that is not the body: mind, or soul, or consciousness. That we are not just our bodies is Socrates' point in the *Alcibiades* I, which, if it is genuine, is probably one of Plato's earliest works. Socrates gets Alcibiades to agree that because the *sōma* can neither use nor rule itself, it must have a user and a ruler. Socrates calls this user and ruler *psukhē* and equates it with the person.[21] In the Homeric poems, however, duality of this kind is not in evidence. It is true that at the moment of death, the person splits into a corpse, which remains on the battlefield until something happens to it, and a *psukhē*, which flits off to Hades.[22] But interestingly, when Odysseus's men are transformed by Circe into swine, we find an opposition between the mind (*noos*), which remains intact, "as it was before," and not the body but a list of (now porcine) features that perhaps add up to Descola's notion of physicality: head, voice, hair, and

---

20 In several cases, Snell's critics have tried to argue that Homer refers to a living body, unsuccessfully in my view. See further Holmes, *The Symptom and the Subject*.
21 Plato, *Alcibiades* 130a-c.
22 See, e.g. *Iliad* 1.3–5.

shape.²³ Homeric heroes may be embodied from our perspective, but they do not seem to "have" bodies and certainly not the bodies that people have in later Greek texts.

Snell, then, is right that *sōma* does not designate "body" in any simple way in the Homeric poems, and he is right to stress that its limited semantic field matters to how we interpret its appearances. Indeed, I would argue he does not go far enough. Not only does *sōma* refer to dead bodies. It is a rare and marked term for dead bodies, referring to corpses that have been (or are imagined to be) denied proper burial and so are destined to enter into the animal economy of circulating flesh. This aspect of *sōma* has long gone unrecognized. But it is worth noting because it suggests that ideas about vulnerability and care are part of the semantic range of *sōma* from early on.²⁴ The absence of "the" body in our Homeric texts thus encourages us to think about what is gained by the concept of the physical body and what is lost.

For Snell, the answer to the first of these questions is easy. What is gained by the concept of body is dependent on what is gained by a concept of soul or mind—namely, a unity of parts that is itself abstracted from material being. Once mind is discovered, a concept of body emerges to cover what of the person remains in the material world. Prior to these discoveries, as Homer's poems ostensibly show, there can be no concept of the person. Rather, there are only fragmented aggregates. Framed in these terms, the teleological thrust of Snell's argument is apparent. For what Snell wants to show is that Homer "was *not yet* capable of understanding the soul as basically opposed to the body."²⁵

Let us unpack this claim. Homer is limited, on Snell's analysis, in two ways. On the one hand, he lacks awareness of the body and the soul as

---

23 Homer, *Odyssey* 10.240.
24 See Holmes, *The Symptom and the Subject*, 29–37. It has to be said that we do find *sōma* used with reference to the living body in Hesiod (*Works and Days* 539–540), who is a rough contemporary of Homer, as well as in the sixth-century BCE poet Archilochus (fr. 196a Merkelbach-West). Even here, though, the *sōma* is not "body" in our sense of a biological object.
25 Snell, *The Discovery of the Mind*, 69, my italics.

the natural halves of the person. On the other hand, if the definition of the soul requires us to recognize what is not body, then "body" must be logically prior to soul. It is, in other words, all there is before soul. Here body is not an organic unity but, rather, an unthought materialism—that is, an inability to get beyond the sensible world—that constrains Homer's concept of a person. Some scholars have argued that the continuity of functions in Homer make his persons more, not less unified. But Snell would disagree. Unity arises only when corporeality has been disciplined by an incorporeal mind or soul. The dramatic gesture of withholding the concept of the body from Homer thus meets a deflationary end in *Discovery of the Mind*. For as much as Snell sees the discovery of the mind as caught up in the discovery of the body, he, like virtually all other historians who have told this story, is committed to seeing speculation about the immortal or immaterial mind or soul as the active partner in the development of western dualistic thinking. This story leaves little space to speculation about the body.[26] If, however, we approach the physical body not as a self-evident fact but rather as itself a partially hidden object subject to speculation, then its history becomes newly important for the larger history of embodiment in classical antiquity and the intellectual traditions that descend from it up to the present day.

Before turning to that history, I want to consider what the consequences of accepting that Homer does not have a concept of "the body" are for thinking about embodiment. If Snell is right that there is no dualism of body and soul in Homer, is he also right that the Homeric hero is consigned to being nothing but a fragmented, un-self-reflective

---

[26] Instructive here are the remarks about the "discovery of the body" made by the important postwar historian of ancient thought Jean-Pierre Vernant, who accepted Snell's conclusions. Vernant writes of that discovery that it refers to "a progressive conquest of its form ... what is meant is evidently not a question of the human body as an organic and physiological reality on which the self relies for its support" (Jean-Pierre Vernant, *Mortals and Immortals*, ed. and trans. F. I. Zeitlin [Princeton, NJ: Princeton University Press, 1991], 159). Vernant does elsewhere make brief mention of the contributions of Greek medicine to objectifying the body in anatomical and physiological terms (28).

aggregate? The critiques of Snell have been largely constrained by his terms with the result that one either defends the unity of the Homeric subject or else defends disunity as a feature of subjectivity understood as a transhistorical condition.[27] These terms, unity and disunity, are not, however, all that helpful. It may be a more promising approach to recognize that descriptions of persons in Homer enact a fundamental multiplicity even as they seem to assume the functional unity of an "I."

These descriptions also seem to recognize at least two modalities of being. On the one hand, a person has a form (*demas, eidos*) that is visible to others; she has skin or flesh (*chrōs, rhinos, sarx*) that can be touched;[28] he has limbs that can be observed in action (*guia, melea*).[29] If a warrior is cut open, internal parts sometimes spill out. On the other hand, the flesh and the limbs are also sensed from within and animated by emotions and forces. What is more, the panoply of parts and forces most active in mental and emotional life are described from a primarily phenomenological perspective: the *phrenes* that jump in the chest, the *ētor* that rises up to the mouth when Andromache learns of Hector's death. The many attempts of scholars to map these "psychological"

---

27 For the former position, see R. Renehan, "The Meaning of ΣΩMA in Homer: A Study in Methodology," *California Studies in Classical Antiquity* 12 (1979): 269–282 (with a philological critique of Snell, though he also recognizes there is no body-soul dualism in Homer); Williams, *Shame and Necessity*; Christopher Gill, *Personality in Greek Epic, Tragedy, and Philosophy: The Self in Dialogue* (Oxford: Oxford University Press, 1996). For the latter, see J. I. Porter and Mark Buchan, "Introduction," in *Special Issue: Before Subjectivity? Lacan and the Classics*, J. I. Porter and Mark Buchan, eds., *Helios* 31 (2004): 1–19.

28 The usual translation of *chrōs* is "skin" but see Valeria Gavrylenko ("The Body without Skin in the Homeric Poems," in *Blood, Sweat, and Tears: The Changing Concepts of Physiology from Antiquity to Early Modern Europe*, eds. Manfred Horstmanshoff, Helen King, and Claus Zittel (Leiden, The Netherlands: Brill, 2013), 479–502) for analysis of its complex semantic range, encompassing not just a concept of surface but also of depth and fleshiness. For Gavrylenko, *chrōs* "is" the body in Homer, a "body without skin."

29 Guillemette Bolens privileges these terms in arguing that the "body" in Homer should be understood primarily in terms of joints and movement as opposed to an idea of the body as an envelope in later texts: see G. Bolens, "Homeric Joints and the Marrow in Plato's *Timaeus*: Two Logics of the Body," *Multilingua* 18 (1999): 149–157; G. Bolens, *La logique du corps articulaire: Les articulations du corps humain dans la littérature occidentale* (Rennes: Presses Universitaires de Rennes, 2000). The latter work captures important aspects of how we would say the Homeric hero is embodied and adds another dimension to what I refer to below as the "felt" body.

terms onto anatomical organs have been largely inconclusive (even the term "organ" is anachronistic and implicated in Aristotelian notions of biological functionality). More promising are approaches that recognize the integrity of first-personal modes of knowing the parts of the self that are often described through the behavior of stuffs and forces outside that self: wind, water, honey, smoke.[30] These stuffs and forces are not alien to the Homeric person. Rather, he participates in and is himself a field of dynamic activity: strength and anger course through him; on the battlefield, he may experience a surge of *menos*, something like a life force. The person has a felt relationship to different aspects of her self that is as important as relationships (to her own body and to other bodies) that are seen and tangible.

We could describe such experience as embodied. But it is important to recognize that the seen and tangible body is not taken as the ground of felt experience. A physical body, in other words, is not the cause of experience or mind, nor when an emotion like anger is described as smoke-like or fluid should we imagine these terms as metaphorical.[31] Instead, aspects of a self can be perceived in different and complementary ways. We are forced here of course to infer ingrained cultural assumptions from two highly stylized epic poems. But what we can glean of these assumptions from Homer as well as from other archaic Greek texts suggest different modalities of experience that are not mapped onto two halves of a human being but are understood, rather, perspectivally.

One place where we can see these differences is in the constitution of the boundaries of a person. These boundaries are created by the skin that can be ripped open by a weapon and indeed, seems often defined

---

30 See Michael Clarke, *Flesh and Spirit in the Songs of Homer* (Oxford: Oxford University Press, 1999), 79–115, esp. 80–83 on the semantic range of the verb *thu(n)ō*.
31 On the gaseous and liquid qualities of anger, see Clarke, *Flesh and Spirit*, 90–97, with, e.g. *Il.* 9.646, 18.110.

by its vulnerability.[32] But a person is also bounded by the parameters of consciousness and, more specifically, a *sense* of self. And just as a weapon can penetrate the skin, so can external forces cross into the field of the self. The perception of a force or feeling as somehow discontinuous with the self—a surge of *menos*, or the idea that "pops" into your head, or a lack of judgment that brings disastrous consequences—often provokes Homeric subjects to infer, in the moment but sometimes retroactively, the presence or interference of a divine agent.[33] The conscious, felt person therefore has boundaries that do not coincide with the seen surface of a person. The felt is, rather, a domain contiguous with the unseen region of gods and daemons. These divine agents have the power to cross the boundaries of this self and act on it in the same way that the weapon can break the skin.

By implicitly classifying space beyond the parameters of the felt self as daemonic, the Homeric poet suggests that early Greek concepts of subjectivity do not carry with them a sense of nonconscious space within the person. Moreover, most early texts assume that incursions into the felt self are sent by anthropomorphic agents or signal the presence of personified alien beings. One of the major shifts we see in medical writing will be precisely the designation of large areas of the embodied self as existing below the threshold of consciousness. The idea of a physical body thus depends in large part on the isolation of a "daemonic" space within the boundaries of the self. At the same time,

---

[32] Gavrylenko, "The Body without Skin in the Homeric Poems," 490, following Nicole Loraux, argues that the boundary of "skin" (*chrōs*) *only* matters at the moment of vulnerability and warns against mistaking it for a neutral delineation of the individual. On this point, see also De Hart, "Hippocratic Medicine and the Greek Body Image," 357–360, who argues that the "atomized" body is a product of Hippocratic medicine and the democratic *polis*. We should consider, too, the ways in which agency and selfhood are distributed through tools and weapons in Homer: see Alex Purves, "Ajax and Other Objects: Homer's Vibrant Materialism," in *Special Issue: New Essays in Homer: Language, Violence, Agency*, Helen Morales and Sara Lindheim, eds., *Ramus* 44.1–2 (2015): 75–94, and, more broadly, C. Knappett, "Beyond Skin: Layering and Networking in Art and Archaeology," *Cambridge Archaeological Journal* 16.2 (2006): 232–259.

[33] Anthropological work on embodiment has yielded important insights into the "abduction" of alien agency: see Csordas, "Embodiment as a Paradigm for Anthropology"; Alfred Gell, *Art and Agency* (Oxford: Clarendon, 1998).

this internalized daemonic space is no longer populated with humanlike agents but by impersonal forces. Especially when these forces cause damage, the question is not *why* they act. Medical attention will shift, rather, to the mechanics of *how* they act. These new explanatory strategies leave implicit the questions of why someone is suffering and what that suffering means. They therefore create space for a new ethics organized around the body and its care. I want to turn now to examine in more detail the distinctive features of the physical body as we see it taking shape in medical writing.

3. Body in the Hippocratic Corpus

I have described the body whose appearance drives the formation of a set of philosophical and ethical problems around an embodied self as "physical" or "biological." I use these terms, on the one hand, in a contemporary sense as a way of capturing salient features of the body as it is problematized in the western tradition. On the other hand, I want to reanimate the Greek roots (*physis*, "nature"; *bios*, "life") of these terms to pick up on salient features of the body within early Greek medical and philosophical writing. For, as one Hippocratic author writes, the starting point (*archē*) of medicine is the nature (*physis*) of the body. What medicine seeks to defend is the life (*bios*) realized through the physical body. What can we say, then, of the body's nature and the life it supports? In this section, I isolate two aspects of the body in medical writing that are fundamental to its status as physical—its impersonal nature and its concealed, nonconscious interior—before touching briefly on the modes of being in this body.

Interest in the nature of the body in fifth-century BCE medicine has to be understood in the context of the broader "inquiry into nature" in the sixth and fifth centuries. The rise of natural philosophy in this period is a complex and in many respects unknown story, long put in the service of maligned but tenacious narratives about the birth of rationality. What is clear is that the thinkers associated with the

Presocratic tradition shared an interest in giving an account of the world and events within it that dispensed with intentional agents—that is, gods, especially Zeus—and imposed homogeneities and regularities on a universal scale.[34] They sought to identify one or more basic stuffs whose changes and/or combinations could account for what we sense and experience. It is probably by trying to understand the pluripotency of these basic stuffs, as well as the dynamic identities of compound or phenomenal objects, that the early physicists got interested in the idea of a thing's nature, helpfully defined by Gregory Vlastos as "that cluster of stable characteristics by which we can recognize that thing and can anticipate the limits within which it can act upon other things or be acted upon by them."[35] The physical body emerges, then, within a landscape populated by a range of different, nonhuman objects and beings in the context of ambitious questions about the nature of the world and being as a whole.

But then again, the body is not just one object among others. That its workings go on so close to home can help explain why medical writing and embryology seem to have been a privileged place for developing the idea of *physis* more generally in the fifth century. Moreover, the professionalization of medicine in this period as a specialized domain for investigating the body and its malfunctioning is no doubt responsible for the interest of some medical writers in hiving off the body from the larger domain of the cosmos as an object whose *physis* requires its own field of inquiry.[36] Finally, the object of such inquiry is often classed not simply as the nature of the body but the nature of a human being. That is, it is through the physical body that human beings are first and most successfully incorporated into the inquiry

---

34 De Hart, "Hippocratic Medicine and the Greek Body Image," 376, draws a helpful contrast between the local "sacral intensities" of archaic space-time and the homogeneous Ionian cosmos.

35 Gregory Vlastos, *Plato's Universe* (Seattle: University of Washington Press, 1975).

19. On the early history of *physis*, see also Gerard Naddaf, *The Greek Concept of Nature* (Albany: SUNY Press, 2005).

36 See, most notably, *On Ancient Medicine* 20.

into nature: as Aristotle writes at the start and close of the *Parva naturalia*, the most accomplished physicists conclude with "medical principles."[37] Medicine remains a master discourse for taking up questions of human nature and its malfunctioning in other late fifth-century discourses, including historiography, ethnography, and rhetoric, in addition to philosophical ethics and moralizing genres. Another way to put this would be to say that in the classical period the physical body works as the bridge between inquiries into nonhuman things and stuffs and new inquiries into the nature of people as both biological beings and social and ethical agents.

What makes the physical body so attractive as a model for understanding human nature is, then as now, that it enables human nature to be reduced to a handful of core elements with ostensibly predictable patterns of behavior subject to manipulation. Despite remarkable variability in the details, virtually all of our extant texts posit a handful of constituent stuffs or "humors" (bile, phlegm, fire, water, "the acid," blood, water, and so on) as the building blocks of human nature. These humors, singly and in interaction with one another, are responsible for health and disease. Their pathological tendencies are triggered by changes of temperature and state—that is, if they grow too hot or cold or wet or dry (because of changes of weather or season; or the ingestion of certain kinds of food or drink; or practices like exercise, sex, and so on) or if their particular power (*dynamis*) grows too strong. Even a slight external stimulus can precipitate a process that, if unchecked, leads to disease. Disease is always incipient in the humoral body, making proactive control of its always shifting composition imperative.

The laws governing whether the body flourishes or suffers are, as I have just emphasized, impersonal, regular, and uniformly applicable to the natural world. The medical writers often back up their claims about the nature of the body and what happens to it by appealing to

---

37 Aristotle, *On Sense and Sensible Objects* 436a17-21; *On Respiration* 480b28-30.

analogies with nonhuman objects and natures: leather bags, clay vessels, trees, a ball of wool. These objects participate in a world without language or negotiation or consent. In the same way, the humors and the parts of the body are cut off from the mind except insofar as they are causally responsible for its functioning. As we have just seen, they respond to forces like heat and cold; they move according to a fluid dynamics. If errant stuffs are to be brought back under control, they have to be managed by technical means—diet, exercise, drugs.

Moreover, by substituting humors and external stimuli for a god's intent to harm, medical writing about disease changes the nature of the causal process.[38] Whereas a god's intention is not just necessary but sufficient to cause a disease to occur (or, less dramatically, to put an idea in someone's head), these causes typically acquire the power to harm by participating in a causal series through which the normal functioning of the body is subverted and appropriated for death not life: one thing leads to another, such that a small stimulus snowballs into a massive harm. The causal series displaces the intentional agent behind the disease as well as the social interactions with gods and godlike figures previously seen as integral to both the origin and the resolution of disease. The fight against the disease now shifts decisively to the body, understood as the terrain of a panoply of forces that have to be managed via ongoing interventions in the body's composition. To be embodied under these conditions entails one of two positions: to be the victim of these forces or their master. The very possibility of mastery colors the management of the body as an ethical responsibility over the course of the fifth and fourth centuries. Embodiment, in other words, is not a neutral condition. At least for the free male subject, it requires labor.

---

38 De Hart, "Hippocratic Medicine and the Greek Body Image," 368–370, sees more continuity between archaic notions of personal power and the Hippocratic concepts but does not deal with the atomization of intention in the latter.

It is not surprising that medical texts and practices encourage the conceptualization of a body that needs the mindful oversight of physicians and well-informed patients. But we also find a growing interest in these texts in the body's own power to be healthy or even to seek health. Some authors make explicit reference to "innate" or "connate" heat in the body that breaks down overly strong humors—anticipations of vital heat in Aristotle and the Stoics—and cooking is the implicit model for digestion and the triumph over malignant humors in a wide range of contexts.[39] The body's nature (or human nature) is sometimes said to be stronger or weaker than external forces.[40] The nature of a body can register as an even more active force, as in a passage from *Epidemics* VI that describes the efforts of "untaught nature" in doing what is needed (sc. to maintain health) "without thought," through automatic behaviors like blinking, salivating, and sneezing.[41] The passage will become influential in the later medical tradition. Galen, for example, is extremely interested in the powers of "untaught nature," as well as in the nonconscious physiological work of the vegetal part of ourselves (and he puzzles over the relationship of this part to our rational minds).[42]

The passage about "untaught nature" also points to another defining aspect of the physical body—namely, the fact that much of it lies below the threshold of consciousness. I suggested above that in archaic Greek poetry, as far as we can determine, the self is bounded in part by a field of consciousness. In other words, there is no nonconscious space

---

[39] On vital heat in post-Hippocratic philosophers, see F. Solmsen, "The Vital Heat, the Inborn Pneuma and the Aether," in *Kleine Schriften* (Hildesheim: Olms, 1968), 605–611.

[40] [Hippocrates] *On Ancient Medicine* 3.

[41] [Hippocrates] *Epidemics* VI 5.1. See further discussion of the passage in relationship to other texts in L. Ayache, "Hippocrate laissait-t-il la nature agir?" in *Tratados Hipocráticos: Actas del VIIe colloque international hippocratique, Madrid, 24-29 de Septiembre de 1990*, ed. J. A. López Férez (Madrid: Universidad Nacional de Educación a Distancia, 1992), 19–35.

[42] See Brooke Holmes, "Galen on the Chances of Life," in *Probabilities, Hypotheticals, and Counterfactuals in Ancient Greek Thought*, ed. Victoria Wohl (Cambridge, UK: Cambridge University Press, 2014), 230–250.

in the self. When the person experiences a rupture in experience, it is created by the incursion of alien minds, rather than the incursion of other, hidden parts of the self. The medical writers, by contrast, make unseen and unfelt space a central part of their account of the body and human nature. Indeed, much of what happens within the body happens not just out of sight—the skin, of course, conceals most everything of the inside—but below the threshold of the embodied person's conscious experience. One text, *On the Technē*, credits the incurability of many diseases to the fact that they first develop deep in the cavities of the body unknown to the physician and to the patient and so get a head start. The "opacity" of the body makes it virtually complicit in the production of disease.[43] Another text, *On Regimen*, speaks of diseases coming into being gradually before becoming manifest with "a sudden spring."[44] In the everyday descriptions of disease in the nosological texts, we regularly encounter stories of disease that begins even before the patient starts to feel symptoms. The author of *On the Use of Liquids* writes that the cavity can be in a state (here, of being overpowered by cold) that the embodied person is "very far from feeling" and so, as a result, actively makes worse (by fulfilling the felt desire for a cold drink).[45]

The casting of the inside of the body as unseen or potentially seen space no doubt owes something to the larger interest in the unseen plane of reality in Presocratic ontologies, and especially in the various pluralist philosophies where the basic building blocks of the world lie below the threshold of our perception even as they are responsible for the nature of what we do see. But it also builds on the understanding of the unseen as the domain of gods and daemons. Given this cultural backdrop, we can see why the unfelt regions of the body could be viewed as potentially threatening spaces. At the same time, the

---

43 [Hippocrates] *On the Technē* 10–11.
44 [Hippocrates] *On Regimen* I 2.
45 [Hippocrates] *On the Use of Liquids* 2.

conceptualization of the physical body as largely unfelt space further establishes the grounds for medicine's epistemic authority over the physical body. The felt experience of the patient remains important, but only as one (potentially unreliable) sign among many others of what is happening in a space defined primarily as unseen, rather than as known primarily through embodied experience. The heightened attention to the inside of the body as a space that could be known better by being opened up and seen directly can help explain the growing interest in internal anatomy in the Hippocratic texts, which culminates in the practice of systematic human dissection and probably vivisection at Alexandria under the Ptolemies in the third century BCE and then ongoing anatomical investigations with animals in later centuries.[46]

The development of anatomy into the first centuries CE strengthens the idea that a body can best be known from the outside looking in. Yet such a perspective is also resisted in antiquity, most notably by the Stoics, whose arguments for cardiocentrism even after detailed dissections of the brain by Herophilus and Erasistratus rely on what it *feels* like to think and speak—that is, to be a rational being. In the Hippocratic texts, we do find, albeit relatively rarely, the view that being in a body confers a unique and perhaps even uniquely valuable perspective on the nature of that body. In the treatise *On Ancient Medicine*, for example, the author allows that everyone has some acquaintance with the specificities of their own nature through daily biofeedback and long practice (e.g., whether they need one meal a day or two, whether they can tolerate cheese). Such knowledge, however, reaches its limits in disease, where you need a more complex understanding of the mechanics of the humors and the various causes affecting the body. The gynecological and embryological texts speak of the woman of experience, who may be a midwife or assistant but may also be the woman who knows her body through the events of

---

[46] See Heinrich von Staden, "The Discovery of the Body: Human Dissection and Its Cultural Contexts in Ancient Greece," *The Yale Journal of Biology and Medicine* 65.3 (1992): 223–241.

menarche, pregnancy, and childbirth and can perhaps serve as an important source of information for the male doctor.[47]

Nevertheless, on the whole, the medical texts do not subscribe to the principle that Socrates puts forth in Plato's *Republic*, namely, that the best doctor is the one who has experienced the most diseases himself.[48] In Plato the doctor's embodied experience is educational because the mind is ostensibly independent from the body. By contrast, in the Hippocratic texts, a sick patient is more likely to be confused and noncompliant when he is "full of disease,"[49] and a number of these texts explain cognitive faculties more generally through the "ridiculous" kinds of causes that Socrates deplores in the *Phaedo*, causes like wetness and dryness, or the condition of the blood or air.[50] From the perspective of the physicist and the physician, thinking is necessarily embodied. Yet at the same time, in the Hippocratic Corpus the best physician is, as I have argued elsewhere, curiously "disembodied."[51] He learns not from his own suffering but from the sufferings of other bodies. He reads signs to figure out what is going on in a hidden interior, whose workings can also be simulated by observing and manipulating analogous nonhuman bodies and objects. The very structural division

---

47 On the "woman of experience," see A. E. Hanson, "The Medical Writers' Woman," in *Before Sexuality: The Construction of Erotic Experience in the Ancient Greek World*, eds. D. Halperin, J. Winkler and F. I. Zeitlin (Princeton, NJ: Princeton University Press, 1990), 309–337. Lesley Dean-Jones ("Autopsia, Historia and What Women Know: The Authority of Women in Hippocratic Gynaecology," in *Knowledge and the Scholarly Medical Tradition*, ed. D. Bates (Cambridge, UK: Cambridge University Press, 1995), 41–59) argues that the Hippocratic writers express greater uncertainty about women's bodies because they lack embodied experience but the evidence she uses is too limited to draw clear conclusions.

48 Plato, *Republic* 3, 408d10–e2.

49 [Hippocrates] *On the Technē* 7. The contrast is with a physician working "with a healthy mind in a healthy body."

50 Beate Gundert gives a full account of the intertwining of *sōma* and *psychē* in the Hippocratic Corpus. See Gundert, "Soma and Psyche in Hippocratic Medicine," in *Psyche and Soma: Physicians and Metaphysicians on the Mind-Body Problem from Antiquity to Enlightenment*, ed. P. Potter and J. P. Wright (Oxford: Oxford University Press, 2000), 14–35.

51 On the disembodiment of the physician, see Brooke Holmes, "In Strange Lands: Disembodied Authority and the Role of the Physician in the Hippocratic Corpus and Beyond," in *Writing Science: Medical and Mathematical Authorship in Ancient Greece*, ed. Markus Asper (Berlin: Walter de Gruyter, 2013), 431–472.

of physician from patient in the clinical relationship exaggerates the difference between the body as an object of knowledge and a knowing, virtually disembodied subject.

To speak of the physical body, then, is to speak of a body that is defined by being available to a particular form of knowledge shaped by the larger inquiry into nature and the professionalization of medicine as a *technē*, as well as to a rapidly developing arsenal of techniques for controlling physical objects in the classical period. To be *in* a body defined in these terms poses epistemic challenges that, from the perspective of physicians at least, have to be addressed by educating oneself, as a layperson, about one's own body through medical texts. The challenges involved are also ethical insofar as mastery of the body and, hence, self-mastery are gaining traction as a cultural ideal in this period.[52] It is largely as an ethical problem that the body becomes important to Plato,[53] to whom I want to turn in the final section.

4. Body in Plato

Plato has long loomed large in the history of bodies, embodiment, and dualism, and with good reason. He undoubtedly plays a foundational role in conceptualizing the person in terms of two parts, body and soul. Yet the standard portrait of western philosophy's original somatophobe, usually drawn from the *Phaedo*, is misleadingly narrow and obscures the extent to which body (*sōma*) is a variable and slippery term in the Platonic dialogues. As the complex reception history of

---

[52] Foucault, *The History of Sexuality, Volume II, The Use of Pleasure*, trans. R. Hurley (New York: Pantheon Books, 1985).

[53] For emphasis on this point, see also Dorothea Frede, "Disintegration and Restoration: Pleasure and Pain in Plato's *Philebus*," in *The Cambridge Companion to Plato*, ed. R. Kraut (Cambridge, UK: Cambridge University Press, 1992), 425–463; Broadie, "Soul and Body in Plato and Descartes," 307; Carlos Steel, "The Moral Purpose of the Human Body: A Reading of *Timaeus* 69–72," *Phronesis* 46.2 (2001): 105–128; Carone, "Mind and Body in Late Plato," 227–269, esp. 229–230 n.9, 259; Lang, "Plato on Divine Art and the Production of Body"; Thomas M. Miller, "Plato's Doctrine of the Immortality of the Soul," Ph.D. diss., Princeton.

Platonic dualism shows, different passages could be used to support very different and even contradictory positions, with Plato at times being labeled a materialist about soul.[54] I cannot hope to map the full range of the meanings of *sōma* here. But I do want to give a better sense of some of the different ways in which the body partners with the soul in Plato, focusing first on its function as a foil to the soul before turning to the implications of being in a body for the soul.[55]

Before addressing these questions, though, it is worth remembering that Plato was not the first to approach the soul from a perspective of embodiment and body from the perspective of ensoulment. Several medical texts seem to assume the soul as the body's counterpart, separable and yet causally entwined. Plato also almost certainly inherits an eschatological tradition, associated with the Orphics and Pythagoreans, that is largely lost to us but seems to have invested ethical importance in the soul and its afterlife existence over and above the body.[56] Moreover, Socrates and Plato seem to be part of a trend in the later fifth and fourth centuries BCE to articulate the soul against the body in ethical philosophy (in the fragments of Democritus, for example, we find the soul and body as complementary parts of the person). Nevertheless, from what we can tell, Plato does play a decisive role in the history of philosophy in establishing body and soul as a pair wherein the latter is superior to the former. Part of the reason for Plato's importance lies in the fact that he takes up the challenge of actively defining the ethical relationship of the soul to the body

---

54 See Aristotle, *De anima* 1.3, 407a2-3. Galen's treatise "That the Affections of the Soul Follow the Mixtures of the Body" offers an extended corporealist reading of Plato.

55 I have discussed the body in Plato further at Holmes, "Body, Soul, and the Medical Analogy in Plato," and Holmes, *The Symptom and the Subject*, 206–210.

56 David B. Claus remains valuable on the prehistory of the Platonic soul, in part because he does not overvalue the eschatological inheritance (about which we must remain speculative and so skeptical), in part because he recognizes the importance of a physiological and medical tradition. See Claus, *Towards the Soul: An Inquiry into the Meaning of ψυχή before Plato* (New Haven, CT: Yale University Press, 1981). T. M. Robinson for his part portrays Socrates as an Orphic sympathizer. See Robinson, "The Defining Features of Mind-Body Dualism in the Writings of Plato," in Potter and Wright, *Psyche and Soma*, 37–55, 38.

(he is also interested in the causal relationship but, as we have seen, its logistics do not receive the kind of attention they will in the later philosophical tradition). I suggested earlier that Plato's interest in establishing the soul as the "true" human being can be understood at least in part as a response to the explanatory work that the physical body as a concept was doing on behalf of human nature in the late fifth century and, perhaps, the cultural authority of medicine. We see him minimizing the body's participation in human life by defining it in simple terms as a tool and by isolating its care from the care of the soul. I look first at these kinds of contexts for the body before turning to the challenges that embodiment poses to psychic flourishing in the Platonic dialogues.

In the *Apology*, Socrates describes his particular brand of political activism as follows: "I go around doing nothing but trying to persuade you, young and old, to care neither for your bodies nor for your possessions before taking care that your soul is as good as possible."[57] What does Socrates mean by soul here? One common association in the speech is between the soul and thought (*phronēsis*). Eric Havelock has also pointed out that Socrates uses the expression "to care for the soul" interchangeably with the expression "to care for oneself," implying that the soul is virtually equivalent to the reflexive pronoun.[58] That the soul's equation with the self is due to its participation in thought is a claim argued for more systematically in the *Alcibiades I*, as we saw earlier. There, Socrates defends the equivalence of soul and self by methodically eliminating objects of care that merely belong to the self, starting with things (shoes, rings), moving to body parts (hands, eyes), and then finally arriving at the body itself as something "other than" (*heteron*) the self. The body is defined as an instrument, leaving the soul to be assigned the role of its user and, in the next phase of the

---

57 Plato, *Apology* 30a7–b2.
58 See 36c3, 39d3, with Eric Havelock, "The Socratic Self As It Is Parodied in Aristophanes' *Clouds*," *Yale Classical Studies* 22 (1972): 1–18, 6–9.

argument, its master. If, as Socrates implies, the self is defined by its exercise of control over the other parts, its care will be paramount.

The authenticity of the *Alcibiades* I is not certain, but Socrates makes a similar argument in Book 3 of the *Republic*. There, he advocates for the care of the soul over and above what he describes at one point as the "excessive" care of the body. The body here is no longer simply a tool, but a more complex, dynamic object that is primarily if problematically under the authority of medicine. For, as Socrates says in Book 1, it is not enough for a body to be a body. It needs "something else," and so the medical art was invented.[59] And yet Socrates' worry is that medicine has gained too much ground. The overinvestment among elites in the care of the body, he argues, comes at the expense of the care of the soul, first because care of the body does not improve the soul, second because it is a distraction from the soul's cultivation.[60] He goes further, in fact, claiming at one point that care of the soul is sufficient for the health of the body, too—no need to "go on at length" about the body's needs.[61] In the *Charmides*, we also find the claim, ascribed to a "Thracian doctor," that curing the soul is most essential in the health of the whole.[62] These passages downplay the need for medicine's complicated precepts and claims about the nature of the body and instead locate bodily health with the control of desires, thereby gaining ground for philosophical ethics. They also strengthen the idea that the soul is the locus of the true self—not just what is human in us but what is divine.

Yet at the same time, medicine's analysis of bodily dysfunction is a model for how to understand disorder in the soul. In dialogues such

---

59 Plato, *Republic* 1, 341e1–6.
60 Plato, *Republic* 3, 407b8-c6. On Plato's rivalry with medicine and attempts to appropriate its cultural authority, see Susan B. Levin, *Plato's Rivalry with Medicine: A Struggle and Its Dissolution* (Oxford: Oxford University Press, 2014), focusing on *Gorgias, Symposium, Republic, Statesman,* and *Laws*.
61 Plato, *Republic* 3 403d1–e2.
62 Plato, *Charmides* 156d.

as the *Protagoras*, the *Crito*, and the *Gorgias*, we find, in arguments on behalf of the ethical practices that are most closely associated with Socrates, the physician or sometimes the trainer put forth as a model. These references give us a glimpse of how the state of being in a body had become a topic of cultural and moral concern, at least among elites, in the classical period. But they sidestep the question of whether being embodied might be a concern for the health of the soul. That is, the structure of the analogy displaces questions about how body affects soul and vice versa. The body and the soul are simply two parallel systems that need to be managed for flourishing.[63]

Elsewhere in Plato, however, the body is neither safely penned up in the structure of an analogy with the soul nor is it a pliable tool to be used by its master. In some of the most famous passages about the body in Plato's dialogues, the body does act causally on the soul, and its effects are malign. Even as these passages get closer to the metaphysical and ontological questions about a relationship between body and soul and the (substantial?) nature of the difference between them, they are primarily ethical questions, embedded within and subordinate to inquiries into the best possible human existence. When Socrates asks in the *Phaedo* what sort of the thing soul is, he does so in order to answer a question about whether we should fear for or be confident about the fate of our soul.[64] If we get clearer on this point, we can see that some of the basic assumptions about Plato's views on the soul's relationship to the body and its nature are not well-grounded in Plato's texts and are heavily colored by later receptions. The very idea that the soul is incorporeal, for example, cannot be securely ascribed to Plato.

---

63 Robinson, "The Defining Features of Mind-Body Dualism in the Writings of Plato," 41–42, describes the position outlined in the *Gorgias* in terms of a rather different parallelism, according to which both body and soul have (potentially harmful) desires and needs of their own. The discussion builds on the medical body, and there is an explicit medical analogy, but treats the body more as a quasi-person than the medical texts do. Its (appetitive) desires will be subsumed into the soul with the *Republic*'s theory of tripartition.

64 Plato, *Phaedo* 78b.

He never makes the claim about incorporeality explicitly, though he describes soul as "more like" the class of invisible things, that is, the Forms, than the class of visible things and ontologically prior to the body.[65] By contrast, the claim that it is risky for our true happiness to associate too closely with the body or to have a body in thrall to the phenomenal world is well established, most famously in the *Phaedo* but also in later texts such as the *Timaeus* and the *Philebus*. Each of these texts, however, articulates the problem in slightly different terms.

The *Phaedo* is often used as the source for Platonic dualism. But the dialogue is unusually vehement in its negative portrayal of the body, which is at one point dismissed simply as "evil." It should be read together with other dialogues for an accurate picture of Plato's views. It is true that ideas we have already seen here recur—that the soul is properly the master of the body, that the body is its instrument. We also find a clearer statement of the claim that the soul is the animating principle of the body. But the body being instrumentalized for sense perception is now capable of dragging the soul around so that it wanders, confused and dizzy, like a drunk man.[66] Embodiment is, in essence, a pathological state. Still, its harms can be mitigated. The practice of philosophy is, Socrates says, to keep the soul as free as possible of the body's concerns, "never willingly associating with the body in life"[67] and instead focusing as much as possible on the Forms. The alternative is to end up dragging a desire for corporeal things into one's next life. The actual mechanics of embodiment, let alone metempsychosis, remain vague in the dialogue. The soul seems to be some stuff that gets caged in a body but perhaps survives its death and

---

65 Plato, *Phaedo*, 79b-c; *Timaeus* 34b-c; *Laws* 10, 892a-c. For the claim about incorporeality, see Miller, "Plato's Doctrine of the Immortality of the Soul," ch. 2; see also Sara Brill, *Plato on the Limits of Human Life* (Bloomington: Indiana University Press, 2013), 19–82. Carone, "Mind and Body in Late Plato," argues against the attribution of substance dualism (as well as attribute dualism) to Plato in the *Phaedo* and elsewhere.

66 *Phaedo* 79c.

67 *Phaedo* 80e-81a.

trails its attachments to corporeality even when it is disembodied. What is clear is that Socrates' ideal is aspirational disembodiment: a turning-inward of the soul that minimizes engagement with the world of "visible" things and the problems they foster (gluttony, violence, drunkenness).

The claim that the body introduces disorder into the soul and life itself is again found in the *Timaeus*, where we are also given a more detailed account of how a soul comes to be embodied. The context of the account is Timaeus's "likely story" of the creation of the cosmos, which turns out to have both a soul and a body of its own. Embodiment at the cosmic level poses few problems. The body of the cosmos eats its own waste in a perfectly calibrated cycle: there is nothing outside to disrupt it, no true intake and output, no problem. By contrast, individual human souls, each of which is imagined to have its proper home in a star, suffer embodiment harshly, at least initially. These souls are by necessity implanted in bodies subject to influx and efflux and, accordingly, rocked by desires and emotions that the soul must master.[68] If it succeeds, it returns to its native star. If it fails, it returns to a female body, from which it may fall even further into animal forms in future lives.[69]

In the *Timaeus*, the terms of success for the embodied soul are spelled out further. It is not just the pursuit of philosophy that is entrusted with saving the soul from the body and establishing it in its proper position as lord and master. Stargazing also plays an important role in aligning the soul's rotations with those of the stars and correcting the disorderly motions that assail the soul when it enters a body at birth. At the same time, despite Timaeus's interest in counteracting the pull of the body by working on the soul, he also thinks it is important to

---

[68] The mechanics involved here are limited to understanding that a soul rules a body by being planted "in" it in some way (as is clear from the prefixed Greek verb *emphuteutheien* at 42a3). See also *Laws* 10, 898e-899a, where in a discussion of how the soul of the sun rules its body, the Stranger makes clear that in human embodiment, the soul rules from within a body.

[69] Plato, *Timaeus* 42b; 90a.

impose order directly on the body in its own idiom, via gymnastics. These kinds of exercises can counteract the pathology of normal embodiment. But Plato also allows that sometimes a body is beyond fixing.[70] In some cases, the body's unhappy condition (the state of the marrow, the disorder of the humors) is responsible even for disorders that seem "psychic," such as lust. As a result, he concludes, in one of the most surprising passages from the annals of Platonic dualism, a person cannot be held responsible for his failings.[71] In this situation, embodiment is a prison from which there is no escape. Under normal conditions, though, embodiment is less traumatic. The body is the obedient vehicle (*ochēma*) of the soul, allowing its wishes to be carried out and transporting it around (though the soul is the principle of motion).[72]

The *Philebus* is unusual in being considered a late dialogue that nevertheless reprises core "Socratic" concerns about pleasure and the good and reintroduces Socrates as the central figure. Its primary task is to determine how to separate false from true pleasures. Socrates wants to classify bodily pleasure—or what he calls at one point "delight in becoming"[73]—as false. But he cannot deny that it derives from the restoration of a natural state after "combinations and divisions and fillings and emptyings and any growths and witherings."[74] He tries to get his interlocutor Protarchus to consider a situation where there are no movements in the body and, so, no pleasure and pain. Unfortunately, Protarchus is up on contemporary physics and points out that "wise men" say the world is always flowing this way and that.

---

[70] The *Timaeus* also includes a long discussion of diseases of the body, which receive humoral explanation. On Plato's relationship to contemporary medicine in this account, see G. E. R. Lloyd, "Plato as a Natural Scientist," *Journal of Hellenic Studies* 88 (1968): 78–92.

[71] Plato, *Timaeus* 86b-87a, discussed usefully by Gill, *Personality in Greek Epic, Tragedy, and Philosophy*; see also Steel, "The Moral Purpose of the Human Body: A Reading of *Timaeus* 69-72," 126–127.

[72] Plato, *Timaeus* 41e2, 69c7.

[73] Plato, *Philebus* 54e5.

[74] Plato, *Philebus* 42c9-d7.

Socrates concedes that we cannot avoid some becoming, but in a now-familiar move recommends trying to minimize movements in the body as much as possible by tamping down on desires.[75] The gauge of success is that those movements will happen without ever reaching an intensity such that they break through into consciousness—that is, into the soul. Disembodiment is again aspirational. Yet it is now a state aided by the cordoning off of the body as nonconscious space, where events might happen without ever erupting into the soul. In articulating a state that he calls "anaesthetic" and that includes physiological processes later allied to the "vegetal" soul or "nature," such as growth, Socrates adds a chapter to Plato's efforts, especially in the later dialogues, to theorize the causal influence of the physical body on the soul. In so doing, he further appropriates the authority of medicine to describe bodily pathologies. He appropriates medicine's claim to control the risks of embodiment, too, in continuing to develop an ethics around practices of minimizing the body's influence as much as possible as a precondition of psychic flourishing.

In these later texts, Plato has no qualms about acknowledging the power exercised by the junior partner in the body-soul relationship. Yet given that he consistently depicts the soul as properly hegemonic, corporeal influence unsurprisingly registers as revolt. If in the Hippocratic texts, embodiment is a precondition of thinking, Plato often casts thinking as something the soul does very well on its own, if the body does not get in the way. He also in various later dialogues, including the *Phaedrus* and the *Laws*, continues to work with the soul, not a nature (*physis*), as a life principle of the body and the cause of its movements—in short, the force behind the imposition of order and limit on what is sometimes defined as lacking in limit. The body left to

---

75 Desires act analogously to humors here and elsewhere in Plato: see Holmes, "Body, Soul, and the Medical Analogy in Plato," 363–364. On the "medical" flavor of the dialogue, see also Dorothea Frede, "Disintegration and Restoration: Pleasure and Pain in Plato's *Philebus*," esp. 456; Carone, "Mind and Body in Late Plato," 248.

its own devices quickly spirals out of control. But of course the body is never completely on its own. Its turmoil always has ethical implications because of its impact on an ensouled person but also because bodies are supposed to be under the control, as much as possible, of persons.

By insisting on desires and "visible" things, rather than the particular powers of food or drink or changes of season as pathogenic, Plato is telling a story about the risks of embodiment that is different from what we find in the medical writers. Nevertheless, in his accounts of the physical body as a source of disruption to the soul and the self, he reinforces medical perceptions of the body as at once disordered and in need of control *and* structured by regularity and so amenable to practices like dietetics, gymnastics, and medicine. Within this history, to have a body is never just a fact about human life. The body is, instead, always a dynamic economy of alien powers. Through the physical body, human nature and the self are produced but also threatened. Its complex nature means that the history of embodiment that unfolds from the physical body's emergence in ancient Greece is a history not only of philosophy but of politics and ethics as well.

CHAPTER TWO

Embodied or Ensouled

ARISTOTLE ON THE RELATION OF SOUL AND BODY

Helen Lang

1. Introduction: The Problem of Soul and The Investigation of It

Aristotle opens *On the Soul* I, 1, praising soul and the study of it; soul is "among first things," remarkable and important to know. Indeed, understanding soul contributes to truth and to the study of nature. His most general definition of soul appears here: soul is "the first principle of animal life."[1] Aristotle sets aside several problems that reappear later in his account: what is soul's genus? Is it a kind of potency or actuality, is it divisible or indivisible, does soul have parts?[2] But one problem cannot be postponed: what relation obtains between soul and the animal of which it is the first principle? Do "the affections of

---

1 Aristotle, *On the Soul* I, 1, 402a6-7.
2 Aristotle, *On the Soul* I, 1, 402a11-b2.

the soul" [τὰ πάθη τῆς ψυχῆς], for example feelings such as anger or even perception, involve the animal as a whole of soul and body, or are they "proper" [ἴδιος] to soul apart from body and so apart from the animal too?[3] For most activities, such as imagination, soul seems connected to body and in these cases the study of soul must include a reference to body.[4] *If* there is something proper to soul, then in regard to it soul might be separated [χωρίζεσθαι] from body and the animal; in this case, soul and what is proper to it would be studied apart from body. Thinking seems to be the best candidate for what is proper to soul and so separable from body; but if thinking requires imagination and imagination requires body, then thinking too requires body.[5] *If* there were nothing proper to soul, it would be inseparable from body and so the study of soul would in every case require a reference to body and the animal as a whole.[6] It does seem, he continues, that all affections of the soul involve body. So the investigation of soul must include body and belongs to the study of nature.[7] But there is no unequivocal answer.

This ambiguity raises a serious problem. Here in the *On the Soul*, Aristotle examines soul as part of natural science which, as he defines it, must include a reference to matter.[8] So if there is something "proper" to soul and so separate from body, in principle it could not be studied in the *On the Soul*. And before proceeding, Aristotle apparently raises this issue by asking what investigation considers things that are or can be thought of apart from matter? Whatever occurs only in body but can be considered without reference to it is investigated by the mathematician (e.g., points and lines); what is actually separate, insofar as

---

[3] Aristotle, *On the Soul* I, 1, 403a3-5.
[4] Aristotle, *On the Soul* I, 1, 403a5-10.
[5] Aristotle, *On the Soul* I, 1, 403a8-10.
[6] Aristotle, *On the Soul* I, 1, 403a10-11.
[7] Aristotle, *On the Soul* I, 1, 403a16-25.
[8] Aristotle, *On the Soul* I, 1, 403b12-13. See *Physics* II, 2, 194b10-15 where Aristotle concludes that the study of nature must always include a reference to matter.

it is such, is considered by "the first philosopher."[9] So *if* there is something "proper" to soul and so separate, then its investigation apparently belongs to "the first philosophy," rather than to the natural science of *On the Soul*. *If* soul possesses something "proper" to itself apart from body, it may be referred to in *On the Soul*, but it cannot be studied there because what is "proper" is by definition separate from matter.[10]

In *On the Soul* I, Aristotle turns to his predecessors, giving us important evidence for their view; his own account is postponed to *On the Soul* II and III. In *On the Soul* II, he pursues neither thinking nor what may be proper to soul; rather, he gives a second definition of soul, "the actuality of a natural body having life potentially in it," and then considers the implications of this definition for body.[11] Thus this book, which is clearly part of natural science, defines the relation of body to soul. I shall turn to it in a moment.

On the Soul III, 1 continues the investigation of sensation. There is no sense in addition to the five: sight, hearing, smell, taste, and touch. Sensation should be defined, Aristotle argues, as a relation between the sensible object and the sense. At *On the Soul* III, 3, he distinguishes "two differences [δύο διαφοραῖς] by which we characterize soul: local movement and thinking, namely understanding and perceiving.[12] He takes up perceiving and thought first (*On the Soul* III, 3-8), and in *On the Soul* III, 9-13, concludes his investigation of soul with an account of soul as originating local motion in the animal.[13] So *On the Soul* III

---

9 Aristotle, *On the Soul* I, 1, 403b8-16: ὁ πρῶτος φιλόσοφος; here Aristotle also mentions the dialectician in contrast to the physicist, although he does not develop the distinction. See *Physics* II, 2, 193b31-194a12; 194b10-15; *Metaphysics* VI, 1, 1025b19-1026a32.

10 Again, the *Physics* provides an important parallel. In *Physics* VIII, Aristotle asks whether or not motion in things is eternal and unequivocally answers "yes"; he raises objections to this view and in resolving them reaches the conclusion that there must be a first unmoved mover [Cf. *Physics* VIII, 1, 252a4-6; 6, 260a15-18; 10, 267b20-26]. Although identified within the bounds of physics, as unmoved this mover lies outside of physics as a science and so remains unexamined in this study [Cf. *Physics* II, 7, 198a27-30].

11 Aristotle, *On the Soul* II, 1, 412a27-28; 2, 413a21-413b4.

12 Aristotle, *On the Soul* III, 3, 427a17-19" "τῷ νοεῖν καὶ τῷ κρίνειν καὶ τῷ αἰσθάνεσθαι."

13 Aristotle, *On the Soul* III, 9, 432a15-18.

clearly continues the investigation of *On the Soul* II; both are natural science.

In effect, *On the Soul* examines the affections of soul, (i.e., soul as connected to body). As natural science, it must include a reference to matter and in principle cannot consider what is proper to soul (i.e., separable from body). If there is something proper to soul, then study of it belongs not to natural science but to first philosophy. I shall suggest in conclusion that the study of soul as it belongs to "the first philosopher" does appear in *Metaphysics* XII, an investigation of substance. By respecting the separation of the sciences, as Aristotle defines them, we can identify what is proper to soul as separate from body. In short, we can first work within the science of nature to define both soul and body as they are linked as well as the nature of this link and then turn to the investigation of substance to identify what is proper to soul as separate from body.

2. Soul as the First Actuality of Body: Body in Relation to Soul

On the Soul II, 1, opens with an important question: "what is soul and what would be the most common definition of it."[14] Aristotle assumes his account of substance, calling on several technical terms to argue that soul is form while body is matter. I turn first to his argument and then consider its terms and implications.

Substance is spoken of in three ways: (1) as matter [ὕλη], which in virtue of itself *is not* "a this"; (2) as form, namely shape [μορφὴν καὶ εἶδος], in virtue of which a thing *is* called "a this" and; (3) as what is from these [τὸ ἐκ τούτων].[15] Body, soul, and living things map onto

---

14 Aristotle, *On the Soul* II, 1, 412a1-5. I may note that Hamlyn translates "κοινότατος" as "comprehensive: τί ἐστι ψυχὴ καὶ τίς ἂν εἴη κοινότατος λόγος αὐτῆς.

15 Aristotle, *On the Soul* 412a6-9. Aristotle often uses the expression "τὸ ἐκ τούτων" for the combination of form and matter; for some examples, see *Physics* I, 3, 186b35; *Metaphysics* VII, 3, 1029a3; 10, 1035a1-2; VIII, 1, 1042a28-30; 3, 1043b17-18.

these kinds of substance. Body most of all is thought to be substance and every natural body that partakes of life (i.e., growth, decay, and self-nutrition) will be from matter and form.[16] So living body is the third kind of substance. Soul cannot be a body because soul distinguishes living from nonliving body.[17] Body is the substrate, the matter (i.e., substance that *is not* a this).[18] If body is matter, soul must be form [εἶδος], substance that *does* make a thing a "this."[19] But substance in the sense of form is also actuality [ἐντελέχεια]; so soul must be "form and actuality of a natural body able to have life." [20] This definition of soul rests on the terms that appear here and are defined in *Metaphysics* VII: "substance," "body," "substrate," "matter," "form," and "actuality."

In *Metaphysics* VII, Aristotle sets out from substance. There are, he says, many senses of being, but "that which is primarily is the 'what' " and indicates a thing's substance; therefore, substance is being that is primary—what a thing is without further qualification.[21] Expressed grammatically, substance is the subject while other kinds of being are predicates. Aristotle's account of substance, like his account of soul, affirms the priority of form (i.e., shape).[22] Matter and the individual composed of matter and form can also be subjects and so are also substance, but not in the primary sense. Form alone is primary substance and soul is form.

The affirmation of form as prior to matter entails a rejection of what Aristotle calls the "most common view": body is most obviously substance.[23] Since he identifies body with the substrate and

---

16 Aristotle, *On the Soul* II, 1, 412a14-16; cf. *Metaphysics* VII, 2, 1028b8.
17 Aristotle, *On the Soul* II, 1, 412a16: . . . οὐκ ἂν εἴη σῶμα ἡ ψυχή.
18 Aristotle, *On the Soul* II, 1, 412a16-19. The key words in Greek read: τὸ ὑποκείμενον καὶ ὕλη.
19 Aristotle, *On the Soul* II, 1, 412a19-21.
20 Aristotle, *On the Soul* II, 1, 412a21.
21 Aristotle, *Metaphysics* VII, 1, 1028a14-15; 30-31.
22 Aristotle, *Physics* II, 1, 193b7; *Metaphysics* VII, 3, 1029a6; 29-30.
23 Aristotle, *Metaphysics* VII, 2, 1028b8-11; on this rejected view, body includes animals, plants, their parts and natural bodies such as fire, water, or earth. Compare this list with "things that are by nature" at *Physics* II, 1, 192b9-11.

matter, if body is primary, matter is primary; "impossible" he says.[24] As the substrate and the matter, body is substance in the secondary sense of what cannot be a "this such"; [25] finally, he makes the compound of form and matter the weakest sense of substance because any compound must be posterior to its parts.[26] Living things have soul as their form and body as their substrate, or matter, and so are substance in the sense of being the combination of form and matter.

The unequivocal identification of soul with form in *On the Soul* II, 1, makes soul the most important kind of substance—what can be a "this such" without further qualification—and so being too. In *Physics* II, 1, Aristotle reaches the same conclusion about nature: it is primarily form.[27] So as part of natural science, *On the Soul* agrees with the definition of what a natural thing is in the *Physics* and as an account of substance it agrees with *Metaphysics* VII.

But what does "this such" mean and why is being "this such" primary? I shall turn to form as a "this such" in a moment. First, further clarification of "body," "matter," and "the substrate" will answer these questions. Again, *Metaphysics* VII, 3, helps us interpret *On the Soul* II, 1. The substrate, he says there, can be thought of in different ways and matter is one of them.[28] As the word implies, the "substrate" is something that underlies; as underlying, it is crucial to all generation and destruction because all life requires something underlying that remains

---

24 Aristotle, *Metaphysics* VII, 3, 1029a26-27.
25 See Aristotle, *Metaphysics* VII, 1, 1028b9-10; 2, 1028b35-1029a2.
26 Aristotle, *Metaphysics* VII, 3, 1029a26-32.
27 See Aristotle, *Physics* II, 1, 193b3-7.
28 Aristotle, *Metaphysics* VII, 3, 1029a2; Hamlyn remarks, citing *Metaphysics* VII, 3, that strictly speaking the identification of the substrate [τὸ ὑποκείμενον] with matter is "incorrect." Hamlyn *Aristotle's On the Soul: Books II and III (with Certain Passages from Book I)*, trans. with Introduction and Notes by D. W. Hamlyn (Oxford: Clarendon, 1968), 83. I may note that the Greek word here "τὸ ὑποκείμενον" may be translated as substrate or subject. Both can be taken to mean "what underlies." Hamlyn translates it as "subject," where I translate "substrate" but of course we read the same Greek both in *On the Soul* and elsewhere.

one and the same.²⁹ So Aristotle concludes: "[m]atter, in the most proper sense of the term, is to be identified with the substrate ..."³⁰ Because it underlies change, the substrate underlies, we might say, different predicates, and so in this sense it is a subject and a substance.

But form is primary substance. In contrast to body as the substrate and matter, soul is form and so must also be actuality. Here we reach the final term in the compressed argument of *On the Soul* II, 1. Identified with form, actuality is central to Aristotle's account of soul and means "fulfillment" or being complete.³¹ As complete, "actuality" contrasts with "potentiality" and matter is potentiality.³² Strictly speaking, "potentiality" means "possibility [for being complete]"; body is identified with matter in *On the Soul* II, 1, because body has the *possibility* of life.³³ "Body as potentially having life" refers only to body such as seeds or fruit.³⁴ Life involves growth, decay, and self-nutrition and body such as seeds or fruit may lead to (i.e., having the possibility of life in exactly this sense).

Growth, decay, and self-nutrition are kinds of motion and together potency and actuality define motion for Aristotle. Motion is always incomplete, the actualization of the potential, as potential, by that which is actual.³⁵ "Potential" means "possible" in the sense that fulfillment may yet be achieved, and motion is the process by which fulfillment is actually achieved, for example, the growth of an individual to full size. So matter, being potential, is moved while form, being actual,

---

29 Aristotle, *On Generation and Corruption* I, 1, 314b2-4. Aristotle is here reporting views of those who construct all things from a single elements, as opposed to those who have multiple kinds and so make generation and corruption mere mingling of these different kinds. He supports, in his own way, the prior view.

30 Aristotle, *On Generation and Corruption* I, 5, 320a2-3; see *On Generation and Corruption*. I, 3, 319a19-20; *Metaphysics* VII, 8, 1033a24-26.

31 Aristotle, *Metaphysics* IX, 3, 1047a30.

32 Aristotle, *On the Soul* II, 1, 412a9.

33 Aristotle, *On the Soul* II, 1, 412a17; see *Metaphysics* IX, 1, 1046a29-30.

34 Aristotle, *On the Soul* II, 1, 412b27-27.

35 Aristotle, *Metaphysics* IX, 6, 1048b28-30. See Aristotle, *Physics* III, 1, 201a11, 28-29; 3, 202a13-16.

is the mover. Now we see Aristotle's three kinds of substance more clearly: body is matter (i.e., it is moved and becomes developed); soul is form (i.e., it is actual and the mover) and the living thing (i.e., the combination of form and matter) is the individual in which motion occurs.

Before pursuing soul and body as mover and moved, I would like to distinguish motion, which involves body and soul, from activity. Motion is defined as a process, the actualization of what is potential [by what is actual]. "Activity" is complete at any moment, never requiring or involving development; Aristotle's examples of activity are sensation or thinking.[36] Thinking, as we saw at *On the Soul* I, 1, may be "proper" to soul and so separate from body. As activity, it does not involve motion, actualization, or matter. It may be proper to soul because it is not clear that it involves body.

The terms raised by the argument of *On the Soul* II, 1, bring us to the relation of body to soul, now defined as matter and the substrate, in relation to form and actuality within the living thing composed of form and matter. As actuality, form acts as mover and body as matter and potentiality is moved, or acted upon by form. But matter is never neutral to form; matter desires form as its good;[37] matter posseses an innate impulse, or appetite, for form as its mover.[38] In living things, since body is matter and soul is form, we must conclude that body desires soul.

Now we can see how this relation plays out in living things. Form and matter are constitutive principles that make a natural thing composed of them what it is. Because form makes a thing actual, form is the primary target of the definition. For example, the form of a human

---

36 Aristotle, *Metaphysics* IX, 6, 1048b18-33.
37 Aristotle, *Physics* I, 9, 192a20-24; see also, *On the Heavens* I, 3, 270b23, where the heavens have "aether" as their matter and Aristotle derives the word "aether" from "to run always."
38 See Aristotle, *Physics* II, 1, 192b18, where the contrasts between what is by nature and what is by art rests on the fact that things that are by art have no innate impulse for change.

is rational and "rational" is the primary term in the definition. Matter constitutes the range of possibilities defined by form and these possibilities always, whenever possible, find expression in the individual, the combination of form and matter. Therefore, the definiton of natural things must include a reference to matter. So for example, if a natural thing is human, the form must be "rational" and any individual has the possibility of hair, which in its turn has a possible range of colors; but a human, John or Jane, being rational has no possibility for scales or feathers, and *a fortiori* the wider range of colors found in birds or reptiles. In this sense, form causes matter—form sets the boundaries making a "this such"—while matter, desiring expression within these boundaries, runs after form, and together they constitute the individual.[39]

In *On the Soul* II, 1, Aristotle says that matter is substance that in virtue of itself cannot be a "this such." Matter cannot be without form to define the range of its possibilities, possibilities for which matter has an appetite. Because matter is actively oriented toward form, they work together to constitute an individual, defined by a single unique form (e.g., rational) and, expressed by the individual, the combination of form and matter. For example, a human is defined as "rational animal" and that definition is expressed by the individual who, being rational, is bipedal, has an opposed thumb, etc.

No part of an individual escapes the mark of form. Here we arrive at form as making a thing a "this such" and matter as failing to do so. For example, if bones are found, a pathologist immediately declares "this is a human," "this is a dog." There is no such thing as a bone or any part of an individual that is not a kind. And so no individual part can either be or be known without reference to the specific kind, the form. But the converse is not true. An expert, for example the pathologist, can know a kind without reference to any given individual, and once the

---

39 Aristotle, *Physics* I, 9.

pathologist knows a specific kind that knowledge may in a sense be independent of any individual. In short, this or that body, either as a whole of any part, can neither be nor be known apart from form. And for living things, form is unequivocally soul. Soul, as form, makes an individual to be a specific kind—dog, cat, human—while body, as matter, cannot be at all except as being the bone or blood of a cat, of a dog, of a human. But if form is able to be apart, then why (at least in nature) is form always found with matter? Matter is actively oriented toward form and, desiring it, matter seizes every opportunity to be with form. So in living things we see soul as shape and kind; we see body as matter that expresses form in relation to shape and growth, decay and self-nutrition. Body expresses the dynamic relation of matter to form; soul as form causes the living body to be alive by being a specific kind.

3. Soul and The Activity of Thinking

Soul is form and form is actuality; so soul must be actuality. But actuality, Aristotle says, is ambiguous. Soul may be like knowledge, which is actual but not fully active and so is capable of further development; or soul may be be like contemplation, which is fully active and so incapable of further development. Knowledge is potency "for the sake of" the activity of contemplation. For example, a trained doctor, when eating or praying, possesses knowledge of "the facts" of medicine, but is not actively practicing medicine. Actuality that is fully active completes potency that is "aimed" at it. So actuality that is fully active completes actuality as knowledge. In an emergency, the doctor immediately starts practicing medicine. Soul is actuality in the sense that knowledge is actuality. It is prior in origin and a prerequisite of complete active actuality. Why is soul actual in the weaker rather than the stronger sense? Aristotle's account of soul in sensation and thinking answers this question. It also returns us to the key question of *On the Soul* I, 1: is there an activity that is "proper" to soul, belonging to soul as separate from body? Sensation is to its object, he claims, as thought is to its object. So the relation of sensation to its object provides a model for the relation of thinking to its object. And thinking, most of all our activities, may be "proper" to soul.

First sensation, then thinking. Sensation, Aristotle says, consists in being moved and acted upon.[40] Much of *On the Soul* II concerns the separate senses, each of which is acted upon by its proper object (e.g., color is the proper object of sight). In each case, the analysis rests on the distinction between what is potential and what is actual, as we have already seen these terms. The sense is potential in the sense of possessing ability (e.g., sight is the ability to see, hearing is the ability to hear). This ability is first produced through generation by a parent.[41] Generation is important for two reasons: (1) There is no ability without a kind just as there is no body without a kind; ability is specified by kind, and (2) individuals of different kinds have different abilities (e.g., humans think, antelopes run). Generation explains different abilities among different kinds and identical ability among individuals of like kind. But actual sensation is not just having the potential defined by generation; actual sensation is an activity that corresponds to contemplation, the activity involved in the full exercise of knowledge.[42] (There are differences between sensation and thought but considering them as alike tells us about contemplation.)

We have already seen potency, actuality, and the dynamic relation between them. In Aristotle's account of sensation (and so thinking too), we see this relation at work. The sense is potentially what the sensible object is actually. For example, the eye is able to see a wide range of colors while the visible object must be an actual specific color; the activity of sight occurs when the eye's capacity is acted upon by the actual color of a sensible object.[43] There is one actuality, that of

---

40 Aristotle, *On the Soul* II, 5, 416b33-34.
41 Aristotle, *On the Soul* II, 5, 417b16-18.
42 Aristotle, *On the Soul* II, 5, 417b18-19.
43 Aristotle, *On the Soul* II, 5, 418a3-5.

the object, and that actuality defines what the eye sees and so defines what the eye becomes when it is actually sees. "Fully active" for the eye means seeing an actual color. Aristotle makes the point unequivocally "at the end, the one acted upon [the eye] is assimilated to the other [the color of the sensed object] and is identical in quality with it."[44] Sensation, then, is the capcity to sense, given by the parent and so defined by kind, fully actualized—made completely active—by its proper object. When the sense becomes identical with its object, no further development is possible: the sense is fully active.

Now thinking. Just as sight is first given by the parent, so humans first receive mind or rationality from their parents. Just as the eye possesses a range of potential colors and is actualized by one specific actual color, so the mind can think all things but is actualized by one specific intelligible object. "Thought must be related to what is thinkable, as sense is to what is sensible."[45] Therefore, mind must be completely unmixed so that it can receive any object and when it receives an object it becomes the actuality of this object. When the mind has acquired knowledge in this way—at *On the Soul* II, 1, as we saw, Aristotle identifies soul with knowledge in this sense—it can actively contemplate. When it engages in this activity, there is no possibility of further development: "thought" Aristotle says, "is able to think itself" [καὶ αὐτὸς δὲ αὐτὸν τότε δύναται νοεῖν].[46]

The identification of soul with knowledge and its transition to contemplation or activity is key. We can take an example of how this transition works. Someone beginning to learn "the facts" of medicine is potential in the sense of rational (possessing mind given by one's parents) but untrained. Someone who has completed their training has

---

44 Aristotle, *On the Soul* II, 5, 418a5-6. At *Metaphysics* IX, 5, 1048a6-7, Aristotle notes that in the case of lifeless things, when agent and patient are in contact, one must act and the other be acted upon, e.g., a flame and a piece of paper.
45 Aristotle, *On the Soul* III, 4, 429a17-18.
46 Aristotle, *On the Soul* III, 4, 429b9.

acquired "the facts" of medicine—now possesses them internally—but may not be actively practicing at the moment. A doctor may be sleeping or eating. If a medical emergency occurs, the doctor who knows the facts is the potential doctor who springs into action; when the doctor diagnoses the problem, the thinking that is occuring must be fully active—that is, thinking as fully active calls on the facts that have been acquired, the facts in virtue of which we say "the doctor has knowledge," and judgment follows. The soul can think itself in this sense: the facts of medicine have been internalized and as internal serve as the basis for the activity of doctoring.

If the soul in a way thinks itself, does this activity constitute something "proper" to soul (i.e., something independent of body)? At *On the Soul* I, 1, Aristotle states the problem clearly. Thinking seems to be the best candidate for what is proper to soul—that is, belonging to it as separate from the body. But if thinking too proves to be impossible without imagination, then thinking too requires body. When soul in a way thinks itself, (e.g., actually practicing medicine) soul uses facts acquired in a prior development. And the acquisition of the facts, as we see in the account of *On the Soul* III, requires that the potency of the mind, its unmixed capacity to know, be actualized by the facts. This actualization explains how external facts, such as those of medicine, enter the soul (thereby becoming internal) and it does require imagination. Aristotle goes on in *On the Soul* III, 5, to explain that thought gains its character by first becoming all things—the acquisition of facts—and then by making all things (i.e., passing judgement on facts by virtue of the knowledge that one possesse)s.

The conclusion of his argument makes the case in an even stronger form. There are objects of thought and objects of sense.[47] How are they related? It seems, he says that there is no "fact" [πράμα] outside of sensible magnitudes and so objects of thought are always abstracted from

---

47 Aristotle, *On the Soul* III, 8, 431b20-23.

sensible things; so, for example, points, lines, and surfaces are found in bodies and the mathematician abstracts them from body.[48] Therefore, knowledge must begin in sensation and all knowledge—even the most abstract—uses images from sensation [ὅταν τε θεωρῇ, ἀνάγκη ἅμα φαντάσματι θεωρεῖν].[49] With this conclusion, Aristotle turns to the soul as originating local motion in animals.

Our examination of soul in *On the Soul*, then, reaches two couclusions: (1) Body depends upon soul as matter or potency depends upon form or actuality; body cannot be at all without being "this kind" of body and in the case of body that is potentially alive, the form or actuality is soul, and (2) soul depends upon body as a necessary condition of thinking because all thinking begins in sensation and requires imagination. In short, in *On the Soul*, Aristotle fails to reach any activity that is "proper" to soul; he fails to reach a sense in which soul can be or act independently of the body.

But *On the Soul*, as we saw, is natural science: the investigation of natural things defined primarily by form that must also include a reference to matter. If there were an examination of soul, or mind, that is not part of natural science, perhaps it would yield something "proper" to soul (or mind), something independent of body or matter. Is there an investigation that can be called "first philosophy" and that includes soul?

4. Conclusion

Metaphysics XII, 1, opens as follows: the inquiry concerns substance, and the inquiry concludes with an analysis of the activity of thinking from which matter is explicitly excluded. The primary problem of *Metaphysics* XII concerns how the cosmos is unified and how it

---

48 Aristotle, *On the Soul* III, 8, 432a3-6.
49 Aristotle, *On the Soul* III, 8, 432a7-9.

contains the good; Aristotle concludes that the fishes, the fowls, and the plants are all ordered together.[50] This conclusion rests on his analysis of the first motion of the cosmos and the cause that originates it. This motion, the motion of the first heaven, must be continuous circular locomotion and it requires a cause that is itself incapable of being moved and so has no matter; having no matter, this cause can only be form and actuality.[51] As in *On the Soul* II, form and actuality are ambiguous. Is this mover actual as knowledge or as contemplation? The first mover is actuality that is fully active, has never undergone motion or process in any sense: perfect activity for all time.[52] It must exercise the highest activity, the only activity capable of being eternal and unchanging: thinking. Indeed, this mover enjoys the best life; it enjoys forever the life of perfect activity, thinking, which we enjoy only for a short time.[53]

But there is a problem. Thinking, as we have seen, becomes identical with the actuality of its object; so the first mover would take on the actuality of whatever it thinks about and becoming actual in this sense is a form of motion. Therefore, the first mover must have the highest possible object as the eternal object of its thinking.[54] The first unmoved mover must forever, unceasingly, actively, without change, contemplate itself: it is perfect activity (i.e., thought thinking thought for all time).[55] Here Aristotle identifies the first mover as god. "If, then, God is always in that good state in which we sometimes are, this compels our wonder; and if in a better this compels it yet more. And god *is* in a better state. And life also belongs to god; for the actuality of thought is life, and god is that actuality; and god's essential actuality is

---

50 Aristotle, *Metaphysics* XII, 10, 1075a15-17.
51 Aristotle, *Metaphysics* XII, 6, 1071b9-22.
52 Aristotle, *Metaphysics* XII, 7,1072a24-26; 1072b4-6.
53 Aristotle, *Metaphysics* XII, 7, 1072b1-15.
54 Aristotle, *Metaphysics* XII, 9, 1074b15-34.
55 Aristotle, *Metaphysics* XII, 9, 1074b35-1075a10.

life most good and eternal. We say therefore that god is a living being, eternal, most good, so that life and duration continuous and eternal belong to god. For this *is* god."[56]

So thinking, as we see in the case of god, can be an activity that is proper to soul in the sense of being independent of all reference to body and to matter. But thinking as proper to soul and without reference to body seems to belong to god and not humans. But Aristotle does say that the activity god enjoys forever humans enjoy for a short time. What does this claim amount to? The activity of thinking enjoyed by god is perfect. When Aristotle takes up perfection for humans, he again compares human activity to the activity that god enjoys.

The highest perfection for humans is is defined in the *Nicomachean Ethics*: happiness. Happiness, Aristotle says at *Nicomachean Ethics* X, 6, is for us the "end" [τέλος] or that for the sake of which. As such happiness is an activity, like sensation or thinking. And "if happiness is activity in accordance with excellence" [εἰ δ' ἐστιν ἡ εὐδαιμονία κατ' ἀρετὴν ἐνέργεια], that must mean the highest excellence which is of the best in us.[57] The best in us is our intellect [ἔννοια] and the intellect should be our natural ruler and guide whether we think it divine or only the most divine thing in us.[58]

Here in the *Ethics*, Aristotle's position emerges unequivocally: complete happiness for humans is the intellect's activity conducted with proper excellence.[59] Within us, it is what is best, most continuous, and most self-sufficient.[60] And when, Aristotle concludes, being mortal, we think of god and of immortal things, we make ourselves identical with an object that is immortal to the highest and fullest extent possible. With god as our object of thought, we become identical to pure and

---

56 Aristotle, *Metaphysics* XII, 7 1072b24-31.
57 Aristotle, *Nicomachean Ethics* X, 7, 1177a12-14.
58 Aristotle, *Nicomachean Ethics* X, 7, 1177a14-16.
59 Aristotle, *Nicomachean Ethics* X, 7, 1177a17.
60 Aristotle, *Nicomachean Ethics* X, 7, 1177a23-34.

perfect activity. The only difference between humans and god is that the first unmoved mover is perfect forever while we are perfect only for a little while. But for that little while, we apparently experience thinking that is "proper" to the soul: thinking of the highest being, itself perfect activity, free of body or matter. When we become identical with this mover as our object of thought, i.e., we are free of all reference to matter or to body, engaging in our highest excellence. By engaging in the thinking proper to soul, we exercise soul as it is apart from body: we are active in the sense proper to soul.

CHAPTER THREE

Beautiful Bodies and Shameful Embodiment in Plotinus's *Enneads*

Lesley-Anne Dyer Williams

1. Introduction

The reception of Plotinus (204/5–270 CE) and his concept of embodiment has tended to emphasize two seemingly contradictory aspects of his thought. The accounts of Plotinus's life supplied by Porphyry have given his philosophy a general reputation for disdaining the body.[1] Plotinus's refusal to have a portrait taken and other stories by Porphory used to illustrate his shame in embodiment are often cited in order to argue that his

---

1 While some consider Plotinus to be an influence on Christian asceticism, the renowned classicist E. R. Dodds sees Plotinus's shame in embodiment as indicative of the general spirit of the time, manifest in both Neoplatonic and Christian asceticism. E. R. Dodds, *Pagan and Christian in an Age of Anxiety: Some Aspects of Religious Experience from Marcus Aurelius to Constantine*, reprint edition (Cambridge and New York: Cambridge University Press, 1991). For a more extensive bibliographical account, see Daniel A. Dombrowski, "Asceticism in Plotinus," in *Philosophie: Historische Einleitung, Platonismus*, ed. Hildegard Temporini and Wolfgang Haase (Berlin: Walter de Gruyter, 1987), 703–704.

asceticism was motivated by hatred of the body rather than by athletic philosophical rigor.² And yet, scholars also credit him with the voluptuous aesthetics at the heart of the Italian Renaissance and nineteenth-century Romanticism.³ Depending upon the discipline—philosophy, theology, or art—Plotinus may be viewed as either a Gnostic that hates bodies or a grand theorizer of bodily beauty.

Although Plotinus's concept of embodiment is often associated with Gnosticism and a sense of shame, these common generalizations overlook key metaphysical distinctions in his philosophy made between matter, body, and soul.⁴ His motivations for these distinctions are best seen in his attacks upon the Gnostics, Materialists, and the Simple Hylomorphists (not to be confused with all Aristotelians).⁵ Once these distinctions are grasped, it is possible to reconcile his

---

2 All citations of the *Life of Plotinus* and the *Enneads* are in the Armstrong translation with reference to the Greek in Plotinus and Arthur Hilary Armstrong, *Ennead*, vol. 1–6, Loeb Library (Cambridge, MA: Harvard University Press, 1966).

3 Stephen Halliwell, *The Aesthetics of Mimesis: Ancient Texts and Modern Problems* (Princeton, NJ: Princeton University Press, 2009); Douglas Hedley, *Coleridge, Philosophy and Religion: Aids to Reflection and the Mirror of the Spirit* (Cambridge and New York: Cambridge University Press, 2000); Aphrodite Alexandrakis and Nicholas J. Moutafakis, *Neoplatonism and Western Aesthetics* (Albany: SUNY Press, 2002); Michael J. B. Allen, V. Rees, and Martin Davies, *Marsilio Ficino: His Theology, His Philosophy, His Legacy* (Leiden, The Netherlands: Brill, 2002); John Hendrix, *Aesthetics & The Philosophy Of Spirit* (New York: Peter Lang, 2005); Stephen Gersh and Bert Roest, *Medieval and Renaissance Humanism: Rhetoric, Representation and Reform* (Boston: Brill, 2003).

4 I generally follow Margaret Miles in preferring to avoid "the body" because it refers to a generic human body, except in those circumstances where the body is spoken of generically in relationship to the soul. Her book gives a much fuller exposition of Plotinus's life and treatises than is possible here: Margaret R. Miles, *Plotinus on Body and Beauty: Society, Philosophy, and Religion in Third-Century Rome*, 1st ed. (Oxford and Malden, MA: Wiley-Blackwell, 1999), xii. Although it is not possible to discuss it here, embodiment in Plotinus's philosophy is a concept that would pertain to both human bodies and the physical world as a whole.

5 This chapter contrasts Plotinus with views of his contemporaries. It does not deal with the relationship between Plotinus and Christianity on embodiment. Augustine contrasts the two in the *City of God*, pointing out the pride of Platonists when they think their own effort can help them attain salvation. Stephen Gersh has written the best comparative study of Neoplatonist and Christian concepts of transcendence and immanence: *From Iamblichus to Eriugena: An Investigation of the Prehistory and Evolution of the Pseudo-Dionysian Tradition* (Leiden, The Netherlands: Brill, 1978). The following work is helpful when trying to compare it with modern philosophers like Descartes and Hegel: Kevin Corrigan and John Douglas Turner, *Platonisms: Ancient, Modern, and Postmodern* (Boston: Brill, 2007).

phenomenological experience of bodily shame (and his rejection of having a portrait made) with his clear aesthetic appreciation of beautiful bodies and unsentimental art. Plotinus valued ensouled and enformed bodies for their capacity to bring order and life to the physical world and for their ability to turn human souls towards their divine origins. However, he experienced and taught a problematic view of *human* embodiment because human souls could easily become distracted from their proper objects of philosophical contemplation by temporal, transient bodies. He theorized that the human embodied state resulted from an original fall of soul's into bodies when those same souls became distracted from the One.

2. Against a Variety of Materialisms, including the Simple Hylomorphists

Plotinus begins his treatise on matter by assuming that he is addressing an audience that believes there is a distinction between matter and form and that disagrees primarily over the definition of each and how they are related.[6] The matter-form composite is assumed by Plotinus because the process of decay is self-evident and this decay indicates a distinction between matter and form.[7] The two kinds of materialists he addresses most particularly are the Stoics who think all beings, including the gods, are matter-form composites and those who confuse matter with atoms or elements.[8] He further opposes what I will call the simple hylomorphists, that is, those who admit to immaterial entities but think these immaterial entities, including souls, arise out of matter. Two criticisms of these positions by Plotinus are particularly relevant to his concept of embodiment. First, he criticizes those who would

---

6 *Enneads*, II.4.1.
7 *Enneads*, II.4.6.
8 *Enneads*, II.4.1.

conflate matter and body. Second, he criticizes those who do not see that neither form nor life (i.e., soul) could arise from matter itself.

The conflation of matter and body is particularly an issue for modern readings of Plotinus because our common definition of matter tends to consist of what Plotinus would call body. Bodies need matter because without them they would have no mass or magnitude, but they cannot be reduced simply to matter.[9] Plotinus defines matter in a way that distinguishes it from Empedoclean elements, Democritean atoms, and any other theory that proposes its existence as body without the influence of Mind. Matter cannot be Empedoclean elements, as the Stoic believed, because elements can decay.[10] Some further principle is necessary to explain this change. Democritean atoms cannot be base matter either, as the Epicureans believed, because all bodies are endlessly divisible. In addition, Plotinus thought that it is impossible to explain the continuity of things apart from Mind, and it is impossible for a creative power to produce anything out of a matter that is not continuous.

"Matter," for Plotinus as for Plato, does not mean atoms or elements. It does not mean a mass that needs to be shaped. Any analogy drawn between the creation of the universe and a potter making something out of clay ignores the fact that bodiliness is a quality that must be made out of matter first.[11] That is, matter is not a body. It only becomes corporeal when it is formed in some way. Matter is mere privation or negativity, the absence of all form and the precondition for change.[12]

---

9 *Enneads*, II.4.6.
10 *Enneads*, II.4.7.
11 *Enneads*, II.4.8.
12 Its origin is contested. See for example, Denis O'Brien, *Plotinus on the Origin of Matter: An Exercise in the Interpretation of the Enneads* (Berkeley, CA: Bibliopolis, 1991); Denis O'Brien, "Plotinus on the Making of Matter Part I: The Identity of Darkness," *International Journal of Platonic Tradition* 5, no. 1 (2011): 6–57; Denis O'Brien, "Plotinus on the Making of Matter Part II: 'A Corpse Adorned' (Enn. II 4 [12] 5.18)," *International Journal of Platonic Tradition* 5, no. 2 (2011): 209–261(53);' Denis O'Brien, "Plotinus on the Making of Matter Part III: The Essential Background," *International Journal of Platonic Tradition* 6, no. 1 (2012): 27–80; John F. Phillips, "Plotinus on the Generation of Matter," *International Journal of Platonic Tradition* 3, no. 2 (2009): 103–137.

Matter is purely a substratum, and what we often consider matter—atoms, elements, etc.—are already bodies with some form.[13]

Ultimately, matter has no existence prior to being formed. Plotinus was a Monist, not a Dualist, believing that there was only one first principle, the One or the Good. Monism entails that there is only one principle of the universe—the Good. Matter cannot therefore exist independently of form as if it were a first principle alongside the One.

It is worth noting here that although Plotinus denies that bodies are inherently evil (as will be seen in the next section) he does at times speak about matter as evil.[14] Proclus even criticizes Plotinus for verging upon Dualism because of this tendency.[15] Matter is only evil when considered as a privation or perversion of something that ought to be there. This privation generally considered is absolute evil, and when there is a "negation of something that ought to be present" in the soul, that soul is evil. Even when matter is considered as something evil, Plotinus writes:

> [E]vil is not alone: by virtue of the nature of Good, the power of Good, it is not Evil only: it appears, necessarily, bound around with the bonds of Beauty, like some captive bound in fetters of gold; and beneath these it is hidden so that, while it must exist, it may not be seen by the gods, and that men need not always have evil before their eyes, but that when it comes before them they may still be not destitute of Images of the Good and Beautiful for their Remembrance.[16]

---

13 *Enneads*, II.4.14. While he does not think matter is potentiality, Plotinus does employ Aristotle's matter to explain Plato's receptacle; see Gary M. Gurtler, "Plotinus: Matter and Otherness, on Matter (II 4 [12])," *Epoché: A Journal for the History of Philosophy* 9, no. 2 (2005): 197–214.
14 *Enneads*, I.8.
15 Jan Opsomer, "Proclus vs Plotinus on Matter ('De Mal. Subs.' 30-7)," *Phronesis: A Journal of Ancient Philosophy* 46, no. 2 (2001): 154–188.
16 *Enneads*, I.8.15.

There is never any time when any body or any soul exists without some Good or Beauty present there alongside it. Although to the rebellious this Beauty appears as a chain, it is actually a vestige of the Good, calling the soul to remember. This presence of the Good occurs because matter is never present without body and bodies are inherently good because they have the gift of form from the intelligible world.

Kalogirotou adequately summarizes Plotinus on the existence of evil when he writes, "Matter is only evil in other than a purely metaphysical sense when it becomes an impediment to return to the One."[17] The body is inherently good and is only improved when it receives a soul. The problem with bodies concerns their effect upon souls. Furthermore, all evils ultimately fit within a larger whole that is good. In a treatise on Providence, Plotinus compares the relationship of the aesthetically beautiful whole of the world and individual "evils" to a stage-production:

> In the dramas of human art, the poet provides the words but the actors add their own quality, good or bad—for they have more to do than merely repeat the author's words—in the truer drama which dramatic genius imitates in its degree, the Soul displays itself in a part assigned by the creator of the piece.
>
> As the actors of our stages get their masks and their costume, robes of state or rags, so a Soul is allotted its fortunes, and not at haphazard but always under a Reason: it adapts itself to the fortunes assigned to it, attunes itself, ranges itself rightly to the drama, to the whole Principle of the piece: then it speaks out its business, exhibiting at the same time all that a Soul can express of its own quality, as a singer in a song. A voice, a bearing, naturally fine or vulgar, may

---

17 Androniki Kalogiratou, "Plotinus' Views on Soul, Suicide, and Incarnation," *Schole* 3, no. 2 (2009): 394.

increase the charm of a piece; on the other hand, an actor with his ugly voice may make a sorry exhibition of himself, yet the drama stands as good a work as ever.[18]

Individual evils perceived in the world—cries, wars, and all ugliness—all play a part in the divine plan, which is inherently good.

In addition to conflating matter and body, materialism does not, according to Plotinus, give an adequate explanation for the origin of life. When addressing this concern, Plotinus asks, "How could the composition of the elements have any sort of life?"[19] Life never arises spontaneously, since there is always some origin of motion. This origin is the soul:

> For soul is the "origin of motion" and is responsible for the motion of other things ... For certainly all things cannot have a borrowed life: or it will go on to infinity; but there must be some nature which is primarily alive, which must be indestructible and immortal of necessity since it is also the origin of life to others. Here, assuredly, all that is divine and blessed must be situated, living itself and existing of itself, existing primarily and living primarily, without any part in essential change, neither coming to be nor perishing ... This then which is primarily and always existent cannot be dead, like a store or wood, but must be alive, and have a pure life, as much of it as remains alone; but whatever is mixed with what is worse has an impeded relationship to the best—yet it certainly cannot lose its own nature—but recovers its "ancient state" when it runs up to its own.[20]

---

18 *Enneads*, III.2.17.
19 *Enneads*, II.9.5.18–19; cf.: Stephen R. L. Clark, "Plotinus; Body and Soul," in *The Cambridge Companion to Plotinus*, ed. Lloyd Gerson (Cambridge, UK: Cambridge University Press, 1996), 277.
20 *Enneads*, II.7.9–29.

This argument resembles the Aristotelian argument for the existence of God from motion, but it arrives at a stronger conclusion than an "Unmoved Mover," "Uncaused Cause," "Necessary Being," or "Pure Act." All motion, even bodily motion, originates with life. Life, which is something possessed by a soul, gives birth to other life and to motion. Just as there cannot be an infinite regress of motion, so there has to be one life that is the origin of all life and motion. This argument, unlike the Unmoved Mover argument, ascribes a single origin to two phenomena—life and motion. Plotinus shared the general understanding common among his philosophical predecessors that soul, in its most basic sense, means "life-giving force." He may have differed from them in the degree to which he would allow body and soul to be associated, but he shared this basic sense of soul as the gift of life.[21] Thus, he defines Universal Soul as the principle of form and life as it exists in the world. Insofar as Universal Soul is embodied in the world as Nature, it is the ultimate source of movement and life to all of the world. Universal Soul is not, however, the ultimate cause of things. Rather, the Universal Soul emanates from the Intellect, which emanates from the Life surrounding the One.[22]

While simple hylomorphism does not conflate matter and form in the way that most materialism does, Plotinus considers it to be equally problematic in accounting for the origin of life. Pure entelechy (the matter-form composite analogously applied to body and soul) does not have the capacity to explain what a soul is or where it came from.[23]

---

21 Paul Kalligas, "Living Body, Soul, and Virtue in the Philosophy of Plotinus," *Dionysius* 18 (2000): 25–37; Paul Kalligas, "Plotinus against the Corporealists on the Soul. A Commentary on Enn. IV 7 [2], 8.1–23," in *Studi sull'anima in Plotino*, ed. Riccardo Chiaradonna (Naples, Italy: Bibliopolis, 2005), 95–112.

22 The theory of the three hypostases can be read about in more detail in the following handbooks: A. H Armstrong, *The Cambridge History of Later Greek and Early Medieval Philosophy* (Cambridge, UK: Cambridge University Press, 1967); Lloyd P. Gerson, ed., *The Cambridge History of Philosophy in Late Antiquity*, 2 vols. (Cambridge, UK: Cambridge University Press, 2011); *Alcinous: The Handbook of Platonism*, trans. and ed. John Dillon (Oxford: Clarendon, 1996).

23 *Enneads*, IV.1.1; *Enneads*, IV.7.8.

According to Plotinus, no theory of the soul in which life comes from non-life is a sufficient explanation for the origin of life. Pure entelechy, like materialism, is unsustainable for Plotinus because it makes several claims that he considers improbable: that life can come from nonlife and that nonliving elements might form living bodies merely by their union. Thus, hylomorphism in the sense of pure entelechy, suffers from the same problems as materialism because it posits a material origin for nonmaterial and living things.[24] All bodies are, of course, for Plotinus, some kind of entelechy, and at the end of the day pure matter never exists without form. Furthermore, soul is the source of all form in bodies and therefore the source of entelechy. Plotinus rejects, however, any conception of body and soul that reduces it to entelechy on the grounds that it is another form of materialism.

The denial of entelechy as a sufficient explanation for the soul-body relationship does not necessarily entail a full rejection of Aristotle's concept of the soul. The principle cause for concern is not Aristotelian hylomorphism, but entelechy as a physicalist explanation of soul. Plotinus believed that human souls have a twofold nature: they are embodied, and they transcend bodies.[25] Simplistic hylomorphism does not account for this two-fold nature. Nevertheless, while the soul can never in itself be an entelechy—that is, the form of a body—Pino argues that for Plotinus "the psychosomatic composite does admit of a certain hylomorphic character so that soul indeed informs body and supplies its entelechy."[26] Lloyd Gerson argues that Plotinus

---

[24] It is also not sufficient to explain the soul in terms of the logic of participation; rather, Christopher Horn argues, Plotinus employs the Aristotelian concept of *energeia* to articulate a Platonist biology while continuing to defend a form of psychophysical dualism. Christopher Horn, "Aspects of biology in Plotinus," in *Neoplatonism and the Philosophy of Nature*, eds. J. Wilberding and C. Horn (Oxford: Oxford University Press, 2012), 214–228.

[25] Suzanne Stern-Gillet, "Dual Selfhood and Self-Perfection in the Enneads," *Epoché: A Journal for the History of Philosophy* 13, no. 2 (2009): 331–345.

[26] Tikhon Alexander Pino, "Plotinus and the Aristotelian Hylomorphic Body: Making Room in Entelechy for the Soul as Substantial Form," *Dionysius* 31 (2013): 41–56.

misinterpreted Aristotle, who can be interpreted in a way that is consonant with this position because of his belief in the separable intellect.[27] In a certain sense, the soul may be said to exist in a hylomorphic relationship to the body as long as the soul is not said to arise from the body and to be reducible to the embodied soul. The soul has its ultimate origins in the Nous, and in a certain sense, remains there even when it forgets it has fallen.

3. In Praise of Bodily Beauty Against the Gnostics

While the materialists and simple hylomorphists both receive critiques from Plotinus because of their lack of a sufficient explanation for soul and life, the Gnostics receive even harsher criticism because they emphasize the importance of soul to the denigration of body. A. H. Armstrong notes that the "passionate intensity" with which Plotinus opposed the Gnostics was "fiercer than the sharpest of his school-polemic against Stoic materialism or Epicurean denial of Providence."[28] Furthermore, Armstrong surmises that some of the "Gnostics" were called "friends" by Plotinus because they attended his lectures and may have claimed him as an ally, but he vehemently opposes the beliefs of these "friends" because they twist the words of Plato and syncretistically unite them with Christian teachings.[29]

---

27 Lloyd P. Gerson, *Plotinus* (London: Routledge, 1999), 135. Gerson believes that Aristotle is actually working with the tradition of Plato. See Gerson, *Aristotle and Other Platonists* (Ithaca, NY: Cornell University Press, 2006).

28 A. H. Armstrong, *The Cambridge History of Later Greek and Early Medieval Philosophy* (Cambridge, UK: Cambridge University Press, 1967), 206.

29 The field of Gnostic studies changed dramatically with the rediscovery of Gnostic texts in Nag Hammadi, Egypt, in 1945. These texts point to a Jewish origin for the sect, but their syncretistic tendencies meant that they drew upon Christian and Platonist writings for their beliefs. Of those discovered, the Sethians, "whose teaching stood very close to the Christian heretic Valentinus" and who Porphyry simply calls "Christians," appear to be Plotinus's most likely opponents. James M. Robinson, editor of *The Nag Hammadi Library*, suggests that he had read *Zostianos, Allogenes, Three Steles of Seth,* and the *Trimorphic Protennoia*.

Plotinus' primary objection to Gnosticism concerned the way its teaching that embodiment is evil ignored the clear presence of beauty in the world:

> What other more fairer image of the intelligible world could there be? For what other fire could be a better image of the intelligible fire than this fire here? Or what other earth could be better than this, after the intelligible earth? And what sphere could be more exact or more dignified or better ordered in its circuit [than the sphere of this universe] after the self-enclosed circle there of the intelligible universe? And what other sun could there be which ranked after the intelligible sun and before this visible sun here?[30]

No other world could be a better image of the intelligible world than the one that exists right now. This present world, he writes, is second only to that higher one.

To understand the impact of this praise, it is important to note that Plotinus, like Plato, teaches that there are two worlds, a visible one and an intelligible one. The visible world is embodied and is perceived through the five senses. The intelligible world is invisible and can only be perceived by means of the intellect. This intelligible world is the first emanation from the Good, also known as the One, from which all things come into existence. The Intellect, its Ideas, the Universal Soul, and Individual Souls are all inhabitants of this intelligible world.

When Plotinus argues with the Gnostics that no "fairer image" of the intelligible world exists, he is arguing for both the beauty of the physical world and for what that beauty entails. The beauty (and imperfection) of fire on earth points to an even more beautiful fire. The beauty (and imperfection) of geometric shapes likes spheres and circles in the sensible world points to the existence of perfect geometric shapes. The

---

30 *Enneads*, II.9.4.25–32.

ability for the visible sun to give light in order to aid human perception by the senses points to an invisible sun that gives light by illumining the mind. The near perfection of this present world points to the pure perfection of the intelligible one. Sensible beauty indicates the existence of intelligible beauty.

The perception of sensible beauty has theological consequences for Plotinus. Just as the beauty of a piece of art is evidence for the craftsman's skill, so the beauty of the physical world is evidence of the craftsmanship of the universe's maker. Plotinus thinks that the beauty of the physical world is the primary communication of the divine to the human. Any claims to special revelation that undermined this communication are suspect. The Gnostics claimed that they knew the embodied world is evil because they had special communication from God intended for them personally. Plotinus mocks the Gnostics for supposing that they could trust a god that would allow the existence of an abjectly evil world. For this reason, Plotinus asked the Gnostics, "God, in his providence cares for you; why does he neglect the whole universe in which you yourselves are in?"[31] Their inability to see the living work of the creator in the world baffled Plotinus because he believed that nature, as the visage of the World Soul's benevolent work in the world, testifies to the providential care of the Intellect for the universe.[32] Thus, Plotinus asks, "why do they feel the need to be there in the archetype of the universe which they hate? And where did this archetype come from?"[33] The Gnostic claim that embodiment is evil "because God told them so" contradicts all evidence from nature concerning the nature of the divine. The failure (or refusal) of the Gnostics to perceive and rightly attribute beauty in the sensible world is a fatal mistake.

---

31 *Enneads*, II.9.9.64–66.
32 *Enneads*, II.9.3–4, 7–8, 10, 12, 17–18.
33 *Enneads*, II.9.5.27–30.

Gnostic rejection of bodily beauty entails a denial of the only *known* channel of communication between human and divine. Gnostics taught that they had direct communication from the divine, and this appeal to authority served as the basis for their philosophy of embodiment. Plotinus, following the inductive logic of Plato's *Timaeus*, saw that this philosophy of embodiment contradicted what could be known about the creator from observing the physical world. The Gnostic appeal to divine revelation contradicted what could be gathered about the divine by reason. The beauty of the physical world suggested to Plotinus that the maker of the world had used a beautiful template for it and therefore might be supposed to have good intentions for it, regardless of whether the human soul sees or remembers this goodness through the contemplation of beauty.

The Gnostic does not consider that the beautiful nature of a work reflects the good intention of its maker. The beauty of ensouled and enformed bodies in the universe is the primary justification that a person might have to believe in a good creator. For this reason, in stark contrast with the Gnostics, bodies, especially beautiful ones, are inherently good things for Plotinus. Not only are they constructed by means of form (something inherently good), but they also reveal the good intent of the maker of the universe.

4. The Aesthetic Shame of Embodiment in Porphyry's *Life of Plotinus*

Although Plotinus writes very positively about embodied life when writing against Gnostics, materialists, and simplistic hylomorphists, it can appear difficult to reconcile these writings with accounts of Plotinus's attitudes towards embodiment found in Porphyry's *Life of Plotinus*. If Plotinus valued bodily existence, why did he feel ashamed to be embodied? Most of our knowledge of Plotinus's life comes from the account given by his student, Porphyry, because Plotinus did not write about his own life. It is not possible to address here all instances of possible shame over embodiment described in the *Life of Plotinus*. The most relevant one for issues of aesthetics, however, concerns his refusal to get a portrait taken.

In his *Life of Plotinus*, Porphyry recalls his teacher's disconcerted preoccupation with embodiment and associates it with his aesthetics of image:

> Plotinus, the philosopher of our times, seemed ashamed of being in the body. As a result of this state of mind he could never bear to talk about his race or his parents or his native country. And he objected so strongly to sitting to a painter or sculptor that he said to Amelius, who was urging him to allow a portrait of himself to be made, "Why really, is it not enough to have to carry the image in which nature has encased us, without your requesting me to agree to leave behind me a longer-lasting image of the image, as if it was something genuinely worth looking at?"[34]

To illustrate the shame that Porphyry claims Plotinus possessed concerning his body, he gives a few pieces of evidence. First, Plotinus would never speak about where he came from and whom he descended from. Second, he was adamantly opposed to having his portrait taken, so much so that his students had to make one surreptitiously.

These two examples, however, do not necessarily imply that his shame originated from a hatred of body per se (although they might imply that he was ashamed of his own particular body, thinking it not particularly beautiful). They should instead be read alongside Plotinus own writings in the *Enneads* on embodiment, especially his stated belief that the most beautiful aspect of the human body is the human face because it is the window to the human soul.[35]

---

34 Porphyry, *Life of Plotinus*, 1.1–10.
35 Annick Charles-Saget, "Le Moi et son visage: Visage et lumière selon Plotin," *Chora: Revue d'études anciennes et médiévales* 5, no. 5 (2007): 65–78.

Concerning the limitations Plotinus placed upon his self-narration, what he would not say about his origin ought to be compared to what he did say. Plotinus did speak of his own education to his students. For example, he recounted his experiences studying philosophy in Alexandria at the age of 28. He was initially dissatisfied with all the teachers he encountered. Then he met Ammonius, who taught the fundamental agreement between Platonic and Aristotelian philosophy, and he found his philosophical home. The difference between Plotinus's story about his education and his failure to give an account of parental lineage rests in the purpose of the individual stories. Plotinus's account of his education had the potential to help his students, whereas stories about lineage and geographical origin pertained merely to the accidents of change, parts of the world that were not important in the pursuit of the cause and nature of it. They were by-products of matter. The fact that the lineage and geographical origin of personhood vary from individual to individual demonstrates that bodily origin comes from the world of change and becoming, not the world of being. The story about his education had value for Plotinus because it reflected intelligible realities as revealed on earth, unlike his physical appearance and human parentage, which were mere necessities of being a temporal and embodied creature.

If this interpretation of Plotinus's shame is true, he was unashamed of telling things that might help others, but he considered the particulars of his own individual existence to be unimportant. He would have approved of Porphyry's description of his education, but he would have disapproved of Porphyry's recounting his frequent stomach problems and personality quirks. Plotinus suffered a common affliction among popular teachers: his students were hungry for every detail of his personal life even though he thought these details distracted from their own philosophical pursuits.

Concerning his shame at having his portrait taken, Plotinus' remarks about his body being an image of an image allude to Plato's critique of the poets. In the *Republic* Bks. 2, 3 and 10, Plato famously argues that the poets are mere imitators of imitations.[36] The maker of the world made everything according to the form of his divine plan, and when a carpenter makes a chair, he makes it with the idea of a chair in mind. When a poet or painter makes a chair, however, he makes only an imitation of an imitation. Plotinus does not want his portrait taken because the goal is to capture his physical likeness, a temporary state of affairs. Just as genealogical and geographical representations focus upon the changing aspects of the physical world, so a portrait is capturing the temporary reality that Plotinus was embodied.

Plotinus's own treatises show that he did not condemn the arts of painting or sculpture. It seems what is being condemned in this disagreement with his student is merely sentimental portraiture. The *Enneads* contain a more sophisticated account of the image-reality relationship. In the treatise on intelligible beauty, Plotinus writes that the arts "do not simply imitate what they see, but they run back up to the forming principles from which nature derives; then also that they do a great deal by themselves, and, since they possess beauty, they make up what is defective in things."[37] This statement suggests that Plotinus did not think artists merely imitated imitations. Rather, they created beautiful things by imitating not only beautiful bodies but also intelligible beauty.

Although metaphysical assumptions today about intelligible realities and beauty are not identical with those of Plotinus, some contemporary analogies can be made with his concept of embodiment and art. Modern photography, for example, trends toward capturing the spirit of an occasion, not just the people involved. Analogies can also be made between Plotinus's refusal to give a parental lineage and the way historians today would never be content to be called genealogists,

---

36 A good introduction to this issue can be found in Charles L. Griswold, "Plato on Rhetoric and Poetry," in *The Stanford Encyclopedia of Philosophy*, ed. Edward N. Zalta, Fall 2014, http://plato.stanford.edu/archives/fall2014/entries/plato-rhetoric/.

37 *Enneads*, V.8.1.35–39, 239.

antiquarians, or journalists. In the case of modern artistry and the historian's craft, mimesis aims at more than mere imitation or description of physical objects or events. It reaches toward something more, maybe not a metaphysical reality in the Plotinian sense but certainly some communication of meaning beyond physical likeness or genealogical exactitude.

Plotinus's aesthetic theory distinguished types of mimetic acts based upon the ultimate use of a given image as well as the object imitated. This distinction between mimetic acts reflects the perspectival nature of Plotinus's philosophy. The same thing, the same object, the same image—a body—can be evil when viewed from the perspective of dissimilitude and good from the perspective of similitude. Is the body used by the soul to reveal unchanging realities, even though the body is itself changing? Then the body in that case is a good. Or is the body considered a good in itself and an occasion for the soul's distraction? In this case, the body is an evil. The desire to know about his parentage and to preserve his physical likeness were extraneous to what mattered most to him, the soul's ascent through the pursuit of philosophy. Bodies are not evil, but they can be a distraction from the soul's proper pursuit.

When Plotinus refused to sit for a portrait, asking Amelius why he wanted an image of an image, he was not repudiating art or even bodies. Rather, he was critiquing the imitation of bodily things for their own sake. Portraits of the sort that he desired were not designed to capture beauty or communicate intelligible ideas. They merely captured the physical likeness of a person for sentimental reasons. True art imitates the intelligible world and not the sensible one.

5. Conclusion

Taken out of context, Plotinus's refusal to have a portrait taken or to relate his parentage, his attacks upon matter as evil, and his references to the fall of souls into bodies can give the impression that he hates the body and embodied life. When such things are taken into account alongside his more positive statements on embodied life, however, the idea that Plotinus hates the body and embodiment appears much too simplistic. While it is a mistake to overvalue the body, it is equally problematic in Plotinian philosophy for Gnostics, materialists, and simple hylomorphists to not appreciate the beauties of embodied life.

It might be better to say that Plotinus hates the body only insofar as it is hindrance to the soul's ascent. The body in itself is a good. Its beauty is a testimony to the craftsmanship of its maker, and the way Nature guides it is evidence of the providential care of the Intellect. The placement of souls into bodies can be a good because the soul has the capacity to elevate the body by perfecting its form and giving it life; nevertheless, embodiment is a temporary state for the human soul and to cling to the body is to cling futilely to changeable matter.

CHAPTER FOUR

Augustinian Puzzles about Body, Soul, Flesh, and Death

Sarah Catherine Byers

Book Thirteen of the *City of God* contains a series of philosophical puzzles about embodiment. Some of these riddles Augustine himself poses; others arise for the reader, given the perplexing character of Augustine's assertions. My aim here will be to articulate the questions at issue and investigate whether, and if so how, we can piece together a coherent Augustinian account of embodiment. The particular approach I employ in doing so will also, I hope, advance the scholarship on Augustine by drawing attention to his role as a figure informed by the Aristotelian commentary tradition.

The overly simplistic view of Augustine as exclusively a "Christian Platonist" that long dominated secondary treatments has more recently been supplemented by research on Augustine's use of Stoicism and Aristotelianism; but there is more to be done.[1] Augustine knew Aristotle's *Categories* from the time he was a young man, as he tells us

---

[1] For Augustine and Stoicism, see Charles Brittain, "Non-Rational Perception in the Stoics and Augustine," *Oxford Studies in Ancient Philosophy* 22 (2002): 253–308; Sarah Byers, *Perception,*

in the *Confessions*.² Furthermore, it is clear that at least from the time of his anti-Manichean works and the early books of his *Literal Meaning of Genesis* he knew and used a number of basic concepts from classical physics and metaphysics, including some that were first articulated by Aristotle in the *Physics, Metaphysics*, and *On the Soul*.³ These could have been transmitted to him by anthologies of classical philosophical texts,⁴ or by commentators such as Plotinus and Victorinus.⁵

Sensibility, and Moral Motivation in Augustine (New York: Cambridge University Press, 2013). For Augustine and Aristotelianism, see Ilsetraut Hadot, *Arts libéraux et philosophie dans la pensée antique: contribution à l'histoire de l'éducation et de la culture dans l'Antiquité*, 2nd ed. (Paris: J. Vrin, 2005), 127–128; Timothy Chappell, *Aristotle and Augustine on Freedom* (New York: St. Martin's Press, 1995), 160–162; Montague Brown, "Augustine and Aristotle on Causality," in *Augustine: Presbyter Factus Sum*, eds. Joseph Lienhard, Earl Muller, and Roland Teske (New York: P. Lang, 1993), 473, 468–469; and William Mann, "Immutability and Predication: What Aristotle Taught Philo and Augustine," *International Journal for Philosophy of Religion* 22, no. 1–2 (1987), 29–30.

2 *Confessions* 4.16.28. This text was apparently the Latin translation made by Victorinus, or perhaps was the *Categoriae Decem*. In the *Confessions*, Augustine presents the *Categories* as an easy but uninteresting book unrelated to the momentous existential questions about human life and the nature of God that he needed to have addressed in his young adulthood. It does not follow from this, of course, that Augustine thought it was wholly without utility in other areas of philosophy such as physics or metaphysics. In his *Letter* 66.2.4 he endorses the definition of (primary) substance given by Aristotle in *Categories* 5 2a11-14. In his *Against Julian* 6.18.53-56 he is willing to use the category "dispositional quality" (*affectionalis qualitas*) introduced by Julian from *Categories* 8 9b34-10a5 to describe an enduring condition of the soul (as distinct from a passing feeling, a passion). In the prologue of *On the Trinity* Book 8, he presses the category "relation" (*Categories* 7 6a36ff.) into service to define the Father, Son, and Holy Spirit.

3 The concepts used by Augustine, not all of which will be examined in this paper, include matter (including ultimate matter) and form; substance; quality; quantity; life as self-motion; potentiality; and efficient causality.

4 Augustine says that he has six large volumes (in Latin) relating the opinions of philosophers living up to the time of "a certain Celsus" (*On Heresies* prologue; cf. the contents of *Letter* 118.2.10ff. and parts of *City of God* 8). This philosophical source is distinct from the "Platonic books" and "books of Plotinus" that he mentions in *Confessions* 7.9.13, 8.2.3 and *On the Happy Life* 1.4. Scholars have debated who the compendium's editor ("Celsus") was, and whether he was actually the same as the "Celsinus" whom Augustine mentions in *Against the Academics* 2.2.5 (there being a misspelling by Augustine in one or the other case, it has been claimed). See Pierre Courcelle, *Late Latin Writers and Their Greek Sources*, trans. Harry Wedeck (Cambridge, MA: Harvard University Press, 1969), 192–194. Works of Aristotle (and not just the *Categories*) were in circulation well before Augustine's time; see next note and Jonathan Barnes, "Roman Aristotle," in *Philosophia Togata* II, eds. J. Barnes and M. Griffin (Oxford: Clarendon, 1996), esp. 65–66. Thus the popular perception that Augustine could not have known any material from Aristotle apart from the *Categories* is not a reliable guide (*pace* Juhana Toivanen, "Perceptual Self-Awareness in Seneca, Augustine, and Olivi," *Journal of the History of Philosophy* 51, no. 3–4 [2013], 368).

5 There were commentaries on the *Categories* beginning in the first century BCE, on the *Metaphysics* and *Physics* beginning in the early second century CE, and on the *On the Soul* beginning at the turn of the third century CE. Victorinus, mentioned by Augustine in *Confessions* 8.2.3, is recognized as belonging to the commentary tradition on Aristotle, as is Plotinus.

With regard to the topic of embodiment in particular, it will emerge that Augustine's employment of some (ultimately) Aristotelian concepts and distinctions helped him to develop a clearly discernible account of a human being as a single-substance body-soul compound, and an account of death that is correlative with this. He also analyzes death and dying in a way that appears to be informed by the Aristotelian categories.

However, Augustine does not always follow through in explaining how he thinks these core Aristotelian insights play out in the details. Consequently, sometimes it is not immediately obvious how his position is consistent, even within the same text. In such cases, it is possible for us to construct a plausible account of what an Augustinian position would be, even one that it is reasonable to suppose that Augustine actually held. But this rendering takes some work on the part of the reader.

1. Dualism and the Nature of Flesh

The first set of puzzling texts I wish to investigate will serve to address the question whether, or in what sense, Augustine is a dualist. By "dualism" I mean substance dualism, the thesis that the soul and the body are each substances, where "substance" is understood with Aristotle and Augustine to be a thing that exists in its own right and not merely in another.[6] That is, by "substance" I mean what is called "primary substance" in Aristotle's *Categories*. It would follow from this substance dualism that the soul can survive the death of the body, *and* the body can survive the death of the soul, since each has its own proper existence. In his anti-Manichean works, Augustine indicates that he is not a substance dualist. He points out repeatedly that the body cannot survive without the soul, which is tantamount to saying that the body is not a substance in the relevant sense[7] and so there are not two substances

---

6 For this definition, see Augustine *Letter* 66.2.4; cf. Aristotle, *Categories* 5 2a11-14.

7 *Pace* Etienne Gilson, *The Christian Philosophy of Saint Augustine* (New York: Random House, 1960), 44–45. Gilson cites *On the Catholic and Manichean Ways of Life* 1.4.6 as evidence that Augustine held

in the human being. On the other hand, Augustine obviously does not subscribe to materialism, the alternative to dualism in contemporary philosophy of mind. Nor is he merely a property dualist, holding that conscious experience, imagination, and mental acts are qualities or byproducts of the body and its processes; instead, he argues that these must occur in a substantial immaterial subject.[8] His position constitutes a fourth way. He posits that the soul is an immaterial substance while the body is not a substance at all in the sense alluded to at the outset of this paragraph. This does not entail that the body is unreal or unimportant, but it does mean that "the body" is a name for the continuously produced effect of soul's natural activity on matter.

I have in the past drawn attention to this Augustinian position found in his anti-Manichean works,[9] but did not examine how it might be compatible with some key passages of the *City of God*, perhaps the most widely-read text that records Augustine's mature views on embodiment. Book 13 contains statements about flesh and the human being which seem to alternately support and conflict with the single-substance account of the anti-Manichean works. These can be illuminated by the *Literal Meaning of Genesis*, whose latter book(s)

---

that "the body" is a (primary) substance, as well as the soul. However, Augustine does not actually say that therein. He says that the definition of a human being is, a compostion of soul and body. Here it should be remembered that "body" for Augustine means matter with extension (see note 25 below), and that there is no article (cf. Gilson's "the") in the Latin. (Compare the discussion of "the body" by Brooke Holmes in this volume.) In this passage, Augustine goes on to note that although this is the definition of the term (*homo*), the term has a synecdochic use to refer to one or the other of the parts of the human being, as in "That man [actually the man's body] lies buried in such-and-such a place." Cf. Augustine's discussion of the ordinary language uses of the term in *City of God* 13.24. Augustine also here (*On the Catholic and Manichean Ways of Life* 1.4.6) mentions the question of how soul is united with body (like a centaur, or like two yoked horses?), but does not choose the latter option. He merely says that it would take a long time to explain the relation, and that such an explanation is apart from his immediate goal.

8 Augustine's arguments are collected in Ludger Hölscher, *The Reality of the Mind: Augustine's Philosophical Arguments for the Human Soul as a Spiritual Substance* (New York: Routledge & Kegan Paul, 1986). For comparisons with contemporary philosophers (Meixner, Swinburne, Shoemaker, Lowe) see Bruno Niederbaccher, "The Human Soul: Augustine's Case for Soul-Body Dualism" in *The Cambridge Companion to Augustine*, 2nd ed., eds. David Meconi and Eleonore Stump (Cambridge, UK: Cambridge University Press, 2014), 125–141.

9 Sarah Byers, "Augustine and the Philosophers," in *A Companion to Augustine*, ed. Mark Vessey (Malden, MA: Wiley Blackwell, 2015), 177–179.

Augustine composed while he was writing the initial book(s) of the *City of God*.[10] Of all the works in Augustine's corpus, the *Literal Meaning of Genesis* contains the most detail about his natural philosophy, and Augustine generally sticks to the views that he put forward there, still summarizing or alluding to them in his *City of God*.

To proceed with an examination of the concept of flesh, we note first of all that in *City of God* 13.3 Augustine tells us that the reason why mortality[11] is inherited is because flesh is not dust. The way in which flesh differs from dust makes it able to be a carrier of mortality, then.

Abstracting Augustine's statement from its theological context about original sin and examining the physics that it implies, we find that his distinction between dust on the one hand, and flesh on the other, is intended to mark out the difference between elements and things that are composed of elements. He tells us that flesh is made from dust, that is, from earth (*ex terra facta est caro*). If we ask exactly how flesh differs from elemental earth, the answer seems to be given in *City of God* 13.24, namely that it differs both by having another element in addition to earth, and by being formed in such as way as to be flesh—that is, to have the nature of flesh. The additional matter that is in flesh besides earth is water: flesh has earth plus water. But mud, too, is composed of earth and water, and flesh is distinct from mud. The human being was formed from earth or from mud, or to put it more clearly, Augustine says, the human body was formed from this.[12] Flesh differs from mud, then, in virtue of its nature (*natura carnis*) or form; moistened dust formed (*formatus*) in a certain way is a human body.[13]

---

10 *City of God* (413-426/427); *Literal Meaning of Genesis* (401-414/415). The anti-Manichean works were written in the late 380s and 390s.

11 By "mortality" in this paper, I mean the "necessity of dying" (Augustine, *City of God* 13.3; cf. *Literal Meaning of Genesis* 6.25.36-6.26.37). I thus mean to exclude reference to the mere capacity to die, which Augustine thinks was characteristic of the original human body before the Fall (able to die and able not to die).

12 *City of God* 13.24.

13 *City of God* 13.24.

We begin to see here that Augustine's understanding of the matter of embodied human existence is complex. He says in succession that dust, that is, earth, served as the material (*materies*) for the formation of the human being, and that flesh was manufactured from earth, and that the body was made from earth or mud.[14] These statements will be compatible if dust or earth is the matter of mud, which is in turn the matter of flesh (which is the same as the "body"[15]), which is in turn the matter of the human being. Such a "nesting" of kinds of matter in one thing[16] (the human being) would evoke Aristotle's observation that "there come to be many matters for the same thing, when the one matter is the matter of another."[17] These levels of matter are also levels of structure, given that earth and water each have a nature or structure, but when formed into flesh together constitute matter of a different nature.

This is important for the larger question of Augustine's "dualism" or lack thereof because it is connected to the question of what the form of the body is. According to Augustine, does flesh, also known as the body, have its own form, or is it continuously formed by soul? Is it a substance in its own right, or not? To confirm that Augustine is in fact conceptualizing the human being as composed of proximate and remote matter,

---

14 *City of God* 13.3, 13.3, and 13.24 respectively.

15 This is uncontroversial given that Augustine consistently treats "flesh" and "body" as two names for the same thing, interchanging these terms in *City of God* Book 13, *passim*, and in the *Literal Meaning of Genesis*. This interchanging occurs too in his definition of a human being, which we will consider below.

16 Someone might ask here what the justification is for taking Augustine's statements that flesh was *made from* earth to imply that it is *made up of* earth. The question arises particularly in the context of scholarly debate about the Aristotelian account of matter. According to one interpretation, Aristotle had two conceptions of matter, each playing a distinct role in his metaphysics: matter as preexisting substrate of the substance versus the constitutive matter of a substance. According to another interpretation, he had one conception of matter, holding that the same matter (though not the perceptible matter) persists through a substantial change and is constitutive of the substance. Augustine thinks that the elements persist through the substantial change (generation and death) of a human being (see, e.g. *Literal Meaning of Genesis* 10.9.15.). Hence the elemental matter from which the human being is made is also constitutive (remotely) of the human being.

17 *Metaphysics* 8.4 1044a20-23; cf. 1044b1-3.

each of which has its own 'level' of form, it will be profitable to investigate further Augustine's analysis of matter in the *Literal Meaning of Genesis*, comparing it to the *City of God* and to the classical Aristotelian account. In order to set up the comparison, however, we should first briefly revert to Aristotle's presentation of the distinction between the proper or proximate matter of a substance and its remote matter.

Aristotle observes that, in any complex entity, there are levels of matter. Phlegm is composed of what is fat and what is sweet, if what is fat is composed of what is sweet, he tells us. The former is proximate (to the substantial form, in this case the form of phlegm) while the latter is remote. The more complex the substance, the more levels it has. Most basically, for Aristotle, substances are made up of elements, but the elements themselves are simple bodies; they are matter having the form of earth, water, air, or fire. To give a more updated example, in the case of water, the proximate matter is hydrogen and oxygen, and the nonproximate matter is the subatomic particles. We can even analyze entities down to their ultimate matter, completely stripped of all properties and form, which Aristotle sometimes calls "primitive" matter (so-called "prime" matter).[18] It does not exist independently in nature, of course; according to Aristotle, everything that actually exists exists as some kind of thing.

The distinction between proximate and remote matter can be made in cases of inorganic and organic substances, in addition to artifacts.

---

18 *Metaphysics* 7.3 1029a24; *On the Generation of Animals* 729a32. Currently the question of whether Aristotle was committed to a concept of "prime matter" is controversial among some scholars, but in late antiquity and thus for Augustine and his sources, it was not. (The ancient interpreters did differ on how exactly to define prime matter, however. Augustine seems to have followed Plotinus's view that it is absolutely without extension; see note 25 below.) Cf. Richard Sorabji, ed., *The Philosophy of the Commentators, 200–600 AD: A Sourcebook*, vol. 2 (London: Duckworth, 2004), 253. According to the late antique interpretations, prime matter has an essential conceptual function in Aristotle's schema because it makes possible the conservation of matter through substantial change at the most elementary level. An updated example of the kind of case for which prime matter might have explanatory relevance is that of the conversion of subatomic particles into other kinds of subatomic particles, with the energy being conserved (e.g., a muon and anti-muon together convert to two photons, with the mass-energy of the muon being equal to the motion-energy of the photons).

Regarding the human being, the organic substance which particularly interests us, Aristotle says that the proximate matter is flesh.[19] Obviously, there are many levels of nonproximate matter: each organ is composed of a particular kind of tissue, the fabric of which is certain kinds of cells having particular molecular constituents (as we know today but Aristotle did not), which are in turn made up of elements. These various levels of matter are compounded and arranged by an overarching organizing principle provided by soul, making it be a systemic unity rather than a mere pile of different types of matter.

Of course, as has already been indicated obliquely in the previous two paragraphs, to say that there are "levels" of matter in things is the same as saying that there are levels of structure or form in things, given that what makes matter be the kind of matter it is, is form. So substances have at least two "levels" of form: the substantial form and the forms of the various kinds of elements that are in the substance. In the case of organisms, the substantial form is provided by its soul, but soul can only work on certain *kinds* of matter. "Soul is the first actuality of body potentially possessing life,"[20] which is to say that only matter having the right structure and constituents is capable of being made alive. In organisms, however, the form of the organism as a whole (so, the form of the human being) also makes the *proximate* matter be the kind of matter it is. That is, the substantial form provides the form of the proximate matter; it does not add a substantial form to the proximate matter. Hence the decomposition that immediately ensues at death results in the subsistence not of the proximate matter, but of the more basic matter. (This is unlike the destruction of a nonorganic compound such as water. For instance, the thermal decomposition of water results in the subsistence of its proximate matter, hydrogen and oxygen.) This is why Aristotle at the same time asserts that "flesh and

---

19 *Metaphysics* 7.8, 1034 a6.
20 *On the Soul* 2.1 412a27-28.

bones" is the proximate matter of an organism[21] and denies that the corpse that results from death is the proximate matter of the body.[22] The composition of the tissues is so changed by the rotting that begins immediately upon cessation of circulation, that it is no longer flesh.

Augustine's *Literal Meaning of Genesis* contains an account of matter and form that recapitulates the basics of the Aristotelian analysis. Here Augustine shows that he knows and uses the concept of ultimate matter, that is, completely unformed matter (*informis materia/materies*). He also asserts that it does not exist independently of form:[23] it is "first" or "primary" not in the temporal sense, "but because that from which something is made is still prior as its source, even if not in time, to what is made from it.... When we say 'matter' and 'form,' we understand them as being together simultaneously, although we are unable to state them simultaneously."[24] Matter as such has no three-dimensional extension; length, width, and depth are characteristics of "body,"[25] which is formed matter.[26] The most basic bodies are the elements.[27]

With regard to the human body in particular, Augustine's position in the *Literal Meaning of Genesis* matches that of the *City of God* when he claims that the human body or flesh is formed from earth[28] or from mud (water and earth).[29] Similarly, he again treats the term human "body" (*corpus*) as a synonym for human "flesh," indicating that he

---

[21] *Metaphysics* 7.8, 1034 a6.

[22] Cf. *Metaphysics* 8.5 1044b34-1045a3.

[23] *Literal Meaning of Genesis* 1.15.29, e.g. [*Deus*] *formatam creavit materiam*.

[24] *Literal Meaning of Genesis* 1.15.29 (trans. Edmund Hill, *On Genesis* [Hyde Park, NY: New City Press, 2002], amended); cf. 1.4.9, 7.27.39, 8.20.39; *Confessions* 12.3.3–12.6.6.

[25] *Literal Meaning of Genesis* 7.21.27; cf. *On the Magnitude of the Soul* 4.6 and 14.23; *On Music* 6; *On 83 Different Questions* #20 and #57; *On the Soul and Its Origin* 4.21.35. Cf. Plotinus *Ennead* 2.4.11 ll. 13–15.

[26] See the distinction between matter and body, the latter of which has form added to matter, *Against Faustus* 20.14 and 21.4; *Literal Meaning of Genesis* 1.1.2, 8.20.39.

[27] *Literal Meaning of Genesis* 1.15.30.

[28] *Literal Meaning of Genesis* 7.5.8, 10.1.1, 10.9.15.

[29] *Literal Meaning of Genesis* 7.12.18.

thinks that flesh is not the material of which a living body is made, but simply is the live human body.[30]

More importantly, for our purposes, Augustine makes clear in both the *Literal Meaning of Genesis* and the *City of God* that he thinks that flesh/body, the *proximate* matter of the *human being*, lacks a form of its own apart from the soul. Thus the human body itself is not a formed substance in its own right. Like Aristotle, he notes that at death (separation of the soul) "the flesh does not return to the human beings from whom it was created, but to earth, from which it was formed for the first human."[31] That is, the decomposition that immediately ensues at death results in the subsistence not of flesh, but of the more basic (elemental) matter. We could add to this the evidence of *City of God* 13.24, where in describing the creation of the human being he asserts that the elements (earth and water) were not formed into the human body before the human soul was added. Flesh did not preexist the soul. Flesh or body is "before" ensoulment only in the sense that this is what is being informed by the soul:[32] moistened dust formed (*formatus*) by soul (*anima*) is a human body.[33] This is consistent with his earlier anti-Manichean writings, in which he repeatedly states that when something dies—that is, its soul departs—the body loses its form, disintegrates, and is not the same kind of thing that it was. It is implied by this position that the form of flesh/body is provided by the soul. All of these claims are of a piece with his formal definition of "human being" in *City of God* 15.7: a human being is "a [single] rational substance consisting of body and soul."[34]

---

30 *Literal Meaning of Genesis* 7.5.8, 10.1.1, 10.9.15.

31 *Literal Meaning of Genesis* 10.9.15. Although these words are placed by Augustine into the mouth of interlocutors, he does not disagree with them on this point.

32 Cf. Augustine's use of the sense of "before" when he stipulates that matter is prior to form as source, rather than prior in time (*Literal Meaning of Genesis* 1.15.29).

33 *City of God* 13.24.

34 Cf. *Tractates on the Gospel of John* 47.11: "the community of the flesh and the soul (*consortium carnis et animae*) has received the name of human being."

The weight of the evidence, then, would seem to put it beyond a reasonable doubt that Augustine consistently holds a single-substance account of the human being.

However, if we return at last to where we started, to Augustine's claim that the reason why mortality is *inherited* is because flesh differs in nature from dust (*City of God* 13.3), it is not immediately obvious how this is compatible with the single-substance account. Given that Augustine is insisting here that mud and earth, which are present in flesh, are not the bearers of this accident (mortality), he might seem to imply that flesh is a bearer of accidents which it retains while it is in transit between parent and child, and thus that it has its own characteristics independently of any soul. This would mean that flesh/body is a substance in itself, a subject of accidents. But according to Augustine's single-substance account, the proximate matter of the human being, flesh, is not supposed to retain its accidents apart from the soul, because it does not subsist as flesh apart from the soul, and thus cannot be a subject of accidents. Has Augustine contradicted himself within the *City of God* Book 13, holding on the one hand that the form of the body/flesh is provided by soul (yielding a single-substance account of the living human being), and on the other that the body has its own form and matter (yielding substance dualism)?

It is likely instead that Augustine's claim in *City of God* 13.3—the reason why mortality is inherited is because flesh is not dust—should be taken to mean that the forming substance (soul) from which matter receives its animation and structure (and thus is constituted as flesh) has itself become distorted. The accident of mortality belongs to the human being by virtue of acquired characteristics of the soul. Augustine says in 13.3 that mortality is inheritable owing to the fact that in procreation a human being comes from a human being, unlike the case of creation, wherein a human being came from dust. Given his stated position that soul informs flesh (*City of God* 13.24), when he says here that generation is the passing on of human nature, he would seem to mean that inherited mortality is somehow owing to the human being's intellectual soul, the source of form or essence in the human being.

In order to see exactly how this is supposed to work in Augustine's account we need to look elsewhere in *City of God* and in *Literal Meaning of Genesis*. Consider *Literal Meaning of Genesis* 7.6.9:

> ... If the soul, you see, were something unchangeable, we ought not to be inquiring in any way at all about its quasi-material; but as it is, its changeableness is obvious enough through its sometimes being rendered misshapen by vices and errors, sometimes being put into proper shape by virtues and the teaching of truth, but all within the nature it has of being soul. In the same way flesh, in its own nature by which it is flesh, is both embellished with health and disfigured by diseases and wounds.[35]

Given the exegetical work we have already done on Augustine, the most plausible reading of this text is that while there are two kinds of changeable stuff in a human being—physical matter, and quasi-matter[36]—there is only one substantial form, the form of human being, animating and structuring both at once. That is, the soul's form is the intellect, and this also provides the form of the body/flesh. This reading is supported by *Literal Meaning of Genesis* 12.35.68, where Augustine says that the human mind (*mens*[37]) has a natural impulse to make a body. The human being is thus one substance, having one

---

[35] *Literal Meaning of Genesis* 7.6.9: "... si enim quiddam incommutabile esset anima, nullo modo eius quasi materiem quaerere deberemus; nunc autem mutabilitas eius satis indicat eam interim uitiis atque fallaciis deformem reddi, formari autem uirtutibus ueritatis que doctrina, sed in sua iam natura, qua est anima, sicut etiam caro in sua natura, qua iam caro est, et salute decoratur et morbis uulneribus que foedatur." Translation by Hill, amended.

[36] That Augustine thought there was "soul matter" (i.e., changeability) was pointed out by Roland Teske, *Studies in the Philosophy of William of Auvergne, Bishop of Paris (1228–1249)* (Milwaukee, WI: Marquette University Press, 2006), 229, although he cites not this text but *Conf.* 12.3.3–12.6.6, a text which does not in fact refer to the human soul.

[37] *Pace* Hill, who translates "soul" here. O'Callaghan's reading of Augustine would have benefited from attention to this passage—see John O'Callaghan, "Imago Dei: A Test Case for St. Thomas's Augustinianism," in *Aquinas the Augustinian*, ed. M. Dauphinais, et al. (Washington, DC: Catholic University of America Press, 2007) 103, 106. In *Literal Meaning of Genesis* 7.27.38 and 7.25.36 Augustine says that if the soul (*anima*) were to preexist the body then we should think that it came to

substantial form (the mind) but two kinds of proximate matter (physical and incorporeal).

We can construct, then, the following interpretation of how mortality is handed on even though flesh is not a substance in its own right with its own accidents. The mortality of post-Fall flesh is owing to the human intellectual soul, in the sense that it is owing to changes in the soul's quasi-matter, which are themselves results of the original sin. An act of assent in the mind of the first human beings (the original sin) affected those persons' quasi-matter (changed their habitual attitudes and desires, their moral character), which in turn affected the physical matter of their soul-body compounds. In subsequent human generation, both physical material and quasi-material from the parents' souls are donated by the mother and father. The formation of the new human being is effected by the addition of the intellect (directly by God) to the inherited quasi-matter from the parents' souls and to their donor physical matter. [38] This new human being is thus one substance having two kinds of proximate matter (incorporeal and physical), the accident of mortality belonging to it in virtue of the latter's contact with the former. This would be the way to understand Augustine's assertion in *City of God* 13.3 that that the stock (*stirps*) of the human race was contaminated when the human nature was changed for the worse by the original sin, and that this damage was passed on to all those descended from Eve. The question we asked earlier, how Augustine can avoid substance dualism given that he seems to suggest in *City of God* 13.3 that flesh is a bearer of accidents (specifically mortality) which it retains even when it

---

body by a natural rational desire (*nauraliter velle, voluntate propria*), and in *City of God* 13.20 he says that after death souls (*animae*) desire their bodies. *Literal Meaning of Genesis* 12.35.68 shows that he thinks it is in virtue of its mind (*mens*) that the soul wants to make a body. *City of God* 13.20 is cited by Gareth Matthews, "Augustine and Ibn Sina on Souls in the Afterlife," *Philosophy* 89, no. 3–4 (2014), 473, responding to Richard Sorabji, *Self: Ancient and Modern Insights about Individuality, Life, and Death* (Chicago: University of Chicago Press, 2006), 37.

38 Augustine argues that the thesis that children's souls are created by God from parents' souls (i.e., that quasi-matter is inherited) is more likely true than that each individual human soul is created entirely from nothing; see *Literal Meaning of Genesis* 9.11.19, 10.11.18-19, 10.14.23, 10.16.29, 10.23.39.

is *in transit* between parent and child, would be answered by Augustine as follows. Flesh is never "in transit" as flesh. Flesh itself is not inherited. The corporeal matter that is provided by the mother and father (which is not yet flesh[39]) becomes flesh at the formation of the new human being, at which point it takes on the attribute of mortality by coming into contact with the quasi-matter of the parents' souls.

The likelihood that this account lies behind *City of God* 13.3 is increased by the fact that the basic model of a "trickle down" of qualities from the soul to body has a precedent in Plotinus, and was used by Augustine in other texts. Plotinus speaks of physical order and beauty coming to the body from the soul, and the soul's beauty (moral virtue) in turn coming to it from the right use of its intellect.[40] Augustine employs this emanation model when speaking about why the resurrected body will be perfectly healthy flesh:

> [T]he perfect health of the body is that final immortality of the whole human being. For God made the soul with so powerful a nature that from its full happiness, which is promised to the saints in the end of time, there will also overflow into the inferior nature, that is, into the body ... the fullness of health, that is, the strength of incorruptibility.[41]

More generally, the Plotinian notion that the body is an image of the soul[42] is implied in other works of Augustine.[43] Augustine's way

---

39 *On the Catholic and the Manichean Ways of Life* 2.49.
40 *Ennead* 5.9.2 ll. 12-23.
41 *Letter* 118.3.14, trans. Roland Teske, *Letters*, vol. 2 (Hyde Park, NY: New City Press, 2002).
42 So Porphyry, *Life of Plotinus* 1. Augustine does not, however, agree with the Plotinian sentiment that embodiment is shameful per se.
43 *City of God* 1.13 and *On the Care to Be Taken of the Dead* 3.5, arguing that the bodies of humans should be treated with respect because they were worn by human soul, though not as external ornaments but as pertaining to human nature, and that corpses of particularly virtuous souls are to be shown special honor (this latter assertion seems to be a reference to the quasi-matter of the soul having lent a particular quality to the body).

of conceiving of the effects of original sin and their inheritance would thus seem to be a creative appropriation of this kind of emanation account.

2. Death, Dying, and Being "in Death"

A second puzzle in *City of God* Book 13 is, exactly how does Augustine understand death, dying, and being "in death" in relation to the single-substance-compound account we have just seen in Section One?

In *City of God* 13.9-13.11, Augustine goes on a quest to identify when a person is "in death." By "in death" he says that he means the process of dying.[44] Then he points out that a person in process of dying is actually alive: she is alive ("in life") until the moment she is dead. So while she is dying, she is not in death but in life. Yet when she is dead, her death has passed; so she is, in fact, not in death after death, either. How, then, is anyone ever in death?

Augustine claims to see this as a genuine *aporia* about the diminishment of life (*vitae detractio*), asserting that it is "extremely difficult to define when one is in death or dying: that is, in a state when one is neither living, which is before death, nor dead, which is after death, but dying, which is in death."[45] He suggests that this will violate the principle of noncontradiction. How can those who are dying be said to be living?[46] To speak of a person as both living and dying at the same time seems as absurd as saying that she can be awake and asleep at the same time.[47] We are left with the absurd conclusion that either no one is dying, or no one is living.[48]

---

44 *moriens, id est in morte,*13.11; cf. 3.10-13.11 *passim*.
45 *City of God* 13.11. Translations of *City of God* 13 are (sometimes amended) from R. W. Dyson, *Augustine: The City of God Against the Pagans* (Cambridge, UK: Cambridge University Press, 1998).
46 *City of God* 13.11; cf. 13.9–13.10 where Augustine reiterates the premise three times: "if it is impossible to be both living and dying simultaneously . . . "
47 *City of God* 13.11.
48 *City of God* 13.9.

This problem, "How can anyone ever be in death while alive?" is relatively easy to solve by using Augustine's own principles, and by properly distinguishing "dying" from "death." The *aporia* is a pseudo-problem given that there are different parts of the human being, in which it can be undergoing or doing opposites simultaneously. Augustine defines the soul as the life principle of the human body and death as the departure of the soul from the body (i.e., flesh).[49] So, he could say that those parts of flesh from which soul has receded are dead (thus no longer an integral part of the human being), while those to which it is present are alive. The death of the organism *as a whole integrated unit* is not a process having duration over an extent of time, but occurs at the moment at which the soul finally entirely departs from the body (ceases to be present to any *part* of the body).

Although Augustine does not explicitly invoke various parts of the body as a way of resolving the paradox he poses, he does distinguish life's "diminishment" (*detractio*) from its being "wholly removed,"[50] and "diminishment" would presumably need to be cashed out in terms of parts.[51] In his *Letter* 166.2.4 he claims that the "vital attention" of the soul can be more present at some places of the body than at others in the case of sensation. So presumably he thinks that likewise, the vivifying power of the soul can be present to some areas of the body and not present to others, and that this is what we call the dying process. So, being in life and in death at the same time is possible. This "dying" is distinct from "death," which is defined as the full removal of life—that is, the soul's final and complete disengagement of its presence from all parts of the body. Death, Augustine goes on to point out, occurs instantaneously.

---

49 *Tractates on the Gospel of John* 47.11; *City of God* 13.9.
50 *City of God* 13.10: "Or shall we, after all, say that he is in life and death simultaneously? – in life, that is, which he lives until it is entirely taken away ([*vita*] *tota detrahatur*), but in death also, because he is dying while his life is being diminished?"
51 In his *Letter* 166.2.4 he claims that the "vital attention" of the soul can be more present at some places of the body than at others in the case of sensation. So presumably he thinks that likewise, the vivifying power of the soul can be present to some areas of the body and not present to others, and that this is what we call the dying process.

Death, then, is not a process. It occurs in a moment, but a moment has no duration; so the moment of death has no duration.[52]

Given that the overarching problem "How can anyone ever be in death (dying) while alive?" is relatively easy to resolve by using Augustine's own principles, and by properly distinguishing "dying" from "death," it is strange that Augustine should insist on the great "difficulty" of his alleged problem. Why does he even suggest that it is important to examine the idea that people who are dying are "in death?"

It is at first tempting to think that Augustine's alleged *aporia* arises from an engagement with Epicureanism. Epicurus claims that "when we exist death is not present, and when death is present we do not exist."[53] This is superficially like the problem Augustine poses, that one cannot be in life and death at the same time. However, Epicurus' point (conveyed to Augustine in Latin sources such as Lucretius and Cicero) differs conceptually from Augustine's philosophical exercise in *City of God* 13.9-13.11. Epicurus's point is that there is no personal identity for us once we die, since death separates the soul from the body, and the atoms which comprise the soul are scattered; sensation, and therefore consciousness, is impossible under these circumstances.[54] Hence "we" no longer exist (*einai*) after death. Augustine's interest is, instead, about the process of dying itself—what it is and how it is related to animation.

Likewise, it is worth noting that the other major candidate for a motivator of Augustine here in *City of God*, namely his theological commitments and reverence for the Biblical text, is not operative in this particular *aporia*.[55] Nor do Plotinus or earlier Christian ecclesiastical

---

52 *City of God* 13.11; cf. *Confessions* 11.15.20.
53 *Letter to Menoeceus* 124–127 in *The Hellenistic Philosophers*, Vol. 1, trans. A. A. Long and D. N. Sedley (New York: Cambridge University Press, 1987), sec. 24A5. Cf. Lucretius, *On the Nature of Things* 3.830-869.
54 Cf. Lucretius, *On the Nature of Things* 3.830.
55 2 Corinthians 4:10, Romans 8:10, and 1 Timothy 5:6 speak of the living being in death or dead, but employ metaphorical senses of "death." Augustine, of course, uses the phrase "in death" with these other senses elsewhere, e.g. *Commentaries on the Psalms* 145.5.

writers speak of the living being "in death" in the biological sense that Augustine is using it here.

By the process of elimination regarding Augustine's intellectual context, then, we are left with the possibility that what is motivating him is an interest in classifying death and dying according to Aristotle's *Categories*. *City of God* 13.9-11 can be read as an effort to think through the following set of questions. Is dying a passion, that is, the undergoing of a change introduced into the patient from the outside? Is it an activity, a self-induced change? Is being dead a state? Is "dying" a quality of human beings?

If we look back at the "three things" that Augustine distinguishes—living, dying, and dead (i.e., before death, in death, and after death respectively)—we find that he describes these in such a way as to show that he thinks they are classifiable as follows: Living, or "being in life," is a passion of the constitutive matter of the human being; the soul is acting on matter to hold it together and initiate biological processes. Death is also a passion; it is what happens to the body when the soul "departs"—that is, terminates its presence to the matter.[56] The soul does this when the matter ceases to be of the kind that it can act upon, through disease or some other type of corruption (these, again, are passions affecting the matter of the human being). In the time during which the body is partially dead and partially alive (having some functional and some nonfunctional tissues), the body as a whole is qualified as variegated in its animation: part of it is undergoing the passion of death and part of it is undergoing the passion of being enlivened. "Dying" is thus a quality of the human being as a whole, in virtue of changes being undergone in various parts of its constitutive matter.

We encounter greater difficulty in understanding what Augustine has in mind when he claims in *City of God* 13.11 that there is another *aporia* about being "in death," arguing that it "cannot be explained in

---

56 *City of God* 13.2, *deserit anima*.

language" how those who are already dead are in death. This second sense of "in death" does not refer to the process of dying, but to the condition of those who have already died.

This way of talking is occasioned by a text from the Bible,[57] but that passage could be taken to mean a number of things.[58] Augustine, for his part, glosses this "in death" as a state of the disembodied soul. "[U]ntil they are brought to life again, they are rightly said to be in death, just as everyone is said to be in slumber until he wakes up."[59] In comparing being "in death" to a state of slumber, presumably Augustine has in mind other Biblical passages which describe the dead as being asleep.[60] But what exactly does this sleep-like state amount to in Augustine's Aristotelian-Plotinian account of the soul-body compound, which we reconstructed in section 1?

It is puzzling that Augustine should characterize "in death" as a state into which people (or souls) enter when they die, given that in the Augustinian schema that we saw in section 1 there seems to be no existing subject for the state of "death." After death, the human being (compound of soul-body) no longer exists to be a subject of properties such as "death." Nor is the soul "in death" in the sense of being in a dead thing, since when the body is dead the soul is not "in" the body any longer. It is not immediately obvious how the disembodied soul could be "in death," since it is a life principle by nature.

At first it looks as though Augustine may be influenced here by the fallacious first argument for the immortality of the soul in Plato's *Phaedo* (70c-72a), which begs the question of whether the soul is immortal by treating death as a state of the soul.[61] However, Augustine

---

57 Psalm 6:6 of his LXX text, "For in death no one remembers you."
58 For instance: that "death" is another name for Hades, an actual place (Psalm 6:6 continues, "and who will give you thanks in Hades?"); or that "those in death" is simply a way of referring to "those who were alive but are no longer alive" rather than a description of the state of enduring subjects.
59 *City of God* 13.11.
60 Daniel 12:2; Job 3:11-13; John 11:11-14.
61 It assumes that the soul is an enduring subject of the properties of life and death (which characterize it successively and repeatedly), rather than addressing the possibility that the soul is destroyed, which is what is at issue in arguments concerning the soul's immortality.

has already rejected this model in *City of God* 10.30, when he commends Porphyry for rejecting the Platonic claim that the living come from the dead and the dead come from the living.

As it turns out, in order to understand what Augustine has in mind with the dead being "in death," we must again supplement the *City of God* with his *Literal Meaning of Genesis*. In the *Literal Meaning of Genesis* he claims that after death the mind (*mens*) of a just person is active, engaged in intellectual contemplation. The disembodied mind, however, lacks the full measure of its nature (*naturae modum*) because it is hindered (*retardatur*) in its impulse to make and manage a body, since it does not have the requisite kind of physical matter at hand (. . . *quamdiu non subest corpus, cuius administratione adpetitus ille conquiescat*).[62] So the human mind is alive, and in being alive it has the capacity and inclination to initiate life functions in the right kind of matter. Now let us compare this to the *City of God*, specifically to *City of God* 13.19. Here he says that the soul (*anima*) of a just person who has died "lives in rest," echoing the idea that he articulates in *City of God* 13.11, namely that "until they are brought to life again, they are rightly said to be in death, just as everyone is said to be in slumber until he wakes up." Putting the *Literal Meaning of Genesis* and *City of God* together, we have a model in which the mind of the disembodied soul is active, but the non-rational powers of the soul (*anima*) are at rest, or "asleep," because they are not operational. Augustine's claim that the soul of a dead person lives but is 'asleep' may remind us of Aristotle's conceptual distinction between first and second actuality of life, which he compares respectively to sleep and wakefulness.[63] We certainly cannot infer from the fact that the

---

62 The *Literal Meaning of Genesis* 12.35.68.
63 *On the Soul* 2.1 412a22-28: Soul is the life principle of the body (first actuality), while particular life functions caused by the soul are a second actuality. Augustine differs in his claim that the mind has not merely the capacity to initiate life functions in matter, but the intent or impulse (*adpetitus, voluntas*) to do so. Intellectual contemplation and the intent to administer a body are apparently conceived of as two (mental) acts of one (mental) power.

metaphor of sleep-wakefulness occurs in both authors that Augustine knew Aristotle's text in translation, and in any case, whether he did or not is beside the point. Conceptually it is clear enough that for Augustine to say that the disembodied soul exists in a state of "being in death" means that this soul is alive and engaged in the activity of thinking, that it has the capacity to enliven matter, but that it is not actually enlivening matter.

3. Conclusions

We have seen two cases in which Augustine's sometimes obscurely expressed views on embodiment can be elucidated when we take seriously the possibility that he is employing ultimately Aristotelian concepts such as substance, form, matter, passion, action, quality, and potentiality. What these instances have in common is that Augustine enunciates the basics of his position, but does not spell out on the spot how the theory he espouses works in its details. We can, however, put together a consistent Augustinian account of embodiment and disembodied existence by using the *Literal Meaning of Genesis* as an interpretative tool for the *City of God*.

As to why Augustine does not make all the relevant details explicit on every occasion, it would seem that the answer is twofold. First, if something has been explained at greater length in a prior text, he may not feel the need or have the inclination to repeat the entire explanation. His position on spiritual traducianism, for example, is spelled out in the *Literal Meaning of Genesis*, so it is merely alluded to in the *City of God* Book 13. Similarly, Plotinus had already explained that emanation of qualities occurs from intellect to soul to body, and so Augustine uses the model without explaining the model itself. An educated reader is supposed to know, or at least know where to find, what Augustine has said in prior works, and what great philosophers such as Plotinus have said. Second, although Augustine does have a strong interest in natural philosophy generally and in human embodiment particularly, the *City of God* is basically a (high-level) apologetical work, and hence Augustine gives greater attention to articulating theses in theological ethics than to pursuing an analysis of the Aristotelian categories to its final conclusions. The fundamental propositions he wishes to communicate in Book 13 are that human death is unnatural (*City of God* 13.3), and that because human life is fleeting we all have an urgent need of moral conversion (*City of God* 13.10-11[64]).

We may find ourselves becoming impatient with Augustine for leaving so much interpretative work to the charitable reader when he writes about embodiment, but his desire to emphasize the fleetingness of life and ethical ideals is evidence of a reflective, philosophical stance. Indeed, his approach here is characteristic of philosophy in late antiquity, insofar as answering the question of how to live one's life ultimately takes precedence over physics.

---

[64] This interest becomes clear when, in 13.10, he becomes distracted by the verbal similarity between the phrases "dying while living" and "mortal life." This involves his going on a tangent based on an amphibolous use of the phrase "diminishment of life," equivocating both on "life" (lifespan *versus* biological life functions) and on "diminishment" (reduction in the duration of the overall lifespan *versus* cessation of biological functions in various parts of the body successively). The point of the tangent is that time is running out for moral conversion.

CHAPTER FIVE

Medieval Jewish Philosophers and the Human Body

Yoav Meyrav[1]

> Wonder not when he says: "eat the fat, and drink the sweet" (Neh. 8.10). For since the intellect uses bodily instruments, doubtlessly the joy of the body is a prelude and a preparation for the joy of the soul.[2]

1. Introduction

Judaism is very much about the body. The Jewish body of knowledge—most notably scripture and the Talmud—aspires to determine everything about a Jew's bodily existence: what you are allowed to wear, what you are allowed to eat, when (and how) you are allowed to have

---

1 This essay is dedicated to the memory of my grandfather Yosef Kaminsky. After spending Yom Kippur 1941 as a Red Army soldier stuck three days on a ship during a storm on the Caspian Sea without any food or water, he swore to never fast again.

2 Hasdai Crescas, "Passover Sermon," in *Crescas' Sermon on the Passover and Studies in his Philosophy* (in Hebrew), ed. A. Ravitzky (Jerusalem: Magnes, 2005), 157.

sex, whether or not you are allowed to cut your hair, when and why you are supposed to be happy, sad, and even drunk. The body of law of the practising Jew permeates his or her entire body, from head to toenail, with rabbinic authorities ceaselessly enriching the corpus of religious "halakhot" pertaining to different circumstances in an attempt to interpret a set of rules written thousands of years ago in light of all the changes the world had undergone since. It is safe to say that Judaism is fundamentally an embodied religion.[3]

In present times there are several different interpretations of what it means to be a Jew, some of which take liberties with the ancient regulations and offer a more relaxed approach to Jewish law, and others which take orthodoxy to new reactionary extremes (and many middle-ground options). In recent centuries there have been many attempts to "release" Judaism from the strains of embodiment and "elevate" it to a place which would render it less mundane. As Howard Eilberg-Schwartz puts it,

> The designation "People of the Book" is ... one of the visible expressions of a larger modern strategy that attempts to disembody Jews and Judaism in hopes of spiritualizing them. ... In the modern period, the majority of Jews came to regard various parts of Judaism, particularly those having to do with the body and sexuality, as primitive and embarrassing. These sorts of feelings and judgments partially explain why Jews have been so enthralled with the designation "People of the Book" in the post-Enlightenment period. Since the late eighteenth century when Jews were able to join European intellectual life, there has been an embarrassment over parts of Jewish tradition dealing with the body, despite the importance of such matters in Jewish sources. Texts dealing with bodily emissions,

---

[3] For a short and useful overview of the body in Jewish scripture and onwards see Louis Jacobs, "The Body in Jewish Worship: Three Rituals Examined," in *Religion and the Body*, ed. Sarah Coakley (Cambridge, MA: Cambridge University Press, 1997), 71–77.

circumcision, rules for defecation and urination, rules about how to perform sexual intercourse, and so forth evoked embarrassment and shame.[4]

But this is all rather recent. Medieval Jewish philosophers, who mostly wrote to a Jewish audience, were no strangers to spiritual aspirations, eternal bliss, or intellectual elitism. It was always a part of the tradition to a certain extent, and even more so once they became exposed to new ideas that they found around them, be it Muslim theology, Graeco-Arabic philosophy, or Christian scholasticism. These new, fascinating bodies of knowledge were thoroughly examined, digested, accepted, rejected, adapted, or incorporated, sometimes for what they were, and in many cases for how they could relate to the Jewish scriptural and rabbinic tradition. Although it was a somewhat less attractive philosophical topic than, say, divine attributes, angels, or the human intellect, the human body was also reinterpreted in the face of these new ideas, though perhaps less systematically, surely less thoroughly, than other topics.

Facing the philosophical ideas about the ontology, psychology, and ethics of the human body was the huge body of Jewish law concerning its regulation and day-to-day practise. In what follows I hope to show that this encounter was a fruitful one, and that in many cases the "embodiment" of Jewish law stood as a moderating factor which restrained the philosophical temperament's eagerness to "do away" with the body and flee to the realm of the metaphysical and the divine.

I will discuss four topics: the assessment of the human body; the relation between body, soul, and character; how the body should be treated; and bodily resurrection. My method, with all of its shortcomings, somewhat decontextualizes the thinkers I discuss. All of them

---

4 Howard Eilberg-Schwartz, "Introduction: People of the Body," in *People of the Body: Jews and Judaism from an Embodied Perspective*, ed. Howard Eilberg-Schwartz (Albany: SUNY Press, 1992), 3.

have a lot to say about "traditional" philosophical topics, and their opinions about these matters have bearings about their opinions about the human body. They are also, obviously, influenced by many different traditions, which in many cases I shamelessly ignore. What I'm trying to do is explore a representative, but by no means exhaustive, array of philosophical discussions of the human body in medieval Jewish philosophy, side by side, and invite the reader to appreciate their philosophical merit, and sometimes their "Jewishness," assuming that there is legitimacy to such a term.

2. The Ontology and Assessment of the Human Body

Is the human body a good body or a bad body? And how do we decide? Answers to this question, and justifications for these answers, vary wildly, and I will now present some of them in a descending sequence—from better to worse. As will immediately be noticed, every answer is justified, and in many cases the justification has to do with the divine plan.

An early example of the supremacy of the human body over other natural bodies is found in the work of the North African Platonic philosopher Isaac Israeli (855–955), who draws connections between the blend of the elements in the living being, its stature, and its quality, leading to the conclusion that the human body is the best, and the only living being able to attain perfection:

> Every animal inclines towards the element which predominates it ... Those animals in which earth predominates incline towards that particular nature; such as cattle ... For this reason they are four-footed and their face is continually turned towards the earth. The nature of man, however, is balanced and blended, and no one element holds sway over him more than the other. Hence the fire takes its path upward toward his head, and, similarly, the earth

drops downward towards his feet. His being is therefore balanced and blended by virtue of the equality of the elements and roots in him. But no one lacking such equality can be perfect in being and existence.[5]

As can be immediately noticed, the main criterion for the assessment of a body is a balance between its elements, or a capacity to reach a certain state of equilibrium among its different parts. Balance and proportion, as well as a somewhat aesthetic advantage, are the reasons another Platonic philosopher, Solomon ibn Gabirol (c. 1020–1070) of Andalusia, labels man as "the best of all the creatures of the Creator" and "the object aimed at in the creation of all substances and beings." The human being, ibn Gabirol writes, "is best proportioned, as regards constitution, of all living beings … most perfect and most beautiful of form, and most completely fashioned."[6] About a century later, the Cordoban Aristotelian Abraham ibn Daud (c. 1110–1180) echoes these sentiments, along with an elaboration about the material causality of the elemental mixture in creatures and things:

> There is in the matter of bodies a difference, and in their mixture there is diversity and distinction. Since some of the mixtures contain some evil and they are remote from parity in this sense, it is only possible for them to receive the forms of minerals. But some of the mixtures are closer to parity, so that it is possible for them to receive the soul of plants. And some of them are [even] closer to parity, so that it is possible for them to receive the souls of animals. And some mixtures are the closest to parity and more remote from

---

5 Isaac Israeli, "The Mantua Text," sec. 4, in A. Altmann and S. M. Stern, *Isaac Israeli—A Neoplatonic Philosopher of the Early Tenth Century* (Oxford: Oxford University Press, 1958), 121–122.

6 Solomon ibn Gabirol, *The Improvement of Moral Qualities*, trans. Stephen S. Wise (New York: Columbia University Press, 1901), 29.

the extension of the qualities that exist in the elements, so that it is possible for them to receive the soul of man.[7]

As with the previous thinkers introduced so far, ibn Daud adopts the level of balance (the "parity") achieved in the mixture of the elements that compose a given body as a means to assess its quality. What is added to the argumentation is the idea of some sort of material causation, namely that the quality of the body determines the quality of the form it receives. Since the human body is the best body in the world, it receives the best form in the world, which is the rational soul. What is implied here is a certain dependability of the form (which, in living creatures, is the soul), upon the material composition of the body. In order for a member of a given species to become actualized, it should have the appropriate matter. But should the material composition of the body be taken merely as a necessary starting point for the organism, or perhaps it has further ongoing implications on the activity of—in our case—the human soul? In other words, how far does the determinative power of man's bodily composition extend? I will return to this question in the next section.

While ibn Daud's approach to the human body's advantage underscores the difference between it and other bodies, his contemporary Yoseph ibn Tzaddiq (d. 1149), of Spain, offers an inclusive argument:

> The demonstration that man is perfect in this world is that he shares the perfection of all kinds of plants, which, however diverse, are included within the class of things that feed and grow. He has the quality of the great terebinth, whose mighty branches invite comparison with the body of man; and the hair that grows on his body

---

7 Abraham Ibn Daud, *The Exalted Faith*, trans. N.M. Samuelson (London and Toronto: Associated University Presses, 1986), 113–114. I have slightly modified the English translation. See discussion in A. Eran, *Me-Emunah Tamah Le-Emunah Ramah (From Simple Faith to Sublime Faith): Ibn Daud's Pre-Maimonidean Thought* (in Hebrew) (Tel-Aviv: Hakibbutz Hameuchad, 1998), 72–75.

has the same quality as the grasses and shrubs ... It is with reference to [the] animal soul, and not the rational soul, that philosophers have remarked that the lion is brave, the hare is weak, the lamb is meek, and the fox is shrewd. But all these qualities are to be found in man, of whom some are brave, some weak, and so forth.[8]

The human being, ibn Tzaddiq writes, is the culmination of the perfection of all living beings. It expresses the perfection of all plants and animals, so its own perfection is both individual and general. That is why ibn Tzaddiq describes it as a "microcosm"; the human being embodies not only its own body, but, in a way, encompasses all living beings. Philosophically speaking, this view can perhaps be seen as equivalent to the claim that man is the end of nature.

These optimistic views about the human body are obviously not the only ones. Some philosophers distinguished between the intrinsic worth of the body, labeled as the "purest" or the most refined of all bodies, and its fragility and weakness. In other words, the fact that the human body is the best overall does not necessarily mean that it is the strongest, healthiest, or freest from harm. This might lead to concern about man's fitness to be the end of creation, or even about God's good intentions and power. One of the earliest and most original Medieval Jewish philosophers, Saadya Gaon (882–942), head of the Sura academy in what is today Iraq, offers two different responses to this issue. First, after presenting the problem, he states a somewhat tautological response:

> Why, with all the distinction accorded to man, he came to have this feeble frame of a body composed of blood and phlegm and two

---

8 Joseph ibn Saddiq, *The Microcosm of Joseph ibn Saddiq*, ed. & trans. J. Haberman (Madison, NJ: Fairleigh Dickinson University Press, 2003), sec. 15, 75–76. Later on ibn Tzaddiq refers also to the equilibrium argument: "[W]hile man is included among the plants and animals, he alone is found among all living things to have an erect stance ... his nature is more in equilibrium, and his body is purer and finer than other bodies" (Ibid., 81).

galls? ... Why was it not constituted of pure elements resembling each other? For what is known as the human body is this thing, created of these mixtures, which is of all earthly beings the purest ... Whoever ... insists upon man's body being composed of elements other than those of which it consists is only demanding his nonexistence, just as he does who demands that the heaven be made of nothing except dirt or that the earth consists solely of fire. That is, of course, demanding the absurd.[9]

Saadya's point is simple; the demand that the human body be compounded differently amounts to the demand that it be something else, hence no longer the human body. This is how, in nature, the human being is built, and the fact remains that it is still the purest of earthly beings. But he offers another response, which interprets man's weakness as an opportunity, an occasion to live a life according to God's plan. Man's maladies, Saadya writes, are "really salutary for him because they keep him away from sin, and render him submissive to his Master, and introduce balance into his affairs."[10] Susceptibility to weather, poison, and other kinds of turmoil is essential for human well-being: "For had he felt no pain, he would not have been afraid of his Master's punishment, because if the latter had said to him, 'I shall inflict pain on thee,' he would not have known what pain was."[11] The same holds for bodily urges and appetites, whose moderation requires "the help of the reasoning faculty which God has granted him ... the craving for food [should be used] for the purpose of sustaining the individual organism, and the sex impulse for the maintenance of the human species as a whole."[12] As we will see in the next section, for Saadya, the human soul's mission in

---

9 Saadia Gaon, *The Book of Beliefs and Opinions*, trans. S. Rosenblatt (New Haven, CT: Yale University Press, 1948), II.4, 184.
10 Ibid.
11 Ibid.
12 Ibid., 185.

this world is to purify itself as much as it can, which is a different of way of saying that it should constantly improve itself. The tools for its improvement are obedience to God's order and the use of its rational powers. The site of the soul's activity is the body with which it is united. The body's shortcoming should be taken as incentives for improvement or pointers to areas of improvement. In short, the human body is composed in a way that fits the human mission in this world.

Some of Saadya's remarks refer to the connection between the human body and the need for rationality in handling it. This becomes a central theme in Moses Maimonides (1135–1204), perhaps the greatest Medieval Jewish philosopher. Maimonides, born in Cordoba, spent most of his life in Egypt, where he was a prominent religious leader and authority in Jewish law (to this day), as well as a court physician.[13] His medical training will become relevant in the third part of this essay.

In a lengthy passage in the *Guide of the Perplexed*, his most celebrated philosophical work, Maimonides meditates on the relation between a species' individuals and its survival, stating that except for human beings, every individual animal "goes about and runs in accordance with its nature, eating what it finds from among the things suitable to it, inhabiting any place to which it has happened to come, and copulating with any female it finds during its heat."[14] The continuance of the species proceeds naturally with no need for the help of other individuals or tools. But the human being is different:

> Let us suppose the case of an individual belonging to the human species that existed alone, had lost the governance of its conduct,

---

13 Perhaps more than any other figure discussed in this essay, how Maimonides should be read and understood is a subject of an ongoing and heated debate since his own times, especially the *Guide of the Perplexed*. In the context of the present discussion I am strictly limiting myself to analyze interesting arguments concerning the human body found in Maimonides' writings, with no attempt to unify them by some hermeneutical principle and no presumption to present them as his definitive position about the matter.

14 Moses Maimonides, *The Guide of the Perplexed*, trans. S. Pines (Chicago: University of Chicago Press, 1963), I.72 (vol. 1, 190).

and had become like the beasts. Such an individual would perish immediately; he could not last even one day except by accident.[15]

Maimonides' point, as he elaborates, is that the human body, for its survival, cannot depend only on its animal qualities, because even its nutrition requires "the application of some art and a lengthy management that cannot be made perfect except through thought and perspicacity, as well as with the help of many tools and many individuals." The human body, in order to survive, needs many things that can be acquired only through the mediation of rationality:

> [T]he precautions against heat in the hot season and against cold in the cold season and the finding of protection against the rains, the snow, and the blowing of winds, require arrangements for many preparations, none of which can be perfected except through thought and perspicacity. Because of this one finds in man the rational faculty in virtue of which he thinks, exerts his perspicacity, works, and prepares by means of various arts his food, his habitation, and his clothing ... a human individual who, according to a supposition you might make, would be deprived of this faculty and left only with the animal faculties, would perish and be destroyed immediately.[16]

There is no question that for Maimonides the shortcomings of the human body are intimately related to rationality. He goes beyond Saadya's conception of directing the soul toward obedience and moderation to a considerably more fundamental point, namely the question of human survival. But if this is the case, the question of natural priority immediately arises: does the rational capacity exist for the

---
15 Ibid., 191
16 Ibid.

sake of the survival of the human body, or is it the other way around? In a way, Maimonides' argument makes the possession of the human rational soul a question of necessity rather than entitlement. Ibn Daud, for instance, maintains that man receives the human soul because man has the best body; Maimonides says that man has a rational capacity because man's body needs it the most. Paradoxically, human bodily weakness is the key for the fundamental advantage human beings have over all of the other natural creatures. This is, in a way, the point that the philosopher and scientists Gersonides (Levi ben Gershon, 1288–1344), who was active in southern France, tries to communicate:

> Since man, because of his rarified matter, has no bodily material for perfection, such as wool or feathers, he has been given the capacity to make clothing and houses. And since for the same reason man has no natural organs for self-defense or for conquest over those animals he desires to eat, he has been given the ability to make weapons of war and for hunting. And since he cannot find proper food without labor, he was given the capacity to work the earth and to prepare food.[17]

Gersonides, like Saadya, distinguishes between purity and utility; and like Maimonides, opines that man's natural fragility sets him apart from other animals in that this fragility is the key for the move from nature to art. Man's turn to labor and art is a necessary compensation for his physical shortcomings, which are the result of his "rarified matter." Somehow, his body is inferior *because* it is purer, and this physical constraint opens up the first step in man's journey from nature toward rationality. So here, again, it can be seen that features of the human body have a determining role in man's overall nature.

---

17 Gersonides, *The Wars of the Lord*, trans. S. Feldman, vol. 2 (Philadelphia: Jewish Publication Society, 1987), IV.6, 167.

It would be a mistake to think that all of the Jewish philosophers shared a positive, or at least constructive, assessment of the human body. There is no shortage of polar opposites. Perhaps the most famous negative assessment of the body is found in the work of the Zaragozan mystic Bahya ibn Paquda (*c.* mid-eleventh-century), whose remarks leave little room for imagination:

> [W]e find man to be the most imperfect and weak of creatures in three ways: in terms of his development (in that other creatures are stronger than he, more able to endure tribulation and more able to provide for themselves without burdening their parents as much as he does); in terms of how filthy his body is (which is easily detected by those close by when he has not washed in a few days, and because his corpse decomposes more offensively than any other creature's when he dies, because his fecal matter is more offensive than theirs, etc.); and for the fact that his capacities become so limited when, subject to a head injury (for example), he seems to be incapacitated when he is no longer able to speak, and hence use an advantage the Creator gave him over other creatures… Note man's weakness and faults: that he never comes to perfection, and on how needy and impoverished he is of things he needs.[18]

Man is not the best creature, but the worst. He is weak, filthy, and easily incapacitated. But although this is a miserable state, it is a miserable state for a good reason:

> Discern all the good and kind things the Creator has done for us, as well as the fact that He created us the way He did with innate defects, destitute, and in need of the things that will perfect us … because the Creator has compassion on us, wants us to know ourselves, wants

---

18 Bachya ibn Pakuda, "Introduction," in *The Duties of the Heart*, trans. Y. Feldman, vol. 3 (Northvale, NJ: Aronson, 1996), 112.

us to be reflective about our environment and to clutch unto the service of God and nonetheless earn a reward in the world to come, for which we were created.[19]

All dramatics aside, Bahya is essentially repeating Saadya's argument, only pushed to the extreme. The physical shortcomings of the human being direct him toward obedience to God and proper behavior. The reason Bahya's assessment is significantly more severe than Saadya's lies in their different ethical agendas, which I return to in the next sections.

3. Body, Soul, and Character

It shouldn't come as a surprise that there is a correlation between the assessment of the human body and its relation with the human soul. The higher the body is regarded, the more it would be "allowed" to contribute to man's work toward his end. I will start the discussion with a fresh look at Saadya's concept of soul, and then move on to other thinkers.

The first thing to keep in mind when discussing Saadya's conception of the relation between body and the soul is that he puts them both on the same ontological plane. For theological considerations, and fear of Christian elements, Saadya asserts that "it would be wrong to ascribe eternity to aught except the Creator."[20] Therefore, soul is created. It is a substance just like physical substances, save the fact that it is the purest among them. According to Saadya, the creation of the soul "first takes place with the completion of the bodily

---

19 Ibid., 112–113.
20 Saadya, *Beliefs*, 6, 3 (p. 241). For Saadya's view about the soul see the discussion in Esti Eisenmann, "Body and Soul, Materiality and Spirituality in R. Sa'adia's Thought" (in Hebrew), *Mo'ed* 20 (2010), 135–152. For the theories of soul he enumerates and rejects see H. Davidson, "Saadia's List of Theories of Soul," in *Jewish Medieval and Renaissance Studies*, ed. A. Altmann (Cambridge, MA: Harvard University Press, 1967), 75–94.

form of the human being."[21] The quality of the soul "is comparable in purity to that of the heavenly spheres. Like the latter, it attains luminosity as a result of the light which it receives from God, except that its substance becomes, in consequence hereof, even finer than that of the spheres. That is how it came to be endowed with the power of speech." The power of speech, namely rationality, is what makes the soul better even than the heavenly spheres, which don't have this power.[22] Although the human body is the best "terrestrial" body, it still can't do anything without the soul, so the soul is better than all terrestrial things. It is either of the same composition of the celestial bodies—the spheres—or better than them. But the first option is rejected by the fact that celestial bodies are deprived of speech. The conclusion is that "it must be a fine substance that is clearer and purer and simpler than that of the spheres."[23] In another place, Saadya remarks that since the soul's substance is "finer even that that of the stars and the heavenly spheres, it is impossible for us to see it with our senses."[24]

Besides the power of speech, the soul also provides the bodily sense organs with the sense faculties. The proof for that is that blind men can see in their dreams although they don't have the power of sight.[25] Since the difference between soul and body is not categorical but qualitative, it does not pose an ontological difficulty to situate the soul physically within the body, and Saadya finds it in the heart, providing some biological justification. The soul has three faculties—reason, appetition, and anger—which respectively reflect the biblical nouns *nefesh, ruah*, and *neshama*. The three faculties are not to be taken as different substances, but all belong to one soul.

---

21 Saadya, *Beliefs*, VI.3 , 241–242.
22 Ibid., 242.
23 Ibid.
24 Ibid., V.1, 206.
25 Ibid., VI.3, 242.

At this point one may ask why, if at all, the soul needs the body, or to be situated in a body. This has to do with its mission in this world, which is to improve until it is worthy of God's reward; in Saadya's words, the soul has to increase its "luminosity." However, the soul needs an instrument through which it will improve, and that is why it is attached to the body:

> [I]nasmuch as the soul cannot, by virtue of its constitution, function by itself, it must needs be united with something that will enable it to work toward its improvement. For it is such actions alone that are conducive to permanent well-being and perfect bliss ... obedience [to God's commandments] increases the luminosity of the soul's substance, whereas sin renders its substance turbid and black ... The pure, clean souls that have been refined are thereupon exalted and ennobled ... those that resemble dross and base metals ... are degraded and debased.[26]

In this critical junction is the need for the body: the soul's activity within it is the only way for it to be purified, by acting according to the law and obeying God in this world. This opens up the option for even the basest of souls to achieve repentance. However, once the human body dies, once the soul departs from it, it is—for the purpose of judgment—the end of the story: the soul "is incapable of being cleansed any longer of the corruption that has accumulated in it."[27] Without being attached to the body, the soul would have never been able to improve. Although bodily existence might summon "sin, defilement, and pain," it is indispensable for soul:

> [I]f God had allowed the soul to remain unattached, it would not have been able to attain well-being or bliss or life eternal. For the

---

26 Ibid., VI.4, 246–247.
27 Ibid., 247.

attainment of these things can be effected by it only by serving its Master, and the soul has no means, by virtue of its nature, of rendering this service except through the instrumentality of the body."[28]

The soul, Saadya stresses, can only act within a body, and vice versa; the human body cannot do anything without the soul. Without having each other, there would be no point to create either of them.[29]

As we have seen in the previous section, Saadya has an overall positive assessment of the human body, as the purest body, and he explains the body's shortcomings as a means to point man toward the right path. So it is not surprising that he defends the body from those who maintain that it is unworthy to be the bearer of the soul:

> I have encountered certain people who asked how it was compatible with the wisdom of the Creator, magnified and exalted be He, to place a being as noble as the soul, which exceeds in purity even the heavenly spheres, in something as turbid as the body. In fact, they began to think in their hearts that God has wronged the soul by so doing.[30]

To this he responds:

> [T]he body of man contains no impurity in and by itself. It is, on the contrary, entirely pure, for defilement is neither a thing that is subject to sense perception nor a requirement of logic. It is purely a decree of the law of the Torah. This law has declared unclean certain secretions of human beings after their discharge from the body, although they do not defile while they are within the body. The aforementioned allegation can be maintained only if he that makes

---

28 Ibid.
29 Ibid., 247–248.
30 Ibid., 245

it will impose upon us rules that he has invented out his own mind and make it obligatory upon us to consider as reprehensible what he so regards.[31]

The picture that Saadya paints is one of complete cooperation between the human body and the human soul. He makes clear that it would be a mistake to ascribe any human action either strictly to the body, or strictly to the soul; the soul provides the person his vocation and powers, while the body makes possible for him to exercise these powers, improve, and be eligible for God's reward.[32] This reward (or punishment), accordingly, pertains to both body and soul: "the reward and punishment in the hereafter is meted out upon the body and soul unitedly, since they constitute together a single agent"[33]

Unsurprisingly, when one turns to Bahya ibn Paquda, who has already expressed a very negative assessment of the human body, his attitude to the relation between the soul and the body would not be as harmonious:

[Y]ou were created with two distinctive components whose tempers contradict and resist each other: a soul and a body. They contradict each other because the Creator introduced a trait and certain abilities in you that, when activated, have you desire certain body-enhancing things that ensure the development of the world and humankind. It is the desire for physical pleasure that all living things

---

31 Ibid., 249.

32 See Ibid., VI.5, 252: "whoever attributes actions to the soul only, or to the body alone or to the bones exclusively, does so out of ignorance of the rules of the language of Scripture and its usage. It is, namely, one of the peculiarities of the style of Holy Writ that an act is performed by three or four or five different things is sometimes related to it by the first alone, and sometimes to the second alone, and sometimes to the third alone."

33 Ibid., IX.5, 336. See also the brief remark by the very early philosopher Dawud ibn Marwan al-Muqammitz al-Raqqi (first half of 9th century): "A human being is composed of body and soul. By their collaboration in any act, the reward for the good or wicked deed is earned. Hence we say that the reward and punishment are both corporeal and spiritual. And just as they are spiritual in a way we cannot grasp, so they are corporeal in a way we cannot grasp." Sarah Stroumsa, *Dāwūd ibn Marwān al-Muqammiṣ's* Twenty Chapters *(ʿIshrūn Maqāla)* (Leiden, The Netherlands: Brill, 1989), 300.

have. But He included another trait and series of abilities in you as well (i.e., perfect wisdom) that, when activated, have you despise life in this world and want to separate yourself from it.[34]

The body is about this world, sustaining the species, and being attracted to other bodies as a means of pleasure. The soul is about despising this world and wanting to flee; "the mind is essentially a spiritual thing that is derived from the immaterial worlds above, so it is a stranger to this gross physical world."[35] The relation between body and soul is one of hostility; their needs are irreconcilable. For Bahya, one of the major problems is that bodily needs and desires arise in life before the needs of the soul, and therefore have an early advantage. They bind the body to this world, and once the needs of the soul appear, man's power of reason and judgment is already clouded by bodily desires. That is why man's endeavor is not cooperation between body and soul, but rather the repression of desires and advancement of reason. Man cannot achieve this on his own; he needs external help, which is offered by the Torah and the law: "the external things you should use are the principles of Torah that were presented through the prophets and God's other messengers. For it was by means of them that God taught His creations how to serve Him."[36] It is no wonder, then, that Torah and Jewish law deal so much with the regulations of the body:

> It cautions us against many foods, clothes, sexual relations, possessions, and actions that stimulate our desires. That is also why it

---

34 Bahya, *Duties*, III.2, 116.

35 Ibid., 117. He continues: "Because it is a stranger to the world, the mind is not consoled there, it has no help and everything opposes it. So it is only natural that the mind would grow weak and need something to relieve it of the oppression of physical desire and fortify it." A similar sentiment is put forth by a contemporary of Bahya, Abraham bar Hayya of Barcelona: "The wise and rational soul has no joy in this world, but is angry and bitter for its imprisonment; the Holy Lord comforts it, speaks to its heart and awards it a rightful place in the world to come as a consolation for its anger and bitterness." Abraham bar-Hayya, *Hegyon Ha-Nephesch Ha-Atzuvah (The Meditation of the Sorrowful Soul)*, ed. Geoffrey Wigoder (Jerusalem: Bialik Institute, 1971), 67.

36 Bahya, *Duties*, III.2, 116.

commands us to occupy ourself with things that resist and oppose them like prayer, fasting, charity, kindness to fortify the mind and to elevate you in this world and the world to come.[37]

In the course of his discussion, Bahya remarks that since the physical composition the body is ontologically linked to this world: "your desires ... are a combination of your character and a composite of the elements. So they are affixed to and rooted in this world. They derive their energy from food, and are fortified by physical gratification."[38] This turns us to the question of whether and how the human body has a determining affect on human character, or perhaps human character has a physical expression. In the previous section it was noted that the human body is often commended for being the best body owing to its constitution and proportion. Philosophically speaking, since no two human beings are exactly the same, do their bodily differences have any kind of ethical import?

In his *Improvement of the Moral Qualities*, ibn Gabirol presents an interesting theory that explains how human character traits express its bodily composition. Understanding the physics behinds human virtues and vices, ibn Gabirol writes, will help us refine our characters and better ourselves. Ibn Gabirol notices that young people are naturally inclined to certain behavior—some praiseworthy, some blameworthy—and only during their maturity does their rationality actually kick in:

> All the qualities of man, of the possession of which he gives evidence at the period of his youth and manhood, are in him during his infancy and boyhood ... Thou wilt observe that in some boys the

---

37 Ibid., 116–117. This is only the first step of Bahya's mystical quest: "Torah-induced service to God manifests itself more in good deeds that affect the body than in the service to God that lies hidden within" (Ibid., III.3, 120).
38 Ibid., III.2, 117.

quality of pudency manifests itself, and in others impudence; some incline to enjoyment, others aspire to virtue, and still others are disposed to vices; these qualities above mentioned and others similar to them being among those of the animal soul; and when men reach unto the stage of maturity, the strength of the rational soul displays its activity and it directs him that possesses it to a proper understanding with regard to the improvement of the qualities, since it is not the practice of the animal soul to improve these.[39]

However, if one wants to correct character traits, it is advisable to do so "as long as the limits of childhood have not been passed."[40] Once the body is fully grown, "it becomes difficult to set them along a good course, just as a sprig may be made to stand erect before it is full grown; but when it has become a tree, it is difficult to bend or move it."[41] But besides this practical advice, which aligns moral development with bodily development, ibn Gabirol proceeds to discuss each moral quality (good or bad) in light of two physical aspects: the bodily humours and the senses. The human body is composed of four domains, each of which corresponds to one of the four elements: "blood corresponding to air, yellow gall corresponding to fire, black gall corresponding to earth, and white moisture corresponding to water."[42] This idea, in itself, has nothing novel about it. But ibn Gabirol takes a step further and claims that each moral quality proceeds from a certain blending of these: pride, for instance, as well as, for example, impudence, hate, and cowardice, stem from the combination of yellow gall and blood, which are both hot, but one is dry and the other moist. To take another example, white gall and blood are both moist, but the former is cold while the latter hot, and together they produce valor, joy, liberality,

---

39 Ibn Gabirol, *Improvement*, 44.
40 Ibid., 55.
41 Ibid.
42 Ibid., 33.

and goodwill. Other types of combinations result in the rest of the qualities, which are overall twenty in number. But this is not the only physical origin of the qualities; they also arise out of our senses: sight can bring forth pride, meekness, prudency, and impudence; from smell can arise wrath, goodwill, jealousy, and alertness, and so forth. All in all, the twenty moral qualities are distributed evenly among the five senses. Every quality, then, stems from a certain bodily blend, and arises through a certain sense. Joy, for instance, stems from the combination of blood and white gall, both of which are moist, but one of which is hot, and the other—cold, and arises through the sense of taste: "Speech, consisting as it does of words, which are of a kind with (the objects of) taste, sometimes gives rise to joy."[43] The same analysis is offered for the rest of the qualities. Knowledge of the qualities and their origins will help man better himself:

> Man ought to consider carefully the qualities which belong to his senses and not employ them except when it is necessary; for God, exalted be He, has so constituted them in man that he can wisely order them, since through them he guards the normal condition of his life. By their means he sees colors, hears sounds, tastes food (flavors), smells odors, distinguishes between hard and soft, and all other things which are necessary to his life; and many which are useful we will mention when we commence (the subject), please God. We will now describe the senses and the various advantages to be derived from their use and the necessity of refraining from the use of them when they would cause harm.[44]

As can be seen from ibn Gabirol's mode of presentation, he locates a continuation between the human being's embodiment and his moral

---

43 Ibid., 50.
44 Ibid., 37.

qualities. This is expressed by his constitution, in the blending of the humours, as well as in the manner he experiences the world, through his sense organs. To this one may add his claim about the importance of timing for moral habituation, namely before the body has fully developed. All these add up to an approach which grounds the scope of human behavior within the scope of human bodily composition, which means that the body itself opens the door for virtue and vice. Whether and to what extent the body determines the moral character of the person, or perhaps only expresses it—or some interplay between these options—remains an open question.[45]

As we have seen in the previous section, ibn Daud maintains that the hierarchical arrangement of bodily mixtures determines the kind of soul each given individual receives. But can this criterion be used to assess differences within members of the same species? It seems that it can. From ibn Daud's discussion it can be inferred that people's entry points to the world are not identical, and some—owing to their material inferiority—have to work harder to diminish their dependency on matter and move toward parity. While in ibn Gabirol the material arrangement of the body expresses its moral qualities, and it is uncertain if a stronger claim is warranted, in ibn Daud it seems that the body does indeed have a determining affect on the individual's

---

45 A similar sentiment is expressed by the Andalusian poet and philosopher Judah Halevi (1075–1141), but it is unclear to what extent he subscribes to it, as it is part of a discussion of the philosophical account of the soul that he ultimately rejects, although the position presented here is not argued against specifically: "Men differ from each other, because most of them are physically of different constitutions, and the intellect follows the latter. If his gall be yellowish, he is quick and alert; if blackish, he is quiet and sedate. The temperament follows the mixture of humours. If an individual is found of evenly balanced humour, which controls his contrasting dispositions ... such a person possesses without doubt a heart which is free from strong passions. He covets a degree of divine character above his own. He is perplexed, not knowing which inclination should have preponderance. He does not give way either to anger, or to lust, or to any other passion, but controls himself, and seeks divine inspiration to walk the right path." Judah Halevi, *The Kuzari*, trans. H. Hirschfeld (New York: Schocken, 1964), V.10, pp. 258–259. Maimonides also thinks that "some character traits a man has from the beginning of his creation, depending upon the nature of his body," but these traits can be rectified if they are addressed. See Maimonides, "Laws Concerning Character Traits," in R. L. Weiss and C. E. Butterworth, *Ethical Writings of Maimonides* (New York: New York University Press, 1975), I.2, 28–29.

moral quality.⁴⁶ But if this is so, aren't we in danger of making the soul *too* dependent on the body? This would be unacceptable to ibn Daud, who maintains that although advancement of the rational soul depends on the body, because knowledge proceeds by abstraction from the senses, the soul can advance to a stage where it no longer has need for the body, and thus it can be concluded that soul's dependency on the body is not absolute.⁴⁷ So what is the ontological status of the soul? According to ibn Daud, the soul is created simultaneously with the body which is fit to receive it, but it is independent of matter; it is created, but does not perish with the body. Ibn Daud arrives at this conclusion by eliminating the other options. It would make no sense to say that the soul existed before the body, entered it, and then perished with it, because in that case the divine plan is flawed, as the association with the body has nothing but a negative effect on the soul. On the other hand, if it were able to persist before the body, and then able to persist after it, what was the point in joining them in the first place? Therefore the soul is created with the body, and can continue to exist after the body perishes. The body serves as the soul's launching pad to the divine realm.⁴⁸

4. Treating or Mistreating the Body

In the previous sections we have seen that, although approaches to the human body vary from thinker to thinker, it is always important and always needs to be addressed—friend or foe, it is part of us, and its relation to our soul is intimate, more often than not with a causal role. In this context, it would be interesting to inquire into how it should

---

46 Ibn Daud, *Exalted Faith*, 246–247.
47 Ibid., 114.
48 Ibn Daud, *Exalted Faith*, 102. For the inner tension within ibn Daud on this point see T.A.M. Fontaine, *In Defence of Judaism: Abraham ibn Daud: Sources and Structures of Ha-Emunah Ha-Ramah* (Assen, The Netherlands: Van Gorcum, 1990), 79–80. See also Eran, *Me-Emunah Tamah*, 69–70.

be treated. This question is interesting not only for purely philosophically reasons, but also in light of everyday Jewish practise, which I have already mentioned has a lot to say about how to moderate the body. In this sense, the philosophical discussion and Jewish law overlap, causing an interesting dialectic. I will divide my discussion into two topics—how to take care of the body, and the coherence of asceticism. I will discuss Bahya ibn Paquda, Judah Halevi, and Maimonides regarding both issues.

All three thinkers—and perhaps this can be extended to every medieval Jewish philosopher—advocate the superiority of the soul over the body. Be this at it may, it is insufficient to cultivate only the soul and neglect the body. Even Bahya, which never hides his disdain toward the body, stresses the importance of caring for it:

> Your body and your soul both need consideration . . . You strengthen and improve your soul by accustoming it to discipline and study, by offering it wise guidance, by training it in good character traits, and by preventing it from acquiring animal desires. But you strengthen and improve your body by providing it with good, appetizing food and with liquids that agree with it, by bathing it in warm water and by being ever sensitive to what is good for it and what it needs.[49]

But why? Not because the body has inherent value, but because caring for the body is a way of caring for the soul, and neglecting the body amounts to neglecting the soul: "The best thing to do," Bahya writes, "is to have your immortal soul govern your mortal body, pay attention and be sensitive to it, and not neglect the things that are so important for your body. For if you do, you will overburden and weaken it, and eventually weaken both body and soul."[50] For the soul to function well, the body has to be taken care of.

---

49 Bahya, *Duties*, VIII.3, 380.
50 Ibid.

But how does the demand to care for the body and the soul justify the long list of worldly precepts in Jewish law? Judah Halevi explains:

> [I]t is not in the power of mortal man to apportion to each faculty of the soul and body its right measure, nor to decide what amount of rest and exertion is good, or to determine how long the ground should be cultivated till it finds rest in the years of release and jubilee, or the amount of tithe to be given, etc.[51]

The answer is simple: it is beyond our power to figure it out by ourselves. Observing the commandments is entrusting our well-being in the hands of God. Maimonides believes that it is important to take care of the body for the sake of man's ultimate goal:

> Man needs to subordinate all his soul's power to thought ... and to set his sight on a single goal: the perception of God ... The purpose of his body's health is that the soul find its instruments healthy and sound in order that it can be directed toward the sciences and toward acquiring the moral and rational virtues, so that he might arrive at that goal.[52]

Without a healthy body, Maimonides reiterates, arrival at this goal would be impossible: "Since preserving the body's health and strength is among the ways of the Lords—for to attain understanding and knowledge is impossible when one is sick—a man needs to keep away from things that destroy the body and to accustom himself to things that make him healthy and vigorous."[53] Maimonides, as we can see, goes as far as connecting a healthy body to the ways of the Lords. Accordingly, the art of medicine becomes crucial for achieving man's

---

51 Halevi, *Kuzari*, II.50, 113–114.
52 Maimonides, "Eight Chapters," in Weiss and Butterworth, *Maimonides*, V.5, 75.
53 Maimonides, "Laws," III.4, 36.

end, so that it attains a religious status, as a form of worship: "the art of medicine is given a very large role with respect to the virtues, the knowledge of God, and attaining true happiness. To study it diligently is among the greatest acts of worship."[54]

But what about the quality of our bodily existence? Here finally we can see that the bodily life should not be merely a life of necessities, but a comfortable one.[55] Maimonides offers many colourful examples and tips for making life easier:

> If the humor of black bile agitates him, he should make it cease by listening to songs and various kinds of melodies, by walking in gardens and fine buildings, by sitting before beautiful forms, and by things like this which delight the soul and make the disturbance of black bile disappear from it. Similarly, if he bestirs himself and sets out to acquire money, his goal in accumulating it should be to spend it in connection with the virtues and to use it to sustain his body and to prolong his existence, so that he perceives and knows of God what is possible for him to know.[56]

The life which Maimonides presents the reader is a pleasant one. Enjoyments, relaxation, and economical prosperity are all included within a life dedicated to worship, for the sake of the body, the soul, and life, as long as man's ultimate end remains in view and is actively sought after.

---

54 Maimonides, "Eight Chapters," V.5, 75.

55 To stress the need for leading a comfortable life, Maimonides lists the necessary requirements for living in a city: "A disciple of wise men is not permitted to live in any city that does not have these ten things: a physician, a surgeon, a bathhouse, a bathroom, a fixed source of water such as a river or spring, a synagogue, a teacher of children, a scribe, a collector of charity, and a court that can punish with lashes and imprisonment" (Maimonides, "Laws," IV.23, 41). It is interesting to see the order in which these requirements are listed. The synagogue appears only after the bodily requirements have been presented.

56 Maimonides' description of the ideal sexual act is also rather uplifting: "Both of them (or one of them) shall not be drunk, lethargic, or sad. She should not be asleep and he should not force her if she is unwilling, but [intercourse shall take place] when both wish it and in a state of mutual joy. He shall

This image is very different than another life option which is to be found, to some extent at least, in probably every existent religion or spiritual institution: the ascetic life. For various reasons, asceticism isn't very popular in the Rabbinic tradition.[57] However, the notion of retreating from worldly affairs for the sake of getting closer to the Divine can seem as an attractive one, especially if one despises the world and the body, a sentiment expressed time and again by Bahya, who prescribes:

> Live the life of an ascetic who abhors the world, and replace the love and preference for the world in your heart with love for the Creator; surrender yourself to Him, and enjoy nothing else but Him; close yourself off to the world and its inhabitants, accustom yourself to the ways of the prophets and the pious; and let your heart trust that God will be as kind to you in the world to come as He is to them.[58]

There's no doubt that Bahya is advocating asceticism. But what exactly does he mean by it? Does the seclusion he advocates amount to neglecting the body? This would be self-defeating, as well as inconsistent, as we have already seen that he believes that it is important to take care of the body for the sake of the soul. As he puts it at least, this abhorance toward the world can be interpreted as some sort of inner experience, not necessarily actual abstinence from bodily

---

converse and play with her a little so that their souls become tranquil, and he shall have sexual intercourse modestly, not shamelessly, and separate [from her] at once" (Maimonides, "Laws," V.4, 43).

57 For a clear overview regarding the scholarly debate about ascetic tendencies in ancient Rabbinic Judaism see Michael L. Satlow, "'And on the Earth You Shall Sleep': 'Talmud Torah' and Rabbinic Asceticism," *Journal of Religion* 83, no. 2 (2003), especially 206–207. For an approach to asceticism in Bahya and Maimonides that differs from my own in its conclusions see H. Kreisel, "Asceticism in the Thought of R. Bahya ibn Paquda and Maimonides," *Da'at* 21 (1988), 5–22. For further discussion of ascetic tendencies in Medieval Jewsih philosophers see Dov Schwartz, "Asceticism and Self-Mortification: Attitudes Held by a Provençal Circle of Commentators of the 'Kuzari'" (in Hebrew), *Jerusalem Studies in Jewish Thought* (1993), 79–99.

58 Bahya, *Duties*, IV.4, 213.

needs. However, later in the text he seems to entertain this option seriously:

> Since everyone has to practice some sort of abstinence to improve himself by only taking what he needs from the world, it is logical that there be some people who are completely ascetic, who separate and cut themselves off from all worldly affairs. While others should learn from their deeds as much as necessary and appropriate for their own good, it would not be to the world's benefit for everybody to practice abstinence to that degree. That would lead to the end of civilization and humanity.[59]

Abstinence here is understood as some kind of religious practise for self-improvement. But Bahya doesn't present it as a religious duty, but as a "regulative ideal" which one should follow for the best of one's ability. Recognizing that some people are more capable of asceticism than others, and serve as role models of sorts, he also makes the obvious point that if applied universally, the result would be the discontinuance of the human race.

Judah Halevi sympathizes, but rejects asceticism as some kind of ideal. True, he explains, historically, in the age of prophecy, there was "divine presence" in the holy land, so "some few persons lived an ascetic life in deserts and associated with people of the same frame of mind. They did not seclude themselves completely, but they endeavored to find support in the knowledge of the Law and in holy and pure actions which brought them near to that high rank. These were the disciples of prophets."[60] But those days are over, and ascetic practise nowadays is tantamount to "distress and sickness for soul and body." The ascetic "has no intercourse with the divine light, and cannot associate

---

59 Ibid., IX.1, 406.
60 Halevi, *Kuzari*, III.1, 136.

himself with it as the prophets." If anything, it moves one away from the divine: "his soul urges him to employ its innate powers in seeing, hearing, speaking, occupation, eating, cohabitation, gain, managing his house, helping the poor, upholding the law with money in case of need. Must he not regret those things to which he has tied his soul, a regret which tends to remove him from the Divine Influence, which he desired to approach?"[61]

Maimonides' approach is both harsher and softer. His discussion of asceticism is related to the ethical doctrine of the mean that he adopts, which calls for correcting deviations from the mean by exaggerating a bit in the contrary direction. To overcome cowardice, for example, one should begin by acting somewhat recklessly. Virtuous people, Maimonides writes, sometimes "incline a little toward the excess or the defect as a precaution." This would sometimes result into activities which can be taken to be ascetic:

> What the virtuous men did at certain times and also what some individuals among them [always] did in inclining toward one extreme—for example, fasting, rising at night, abstaining from eating meat and drinking wine, keeping away from women, wearing garments of wool and hair, dwelling on mountains, and secluding themselves in desolate places—they did only with a view to medical treatment.[62]

The problem arose when these practises—which, incidentally, are not very much unlike what Bahya described—were misunderstood. The "ignorant" saw these actions, but didn't understand the logic behind them, believing that these actions in themselves lead to virtue. Consequently, he writes, "They set about afflicting their bodies with every kind of affliction, thinking they were acquiring virtue and doing

---

61 Ibid., 136–137.
62 Maimonides, "Eight Chapters," IV, 69.

something good and would thereby come near to God—as if God were an enemy of the body and desired its ruin and destruction."[63]

Asceticism, in itself, overrides God's laws, which are already designed to lead man toward virtue. There is already a long list of divine prohibitions and commands, that if one lives according to them, one will attain virtue. The body is already moderated toward the virtuous mean thanks to the Law. Going beyond what is already forbidden is ignoring God's formula for a balanced life. "All of the commandments discipline the power of the soul."[64] Maimonides sums this up quite neatly:

> Only a manifestly ignorant individual would come and wish to add to these things and, for example, prohibit eating and drinking, in addition to the stipulated prohibition about food; and prohibit marriage, in addition to what is prohibited concerning sexual intercourse; and give all of his money to the poor or to the Temple property, in addition to what the Law says about charity, Temple properties, and valuations. His actions are bad and he does not know that he goes all the way to one extreme, completely leaving the mean.[65]

As we have seen, Maimonides believes that moderating the body according to Jewish law sets man on the path toward virtue. Taking care of the body and living a pleasant life need not undermine man's journey to know God, and voluntary suffering is counterproductive, disobedient, and simply misguided. Maimonides permits mild practises of asceticism if they are exercised within the proper context as a precautionary act by people who have already attained virtue.

---

63 Ibid., 70.
64 Ibid., 71.
65 Maimonides, "Eight Chapters," ch. 4, 72.

5. Bodily Resurrection

In the final section of this paper I would like to outline two explanations of bodily resurrection.[66] I think this is important for two reasons. First, because any attempt to analyze the concept of embodiment within the context of Jewish philosophy has to address the traditional Jewish view according to which the existence of the human body does not end with its death; and second, because it is philosophically interesting to see attempts to provide an account of bodily resurrection which is not entirely irrational.

As we have seen earlier, for Saadya a person's reward for their actions in the afterlife is for their body and soul together. People are rewarded when resurrection arrives, and Saadya wants to explain how this works. When a person dies, he writes, their soul is "stored up until the time of retribution."[67] Body and soul are separated, and while the body decomposes and becomes infected by worms and vermin, the soul, which knows this, is pained, "just as a person would be pained by the knowledge that a house in which he used to live is in ruins and that thorns and thistles grow in it."[68] In order to retain man's individuality, for the sake of resurrection the parts to which he dissolves are set aside, "not being mixed with the elemental masses. Rather they remain separate until the time of resurrection."[69] When the time comes, God restores them to their original arrangement in the human body, and reattaches the soul to the body.[70] A potential objection to this would be that it would be wasteful to have elementary parts set aside without being reused to make new people. Saadya, anticipating this objection,

---

66 I am only discussing explanations that understand resurrection in the literal sense. For non-literal interpretations see, for instance, D. Schwartz, "The Neutralization of the Messianic Idea in Medieval Jewish Rationalism" (in Hebrew), *Hebrew Union College Annual* 64 (1994): H1–H22.
67 Saadya, *Beliefs*, VI.7, 257.
68 Ibid.
69 Ibid.
70 Ibid., VII.7, 279.

assuages his audience by explaining that there is plenty of raw material for that:

> The sources of air and fire that are located between the earth and the first part of the heavens were equivalent in volume to 1008 times the entire mass of the earth and its mountains and seas. With such latitude there was certainly no reason for the Creator to compose the bodies of any second generation out of the decomposed parts of the first. Nay, He would merely set the latter aside until He would fulfill for them what He had promised.[71]

Like Saadya, Hasdai Crescas (c. 1340–1410/11), a highly original Spanish rabbinical thinker known primarily for his critique of Aristotelian physics, attempts to provide an account of resurrection which reflects the unity of body and soul, without losing individuality. In his discussion of resurrection, Crescas addresses various problems attached to it in order to remove his reader's doubts about its possibility. The first two problems, which I discuss here, are of a philosophical nature, "pertaining the possibility of the matter itself."[72]

When a human being dies, Crescas writes, his parts are dissolved into their elements. Even if they are reassembled, what promises that they amount to the same person and not to a "new creation"? The whole point of resurrection is that it is personal reward, so if the identity of the individual is not retained, there would be no point to it.[73] What's more, once the dead person's body parts are separated, they move on to different places and different creatures: it could be the center of the earth, the body of an ant, or the corpse of a lion. It would make very

---

[71] Ibid., 278. Saadya maintains that the total number of humans to be created is finite.
[72] Hasdai Crescas, *Or Ha-Shem (The Light of the Lord)*, ed. S. Fisher (Jerusalem: Ramot, 1990), III, I, iv, 4, p. 345.
[73] Ibid.

little sense for them to be removed from their present position for the sake of reassembling the person's body.[74]

Crescas's response to both of these queries is that they assume that it is mandatory that the resurrected body of the dead person will have the exact same parts of the original body. But this assumption is unnecessary, for the important factor is not the parts, but the "temperament and character" of the individual, which can be understood as the proper arrangement of the components rather than the components themselves.[75] It is important to note, Crescas adds, that resurrection has to do with the unifying of body and soul, whereas the soul is already an individual spiritual, stand-alone substance. The soul's powers will use the new body in the same manner that they used the previous one. What's more, memory and imagination belong to the soul rather than the body anyway. Crescas argues that even in this life our bodily components change all the time without turning us into something else; when a person eats and grows, his bodily parts are generated from the food that he consumes, so that they are, in a way, composed out of something that is exterior to his body. Similarly, bodily individuality can be retained, even if an individual's body is composed out of different components once it is reunited with the soul. Since the soul is the principle of individuation, the body that unites with it follows suit, just as food that is consumed by a human being becomes part of that human being. "The body," Crescas concludes, "doesn't have to have the same elemental parts that were dissolved from it, as long as they retain their proportion."[76]

Both Saadya and Crescas accept the miraculous nature of resurrection, but are still concerned how to make rational sense of its mechanics. Saadya proceeds in a somewhat safer route, retaining the identity of the resurrected person by leaving both his bodily components and

---

74 In present times, the completeness of the human corpse for the sake of resurrection is at the center of a huge debate within Orthodox Judaism concerning organ donations.
75 Crescas, *Or Ha-Shem*,, 347.
76 Ibid., 348.

his soul unmixed, but this results in dual ontology, which distinguishes between the physical components of human beings, and the physical components of everything else (the upshot is that it renders more coherent the claim that the human body is the purest), and that would be difficult to defend. For Crescas, the soul is the bearer of identity; the body can be replaced, as long as its original proportions are retained. When all is said and done, the fact that the soul isn't enough of an agent of individuation for Saadya reflects just how seriously he took the union and cooperation of body and soul.

6. Conclusion

Instead of a conclusion, I would like to offer a reflection. Jewish law is not an abstract entity. The practising Jew participates in it whenever he or she eats, clothes, or talks. It accompanies them from the time they wake up to the time they go to bed. When a medieval Jewish philosopher writes about the body, he does so from within a body that is regulated by Jewish law at the very same moment.

The various topics presented in this essay do not—and should not—amount to a unified stance toward the human body. Medieval Jewish philosophers wrote in different places and in different times, within different traditions and according to different agendas. But all of them have Jewish law, either in front of their eyes or in the back of their minds. And if this is indeed the case, they are somehow conditioned to take the body more seriously—devote to it more philosophical space, or ontological import—than they would have without the weight of their embodied religion.

CHAPTER SIX

Scholastic Philosophers on the Role of the Body in Knowledge

Rafael Nájera

Although there has been no systematic treatment of philosophical issues related to embodiment in the medieval period in the Latin West, a number of theological and philosophical problems related to the nature of embodied and disembodied human souls and angels required thinkers of that period to engage with aspects of the problem of what it is for a being to have or to assume a body. In this chapter I will try to elucidate what it means for principal figures in the Scholastic period to be embodied, concentrating on the problem of how embodied beings can attain knowledge. The capacity to know is particularly interesting because it is one of the powers that seem to be associated mainly with noncorporeal entities, yet is shared by embodied entities such as human beings. As we will see, the one thing that characterizes embodied entities when it comes to knowledge is their having to get that knowledge on their own, through or in conjunction with the corporeal senses. To be sure, the processes by which this happens are a point of contention among medieval thinkers. Even though there was no denying that embodiment was the natural state of human beings, and therefore that it this was as good as anything could be in God's creation, the body was seen as a sort of encumbrance to arriving at a purer kind of intellectual activity. Even when their theories entailed that this was not the case, theological concerns often forced medieval philosophers to recant their positions and give human knowledge based on bodily sense perception a lower place, therefore tacitly giving the body a negative role.

The general and extremely important problem of the relation of the soul to the body in human beings stems from the fact that for most medieval Christian thinkers, from Augustine in the 4th century to Suárez in the 16th, humans are first and foremost their soul. Human bodies, and the material in general, are normally considered not only lowly, but also more or less an encumbrance. The emphasis on the body as a hurdle in the path towards God is all the more clear in a figure like Augustine, for whom knowledge (*scientia*) is integral in that path but must necessarily be about the purely intellectual if it is to bring a human being closer to wisdom, that is, closer to a purely intellectual contemplation of God.[1]

By the mid-twelfth century, just before the massive influx of translations of Aristotle's works and their Arabic commentaries into the West, sophisticated thinkers like Hugh of St. Victor would still subscribe to a similar view. Hugh also puts forth a theory of knowledge that captures many Platonic ideas relatively common in the early Middle Ages. In Hugh's view, there is indeed a hierarchy of being going from the lowly material to the much nobler spiritual or intellectual and upwards towards God at the top. In this view, knowledge in humans consists, in essence, in a sort of purification of the material into the spiritual,

---

[1] This is a common theme in Augustine; an extended account of it can be found, for example, in *De Trinitate*, book VIII onwards. To be sure, the body is not simply a hindrance for Augustine, as he is always conscious throughout this and other works that humans are embodied by nature. See Augustine, *On the Trinity*, Books 8–15, ed. Gareth B. Matthews, trans. Stephen McKenna (Cambridge, UK: Cambridge University Press, 2002).

occurring precisely in the head. Hugh is very quick to point out that even though this purification takes place, the material and the spiritual constitute two radically different kinds of being.[2]

Indeed, for Hugh, as for most medieval thinkers, body and soul are of two different and distinct kinds, and thus the interaction between them is especially problematic. Once the Latin West had access to the complete Aristotelian corpus and to commentaries on it by Arab thinkers, answers to this set of problems become more philosophically and technically sophisticated. Certainly, armed with a full arsenal of Aristotelian concepts and terminology, and in particular with Aristotle's theory of the soul and a long tradition of Platonizing commentary on it, Acholastic philosophers from the thirteenth century onwards would engage, although usually not systematically, in complex debates about the nature of the interaction between body and soul. Before we can get into these problems, however, we need to be clear on what exactly the Scholastics were talking about when they talked about body, soul, matter, material and immaterial substances, angels, and a few other related concepts.

Scholastic ontology, a continuation and development of the tradition of Aristotelian metaphysics, is meant to capture the basic idea that the world consists of fairly independent entities, such as cats, dogs, stones, and the like, in which a variety of attributes such as color, height, weight and so on, inhere. The basic ontological distinction is thus between those independent entities, called substances, and their attributes, called accidents.[3] Given that accidents need a substance as

---

[2] This theory can be found in the short treatise *"De unione: Spiritus et Corporis."* Hugh of St. Victor, II, ed. A. M. Piazzoni, 861–868, n.d. Spoleto, Italy: Centro italiano di studi sull'alto medioevo, 1980.

[3] This stands in sharp contrast with early modern corpuscular ontology in which the natural world is taken to consist of mixtures of extended, material particles that compose objects and explain their attributes. Some medieval philosophers, following Aristotle's lead, considered similar ontologies from the ancients and rejected each one them. Some thinkers in the Scholastic period, however, adopted views that approached the corpuscular theory. See Robert Pasnau, *Metaphysical Themes: 1274–1671* (Oxford: Clarendon, 2011).

the subject in which to inhere, accidents are taken to be ontologically dependent on substances. Substances are therefore prior to accidents and are more properly called beings. Reality consists primarily of substances, but these substances are not necessarily material. Indeed, matter is introduced in Aristotelian philosophy independently of the substance/accident distinction in order to explain change in the physical world. Matter is one of the two metaphysical parts that accounts for the generation and corruption of substances; the other one is form. A common argument for the metaphysical composition of substances into form and matter starts with the generally accepted principle that in nature nothing can come out of nothing except through direct creation by God. Unless we assume that God directly creates every single substance that comes into being in nature, which for most medieval philosophers would be absurd, there must be something out of which substances are made, something that remains in every case of substantial generation and corruption. This something, a theoretical entity, is called matter, or prime matter, if taken in the abstract.

The generation of a substance involves therefore some matter that is turned into a specific thing. Nothing of that specific thing must have been present in the matter before the change, otherwise the change would not be a genuine case of substantial generation but just the addition of an integral part of a thing to another integral part. Matter must be completely devoid of any specificity. That specificity is given by the form, which, therefore, accounts for what a thing is.

Another way of expressing the matter/form distinction is by appealing to the notions of potentiality and actuality, which are key to understanding the distinction between active and potential intellect in the Aristotelian theory of the soul to which Scholastic philosophers subscribe. We can say that an acorn is potentially a tree on account of the fact that the acorn, given the right circumstances, can become a tree. Similarly, in the case of substantial generation, matter is potentially the substance that will come into being. Since matter does not have any specificity, it can actually receive any form and thus serve as the substrate for any kind of substantial generation. Matter is therefore potentially *any* thing and indeed it cannot actually exist without having been given a form. Matter is said therefore to be pure potentiality whereas form is said to be pure actuality.

This result is essential to understanding the difference between material and immaterial substances. Medieval philosophers took for granted that some substances, that is, some actual, independent things, do not have any matter. Aristotle himself held that view as well, and it was by appealing to immaterial substances that he accounted for the way in which stars, planets, and the celestial sphere moved around the Earth, as was commonly believed.[4] In Aristotelian cosmology, the Earth is at the center of the universe and is surrounded by a series of concentric spheres that move continuously and eternally. Some of these correspond to the planets, which for Aristotle and the Greeks include the moon and the sun, with the outermost sphere corresponding to the stars. According to Aristotle, each of these spheres is governed by an immaterial substance. Given that immaterial substances, by definition, do not have matter, they do not have any potentiality and are thus pure actualities. From this it presumably follows that they should move eternally and that their motion should be circular. Aristotle thus tied his matter/form distinction to his cosmology. Later generations of commentators would readily adopt this cosmology and give it a Platonic taint by establishing also a causal hierarchy based on the immaterial substances, taken to be intellectual in nature and therefore called intelligences, starting with the First Cause, that is, with God, at the top. The First Cause gives rise to a First Intelligence, and this one in turn to a second and so forth, down until humans, who are intelligent but also material, and continuing down to material substances all the way down to the four elements (earth, water, air and fire) and prime matter.

---

[4] Aristotle's cosmology is put forth in several different places, important are *Metaphysics* XII, *On the Heavens*, and *Metereology*.

Christian medieval philosophers were aware of this cosmology and of Platonic interpretations of it. They also used the idea of separate, immaterial intelligences to explain the nature of angels, which appear many times in key roles in the Scriptures.[5] The Pseudo-Dionysius's treatise *On Celestial Hierarchy*, commented on many times throughout the centuries, also gave them an account of the hierarchy among angels, together with the idea of angels as mediators between God and humans as messengers, and between humans and God as conductors toward the divinity.[6] The accepted fact that angels occasionally took on bodies presented particular problems in the context of Aristotelian philosophy, as we will see.

Christian medieval philosophers believed in the separation between the realms of immaterial and material substances, the latter constituting the realm of change, also called the physical or natural world. In this picture, body (*corpus*) is matter to which extension is added— that is, matter with some specific dimensions. Extension is taken to be an accident in the category of quantity, and therefore something that inheres in a substance and cannot exist on its own. This seems intuitive enough given that any material substance, any particular material thing, up to a certain extent continues to be the same particular thing even if it grows or shrinks. The thing's size is not what makes it the thing it is. The question lingers however whether, even if that's the case, do material things need a size. That is, whether dimensions are something that a material thing cannot fail to have.

Just as matter, body in the abstract does not entail any specific kind of thing. Saying, for example, that Fido the dog has a body in the strict sense does not say anything about the kind of stuff Fido is made of

---

[5] Most of the connections between Platonic conceptions and angelology in the Latin world was made through the mediation of the *Liber de Causis*, a treatise translated from the Arabic in the twelfth century, originally attributed to Aristotle but whose contents come mostly from the Greek philosopher Proclus. See Tiziana Suarez-Nani, *Les anges et la philosophie* (Paris: Vrin, 2002), 19–20.

[6] Suarez-Nani, *Les anges*, 16.

beyond that he is a material substance with a certain height, length, and depth. That Fido's body includes integral parts such as bones and flesh is not explained by Fido's corporeality but, in fact, by Fido's form, which determines exactly the specific, and most likely dynamic, mixture of basic elements that makes it possible for Fido to be Fido and not any other particular dog and certainly not Tibbles the cat or Pi the tiger.

In a very strict sense, therefore, embodiment for the medieval philosophers is simply a fact of material substances, namely that they have specific dimensions. Scholastics had to deal with a number of problems related to that. The problems they faced were metaphysical, including the question raised a short while ago as to whether materiality implies corporeality, and also, if that is the case, what is the nature of corporeality itself: is it some special specificity in prime matter that is akin to a form, or has matter itself some specificity or actuality? A number of Scholastics came up with sophisticated and complex answers to these and other questions.[7]

Be that as it may, the main set of problems that concern us here have to do rather with the status of different embodied things. In the normal course of nature Scholastics accepted the obvious fact that only humans, animals, plants, and nonanimated beings have bodies. The embodiment of all these entities besides humans is nonproblematic beyond the metaphysical issues regarding corporeality. Embodiment is simply and naturally their state of being, and there is nothing, save perhaps God's direct intervention, that would make them be immaterial. Humans, however, are special because they are, by definition, rational beings, and rationality is taken to be purely intellectual and therefore immaterial. On this view, humans therefore are partly immaterial and partly material. The other immaterial entities are God and the angels, which from the point of view of the normal course of nature are not

---

7 See Pasnau, *Metaphysical Themes*, for a detailed account of many of these problems and the different answers to them.

an issue as far as embodiment is concerned because they are naturally nonembodied. Their cases become interesting because, according to Christian doctrine, both God and the angels assume bodies once in a while. Since they are endowed with intellect, and indeed, since they are intellects, when they become embodied the immediate question is how their intellects are affected by their assumed bodies. Naturally, too, since one of the important powers of the intellect is to know things, another important question is what is the role of their bodies in their knowledge.

We have to be careful, however, when speaking about knowledge in the context of Scholastic philosophy. Medieval philosophers did not have a single conception of knowledge, nor, indeed, a particular preoccupation with all the aspects of knowledge that contemporary philosophers may find interesting.[8] One way of understanding the medieval philosophers' way of talking about this issue is by starting with the traditional and perhaps intuitive assumption that there is such a thing as knowledge or cognition in humans that lets them normally understand and say or think true propositions about the world outside their minds. The question is then how such knowledge or cognition comes about in humans, and given that humans have bodies, it is taken for granted that the answer to that question should include an account of a number of corporeal features and processes that presumably play an important role. For medieval philosophers the question turns out to be mainly about the cognition of extramental objects, where cognition is taken to be more than just awareness and recognition of the presence of an object, but the identification of such an object as one of a certain kind and as this specific object as opposed to any other. When I am presented with a coffee mug, I should be able to identify the coffee

---

[8] In fact, there is no simple correspondence between medieval and contemporary conceptions of knowledge. Scholastics simply do not have systematic epistemological treatises. See Martin Pickavé, "Human Knowledge," in *The Oxford Handbook of Aquinas*, eds. Brian Davies and Eleonore Stump (Oxford: Oxford University Press, 2012), 311.

mug as the particular coffee mug it is, including that it is indeed a coffee mug with the accidents it may have and that it is this coffee mug and not that other one. The problem turns out to be very complex and there are numerous debates about many of its details.

In this and other discussions about the Scholastics it is useful to start with Aquinas, who comes at the beginning of the Scholastic period in the 13th century—and who has very detailed, systematic accounts of most of the issues—and next to discuss other figures in comparison and contrast with him. Just like most medieval philosophers, Aquinas's fundamental epistemic category is cognition (*cognitio*) but, as said earlier, this does not correspond exactly to common contemporary conceptions of knowledge. For instance, Aquinas admits of false cognitions, but we normally would not speak of false knowledge.[9] He also speaks of *scientia* in the same sense that Aristotle meant by *epistēmē* in the *Posterior Analytics*, namely, a kind of knowledge of universal propositions that is certain and that is based on immediate knowledge of principles and definitions and universal inferences from them.[10] Aquinas's view of *scientia* is to some extent disconnected from the discussion of how the different living entities can know things. The general idea is that cognition is more fundamental as far as the acquisition of knowledge is concerned, and, as such, the role of the body is exactly the same for cognition and *scientia* in human beings insofar as the latter is basically more complex cognition subject to a number of conditions, such as certainty, explanatory power, and a particular causal origin.[11]

---

9 Pickavé, "Human Knowledge," 312.

10 Aquinas has one of the earliest commentaries on the *Posterior Analytics (Sententia super Posteriora analytica,* volume I of the Leonine Edition), a work that many in the late 12th and early 13th centuries considered extremely difficult.

11 There is no question for Aquinas that humans can acquire knowledge. As Pickavé explains, Aquinas's epistemological optimism is founded on the Aristotelian ideas that nature does nothing in vain and that all things have their proper functions, to which they are directed. The proper function of human beings is to understand and to reason. See Pickavé, "Human Knowledge," 313. Many other philosophers, including Suárez, have the same commitments.

Aquinas subscribes fully to the Aristotelian slogan that all knowledge comes from the senses. He distinguishes, also following Aristotle, between external and internal senses, all of which are corporeal. The former take in what he calls "sensibles," namely accidents of things such as hotness, coldness, rest, movement, shape and size, each one associated with a specific sense (e.g., vision can receive shape but not hotness.) The internal senses, on the other hand, perform different functions. They include the common sense, responsible mainly for differentiating accidents of different kinds; the memorative power, which amounts to memory at the level of sensation; the estimative power, responsible for what we may be called instinctive reactions, for example, the sheep fleeing upon seeing a wolf;[12] imagination, responsible for "creating" sensory experiences without sensory input, as in dreams; and phantasia, responsible for creating phantasms. Phantasms are what the intellect grasps from the senses and transforms into intellectual cognitions.

In a simple case of the cognition of an extramental object, the senses receive what Aquinas calls a "sensible species" and defines as "the form in the matter/form composite."[13] The senses do not assume the actual form of the object since this would mean that the matter in the senses would become the object itself. Rather, this sensible species the senses somehow receive is like a copy of the configuration and attributes of the object, something like a picture of the thing but not exactly because it includes all other attributes besides shape and color. The type of reception that occurs at this stage Aquinas calls "spiritual change," to distinguish it from "natural" change in which matter does assume a

---

12 The general view is that animals other than humans do not think. The estimative power explains why, for example, a sheep seems to understand that a wolf is dangerous. In this view, the sheep's response is not based on understanding but on estimation and it is performed at the sensory level, that is, at the corporeal level.

13 *Sententiae libri De Anima* (henceforth *In DA*) II.24.553. *In DA* is in volume 45 of the Leonine Edition: *Thomas Aquinas, Sancti Thomae Aquinatis Doctoris Angelici:Opera Omnia*. Iussu Leonis XIII (Rome: Vatican Polyglot Press, 1882). Aquinas means here, of course, the individual form of the object with all its specificity, not a general form.

form.¹⁴ In any case, the sensible species is not what the senses sense but rather "that by which a sense senses."¹⁵

Instead of explaining intellectual cognition as a single further step from the reception of a sensible species by the senses, Aquinas adds the additional step of the creation of phantasms by phantasia. Phantasms can be produced by sensible species from either internal or external senses, and so they help to explain cognition during dreams, for example. According to Stump, phantasms also provide the conscious component of sense perception. Neither sensory imagination nor external sensing imply that the would-be knower is conscious of the sensible species presented to her.¹⁶

Once phantasia operates on the sensible species, the knower is conscious of the object. However, this is not yet cognition because cognition, as said earlier, involves knowing the object as the thing it is (e.g., as a cup, a cat, or a dog). In order to accomplish that, the cognitive system must go from the particular that is a phantasm to the universal idea of cup, cat, or dog. Indeed, for Aquinas, as for most medieval philosophers, the intellect can only deal with universals.¹⁷ The universal needed, the counterpart to the sensible species, is called the intelligible species and is totally immaterial.¹⁸

At this point however, according to Aquinas, the causal direction is reversed. In sense-perception, that is, up until the creation of

---

14 *In DA* II.14.418. Aquinas seems to introduce this distinction to deal specifically with the way in which sensation works. He wants to say that understanding an object amounts to getting an account of the object's essence, which includes primordially the object's form. The distinction also lets him deny that any assumption of a form should count as an act of sensation.

15 *Summa Theologiae* (henceforth *ST*) I q85a2. Part I is in volume 4 of the Leonine Edition: *Thomas Aquinas, Sancti Thomae Aquinatis Doctoris Angelici. Opera Omnia*. Iussu Leonis XIII.

16 Eleonore Stump, *Aquinas*. Arguments of the Philosophers. (New York: Routledge, 2005), 259–260.

17 Ockham seems to be an exception. Calvin Normore claims that Ockham was the first philosopher in this tradition to posit the notion of a singular or particular thought. See Normore, "The Invention of Singular Thought," in *Forming the Mind: Essays on the Internal Senses and the Mind/Body Problem from Avicenna to the Medical Enlightenment*, ed. Henrik Lagerlund (Dordrecht, The Netherlands: Springer, 2007), 109–128.

18 ST Iq85a2.

phantasms, the cognitive system responds to input from the senses and is therefore passive. Going back to the extramental object case, it is that extramental object that impinges upon the senses and causes the powers in the senses to receive a sensible species and the phantasia to produce phantasms. Phantasms however, do not impinge upon the intellect in any way. The intellect itself causes its active power, the so-called agent intellect, to take available phantasms and produce an intelligible species by a process Aquinas calls abstraction.[19] The agent intellect delivers the intelligible species to the potential intellect, named in that fashion because it can accept any intelligible species.[20]

The simple cognition of objects out of phantasms is the first act of the intellect. The end product of the process, however, is not the intelligible species, which is characterized in similar terms as the sensible species as that *through which* cognition occurs. The end product is called by Aquinas intellected intention or concept.[21] Several intentions can then be combined to form more complex concepts and propositions, and so it is not only simple objects that the intellect can know. However, according to Aquinas, phantasms are essential for cognition, even for the understanding of incorporeal things, including one's own soul. He says, for example, that "we cognize incorporeal things, for which there are no phantasms, by comparison with sensible bodies, for which there are phantasms."[22] Since phantasms are generated by corporeal senses, and since Aquinas, like many other medieval philosophers and following Aristotle, believes that human intellect starts as a *tabula rasa* without any cognition, the body is therefore essential for knowledge.[23] Indeed, one of Aquinas's arguments against innate

---

[19] ST Iq85a1. The agent intellect is also sometimes called "active intellect."

[20] The potential intellect behaves like matter in natural generation insofar at is not really anything in particular but can accept any intelligible species. For this reason it is called also the material intellect.

[21] ST Iq85ad3.

[22] ST Iq84a7ad3

[23] Aristole *De Anima* III.4 (430a1). The *tabula rasa* view of human intellect is shared by Ockham, Henry of Ghent, and Duns Scotus among others.

knowledge is based on the minor role sense perception would play if there were innate intentions and concepts. It would seem that sense perception is there only to provide an occasion for the retrieval of those concepts. Sense perception would thus be almost unnecessary, which goes against the Aristotelian view that nature does nothing in vain.[24] Even though Aquinas sometimes says that nonempirical principles are innate, according to him what is innate is our intellective power, the "light of reason,"[25] a natural occurrence, not a special act of God.

Aquinas's views preserve the traditional hierarchy of substances insofar as humans are characterized as essentially dependent on their bodies for what is taken to be the perfection of an intellectual being, namely to understand and have knowledge. Such knowledge is accomplished with the mediation of particular sensible species that natural cognitive powers actively use to arrive at universal intelligibles. Later figures, notably William of Ockham, will challenge that view of knowledge as mediated, ascribing to humans the capacity of direct cognition and thus seemingly overriding the body's role. This introduces a series of complications and may even challenge the traditional view that humans are below angels.

The main complication stems primarily from Ockham's view that the intellect and sensitive souls are distinct. Whereas cognition for Aquinas is explained as the interoperation of different powers within a single soul, thereby already including into the human soul itself an essential unity between the material and the immaterial, Ockham needs to explain how two souls of completely different nature can work together to bring about cognition. In Ockham's view extramental

---

[24] Pickavé, "Human Knowledge," 315.

[25] This is very different from divine illumination in the Augustinian sense. As Pasnau points out, after Aquinas the only major figure to defend a version of divine illumination whereby God is directly responsible for the knowledge of humans is Henry of Ghent, but his views rapidly went into disuse. See Robert Pasnau, "Henry of Ghent and the Twilight of Divine Illumination," in *The Review of Metaphysics* 49, no. 1 (September 1995): 49–75. Characteristically, Suárez will still take into account Henry of Ghent's arguments in order to refute them.

objects can be grasped directly by our cognitive systems through what he calls intuitive cognition.[26] Since these simple acts of apprehension, just as for Aquinas, can be used in complex propositions and judgments, it may seem that humans do not need any input from the body. However, this is not the case. Ockham in fact has an account using the phantasms and species vocabulary in which phantasms already include a universal that is impressed into the intellect.[27] In other words, it is not the intellect that reaches "down" to phantasms to produce intelligible species, but in fact phantasms already have the species that causes the intellect to perform the act of cognition. These phantasms, which are nothing but sensory intuitive cognitions, happen at the level of the sensitive soul, and thus the intellect depends on the body insofar as the body causes intellection. According to Ockham sensory intuitive cognitions are a necessary causal condition for the intellect's cognition of a particular. In fact, Ockham is obliterating the species theory of cognition replacing it with a causal account he finds simple and therefore better.[28] Still it is not really clear how a material soul can cause anything in an immaterial one. Suárez, at the end of the Scholastic period, will argue against Ockham's view in connection wiith the knowledge of angels.

---

[26] For a detailed account of Ockham's theory of cognition see Marilyn McCord Adams, *William Ockham*, 2 vols. (Notre Dame, IN: University of Notre Dame Press, 1987), ch 13, 495–550. A succinct account can be found in Eleonore Stump, "The Mechanisms of Cognition: Ockham on Mediating Species," in *The Cambridge Companion to Ockham*, ed. Paul Vincent Spade (Cambridge, UK: Cambridge University Press, 1999), 168–203. Ockham is not the first to talk about intuitive cognition; Duns Scotus had brought that notion to to the fore, although it is present already in thinkers before him. For Scotus, intuitive cognition is an intelligible object immediately present to the intellect, without any intervening species, a sort of intellectual vision. According to Pasnau, Scotus does not have strong arguments for this, so his actual conclusion is modest; it is at least conceivable that humans can have this kind of intuition. See Robert Pasnau, "Cognition," in *The Cambridge Companion to Duns Scotus*, ed. Thomas Williams (Cambridge, UK: Cambridge University Press, 2002), 285–311.

[27] See Stump, "The Mechanisms of Cognition: Ockham on Mediating Species," 178–181.

[28] See, for instance, Sent. II.13, in William of Ockham, *Opera philosophica et theologica*, Gedeon Gál, et al., ed. 17 vols. (St. Bonaventure, New York: The Franciscan Institute, 1967-88) volume VI.). Cf. Adams, *William Ockham*, 508.

Indeed, we can find more clues about the role of the body if we look at the Scholastics' treatment of problems related to disembodied entities. Naturally these entities include God and the angels, as mentioned already, but also there is interesting discussion surrounding disembodied human souls. God, however, is a unique case that forces Scholastics toward very special theories. This is very clear in the case of God's embodiment, the Incarnation. By the time Scholasticism becomes the dominant theological and philosophical tradition in the Latin West, the Church had already established a basic doctrine that called for the Incarnation to be analyzed as the concurrence of two natures, divine and human, in a single individual. This basically precludes any theory that would not want to be labeled as heretical from positing any real influence of Christ's body in His divine intellect. So this case is actually not that fruitful for our discussion.[29] Angels are more promising, and here, again, it is useful to start with Aquinas.

Aquinas's views on angels are systematically given in questions 50 to 64 of the first part of the *Summa Theologiae* after he has talked about God, His essence and persons, and about creatures in general. After angels he will talk about the physical world and about humans, thereby completing an account of God, His creative powers, and the general nature of His creatures.[30] In question 50 he talks about the substance of angels and establishes a few important points. First, angels are naturally incorporeal.[31] There must be intellectual, incorporeal substances because the perfection of the universe and thus the good of creatures

---

29 This, of course, does not mean that the discussion among scholastics was trivial or uninteresting in this respect. Actually, the textual body of discussion is enormous: Aquinas's systematic account of God and Christ in the *Summa Theologiae* spans several hundred pages; Suárez has a few times more pages in volumes 17 and 18 of his complete works—see Francisco Suárez, *Opera Omnia*, 28 vols. (Paris: Ludovicum Vivès, 1856–1878).

30 Part II and III will deal, in turn, with human beings as moral agents and with the mysteries surrounding Christ and the sacraments. For a general account of the structure of the *Summa Theologiae* see Thomas Aquinas, *The Treatise on Human Nature: Summa Theologiae 1a 75–89*, trans. Robert Pasnau (Indianapolis: Hackett, 2002), 16–22.

31 ST Iq50a1.

involves assimilation and therefore imitation of God, who is incorporeal and intellectual. Angels are precisely those necessary incorporeal substances that are a notch below God in the hierarchy and that do not naturally have a body that might compromise their intellectual powers.[32] The proper activity of angels is that of understanding, and understanding does not involve in itself any matter, so angels must be incorporeal.

Second, angels indeed do not have matter, which Aquinas grants might seem, and in fact is, per se incomprehensible to humans. The fact is, Aquinas says, that humans cannot really comprehend either angelic or divine substance since they are above us in intellectuality. Our capacities allow us to fully and positively comprehend only material substances, which are below us. We can, however, understand the angelic nature by means of negations and through the logical consequences of a true account of reality. So since angels do not have matter they should only have form, as even immaterial substances must be explainable in terms of the fundamental matter/form distinction.[33]

Third, as forms, it seems that angels should be pure actuality, but Aquinas says, this is not the case.[34] They have a sort of potentiality with respect to their existence, insofar as they do not exist of themselves but are created by God. Aquinas elaborates on this in *De ente et essentia*, where he argues that the essence of things do not imply existence, there being only one entity in which essence and existence correspond, namely God. All other entities necessarily must have their existence given by something else, which results in a hierarchy of entities based on how close they are in the existential chain with respect to God.[35] This hierarchy, as it turns out, corresponds exactly to the traditional

---

32 Aquinas is, as in the case of human cognition, preoccupied with preserving the traditional hierarchy of substances.
33 ST I q50a2.
34 ST I q50a2obj3.
35 See *De ente et essentia*, ch2.

account in which below angels there are humans, and below them other animate creatures and material substances.

Fourth, each angel has its own species.[36] This is the case because, according to Aquinas, the only way for the same species to have different individuals is for each individual to exist in different matter, which cannot be the case of angels.[37] Each angel is unique in its own kind and so each one is fundamentally different from each other and certainly different from human beings. It is this uniqueness that lets Aquinas explain important issues regarding angelic knowledge, as we will see shortly.

In question 51 Aquinas takes on the problem of the embodiment of angels. The solution is very problematic because Aquinas simply argues that embodied angels do not perform any life functions with their bodies.[38] In fact, their bodies are not even alive because, according to Aquinas, life is what is given by the form of the body, and an angel does not constitute the form of its body. The assumed body of an angel is there, Aquinas says, only for the purpose of manifesting to men the angel's spiritual properties and works.[39] Given that, Aquinas denies, for instance, that angels even speak or eat.[40] A lot of questions are raised by Aquinas's views here, starting with the status of the assumed body of an angel: where does it come from? How is it that it perfectly synchronizes with the angel's will to seem to speak or seem to eat? How does an angel, an immaterial substance that is not the form of its body, move the chunk of matter that is its assumed body? Aquinas does not respond to any of these concerns, but seems to be motivated

---

36 ST I q50a4.
37 Aquinas argues, indeed, that principle of individuation for entities of the same species is what he calls "designated matter" (*materia signata*), which can be understood as matter with specific dimensions and location. Its counterpart, nondesignated matter, is used in the account of the essence of a material thing.
38 ST I q51a3.
39 ST I q51a3ad1.
40 ST I q51a3ad4 and ad5.

primarily in preserving the idea of angels as fundamentally immaterial substances with no natural relation to body. All bodily actions in an embodied angel for Aquinas seem miraculous. The basic idea is, in any case, that the body really cannot have an effect on the intellectual nature of angels.

But what about knowledge? Here also Aquinas argues for the insurmountable gap between the body and the intellect. Unlike in human beings, angels are not naturally conjoined with a body that serves to feed their intellects with the raw materials they need in order to be able to think. In question 54 of the *Summa Theologiae*, Aquinas states this clearly. Since angels do not have bodies they can only have intellectual knowledge, not knowledge from experience. Here we find a statement that nicely captures Aquinas's views on the role of the body in general:

> In our soul there are certain powers whose operations are exercised by corporeal organs; such powers are acts of sundry parts of the body, as sight of the eye, and hearing of the ear. There are some other powers of the soul whose operations are not performed through bodily organs, as intellect and will: these are not acts of any parts of the body. Now the angels have no bodies naturally joined to them, as is manifest from what has been said already. Hence of the soul's powers only intellect and will can belong to them.[41]

Clearly, then, a disembodied entity cannot in any way sense anything and can only exercise intellect and will. The body's role, as far as cognition is concerned, is basically sense-perception.

Unlike in humans, there is neither agent nor potential intellect in angels. Aquinas explains that the distinction between agent and potential intellect applies only to humans in relation to phantasms.[42] It is

---

[41] ST I q54a5.

[42] He provides an interesting analogy regarding phantasms: "[they] are to the potential intellect like colors are to sight, and to the agent intellect like colors are to light" (ST I q54a4)

necessary to posit a potential intellect because the things that humans understand do not exist outside the soul already as immaterial and intelligible, which is how the intellect can consider them. The human intellect must go and build those intelligibles out of phantasms that come and go. So the potential intellect is the power that is in potency with respect to the intelligibles before we actually engage our intellect with them. The active intellect is needed in order to bring the intelligibles to actuality from phantasms. This does not apply to angels because angels do not have knowledge from experience. The things they know are directly available to them insofar as they are always, in a way, present in their intellects.[43]

If this is the case, then, how can an embodied angel know the things around him, or understand the things said to them by humans? Aquinas does not consider this case, but from his discussion in question 55 the answer is that God should actually give them the intelligible species they need to grasp. Just like humans, angels do not know things by their substance—that is, not directly and immediately, as Aquinas says in *ST* q55a1, but by some intelligible species. Only God knows things in their substance since God, in a sense, contains them all. Those species, however, are not drawn from things or phantasms but are given by God.[44] In accordance with Pseudo-Dionysius's celestial hierarchy, the fewer intelligible species an angel needs, the more universal is his knowledge and the closer to God he is. Higher angels therefore need fewer species to know things than lower angels.[45] Humans are far below angels presumably because humans must get those intelligibles themselves through their bodies by means of phantasms: yet another way in which the body is detrimental to the perfection of the soul.[46]

---

43 The discussion is in ST I q54.

44 ST I q55a2.

45 ST I q55a3.

46 It is not clear what is the status of the intelligible species that angels get. Aquinas says that they are "connatural" to them (ST I q57a1), seemingly implying that angelic knowledge is eternal. However, angels cannot know secret thoughts immediately but only through the effect of that secret (ST

Aquinas also says that angels do not understand by reasoning; their understanding is not discursive.[47] This seems to imply that angels are defective in relation to humans, but the thought is that, actually, their knowledge is purer as it is simpler. The fact that human thought and knowledge is the product of a complex mechanism of sense perception, phantasms, agent, and potential intellect, and reasoning—part of which mechanism is not only corporeal but in Aquinas's view inevitably so—actually indicates the less noble status of man in comparison with angels. Bodies, Aquinas says, obtain their perfection by chance and movement; nonbodily things are exempt from that.

Given what we have seen about Ockham's views on cognition, it is not surprising that his views on the knowledge of angels do not align with Aquinas's. One of the main differences is that according to Ockham, angels are not given by God all that they know. Rather God gives them intuitions, and angels reason based on them. Not only that, the discursive nature of angelic reasoning is the same as that of humans. Aquinas's idea of angels having direct access to purer knowledge is therefore out of the picture, and with it one way in which angels are of a nobler nature. The discussion comes in the context of the question of whether one angel can speak to another.[48] Ockham claims that angels can in fact talk to one another because their actual acts of thinking (*cogitatio*) are like speaking mentally, and angels can also hear mentally as thoughts are immediately available to them without any need for intermediate species. Recall that for Ockham species are not really necessary for any creature. One consequence of this is that angels can actually mentally hear whatever a human thinks, and there is nothing a human can do to hide his or her thoughts or to talk to one angel and not to another.[49] Angels, furthermore, can know what another angel

---

I q57a4), implying that angels get to grasp intelligible species of things as they "occur," which goes against the idea that their species are connatural.

47 ST I q58a4.
48 Ockham, *Quodlibeta* I, q6, OTh IX, 36–41.
49 *Quod* I, q6, ad dubium 2, OTh IX, 39.

or a human means by reasoning from more complex or more simple concepts or by cause and effect.[50] The upshot of this is that, unlike for Aquinas, thought and reasoning are of the same kind, independently of the kind of thinker.[51] If there is a difference in status between angels and humans it is not based on their rational capacities.

Suárez, for his part, will argue extensively against Ockham's views, especially when it comes to the role of intelligible species in angelic cognition. In Book II, chapter 3, of his massive treatise *De Angelis*[52] he claims that angels do need intelligible species to understand or to know objects such as material objects that per se cannot unite with the angelic intellect. He starts by considering four contrary opinions, among them one that says that no species is necessary for any creature, which he correctly ascribes to Ockham but also to several other philosophers.[53] The true opinion, he says, is however also the opinion of Aquinas, and he proceeds to lay down his claims in six propositions.[54] Interestingly, Suárez's general argumentative strategy is to assume that indeed angels represent a middle case between God and humans, and so we can infer some truths about, among other things, their cognitive powers, by interpolating between the two extremes. In this way Suárez argues that, first, angelic knowledge should be by way of assimilation or representation in the angelic mind; second, that this assimilation should be due to a faculty that precedes the actual operation of the intellect; third, that cognition certainly implies the concurrence of that faculty with an object of cognition; and, fourth, angels do not have in themselves all the possible objects of cognition.

---

50 *Quod* I, q6, ad dubium 3, OTh IX, 40.
51 Ockham actually does not claim that he has an insight into the thought of angels; his thought is based in what he takes to be the nature of any creature. This point is made by Martin Lenz in his article, "Why Can't Angels Think Properly? Ockham against Chatton and Aquinas," in *Angels in Medieval Philosophical Inquiry: Their Function and Significance*, edited by Isabel Iribarren and Martin Lenz (Farnham, UK: Ashgate, 2008), 159. Ockham's strategy is characteristically to avoid introducing new distinctions when the same could be accomplished in simpler ways.
52 Suárez, *Opera Omnia*, Vol. 2.
53 *De Angelis*, II.3.2–5.
54 *De Angelis*, II.3.7–12.

Following Aquinas's argument in *ST* I q55a1, Suárez also claims that angels cannot cognize objects directly in their substance. The idea is that that through which the intellect cognizes is like a form to the intellect because it is through a form that an agent acts. For example, a plant nourishes itself on account of being a plant—that is, on account of its form, not on account of its matter. So that form must include or must be able to be all that the power in question, in this case the intellect, is capable of accomplishing. Since the intellect can know any universal, the form we are talking about must include or be all there is. However, the form of an angel, being of a specific kind (i.e., an angel being a specific entity) cannot be all things. Angels need something extra to perfect their intellects and attain cognition.

After entertaining some possible objections to Aquinas,[55] Suárez takes on Ockham's position and claims that angels cannot cognize objects immediately, as if the objects somehow could "cooperate" with their intellects. This is what Ockham's intuitions amount to for Suárez. However, this is not possible. Material objects cannot do anything to immaterial entities, they cannot "cooperate" with angels and cause angels to know them.[56] There is indeed a major flaw in Ockham's arguments. Suárez would like Ockham to give an explanation of the supposed causal connection between material objects and the intellect, but he thinks Ockham cannot really have one. In the end, with intuitions out of the way, intelligible species are exactly that which the intellect needs to assimilate or represent external objects.[57]

---

55 *De Angelis*, II.3.13–16.

56 *De Angelis*, II.3.17.

57 Suárez's further positions regarding angels are certainly very much in line with Aquinas's. In further chapters he claims, for instance, that angels are given intelligible species by God since they do not have a way to get them themselves (*De Angelis*, II.4). Species, however, do not simply flow towards angels but are given individually by God, without this constituting a miracle every time (*De Angelis*, II.5). The idea seems to be not that God is constantly paying attention to angels, but that naturally there is some process through which angels receive species from God. Also the intelligible species are universal, not particular (*De Angelis*, II.14).

Suárez also takes on the problem of communication among angels and offers an account that differs from that of Ockham. Angels do not communicate with each other through signs, so there is no question of a mental language. They communicate with each other directly, which means that they cannot lie nor deceive each other. How that communication works, Suárez admits, is hard to explain, but he attempts to give an explanation anyway.[58] Suárez actually posits a kind of "speaking" between angels—speaking insofar as, just as humans do, one angel should be capable of calling the attention of another one, without speaking by an exchange of linguistic signs. Once the second angel attends to the first there is no exchange of intelligible species, but the end result is that the second angel receives the species from God. Suárez's solution surely sounds ad hoc, but the reason why it is necessary to posit this is that otherwise humans would be better equipped than angels.[59] It would be a mistake, certainly, to suppose that a bodily function, namely, being able to utter a sound and thereby calling for the attention of another human being, would allow humans to accomplish something that angels cannot accomplish. In line with the idea that the body is in a way detrimental to the human, the body cannot be allowed to give embodied creatures advantages over disembodied ones. If that means coming up with solutions such as this, so be it.

Disembodied creatures must therefore have an advantage over embodied ones. Consequently, we should expect disembodied human souls to be better off than embodied ones. The problem is not only philosophical. Christian doctrine dictates that the human soul does not die with the death of the body, but actually lingers on until it reunites again with the body in the Final Judgment. Aquinas solves the problem by arguing that the human soul is not dependent on the body

---

58 In *De Angelis*, II.28
59 *De Angelis*, II.28.34 (254).

and that, as far as knowledge is concerned, disembodiment implies adopting a different kind of knowledge.[60]

Suárez, like Aquinas, affirms that the soul is independent of the body, and therefore that it subsists after the death of the body. He thinks the strongest rational argument is the one given by Aquinas in *ST* Iq75a6, which is based on the premise established earlier in that same question, that the soul of man is subsistent on account of its being intellectual. Since the human soul is intellectual and the intellect is in no way material, the human soul has an operation per se independent of matter. Things can be corrupted (i.e., destroyed) either accidentally or per se. Accidental corruption of a thing happens by the corruption of some other thing, for instance, when a color gets destroyed as the thing in which the color inheres gets destroyed. However, Aquinas argues, things get corrupted per se according to their existence. Composite things, for example, get corrupted when the things they are composed of are removed or destroyed. But, the soul's per se existence is that of a form only, which is immaterial; so the destruction of the matter in the body does not affect its existence.[61]

The argument is not very convincing, in light of a powerful objection that comes from Aristotle's own emphasis on the tight link between phantasms and the soul in *On the Soul*: phantasms do not exist without the body and the soul never thinks without phantasms.[62] The objection is, then, that if we take the soul's proper operation to be cognizing and understanding, once the body is removed and phantasms become

---

60 See ST q89a1–3. The metaphysical status of disembodied human souls is also special for Aquinas given that they keep being individuals in spite of lacking matter, which for him is the principle of individuation.

61 *ST* q75a6, paraphrased by Suárez in his commentary on Aristotle's *De Anima* (henceforth *CDA*), disp 2, q3n21: Francisco Suárez, *Commentaria Una Cum Quaestionionibus in Libros Aristotelis "De Anima,"*, 2 vols, ed. Salvador Catellote (Madrid: Labor, 1992).

62 *De Anima* I.1, 403a8–10 and III.7, 431a16–17. South, following Pasnau, thinks Aquinas's argument is flawed, and both Suárez and Aquinas knew it. See James B. South, "Suárez, Immortality, and the Soul's Dependence on the Body," in *The Philosophy of Francisco Suárez*, eds. Henrik Lagerlund and Benjamin Hill (Oxford: Oxford University Press, 2012), 121–137.

unavailable, the soul is not able to perform its proper function and cannot survive. Aquinas's response to this seems, once again, ad hoc, at least philosophically speaking. His view is simply that after the death of the body the soul would have a different way of cognizing, namely one similar to that of other disembodied substances. Aquinas may have got away with this because there was no pressure on him to provide something other than a metaphysical argument for the separation of body and soul. Suárez, on the other hand, as James B. South indicates, had to respond to contemporary arguments such as those of Pomponazzi that stressed the direct relation between intellect and sense-perception. So his response had to rely on a suitable account of cognition, and indeed, a careful interpretation of Aristotle's text.[63]

The strategy Suárez deploys in his *Commentary on De Anima* to get out of the problem is to distinguish three different ways in which the operation of a power can depend on a material power. Two of them, if proved to be the right way in which cognition depends on phantasms, lead to the conclusion that the soul is indeed inseparable from the body and therefore should be rejected. The first way is that the material power is the subject of the operation: phantasia (i.e., the power that generates phantasms) is the subject of cognition if cognition is elicited from the phantasia. The second way is that the material power is the object of the operation: phantasia provides an object for the understanding in the same way that, for example, phantasia is an object for a sensitive appetite. These two ways are not how cognition is related to phantasia. The right relation is of a third kind: they are simply concomitant, and thus there is no real dependency between them.[64]

Later in the treatise, in Disputation 9, Suárez says more about how this works. Basically, the intellect and phantasia coincide in corresponding acts of cognition and imagination because they are rooted

---

63 Ibid., 127.
64 *CDA,* disp 5.

in the same soul and therefore they have an order (*ordo*) and harmony (*consensio*) in their operations. It is not that the potential intellect already has intelligible species of things in itself waiting to be prompted by the senses. Rather, species that correspond to those things the soul senses are produced by the intellectual soul independently of phantasia yet simultaneously. At no point does phantasia cause the species that the intellect needs.[65] It cannot, since, as Suárez emphasizes later on in Disputation 14, the body is of an inferior order compared to the spirituality of the soul.[66] This, of course, amounts to, again, stating the belief in the body's less noble nature with respect to the soul. That the soul and the body do harmonize with each other is just the product of the actual collection (*colligatio*) of their powers during the soul's embodied life.[67]

With this solution Suárez avoids Aquinas's seemingly ad hoc stipulation of two different ways of cognizing, depending on whether the soul is embodied or disembodied. In reality, according to Suárez, cognition is independent from the material power and therefore it makes no difference whether the soul has or does not have a body attached to it. The proper operation of the soul is intellectual, and the body does not give any kind of special or essential support to it. When body and soul are conjoined, at most the body gives the occasion for the soul to cognize extramental things.

This seems to lead to the conclusion that humans, as far as cognition is concerned, are barely, if at all, different from angels, the main difference being related to their existence, with no beginning and no end for angels and with a beginning but also without end for humans. However, this is not the case. According to Suárez, angels are given species of all real things in their intellects whereas humans are not. In

---

[65] *CDA*, disp 9, q2n12. Quoted in South, "Suárez, Immortality, and the Soul's Dependence on the Body," 133.
[66] *CDA*, disp 14, q3n3.
[67] *CDA*, disp 14 q5n5.

humans the species of things flow from the intellect at the same time as they are present in phantasia. Angels are still a notch above humans.

These views, however, get Suárez into other sorts of trouble. While trying to save the notion that the body is inferior to the soul he has also effectively removed the notion that the body is an impediment to the soul's attainment of a higher, purer kind of intellectual activity. Some passages in Aquinas suggest that for him disembodiment of the soul after death grants humans access to a nobler intellectual status. In particular, the soul can finally know itself without the intermission of phantasms.[68] As Cees Leijenhorst explains, Suárez actually seems to attack precisely that notion of the body as an impediment to self-knowledge on the grounds that given that the human soul is naturally inclined to be united with the body as Aquinas says it is, it is strange that the body becomes an impediment to the soul's desire for self-fulfillment in its knowledge of itself. However, at the same time Suárez's views entail that after death the soul still needs some self-mediation, for example, in order to know itself, and as such it is not capable of what should be its natural perfection. When confronted with that theological problem Suárez recants his position, says that the problem is very obscure, that Aquinas is probably right, and we should not deviate from this: "it can be believed that the separate soul knows itself immediately without any other species."[69] The inferiority of the body trumps philosophical results.

To conclude, the discussions of Aquinas, Ockham, and Suárez highlighted here exemplify the tension in the Scholastic period between acknowledging the body's seemingly essential role in cognition and preserving a traditional hierarchy of beings based on the nobility of the immaterial intellect over the corporeal. As we have seen, the discussions are couched in sophisticated Aristotelian terms with their own

---

68 ST Iq89a1–2.
69 *QDA*, disp. 14, q. 5, no. 3. See the discussion in Cees Leijenhorst, "Suárez on Self-Awareness," in *The Philosophy of Francisco Suárez*, ed. Henrik Lagerlund and Benjamin Hill (Oxford: Oxford University Press, 2012), 150–151, where the passage is cited.

internal problems, some of which do not have to do with knowledge itself but with the metaphysical status of matter, form, and body in general. Aquinas seems to be more willing to give the metaphysical explanations more power, whereas later authors challenge some of his conclusions on account of specific issues having to do with human and angelic cognition. In the end, however, theological concerns mandate the body to be put in its proper place below the intellect and to be cast as, in a way, an encumbrance to human perfection, or, more precisely, the perfection of the intellectual soul.[70]

---

70 My thanks to the participants at the workshop on Embodiment at Université Paris Diderot, audiences at the University of North Carolina at Asheville and the University of San Diego, and my colleagues at the Cogut Center for the Humanities at Brown University. Special thanks to Linda Peterson for her insight and suggestions on Aquinas on human knowledge after death.

CHAPTER SEVEN

Hobbes's Embodied God

Geoffrey Gorham

1. Introduction

One of the remarkable features of seventeenth-century natural philosophy was the direct employment of God at the foundations of the both the Cartesian and the Newtonian programs in physics. To ensure that motion was conserved and rectilinear, Descartes stipulated that God continually generated it "in the precise form in which it is occurring at the very moment when he preserves it."[1] Descartes' God was not spatial, of course, though he possessed a virtual extension.[2] But Newton's God actually "constituted" absolute space and time through his real (not just virtual) immensity and eternity.[3]

---

1 Descartes, *Principles of Philosophy* II, 39; AT 8A 63-4 In what follows, references to main primary sources use the abbreviations list. See further G. Gorham, "Descartes on God's Relation to Time," *Religious Studies* 44, no. 4 (2008): 413–431.
2 Letter to Henry More April 15, 1649; AT 5 143.
3 *Principia*, 941. And of course, Newton's God was further called upon as needed to stabilize the system of the world. *Optics*, query 31; PW, 138. See further G. Gorham "Newton on God's Relation

However, although they brought God into space and time, neither Descartes nor Newton were prepared to embody God, since (unlike Spinoza) they considered embodiment to entail divisibility and therefore imperfection. Yet, as I will argue, Hobbes's somewhat neglected "corporeal deity"—derived from the Stoics—offered at least as compelling a conception of God's immanent relation to the world as Descartes or Newton. Given the rise of deism and materialism in France and England at the turn of the eighteenth century, one might have expected a welcome reception for Hobbes's corporeal deity (which was certainly well known). But in fact even radical authors like John Toland—an avowed pantheist—rejected the corporeal god doctrine.

2. Hobbes's Corporeal God

Bishop John Bramhall must have thought he had finally cornered his longtime nemesis Thomas Hobbes when he posed this rhetorical question to the avowed materialist: "When they have taken away all incorporeal spirits, what do they leave God Himself to be?"[4] In his final *Answer to Bramhall*, the aging Hobbes introduced one of the most heterodox deities in the early modern pantheon: "To his lordship's question here: *what I leave God to be?* I answer: I leave him to be a most pure, simple, invisible spirit corporeal."[5] Until recently,[6] scholars have not given serious attention to Hobbes's corporeal deity,

---

to Space and Time: The Cartesian Framework," *Archiv für Geschichte der Philosophie* 93, no. 3 (2011): 281–320.

4 WB iv, 525.

5 EW iv, 313.

6 Agostino Lupoli, "Fluidismo e Corporeal Deity nella filosofia naturale di Thomas Hobbes," *Revista di storia della filosofia*, 54, no. 4 (1999): 573–609; Cees Leijenhorst, "Hobbes's Corporeal Deity," *Revista di storia della filosofia*, 59, no. 1 (2004): 73–95; Dominique Weber, *Hobbes et le corps de Dieu* (Paris: J. Vrin, 2009); Patricia Springborg, "Hobbes's Challenge to Descartes, Bramhall and Boyle: A Corporeal God," *British Journal for the History of Philosophy* 20, no. 5 (2012): 903–934;

since they have shared Bramhall's presumption that his admixture of theism and materialism was *de facto* atheism at best, or a blasphemous joke at worst.[7] Descartes himself set this tone in a 1641 letter to Mersenne, commenting on a (lost) letter from Hobbes: "I leave aside the beginning part about the corporeal soul and God (*anima & Deo corporeis*), the internal spirit, and other matters which don't concern me."[8] Descartes' dismissive remark shows that Hobbes's corporeal theology was not a mere fancy of his dotage. He sincerely hoped his embodied god would supplant the ghostly imposter installed by the Nicene Council and propped up by Scholastic theology ever since.

Hobbes struggled to accommodate a number of traditional divine attributes within his corporeal theology and materialist metaphysics, including infinity, omnipotence, omniscience, and simplicity. In the *Answer to Bramhall*, and earlier works, he insists that God is an "infinite substance,"[9] and for this reason incomprehensible to us.[10] But for Hobbes the notion of an infinite body seems outright contradictory. For he defines body as "that which filleth, or occupieth some certain room, or imagined place."[11] Still he says the infinite can neither be imagined[12] nor in a place.[13] Although this has worried recent commentators,[14] I think Hobbes solves this problem in the *Answer to Bramhall*

Geoffrey Gorham, "The Theological Foundations of Hobbesian Physics: A Defense of Corporeal God," *British Journal for the History of Philosophy* 21 (2013): 240–261.

7 Leo Strauss, *The Political Philosophy of Hobbes* (Chicago: University of Chicago Press, 1952); Edwin Curley, "'I Durst Not Write So Boldly' or How to Read Hobbes' *Theological-Political Treatise*," in *Hobbes e Spinoza*, ed. D. Bostrenghi (Naples, Italy: Bibliopolis, 1992), 497–593; Douglas Jesseph, "Hobbes's Atheism," in *Midwest Studies in Philosophy* 26, no. 1 (2002): 140–166.

8 AT 3 287.

9 EW iv, 302.

10 *Leviathan* I.iii, 12; C 15.

11 *Leviathan* III.xxxiv, 207; C 261.

12 *De Motu* IV.3, 54; *Leviathan* IV, xlv, 15; C 444.

13 *Leviathan* II.XXXI, 190; C 240; *Answer to Bramhall* EW iv, 297, 299.

14 Jesseph, "Hobbes's Atheism," 144. See also Weber, *Hobbes et le corps de Dieu*, 95; Leijenhorst "Hobbes's Corporeal Deity," 82–85; Curley, "'I Durst Not Write So Boldly,'" 587. For additional

itself where he draws an important distinction: "*Body* (Latin: *corpus*; Greek: σώμα) is that substance which hath magnitude indeterminate and is the same with corporeal substance; *A body* is that which hath magnitude determinate and so is understood to be a *totum* or *integrum aliquid*."[15] Unlike "a body," which is a "complete something," mere "body" has no determinate size and so needn't be finite or imaginable.[16] In the English *Answer to Bramhall*, God is never characterized as "a body" but only as "spirit corporeal" (sometimes with and sometimes without the indefinite article).[17] Moreover, although it is true that infinite body does not have a place in Hobbes's sense, there is no reason it cannot occupy infinite space. Placeless bodies are not without historical precedent.[18]

God's omnipotence requires literal omnipresence since for Hobbes motion can be produced or reduced only by a contiguous and moving body (i.e., by collision).[19] So God's body is an all-pervading fluid or "spirit" as subtle and penetrable as a vacuum.[20] Although not literally co-located with ordinary bodies—this is ruled out by Hobbes's

---

objections to Curley's specific arguments that Hobbes's God is incoherent see Leijenhorst, "Hobbes's Corporeal Deity," 81–88.

15 EW iv, 309.

16 "... what has magnitude, whether visible or invisible, finite or infinite, is called by all the learned a body." EW iv, 393.

17 The Latin *Leviathan* has "Affirmat quidem Deus esse Corpus." OL iii, 561. For detailed discussion, see Gorham, "Theological Foundations of Hobbesian Physics."

18 Aristotle's cosmos, Descartes' plenum, and Locke's universe are all bodies that, for different reasons, lack place. Aristotle, *Physics* Bk. IV. 5; Locke, *Essay* II.13.10; 1975, 171. Descartes' notions of "internal" and "external" place (AT 8A 45–49) are both inapplicable to his indefinitely extended plenum. Hobbes himself implies that a world need not be in place, at least not in the Aristotelian sense. *De Motu* III.7, 44.

19 *De Corpore* 2.9.7; OL i, 110; EW i, 124. On the origin and significance of Hobbes's inertial principles, see Frithiof Brandt, *Thomas Hobbes' Mechanical Conception of Nature* (Copenhagen: Levin & Munksgaards, 1917); Leijenhorst *The Mechanisation of Aristotelianism: The Late Aristotelian Setting of Thomas Hobbes' Natural Philosophy* (Leiden, The Netherlands: Brill, 2002), ch. 5; Douglas Jesseph, "Hobbesian Mechanics," in *Oxford Studies in Early Modern Philosophy*, vol. 3, eds. D. Garber and S. Nadler (Oxford: Oxford University Press, 2006), 119–152.

20 *De Corpore* 4.26.3; OL i, 340; EW i, 417.

geometrical conception of body—God does thoroughly intermix with finite things. To illustrate this, Hobbes relies on a memorable analogy:

> I have seen, and so have many others, two waters, one of the river and the other mineral water, so that no man could discern one from the other from his sight; yet when they are both put together the whole substance could not be distinguished from milk. Yet we know the one was not mixed with the other, so as every part of the one to be in every part of the other, for that is impossible, unless two bodies can be in the same place. How then could the change be made in every part, but only by the activity of the mineral water, changing it everywhere to the sense and yet not being everywhere and in every part of the water?[21]

The theological relevance of this elaborate experiment is made explicit in the next few lines of the *Answer*:

> If such gross bodies have such great activity what then can we think of spirits, whose kinds be as many as there are kinds of liquor, and activity greater? Can it then be doubted that God, who is infinitely fine spirit, and withal intelligent, can make and change all species and kinds of bodies as he pleaseth?[22]

It is not easy to grasp how the corporeal god is "withal intelligent," (i.e., omniscient). Given the difference between human bodies and the "spirit corporeal," the analogy between human and divine knowledge will be somewhat strained. In us, sense, desire, deliberation and will are determined by various internal and external physical forces,[23] whereas the corporeal God is fully active and

---

21 EW iv, 310.
22 Ibid.
23 See *Leviathan* i, 1–4; C 6-7; xxxi 27; C 27.

unaffected. Hobbes seems to acknowledge the disanalogy: "when we ascribe to God a will, it is not to be understood as that of man, for a rational appetite, but as the power by which he affecteth everything. Likewise when we attribute to him sight, and other acts of sense, and likewise knowledge and understanding, which in us are nothing but a tumult of the mind."[24] Nevertheless, just as our limited knowledge is ultimately derived from contact with a few bodies,[25] God can be said to be omniscient given his direct contact with all bodies.

Finally, Hobbes's God is supremely simple. Hobbes emphasizes in the discussion surrounding the mineral water analogy that his corporeal God is "most pure, most simple corporeal spirit."[26] A body is pure and simple, he says, when it is "one and the same kind in every part throughout."[27] Such a body can be mixed with other bodies while retaining its simplicity, like wine in water. Thus the traditional attribute of simplicity becomes homogeneity. Such simplicity does not entail partlessness. Although in the *Leviathan* Hobbes says we ought not "attribute to him parts or totality, which are the attributes of things

---

24 *Leviathan* II, xxxi, 25-7; C 240. See also EW v, 14: "... that which we call design, which is reasoning, and thought after thought, cannot be properly attributed to God." Hobbes is not denying that God acts by will, and for a purpose, but only that he deliberates about how to achieve future ends. Thus, in the same paragraph he asserts that "whatsoever is done comes into God's mind, that is into his knowledge, which implies a certainty of the future action, and that certainty an antecedent purpose of God to bring it to pass." (EW v, 14) God has purposes but never needs to think through (design) how to achieve them. The failure to appreciate this disanalogy leads Cudworth, after quoting this chapter of *Leviathan*, to charge that Hobbes "must needs deny the first principle of all things to be any knowing, understanding nature." TIS III, V, i, 60. Cudworth also attributes to the Stoics, at least the later ones, a "Cosmic-Plastic" kind of atheism (Cudworth thinks there are four kinds) for holding that the whole universe is "a body endowed with one plastic or spermatic nature, branching out the whole, orderly and methodically, but without any understanding or sense." TIS I, iii, xxvi, 194. For discussion of Cudworth on the Stoic Theology see Guido Giglioni, "The Cosmoplastic System of the Universe: Ralph Cudworth on Stoic Naturalism," *Revue D' Histoires Des Sciences* 61, no. 2 (2008): 313–338; also J. Sellars, "Is God a Mindless Vegetable? Cudworth on Stoic Theology," *Intellectual History Review* 21, no. 4 (2011): 121–133.
25 *Leviathan*, I; C 6–7.
26 EW iv, 306. See also 313.
27 EW iv, 309.

finite";[28] in the *Answer* he rejects the traditional "partless" conception of God's ubiquity whereby God is "wholly here and wholly there and wholly everywhere."[29] While endorsing the Nicene Creed assertion (as he reads it) that God is not divisible into numerically distinct individuals Hobbes nevertheless insists that God's infinite corporeal magnitude has real parts: "For certainly he that thinks God is in every part of the church does not exclude him out of the churchyard. And is this not considering him by parts?"[30] Hobbes's point seems to be that we can consider God's parts but not separate them.[31]

While Hobbes is concerned to uphold the (mostly) orthodox character of his God, I think Hobbes's God is designed primarily to solve a problem in his natural philosophy. God provides an unremitting source of motion and *conatus* without which Hobbes's universe would reduce to a static, undifferentiated blob. As noted, in Hobbes's world there is no "action at a distance": motion can be produced or reduced only by a contiguous and moving body (i.e., by collision).[32] Hobbes accepts the inertial principles that without interference from other bodies "whatever is at rest will always be at rest and whatever is moved will always be moved."[33] However, in a plenum the motion or *conatus* propagated in collision will constantly diminish: "endeavor, by proceeding, grows weaker and weaker, till at last it can no longer be perceived by sense."[34] But since the actual world is a plenum, according

---

28 *Leviathan* II.xxxi; EW 190, OL 240. See also *De Motu*: "no part of any whole can be infinite." II.2, 31.

29 EW iv, 295. Hobbes regards such a conception impious (as if God were "no greater than to be wholly contained within the least atom of earth") and incoherent ("nor can I conceive how any thing whole can be called whole which has no parts."). EW iv, 300

30 EW iv, 302.

31 "God is nowhere said in the Scriptures to be indivisible, unless his Lordship [Bramhall] meant division to consist only in separation of parts." (Ibid.) On the inseparability of the parts of corporeal God, see further Weber, *Hobbes et le corps de Dieu*, 101–112.

32 *De Corpore* 2.9.7; OL i, 110; EW i, 124.

33 *De Corpore* 2.8.19; OL i, 102; EW i, 115

34 *De Corpore* 3.15.7; OL i, 183; EW i, 217

to Hobbes[35] it follows that any motion will quickly dissipate, contrary to experience. Embodied God solves this problem by providing a continuous, resistance-free supply of motion or *conatus* to the world.[36]

From this perspective, Hobbes's late theology, while certainly heterodox in content, is not so different in function from that of contemporaries like Descartes and More. More tried to avoid both the wholesale materialism of Hobbes and the radical dualism of Descartes by rejecting their shared assumption that anything really extended is body. He allowed God and finite minds to be spatial without being corporeal. But despite their diverse "onto-theologies," More and his two opponents put God into remarkably similar service for the mechanical philosophy. In the creation models of the early *World* (1633) and later *Principles of Philosophy* (1644), Descartes' God produces bodies and diversity by continuously injecting motion into formless extension.[37] The only difference from Hobbes is that whereas Descartes radically separates God from the plenum, as mind from body, Hobbes's God is an immanent cause of change and diversity.[38] The similarity between Hobbes's physico-theology and More's is even more striking. Like Hobbes, More rejects both Descartes' view that God is strictly nowhere and the Scholastics' view that God is wholly in every place.[39] Furthermore, God acts on matter via the "Spirit of Nature" to produce all the changes we perceive: "The *Spirit of Nature* . . . is a substance without sense and animadversion, pervading the whole matter

---

35 *De Corpore* 4.26.2; OL i, 338; EW i, 414–415
36 See further Gorham, "The Theological Foundations of Hobbesian Physics."
37 AT 11, 34; AT 8A 61
38 There is a methodological difference as well. Descartes derives his laws of nature from God being immutable in himself and in his operations (AT 8A 61). Hobbes merely hypothesizes that an "infinitely fine Spirit" can "make and change all species and kinds of bodies as he pleases" (EW i 310). In this respect, Hobbes's God is at the foundations of his physics but not his "first philosophy." See Yves-Charles Zarka, "First Philosophy and the Foundations of Knowledge," in *Cambridge Companion to Hobbes*, ed. Tom Sorell (Cambridge, UK: Cambridge University Press, 2006).
39 For a useful discussion of Hobbes in relation to Cartesian "nullibism" or "nowhereism," see Weber, *Hobbes et le corps de Dieu*, ch. IV.2

of the universe... raising such phenomena in the world, by directing the parts of the matter and their motion."[40] For each philosopher, God produces all the diversity and motions in material things by a direct and ubiquitous operation upon ordinary matter.

3. Looking Backwards: The Stoic Origins of Hobbes's Theory

No doubt one reason for the common scholarly suspicion that Hobbes's embodied god is merely a calculated exercise in dissimulation is the presumed lack of historical precedent for such an unusual godhead. Where in the world did Hobbes get such a strange idea? I think it is clear that Hobbes is reviving the Stoic God. Consider the following account of Stoic theology from Diogenes Laertius:

> They believe there are two principles of the universe, the active and the passive. The passive is unqualified substance, i.e, matter, the active is the rational principle (logos) in it, i.e. God ... God and Mind and Fate and Zeus are one thing but called by many different names. In the beginning he was by himself and turned all substances into water via air and just as the seed is contained in the seminal fluid so this being the spermatic principle of the cosmos remains like this in the fluid and makes the matter easy for itself to work with in the generation of subsequent things. Then it produces the first four elements: fire, water, air and earth.[41]

---

40 1987 Bk. iii, ch. 12, 245. Weber suggests the analogy between the gods of More and Hobbes cannot be so strong because whereas Hobbes says in *de Motu* that God produces natural actions through "secondary causes" (*De Motu* XXXVI.7, 439), for More "Dieu est présent en toutes chose comme l'agent dans sa cause." Weber, *Hobbes et le corps de Dieu*, 119. But More's God does rely on a second cause of sorts, the Spirit of Nature, and Hobbes's corporeal God, at least as depicted in the two-waters analogy, acts directly in the way one body acts on another.

41 Diogenes Laertius *Lives of the Philosophers* Bk. 7, 134, LS 268–269, 275. See also Alexander of Aphrodisias's similar complaint against the Stoics for "claiming the existence of two universal principles, matter and God, of which the latter is active and the former passive; and with saying that God

There are remarkable parallels with Hobbes's "river-water" passages quoted above. Both schemes take God to be a special kind of corporeal substance that produces the diversity among ordinary bodies by actively and thoroughly pervading matter. And both conceive of the divine body as conscious or at least intelligent. The stoic's god is a fiery air (*pneuma*)[42] rather than a Hobbesian fluid but this difference doesn't amount to much since Hobbes emphasizes that a thoroughly homogeneous fluid is indistinguishable from an absolute vacuum in that it neither offers nor suffers resistance.[43] Just prior to offering his model of the infinite spirit's operation, Hobbes hints at the Stoic origin, noting that the word "spirit" in "Latin signifies 'breath, air, wind" and "in Greek πνεῦμα [pneuma]."[44] A more important difference is that the Stoic God is providential whereas Hobbes insists "God has no ends"[45] though it is unclear why it is more plausible to attribute a will and understanding to the Stoic god than the Hobbesian.

It is not surprising that Hobbes would embrace Stoic theology. His philosophy is Stoic in other respects: materialist, plenist, and reductionist about space and time. He was very familiar with sixteenth-century "neo-Stoic" writers like Lipsius and Stoicism was influential

---

is mixed with matter and pervades the whole of it, in this way shaping and forming it and creating the universe." *On Mixture* XI, 224–225, T 139, LS 273, 275.

42 Alexander, *On Mixture* III, 216, 14–20, T 115, LS 290.

43 *De Corpore* 4.26.3; OL i, 340; EW i, 417.

44 Ibid. See also *Leviathan* III, xxxiv, 3; C 242. So it is ironic that Cudworth, in his decidedly anti-Hobbesian tome, *The True Intellectual System of the Universe* (1678), diagnoses atheists as suffering from "pneumatophobia": "an irrational but desperate abhorrence from spirits or incorporeal substances." TIS Vol. I, Bk. 1, Ch. xxx, 200. Cudworth goes on to concede that "all corporealists are not to be accounted atheists." Some "Corporeal Theists," for example, hold "God to be a certain subtle and ethereal, but intellectual, matter pervading it [the world] as a soul. He mentions the Stoics as holding such a view, who are then derided not as atheists but rather 'ignorant, unskilled and childish theists.'" TIS I, Vol. I, Bk. i, Ch. xxx, 202. Cudworth didn't seem to realize Hobbes himself is a corporeal theist in this sense. For a more judicious, though still unsympathetic, contemporaneous treatment of Hobbes's corporeal God doctrine, see CHE, 10–38. On the anti-Hobbesian aims of TIS see John Arthur Passmore, *Ralph Cudworth* (Cambridge, UK: Cambridge University Press, 1951); Samuel I. Mintz, *The Hunting of Leviathan* (Cambridge, UK: Cambridge University Press, 1962); and Sellars, "Is God a Mindless Vegetable?"

45 *Leviathan* xxxi, 13; C 239. See further Dirk Baltzly, "Stoic Pantheism," *Sophia* 42.2 (2003): 3–33.

among his friends in the "Cavendish Circle" (including Margaret). Most importantly, he frequently relied on the authority of Tertullian, an early Christian Stoic. Like Hobbes, Tertullian emphasized the philosophical and Biblical case for materialism about God and souls. And Tertullian's authority was regularly invoked by Hobbes in works that develop and defend the corporeal God doctrine. For example, in a 1662 response to the Oxford mathematician John Wallis, Hobbes answers the charge that his materialism is atheism by consequence, by quoting Tertullian's *De Carne Christi*: "*omne quod est corpus est sui generis: nihil est incorporale nisi quod non est*: that is to say, whatever is anything is a body of its kind. Nothing is incorporeal but that which has no being."[46] The Latin *Leviathan* cites an additional Tertullian text, against the heretic Praxeas (who reportedly preferred an incorporeal God): "every substance is a body of its own kind."[47] Hobbes seems to have in mind the following passage, which explicitly asserts the corporality of God: "Who will deny that God is body (*deum corpus esse*) although God is a spirit? For Spirit has a bodily substance of its own kind, in its own form?"[48] And there are other texts Hobbes might have encountered in his reading of Tertullian that reflect even more closely his form of corporeal theism.[49]

---

46 EW iv, 429. Tertullian, *de Carne Christi* xi, RD 531. He cites the same passage in the two 1668 works that announce the corporeal God doctrine, the Latin *Leviathan* and the *Answer to Bramhall*, as well as in the 1680 *Historical Narration Concerning Heresy: Leviathan*, Appendix, iii, C 540; EW iv, 307, 383; EW iv, 398. See also *Ad Hermogenes* xxxvi; RD 498; Cf. *Ad Marcion* V, xv; RD 463.

47 *Leviathan*, Appendix, iii, C 540.

48 *Quis enim negabit deum corpus esse, etsi deus spiritus est? Spiritus enim corpus sui generis in sua effigie. Ad Praxeas* vii, RD 602. As with finite souls, Tertullian emphasizes the Stoic objection to dualism that an incorporeal substance cannot act on body: "How could He who is empty have made things which are solid, and He who is void have made things which are full, and He who is incorporeal have made things which have body?" (Ibid.) In the preceding chapters, the corporeal God's activity in designing, creating and sustaining the world is said to embody reason, *logos*, intelligence and wisdom. *Ad Praxeas* v, vi, RD, 600-1. See also Evans, *Tertullian's Adversus Praxean Liber* (London: S.P.C.K., 1948), 234–237, for discussion of the Stoic background to these texts. On Hobbes's appeal to these texts in support of materialism, see Riverso, E. "Denotation and Corporeity in Leviathan." *Metalogicon* 4, no. 1 (1991): 78–92, esp. 92.

49 For example, in the tract against yet another heretic, Hermogenes, Tertullian invokes with sympathy the Stoic model of God's mixture with matter: "The Stoics maintained that God pervaded

The Stoic problem of fatalism is central to Hobbes's famous debate with Bramhall about liberty. At one point, Bramhall mentions Lipsius and repudiates Hobbes's view of freedom as Stoic.[50] Hobbes insists that his position is not "from the authority of any sect, but from the nature of things themselves."[51] It is worth noting that in Bramhall's final (1658) word on the liberty debate, he remarks in passing "If he had not been a professed Christian, rather than a plain Stoic, I would not have wondered so much at this answer; for they held that God was corporeal."[52] Although Bramhall's criticism went unanswered, it was appended to another text Hobbes studied closely in preparing his "Answer to Bramhall." It seems that Bramhall might have unwittingly inspired Hobbes to investigate seriously the Stoic roots of his embodied God.

4. Looking Forward: The Deist Reception.

Hobbes's corporeal God seems to have been well known in the second half of the seventeenth century, despite its late and obscure publication. As noted above, Hobbes promulgated the doctrine among the Mersenne circle of Paris as early as the 1630s.[53] Later in the century,

---

matter, just as honey the honeycomb." *Ad Hermogenes* xliv; RD 501. Hobbes hints at broader reading of Tertullian in *Answer to Bramhill*, mentioning that *De Carne Christi* is "now extant among his other works." EW iv, 307. For more on the Stoic origin of Hobbes's God, see Gorham, "Mixing Bodily Fluids: Hobbes's Stoic God," *Sophia: International Journal for the Philosophy of Religion* 53, no. 1 (2014): 33–49.

50 "Discourse of Liberty and Necessity," Section xviii. Bramhall, WB iv, 116. See also "Defence of True Liberty," WB iv, 119. In his Introduction to the defence or "vindication," Bramhall labels Hobbes's position "sublimated stoicism." EW iv, 20. Jamie C. Kassler incorrectly suggests that it was Hobbes who originally invoked and drew upon Lipsius in the debate with Bramhall. See Kassler, "The Paradox of Power: Hobbes and Stoic," in *The Uses of Antiquity: The Scientific Revolution and the Classical Tradition*, ed. Stephen Gaukroger (Dordrecht, The Netherlands: D. Reidel, 1991), 54.

51 EW iv, 260-1; See also EW v, 244-5.

52 WB iv, 426.

53 AT 3, 287. See Curley, "Hobbes versus Descartes," in *Descartes and His Contemporaries: Meditations, Objections and Replies*, eds. R. Ariew and M. Grene (Chicago: University of Chicago Press, 1995), 97–109; and Springborg, "Hobbes's Challenge to Descartes."

Cudworth summarizes the corporeal God doctrine and subjects it to sustained criticism in his *True Intellectual System of the Universe*.[54] Although the *System* is thoroughly and expressly anti-Hobbesian, Cudworth does not explicitly associate corporeal theism with Hobbes, although he rightly emphasizes its Stoic origin. It is unlikely that Cudworth was unaware of Hobbes's position, however. For it was the subject of a public attack by the prominent churchman Thomas Tenison (later Archbishop of Canterbury). In his 1670 pamphlet "Creed of Hobbes Examined," Tenison charged that a corporeal God would have parts and be imaginable, contrary to Hobbes's own theological tenets.[55] In 1690, Anne Conway also mentions "Hobbes' claim that God is material and corporeal," which she notes has been called one of the "worst consequences of the philosophy of Hobbes."[56] Fifteen years later, Leibniz remarks on a recent author espousing "like M. Hobbes that God himself is material," which conception Leibniz dismisses as "impossible."[57]

More surprising than the negative opinion of Cudworth, Conway, and Leibniz, is the tepid reception of Hobbes's embodied God among the emerging class of early eighteenth-century radicals and deists. The Hobbesian theology was probably most thoroughly embraced by the minor English mortalist and materialist William Coward, the author dismissed by Leibniz in the letter mentioned above. In his *Second Thoughts on the Human Soul* (1703), which reduces the soul to the physiological processes that sustain life, Coward makes plain his debt to Hobbes: "If I approve of or concur in the opinion of the learned Mr.

---

54 TIS, 134–136; I, iii, xxx. See Sellars "Is God a Mindless Vegetable?" for an excellent overview of Cudworth's critique.
55 CHE, 12–13. On Tenison's campaign against Hobbes and irreligion, see Mintz, *Hunting of Leviathan*; R. Sullivan, *John Toland and the Deist Controversy* (Cambridge, MA: Harvard University Press, 1982); and A. Thomson, *Bodies of Thought: Science, Religion and the Soul in the Early Enlightenment* (Oxford: Oxford University Press, 2008).
56 *Principles*, Ch. IX, sec. 3; 1996, 64.
57 Letter to Burnet, August 2, 1704; G III, 298.

Hobbs of Malmesbury, that it is a very odd notion to call any created being an immaterial substance, I know I shall be received upon the very account of his name with both censure and prejudice."[58] While Coward's first book concentrates on the materiality of the human soul, his next *Grand Essay* (1704) extends materialism to God (as well as angels and devils). Following Hobbes, whose name is invoked on the first page, Coward argues that "unextended substance" is "as impossible to be conceived as *eternal creature* or *dead animality*."[59] Furthermore, the positive attributes of God are better understood by defining God as an "eternal, omniscient, omnipotent power, or spirit."[60] Spirit is in turn defined merely as "some being which has neither flesh nor bone."[61] For such opinions, Coward seems only to have garnered disdain and persecution, including a public burning of his books in 1704. Locke joined Leibniz in his condemnation of Coward in correspondence with the deist John Collins.[62]

Even the pantheist John Toland was concerned to distance himself from Hobbes's corporeal theism. In the Fifth of his *Letters to Serena* (1704), Toland responds to an objection about the infinity of the universe as follows: "as for the infinity of matter, it only excludes what all reasonable and good men must exclude, an extended corporeal God, but not a pure spirit or immaterial being."[63] Elsewhere in the *Letters to Serena* he vehemently rejects the conception of God, derived from Joseph Raphson and others (presumably Henry More), as somehow assimilated to absolute space: "their unwary zeal refined him into nothing or (what they would as little allow) they made the nature or the universe to be the only God."[64]

---

58 ST, 84.
59 GE, 14.
60 Ibid. 59.
61 Ibid.
62 Locke, *Correspondence*, vol. viii, 198.
63 V, 30; LTS, 236.
64 Ibid, V, 26; LTS, 219–220.

Despite these early misgivings, Toland's view evolves into something closer to Hobbes's. He soon embraces Raphson's neologism "pantheist,"[65] though without elaborating the doctrine. But in his late text *Pantheisticon* (1720), he propounds a definition of pantheism as follows:

> The universe is infinite both in extension and virtue; but one both in the continuation of the whole and the contiguity of the parts; immovable according to the whole as beyond it there's no place or space; but movable according to the parts or by distances in number infinite; incorruptible and necessary both ways, to wit, eternal in excellency and duration; intelligent also by an eminent reason."[66]

Toland proceeds to explain that from the "Motion and Intellect" of the world there arise all species and individuals and that "the force and energy of the whole, the creator and ruler of all, and always tending to the best end, is God."[67] Toland's late view is remarkably close to Raphson's version of "pantheism," which posits "a universal substance, material as well as intelligent, which fashions all that exists out of its own essence."[68] Although Toland conceives God's power in terms of Newtonian force rather than Hobbesian *conatus*, his God shares crucial features with Hobbes's corporeal deity: material, intelligent, responsible for all diversity and change, infinite, indivisible, etc. Acknowledging the pedigree of this theology, Toland ends the first part of his treatise with long quotes from Cicero's summary of the original Stoic version of corporeal theism.[69]

---

65 STS, 1705
66 P 1720, 15
67 Ibid. 16–17.
68 SR, 2
69 Toland P, 58–61; Cicero *Academic Questions*: Book I, Section 6. On Toland's philosophy, see Sullivan *John Toland and the Deist Controversy* and S. Daniel, *John Toland: His Method, Manners and Mind* (Montreal: McGill-Queens University Press, 1984).

The cautious embodiment of God by a few English deists was ultimately swept aside by the immaterialist backlash of the Cambridge Platonists, Leibniz, and Samuel Clarke. The rebirth of corporeal theism required the more radical intellectual soil of the emerging American Republic, where deist and pantheist ideas flourished.[70] God was fully reembodied, in remarkably Hobbesian form, by the 19th-century American founders of Mormonism, which is today the fastest growing religion in the United States.[71]

5. Conclusion

The corporeal theologies we have examined do not embody God because an immaterial god is too remote, abstract, or impersonal. Rather, they take the conceptual incoherence of immaterialism as their starting point: a disembodied god is simply a nonstarter. Furthermore, they assume that theology should comport with the principles of natural science (especially the mechanical philosophy) because God is conceived primarily as the immanent cause of motion and change rather than the transcendent source of being itself. Indeed, each conceive of God by analogy with the most prominent dynamical principles of their time: pneumatic (the Stoics), chemical (Hobbes), and force (Coward and Toland). But although such models could preserve many of the traditional attributes of God (infinity, omnipotence, omnipresence), it was less clear how they could capture God's perfect wisdom and providence. Furthermore, not even the deists (nor for that matter Spinoza) were prepared to accept that an immanent God was divisible (and corruptible)

---

70 See Matthew Stewart, *Nature's God: The Heretical Origins of the American Republic* (New York: W.W. Norton, 2014).
71 On corporeal God within early Mormon theology and natural philosophy, see J. Brooke, *The Refiner's Fire: The Making of Mormon Cosmology: 1644–1844* (Cambridge, UK: Cambridge University Press, 1944); and Erich Paul, *Science, Religion, and Mormon Cosmology* (Urbana: University of Illinois Press, 1992).

into really distinct parts. Because Hobbes was willing to accept all these consequences, it is appropriate to seat his god highest in the materialist pantheon; the Stoic and Deist gods are merely precursors and pretenders.

Abbreviations

Note: Primary source abbreviations are listed beginning with Hobbes, in order of frequency of citation. Following abbreviations are listed in order of reference in the text.

OL = Hobbes, T. *Opera philosophica quae latine scripsit omnia*. 5 vols. Edited by W. Molesworth. London, Joannem Bohn: 1839–1845. Citation by volume and page number.

EW = Hobbes, T. *English Works*. 11 vols. Edited by W. Molesworth. London, 1839–1845. Citation by volume and page number.

De Motu = Hobbes, T. *Critique du De Mundo de Thomas White*. Edited by J. Jaquot and H. Jones. Paris: Vrin, 1973. Citation by chapter, section, and page number of *Thomas White's* De Mundo *Examined*. Edited by. H. Jones. London: Bradford University Press, 1976.

De Corpore = Hobbes, T. *Elementorum Philosophiae, Sectio Prima: De Corpore*, edited by K. Schuhmann. Paris: Vrin, 1999. Citation by part, chapter, section; *Opera philosophica* (OL) by volume and page number; *English Works* (EW) by volume and page number.

C = Hobbes, T.. *Leviathan with Selected Variants from the Latin Edition of 1668*. Edited by Edwin Curley. Indianapolis: Hackett, 1994. Citation by part, chapter, paragraph number and Curley's edition page number.

Elements of Law = Hobbes, T. *Elements of Law*. Edited by F. Tonnies. Cambridge, UK: Cambridge University Press, 1928. Citation by part, chapter, paragraph and page number.

Answer to Bramhall = Hobbes, T.. *An Answer to a Book Published by Dr. Bramhall*. London: Crooke, 1682. Cited by *English Works* (EW) volume and page number.

WB = Bramhall, J.. *Works of John Bramhall*. 4 Vols. Oxford: John Henry Parker, 1842–1844.

LS = *The Hellenistic Philosophers, Vol. 1: Translation of the Principles Sources with Philosophical Commentary*. Edited by A.A. Long and D.N Sedley. Cambridge, UK: Cambridge University Press, 1987. Cited by page number.

IG = *Hellenistic Philosophy: Introductory Readings*. 2nd. Ed. Edited by B. Inwood and L.P. Gerson. Indianapolis: Hackett, 1997. Cited by page number.

T = Robert C. Todd. *Alexander of Aphrodisias on Stoic Physics: A Study of the De Mixtione with Preliminary Essays, Text, Translation and Commentary*. Leiden, The Netherlands: Brill, 1976. Cited by page number.

RD = *The Anti-Nicene Fathers, Vol. 3: Tertullian*. Edited by A. Roberts and J. Donaldson. Buffalo, NY: The Christian Literature Publishing Company, 1885. Cited by page number.

PS = Lipsius. J. *Physiologiae Stoicorum libre tres*. Antwerp, 1604. Cited by book, chapter and page number.

Barnes = *Complete Works of Aristotle*. 2. Vols. Edited by J. Barnes. Princeton, NJ: Princeton University Press, 1971. Cited by volume and page number.

CSM = Descartes, R. *Philosophical Writings of Descartes*. 2 vols. Edited by J. Cottingham, R. Stoothoff, and D. Murdoch. Cambridge, UK: Cambridge University Press. 1985.

AT = Descartes, R.. *Oeuvres de Descartes*. 11 vols. Edited by C. Adam and P. Tannery. Paris: J. Vrin, 1976. Citation by volume and page number.

Principia = Newton, I. *The Principia: Mathematical Principles of Natural Philosophy*. Edited by I.B. Cohen. Berkeley: University of California Press, 1999.

PW = Newton, I. *Philosophical Writings*. Edited by A. Janiak. Cambridge, UK: Cambridge University Press, 2004.

TIS = Cudworth, R. *True Intellectual System of the Universe*. 3 vols. London: Thomas Tegg, 1845. Cited by volume, book, chapter, and page number.

PAM = Conway, A. *The Principles of the Most Ancient and Modern Philosophy*. Edited by A. Coudert and T. Corse. Cambridge, UK: Cambridge University Press, 1996.

CHE = Tenison, T. *The Creed of Mr. Hobbes Examined*. London: Francis Tyton, 1670.

SR = Raphson, J. *De Spatio Reali*. London: Johannem Taylor, 1702.

ST = Coward, W. *Second Thoughts Concerning Human Soul*. London: R. Bassett, 1704.

GE = Coward, W. *The Grand Essay*, London: John Chantry, 1704.

LTS = Toland, J. *Letters to Serena*. London: Bernard Lintot, 1704.

STS = Toland, J. *Socinianism Truly Stated*. London: N.p., 1705.

P = Toland, J. *Pantheisticon*. London: Cosmopoli, 1720.

CHAPTER EIGHT

Leibniz's View of Living Beings

EMBODIED OR NESTED INDIVIDUALS

Ohad Nachtomy

1. Introduction

In the mid-1690s Leibniz presents an intriguing view of living beings.[1] According to Leibniz, a living being involves other living beings, nested one within the other, ad infinitum. This nested structure to infinity characterizes living beings and distinguishes them from nonliving ones. In *New System of Nature* (1695), Leibniz articulates this distinction in terms of a difference between natural machines and artificial ones. Unlike an artificial machine, a natural one remains a machine to

---

[1] In some sections of this chapter (especially 3–6) I draw on my article "Leibniz on Nested Individuals," *British Journal for the History of Philosophy* 15, no. 4 (2007): 709–728. I would like to thank Liat Lavi for assistance with the final version of this paper and acknowledge support of an ISF research grant 469/13.

the least of its parts.² This implies that a natural machine embodies a structure of machines within machines ad infinitum.

This picture gives rise to a number of questions. For example, how does this sort of embodiment serve the constitution of an individual—that is, a unique and unified being? And what exactly does Leibniz have in mind when he talks of machines within machines ad infinitum? In what follows I will argue that the model of embodiment Leibniz deploys in his view of living beings is not a material one, that is, it is not the kind of physical *emboîtement* that we find exemplified in the structure of an onion or in Russian dolls, which are physically encapsulated one within the other. In the course of paper I will examine several models of embodiment: physical, logical, expressive/representative, as well as a model of functional organization. I will conclude that the latter captures most adequately the Leibnizian view of living being and the kind of embodiment it involves. What makes all these nested individuals components of a single individual is that they all follow one dominant program of action, a program that may be seen as composed of many subprograms. But they all serve a single end (*telos*) that informs the developmental program of an individual.

2. "Embodiment" vs. "Nestedness"

As Justin Smith notes in his introduction to this volume, "To speak of embodiment ... is always to speak of a subject that finds itself variously inhabiting, or captaining, or being coextensive with, or even being imprisoned in, a body." When interpreting Leibniz's conception of living being, however, it is not clear that this language is entirely adequate, and I will suggest in this paper an alternative account. To be sure, some very well informed interpreters do conceive the Leibnizian notion of living being in terms of embodiment. For Richard Arthur

---

2 As we shall see, in some important respects, this distinction is coextensive with his distinction between substances and aggregates (developed in his correspondence with Arnauld).

(much like for François Duchesneau), the unity of a corporeal substance is conferred on a body by its dominant monad. And the various stages of the body are seen as various embodiments of the same creature (which account for its unity). In response to my review of his recent book, Richard Arthur has correctly observed that there is a subtle and important disagreement between our positions. He writes:

> I suspect that the source of our disagreement here [...] is that I do not agree that the machinic nature of an organic body makes it into a true unity or substance. The organic body, I believe, is not itself a substantial unity; rather it contains something having substantial unity, namely the monad. The spatial unity conferred on a body by its being ordered into a system is accounted for by the correspondence or cooperation of the various monads; but this consists in an agreement in relations only. The law of the series in the dominant monad constitutes the reason for all the various stages of the body of a living creature being embodiments of the same creature, thus accounting for the living creature's being indestructible. This gives a unity in the sense of threading the various body-stages through time, but it does not produce a real union of the constituents making up a substance's body at any instant.[3]

In my view, however, the corporeal substance in Leibniz is not an embodiment of a spiritual principle. A substance is not an embodiment of a soul or a substantial form or something analogous, but rather a hylomorphic unity, much as in Aristotle. In Leibniz, I will suggest, this substance's unity is provided by an operative principle that governs the infinite structure of nested beings that constitutes the individual. Thus, rather than using the term "embodiment" to describe Leibniz's account of living beings, I will be using the term "nestedness."

---

[3] Richard Arthur, "Reply to Ohad Nachtomy," *The Leibniz Review* 24 (2014): 131–133.

Let me begin with a very rough sketch of Leibniz's view of living beings. Since his early writings, as for instance in *Theory of Concrete Motion* (1670–1671), Leibniz expounds the doctrine that in every bit of matter there are worlds within worlds, to infinity. In the context of this early work, the doctrine appears as a consequence of the idea that matter is divisible to infinity. As he writes, "any atom will be of infinite species, like a sort of world, and there will be worlds within worlds to infinity."[4] A similar view appears several years later in Leibniz's notes from Paris (1676). Here, he writes that every part of the world, regardless of how small, "contains an infinity of creatures," which is itself a kind of "world."[5] Similarly, in the dialogue *Pacidius to Philalethes*, composed in November 1676 (on his way back from Paris to Germany via the Netherlands) Leibniz notes: "in any grain of sand whatever there is not just a world, but an infinity of worlds."[6] On this trip, Leibniz was happy to find his "worlds within worlds" thesis partially confirmed through the microscope's observations of Swammerdam and Leeuwenhoek, whom he visited en route.[7]

In *Primary Truths* (1689–1690), Leibniz notes once again that "every particle of the universe contains a world of an infinity of creatures."[8] As Smith has observed, it is in his correspondence with Arnauld (1686–87) that Leibniz first explicitly identifies these creatures with living entities. Leibniz writes:

> [A]nd since matter is infinitely divisible, no portion can be designated so small that it does not contain animated bodies, or at least bodies endowed with a primitive Entelechy or (if you permit

---

4 A 6.2 N40; LLC, 338–339.
5 A 6.3, 474
6 A 6.3, 555 /LLC, 211.
7 See Arthur, *Leibniz* (Polity, 2014), 69.
8 A 6.4, 1647–1648. In a note on a letter of Michelangelo Fardella from 1690, we find again Leibniz's commitment to the worlds within worlds ad infinitum (AG, 105).

me to use the concept of life so generally), with a vital principle; in short, corporeal substances, of all of which one can say in general that they are.[9]

In a letter to Arnauld from November 28, 1686, Leibniz goes on to suggest that life (or being animate) is the very mark of a true corporeal substance: "I cannot say precisely whether there are true corporeal substances other than those that are animated, but souls at least serve to give us some knowledge of others by analogy."[10] Leibniz holds here that animate things are the only corporeal substances that we know. In the same letter, Leibniz clarifies the reason for this. Given that matter is divisible to infinity, only animate beings could provide a source of true unity:

> For the continuum is not merely divided to infinity, but every part of matter is actually divided into other parts as different among themselves as the aforementioned diamonds. And since we can always go on in this way, we could never reach anything about which we could say, here is truly a being, unless we found animated machines whose soul or substantial form produced a substantial unity independent of the external union arising from contact.[11]

The only things that can be regarded as true beings are animate machines whose soul or substantial form produces substantial unity. As a consequence, they are the only limit, so to speak, to the infinite divisibility of matter. Unlike Pascal, for example, who observes that infinite divisibility lurks in living things as well (see the example of a mite in his *Pensées*[12]), Leibniz considers living beings as the ultimate

---

9 GP II, 118.
10 AG, 79.
11 AG, 80.
12 Blaise Pascal, *Pensées*, in *Œuvres Complètes*, ed. Louis Lafuma (Paris: Éditions du Seuil, 1963), 199.

unities. These unities are indivisible and indestructible because they have an intrinsic source of action and, in this way, they are not susceptible to the divisibility of matter.

In these passages, Leibniz uses the notion of life as a mark of being and of true substantial unity. The notion of life is now connected with the idea of the infinity of beings that Leibniz had previously expounded, so that living beings are found everywhere (or "in the least part of matter").[13] At the same time, living beings form true unities that constitute a limit to the infinite divisibility of matter.

In *New System of Nature* (1695), Leibniz is no longer using infinity merely to describe nature as worlds within worlds to infinity; rather, infinity now becomes one of the defining marks of living beings. Leibniz draws the distinction between living and nonliving things as one between natural and artificial machines. He articulates his position against Descartes's view that living things are nothing but subtle machines, akin to artificial ones though more subtle and complex. Leibniz argues that the difference is not merely of degree. Rather, there is a categorical difference between natural and artificial machines: natural machines differ from artificial machines in being machines to the least of their parts, so that they are machines within machines ad infinitum. As he writes in *New System of Nature*,

> I believe that [Descartes'] conception [in which the difference between natural machines and artificial ones is merely one of degree] does not give us a sufficiently just and worthy idea of nature, and that my system alone allows us to understand the true and immense distance between the least production and mechanisms of divine wisdom and the greatest masterpieces that derive from the craft of a limited mind; this difference is not simply a difference of degree, but a difference in kind. We must then know that the machines of

---

13 GP II, 111–129.

nature have a truly infinite number of organs, and are so well supplied and so resistant to all accidents that it is not possible to destroy them. A natural machine still remains a machine in its least parts, and moreover, it always remains the same machine that it has been, being merely transformed through the different enfolding it undergoes, sometimes extended, sometimes compressed and concentrated as it were, where it is thought to have perished.[14]

In *On Body and Force, Against the Cartesians* (May, 1702), he adds that

> ... a natural machine has the great advantage over an artificial machine, that, displaying the mark of an infinite creator, it is made up of an infinity of entangled organs. And thus, a natural machine can never be absolutely destroyed just as it can never absolutely begin, but it only decreases or increases, enfolds or unfolds, always preserving in itself some degree of life [*vitalitas*] or, if you prefer, some degree of primitive activity [*actuositas*].[15]

By virtue of being a divine creation rather than a result of human production, a natural machine is both infinite (thus presenting the mark of its creator) and an individual, indestructible entity, which remains one and the same as long as it acts.[16] Unlike an artificial machine, a natural machine cannot be composed or decomposed. It is created as one functional unit, however complex it may be. As a consequence, it remains the same as long as it lives—which is forever, unless annihilated by God. Hence, a natural machine always preserves a certain degree of life or primitive activity.

---

14 AG, 142.
15 AG, 253.
16 See *Monadology* § 64, AG, 221.

As Arthur notes, "it is the internal law governing the unfolding of the states of a substance that accounts for it having a genuine unity, as opposed to the accidental unity of an artificial machine."[17] What gives a natural machine—a machine with an infinitely complex structure—its unity is an internal law of production. This internal law functions as a program for self-organization and self-regulation, so that each Leibnizian substance is causally self-sufficient. According to Leibniz, a living being is infinite both in the sense of being ever active and in its nested structure, ad infinitum.[18] The infinity and unity of living beings is intrinsically related, of course, to their being "divine machines," created by an infinite creator.[19]

In *Principles of Nature and Grace, Based on Reason* (1714) § 4, Leibniz writes: "Each monad, together with a particular body, makes up a living substance. Thus, there is not only life everywhere, joined to limbs or organs, but there are also infinite degrees of life in the monads, some dominating more or less over others."[20] The infinite degrees of life correspond to the hierarchy of machines nested within machines to infinity. This turns out to be the distinctive feature of natural machines and ultimately of Leibniz's definition of living beings after 1695.

3. Nested Individuality: Leibniz's Suppositions

Let me now turn to present Leibniz's model of nested individuality—a model that seeks to capture the structure of each living being through the following suppositions:

---

17 Arthur, *Leibniz* (Polity, 2014), 73.
18 See Leibniz's letter to Lady Masham from 1704 (GP III, 356).
19 See also notes on Cordemoy (1685), A 6.4, 1801/LLC, 283; *On Nature Itself*, AG, 158–159 and Leibniz's Fifth Letter to Clarke, arts. 115, 116, in AG, 344–345.
20 AG, 280. See letter to Des Bosses, 29 May, 1716, in Brandon Look and Donald Rutherford (tr. and ed.), *The Leibniz-Des Bosses Correspondence* (New Haven, CT: Yale University Press, 2007), 377.

1. Echoing Aristotle, for Leibniz, an individual substance is a hylomorphic union, so that an active entelechy (or substantial form) animates and organizes receptive matter.[21]
2. An individual substance requires true unity—both in the sense of the unity of form and matter and in the sense of the unity of all its constituents.[22]
3. Organic, complete living beings such as humans, animals, and plants serve Leibniz as paradigmatic examples of substantial unities;[23] they are conceptually distinct from aggregates, such as rocks, lakes, flocks, and armies, which lack such natural and substantial unity.[24]
4. While they are the paradigmatic examples of substantial unity, animals and plants are seen as individual substances that include other such animals (or organic unities) nested within them.[25]
5. The animals nested within an individual substance are themselves complete individuals that have a similar nested structure; they are not mere "parts of the substance but are immediately required for it."[26]

---

21 AG, 175.
22 See Letter 17 to Arnauld, 8 December, 1686 (AG, 77–81).
23 Leibniz's paradigmatic examples include, of course, God, the I, the Ego, and the Soul, but I think he makes it clear enough that the entities denoted by these expressions are seen as the dominating, active aspects of organic beings and not as detached or disembodied entities. As an example, see the following passage from 1691: "L'âme est l'entéléchie première d'un corps naturel ayant la vie en puissance, c'est-à-dire doté d'organes" (*De l'Âme*, II, 1, 412 a 27–29, cited from Fichant's "Leibniz et les machines de la nature," *Studia Leibnitiana* 35, no. 1 (2003): 1–28).
24 See GP VI, 550; Letter to Arnauld, (AG, 80); adn GP VI, 553–554: "... animals are never formed out of nonorganic mass." See also Catherine Wilson's "De Ipsa Natura," *Studia Leibnitiana* 19, no. 2 (1987): 148–172, on p.169.
25 e.g. "... the machines of nature being machines to the least of their parts are indestructible, due to the envelopment of a small machine in a larger one, to infinity" (GP VI, 543); *Monadology* § 67–70 cited above. "I hold that it is enough for the machine of things to have been constructed with such wisdom that, through its very development, those very wonders come to pass, chiefly (as I believe) by means of organisms unfolding themselves through some predetermined plan" ("On Nature Itself," AG, 156). "My view is that every substance whatsoever is a kingdom within kingdom, but one in precise harmony [*conspirans*] with everything else" ("Comments on Spinoza's Philosophy," AG, 280, *c.* 1706).
26 See Letters to de Volder, in AG, 177.

6. The structure of nested individual substances involves a hierarchy of dominating and dominated substances. Such a hierarchy is not accidental but rather typifies the nature of living individuals.
7. The unity of nested individuals is granted by virtue of the activity of a single and dominant entelechy.[27]

Taken together, these suppositions suggest a fascinating picture of individuality manifested in the organic world. Also fascinating, though perhaps less perspicuous, is the claim that the unity of all these nested organisms is grounded in a certain notion of activity. In what follows, I would like to examine the sort of unity and nestedness Leibniz is proposing in his model of individuality by looking at the precise meaning that he ascribes to the notions of nestedness and unity.

In considering the unity of various components, we are inclined to think of material parts being held together as one cohesive spatiotemporal unit. As distinct from the aggregate model, in which unity is relational and external, we tend to seek something that will hold all the constituents together.[28] However compelling this picture may be, it is quite clear that this is *not* the kind of unity Leibniz has in mind. He clearly states that the substances that make up an animal are not *parts* of the substance but rather are required components of the necessary structure of a composite substance. Rather, Leibniz understands the unity of a corporeal substance as a unity of *agency* that derives from the single entelechy animating and organizing the organic body it dominates. Since the organic body of a corporeal substance consists of the individual substances nested within it, this structure seems to imply a hierarchy of activating and activated individuals (active and passive), nested one within the other. So the unity in question does not result

---

27 "[I]t seems probable that animals . . . and similarly plants . . . are not composed of body alone, but also of soul, by which the animal or plant, the single indivisible substance, the permanent subject of its actions, is controlled" (Notes on some comments by M. A. Fardella, AG, 104).
28 We may be inclined to think for example of the model of a molecule in which the atoms are bound together by covalent relations.

from the cohesiveness of parts, but is rather a unity of agency deriving from the entelechy activity. Leibniz's stratified model of the individual requires the domination of an entelechy over the whole organic body and the activation of subordinate entelechies at every level. By definition, *each* substance has such a structure. Leibniz writes:

> What I call a complete monad or individual substance [*substantia singularis*] is not so much the soul as it is the animal itself, or something analogous to it, endowed with a soul or form and organic body.[29]

Let us now examine some implications of Leibniz's model of nested individuals. Leibniz's view is strongly related to views of *emboîtement* endorsed by theorists such as Malebranche and illustrated by the microscope-based observations of Marcello Malpighi (1628–1694) and Antony van Leeuwenhoek (1632–1723).[30] At the same time, Leibniz's model of corporeal substance marks a radical break from the traditional formula of "one body, one substance." Aristotle characterized the individual substance from a logical and grammatical perspective by defining it as that which is "neither said of a subject nor in a subject"[31] and claimed that "no substance is composed of substances."[32] At first glance, Leibniz's idea that an individual consists of other individuals appears to be in tension with Aristotle's tenet that an individual cannot "be said of another" or be in another. Furthermore, Leibniz claims that individuals function as necessary constituents of other

---

29 Letter to Bernoulli 20/30 September 1698 AG, 167–168.
30 It seems to me that what Andrew Pyle says of Malebranche can also be said of Leibniz: "Experimental biology (Leeuwenhoek's microorganisms, Malpighi's chicks, Swammerdam's butterflies) are used to illustrate the theory (of *emboîtement*) rather than to confirm it." See *Malebranche* (London and New York: Routledge, 2003), 172.
31 "A substance—that which is called a substance most strictly, primarily, and most of all—is that which is neither said of a subject nor in a subject (e.g., the individual man or the individual horse")" (*Categories* 5 2a 11–13). See also Strawson's discussion of this point in his *Individuals* (London: Routledge, 1959), ch. 5 and 6.
32 *Metaphysics* 1041a5.

individuals. Therefore it is all the more curious that Leibniz accepts Aristotle's criterion of individuality. He characterizes an individual substance as "not attributed of any other."[33] "A singular substance," he adds, "is that which cannot be said of another thing. If a substance is said of another thing, they would be the same."[34]

That Leibniz finds his view compatible with Aristotle's criterion suggests that he, like Aristotle, employs a *logical* rather than a physical (or material) interpretation of what it means for an individual to be *in* another or to be nested within another. In turn, this suggests a nonphysical interpretation of Leibniz's notion of "nestedness."[35] In developing this point, I will suggest that, for Leibniz, "nested" does not primarily mean being literally and physically within another individual but (more essentially) being activated and functionally organized by another dominating individual.

Aristotle's formulation of the criterion of individuality remains influential even to this day. It not only provides an articulation of our common intuitions about individuals, but also underlies some of our scientific and logical notions of individuality. For example, in first-order logic, individuals are defined as saturated while predicates are to be completed by instantiating individuals. Predicates and individuals are asymmetric, such that an individual cannot take the predicate's place in propositions. In other words, individuals cannot be instantiated; rather, individuals are always unique and universal predicates are instantiated in them. Thus, while Fa and Fb are well-defined formulas, ab, F and GF are not. There is a structural asymmetry in first-order logic between the notion of an individual and that of a predicate, which corresponds to the Aristotelian criteria that an individual cannot be said

---

33 GP IV, 432; L, 307.

34 Cited and translated from G. W. Leibniz, *Recherches générales sur l'analyse des notions et des vérités*, ed. J. B. Rauzy (Paris: Presses Universitaires de France, 1998), 452. See also p. 384.

35 One appealing approach is to view Aristotle's sense of "being in another" as a logical one, so that it primarily pertains to the inclusion of the predicate in the subject. It seems fairly clear that this is precisely the way Leibniz understood the Aristotelian criterion, as his *in esse* principle testifies.

of (or be in) other individuals. Similarly, consider the current notion of biological individuality. We intuitively tend to identify biological individuals as organisms and thereby to exclude groups or parts of organisms from the definition of complete individuals. Both the extreme cases of genes and groups, which have been proposed as biological individuals (and as units of selection), illustrate a common and intuitive reluctance to accept them as individuals. It seems odd to accept a group such as a beehive as an individual precisely because it consists of many organisms even though they can only multiply as a group. It also seems odd for us to accept genes as complete individuals because they are not independent of the organism (or even of the whole genome) in which they are embedded. These two limiting cases are indicative of our intuitive reluctance to predicate individuals of other individuals and to see individuals as nested within others.

For Leibniz, as for Aristotle, individual substances are hylomorphic units characterized by an inherent entelechy or principle of activity, the *form*, determining a principle of passivity, the matter. At the same time, Leibniz holds that each component of an organism, while included in its organic body and subordinated to the dominant entelechy of its substance, has its own entelechy.[36] Thus for Leibniz, as opposed to Aristotle, matter is not a merely passive agent activated by an entelechy. Rather, there are many other entelechies nested within it as well.

The idea that an entelechy activates another entelechy seems initially surprising in the Leibnizian context. Entelechies have their own active force and act spontaneously, so it would seem that the subordinate entelechies, being themselves sources of activity, need not be activated from without. Furthermore, a constituent of an organism and the organism in which it is nested are not only compatible with one another, but are also necessary conditions of their very individuality. For example, an organ is not an accidental part of

---

36 *Monadology* § 70, AG, 222.

a human being; rather, it is a required constituent in the strong sense that it, and only it, completes the individuality of a certain human. Likewise, it is not a mere physical part of the body but a functional constituent of the whole organic unit. Unlike some parasitic worms or viruses that can also exist externally to a certain individual (and vice versa), the nested structure in Leibniz's model is rather constitutive of individuals.[37]

The hierarchical structure indicates that individuals are partly characterized through their place in the hierarchy of individuals. Since the nested hierarchy is not accidental, but rather essential, to the individuality of each individual, the relations each one has with the others are constitutive of it. As I argue elsewhere,[38] these relations are constitutive of the individuals already at the conceptual level of possibility. This implies that the place in the structure constituted by the hierarchy of other individuals partly determines the very individuality and uniqueness of a substance. Indeed, this is precisely what the terminology of nested individuals is meant to flesh out.

4. Analysis and Interpretation: Physical and Metaphysical Considerations

As we have seen, for Leibniz, individuals *not only contain* other individuals as a body of an animal may contain worms or germs but also typically *consist of* other individuals—individuals that are organized in a hierarchical structure and are nested one within another to infinity.[39] As we have also observed, Leibniz's notion of nested individuality

---

[37] As Hidé Ishiguro puts this point: "If x is a constituent of body y, then it is necessarily a constituent of y" (Ishiguro, "Is There a Conflict between the Logical and the Metaphysical Notion of Unity in Leibniz?" *The Monist* 81, no. 4 [1998], 540).

[38] Ohad Nachtomy, *Possibility, Agency, and Individuality in Leibniz's Metaphysics* (Dordecht, The Netherlands: Springer, 2007), chapters 3 and 4.

[39] For the historical background of this notion in relation to life, see Duchesneau, *Les modèles du vivant de Descartes à Leibniz* (Paris: Vrin, 1998), where the chapter on Malpighi is especially

appears in his early writings,[40] but develops in later writings, and especially those that follow the *New System of Nature*, where the notion of a natural machine is introduced. Leibniz expounds the main features of his view of nestedness in the following passage:

> ... Thus we see that each living body has a dominant entelechy, which in the animal is the soul; but the limbs of this living body are full of other living beings, plants, animals, each of which also has its entelechy or its dominant soul.[41]

My interpretation of Leibniz's notion of nestedness differs from the most widely accepted (and perhaps most natural) reading. According to the latter, Leibniz's notion of *emboîtement* applies to the bodies of individual substance but not to the individual substances themselves.[42] For example, François Duchesneau writes:

> In my view, the notion of *emboîtement* does not apply to individuals according to Leibniz. The organic bodies are presented as machines

---

pertinent; see also Pyle, *Malebranche*, chapter 7; Catherine Wilson, *The Invisible World* (Princeton, NJ: Princeton University Press, 1995), chapter 4.

40 In his Paris Notes, Leibniz writes: " ... any part of matter, however small, contains an infinity of creatures (i.e., a world)" (A 478–479; DSR 33). For Leibniz's early views on this point, see Beeley, "Mathematics and Nature in Leibniz's Early Philosophy" in *The Young Leibniz*, ed. S. Brown (Boston: Springer/Kluwer, 1999), 123–145; and Christia Mercer, *Leibniz's Metaphysics: Its Origin and Development* (Cambridge, UK: Cambridge University Press, 2001), chapter 7. Mercer argues "that during the winter of 1670–71 Leibniz invented panorganism, according to which the passive principle in a corporeal substance is constituted of a vast collection of corporeal substances, each of which is itself a corporeal substance whose passive principle is so constituted, and so in *infinitum*" (Mercer, *Leibniz's Metaphysics: Its Origins and Development* [New York, Cambridge University Press, 2001], 256). The main point in this formulation, which was later modified, has to do with the word "collection." Thus, in the model of the nested individual, the passive principle or the body of a corporeal substance is not a collection but an organized structure of corporeal substances which are organized by the substance in which they are nested and at the same time organize the corporeal substances nested in them.

41 *Monadology* § 70, AG, 222. See also letter to Lady Masham (1704), GP III, 356.

42 See Justin Smith, "On the Fate of Composite Substances After 1704," in *Studia Leibnitiana* 31, 1 (1999): 1–7; Justin Smith, "Leibniz, Microscopy, and the Metaphysics of Composite Substance," PhD diss., Columbia University.

of nature, developed to infinity; but these bodies form composed substances only to the extent where they imply a monad of which they constitute the expression in the order of phenomena (in correspondence).

According to Duchesneau, the notion of nestedness is thoroughly mechanistic.[43] This implies that individuals are not nested, and the term "nestedness" can be applied only to bodies or to machines that are not individual substances but rather aggregates. I would suggest, however, that the notion of nestedness is not primarily mechanistic. Rather, in my view, Leibniz's notion of nestedness applies to the metaphysical relations of activation and domination that organize the functions of the nested (and less active) constituents within the same organism. This implies that the relation of nestedness (which turns out to be closely related to domination) is best understood not in physical terms, but rather in metaphysical ones. This suggestion is consistent with viewing the nesting relation as holding between individual substances, so that they can be seen as nested in and/or nesting other individuals.

For Leibniz, the mechanical account of nature (based on the notions of shock, impact, and efficient causation among bodies) does not exclude a metaphysical one (based on those of final causation, activation, and domination). Thus I do not deny the mechanistic account but I would like to stress that the notion of nestedness cannot be properly understood in mechanistic terms alone.[44] It is especially important to keep in mind that Leibniz's position on nestedness does not apply to every physical body or to every machine,

---

43 See also Duchesneau, *Les modèles du vivant de Descartes à Leibniz*, 326–329, 339–343 and his *La physiologie des Lumières* (The Hague: Martinus Nijhoff/Kluwer, 1982), 76–78. As evidence, Duchesneau cites (among others) the following passage: "Et nihil aliud organismus viventium est quam divinior mechanismus in infinitum subtilitate procedens" (Leibniz's fifth letter to Clarke, sections 115 and 116, C, 16, cited from Duchesneau, *Les modèles du vivant de Descartes à Leibniz*, 339); GP VII, 417–418.

44 I thank Justin Smith for clarifying this point.

but only to organic bodies or natural machines. This is especially significant in light of the fact that Leibniz identifies natural machines as corporeal substances that have true unities. As he writes, "I only count machines of nature, which have souls (*âmes*) or something analogous, as corporeal substances; for otherwise there wouldn't be any true unity."[45]

5. The Unity of Nested Individuals

Given Leibniz's commitment to the intrinsic connection between individuality, being, and unity, the structured ensemble of nested individuals must have substantial unity;[46] otherwise, it would not differ from mere aggregates. This implies that an ensemble of nested individuals must be united as *one* single substance, as Leibniz states in a letter to De Volder:

> Although I said that a substance, even though corporeal, contains an infinity of machines, at the same time, I think that we must add that a substance constitutes one machine composed of them, and furthermore, that it is activated by *one* entelechy, without which there would be no principle of true unity in it.[47]

Therefore, a corporeal substance, which contains infinitely many machines, is activated by one entelechy or a single source of action, so that it has a single source of unity. As distinct from artificial machines, natural machines entail infinitely many such machines.

---

45 Letter to Jaquelot, 22 March, 1703, GP III, 457.
46 "... since I am truly a single indivisible substance, unresolvable into any others, the permanent and constant subject of my actions and passions, it is necessary that there be a persisting individual substance over and above the organic body" (Comments on Fardella, A VI 4, 1969; AG, 103).
47 AG, 175, my italics. See also GP II, 252; GP VII, 502 and C, 13–14. In contrast to Duchesneau's view, it seems clear here that what is activated by a single entelechy must itself be a single substance and not a mere single body or a machine.

But unlike aggregates, they form a single unit that has true unity by virtue of its unique source of activity. The very distinction between artificial machines and natural machines[48] indicates that Leibniz sees an intrinsic connection between possessing a natural, organic unity, and possessing a nested structure to infinity. Nonorganic machines do not have a nested structure that develops to infinity.

In addition, the question of unity has to be considered in light of additional constraints, namely, causal independence as well as conceptual relations among *all* individual substances. But it seems that these constraints render Leibniz's notion of nestedness even more puzzling. Though all nested individuals are causally independent of one another, they are all supposed to form one organic unit, such as a fish or a human. In the passage cited above, Leibniz suggests that the unity of a composed substance derives from its single source of activity (i.e., its dominant entelechy). A single and dominating entelechy is supposed to activate and unify the whole hierarchy of causally independent individuals nested within it.

Since Leibniz accounts for the notion of unity in terms of activity, another question arises: What is the precise sense of such activation in a Leibnizian world characterized by causal independence? In the remainder of this paper I will suggest that this sort of activity should be understood primarily in terms of the functional organization of the nested individuals that constitute the organic body of an individual. I will also suggest that it is this organizing activity that Leibniz has in mind when he speaks of the domination of one monad or entelechy over those subordinated to it. Organization and domination are to be understood in terms of functional hierarchy between nested individuals. This will also help account for the differences between organic substances and inorganic aggregates.

---

[48] GP III, 356.

6. Various Senses of Nestedness

We have seen that the organic body of an individual substance is a stratified structure of subordinate substances governed by a dominating one. Let us examine more carefully the kind of nestedness Leibniz has in mind. Given the terms "nested in" or "*emboîté dans*," we tend to think primarily of spatial nestedness as analogous to the way a set of Russian dolls fit together, one within the other. In fact, Leibniz himself invites this interpretation when he uses the imagery of Harlequin in *New Essays*.[49] Let me call this the physical model of nestedness. For x to be nested in y in this model, spatial relations must exist between them such that x is smaller than y and embodied within y. Along with the physical model of nestedness, we can suggest a logical one, which is clearly articulated in Leibniz's complete concept of an individual. For x to be nested in y in this model, x must be logically entailed by y. Here, spatial relations need not play a role. A variant of the logical model would stress semantic implications rather than strictly deductive relations of entailment. For example, we could say that the notion of a street is semantically included in the notion of a town, houses in that of a street, walls in that of a house, etc.

In addition, we should consider the "expression and representation" model of nestetednes, articulated by Duchesneau and evident in his comments cited above.[50] While the "expression relation" clearly plays an important role in Leibniz's notion of corporeal substance, it is too weak for my purposes. As we have seen, Duchesneau denies that nestedness applies to individuals. According to him, the feature of being embodied applies only to bodies in the order of phenomena. While nested individuals indeed express or represent one another, I think

---

49 Book II, ch. VII, §42; GP V, 309.

50 The organic bodies are presented as machines of nature, developed to infinity; but these bodies form composed substances only to the extent that they imply a monad of which they constitute the expression in the order of phenomena. Certainly, the dominant monad of an animal envelopes in its expression the specific expressions of many other monads (in correspondence).

that the relation of expression is not sufficient to account for their unity. Similarly, I do not deny the interpretation of spatial nestedness in the logical or semantic interpretations of nestedness. Rather, I suggest that these interpretations are simply not exhaustive of the primary meaning of nestedness, which Leibniz employs in the context of living individuals. Evidently, the claim that "one individual is *in* another" may have a number of interpretations. For example, one often speaks of logical inclusion as well as physical inclusion. Yet, I think that the most important feature of Leibniz's primary model of nestedness is quite different from both the logical and physical interpretations. An important clue to this question is Leibniz's endorsement of Aristotle's criterion of individuality, namely, that an individual is not *said of* and is not *in* another, while at the same time espousing the view that a structure of nested individuals is constitutive of organic or living beings. I suggest that the primary meaning of nestedness involves degrees of activity versus passivity, as well as functional hierarchy and organization, which are typical of living beings.

7. Activation, Domination, and Functional Organization

This point refers us back to Leibniz's (noncausal) notion of activity. Let us recall that each substance activates all the other individuals that constitute its organic body while each individual also activates itself.[51] Since Leibnizian individuals are causally independent of one another, however, the notion of activation has to be explained in noncausal terms (that is, not through efficient causation). This point clearly applies to the domination/subordination relation. I believe that the key concept in glossing this notion of activation is that of functional organization. The notion of functional organization is nicely exemplified in living

---

51 e.g., see WFN, 138.

things, which partly explains why Leibniz employs organic units or animals as his favorite examples of individual substances.[52]

We can further clarify Leibniz's sense of nestedness by reflecting on why, according to him, the nested structure, ad infinitum, is what distinguishes natural machines from artificial ones, which, like aggregates, do not possess true unity. Animals and plants vividly exemplify a functional hierarchy, which is consistent with Leibniz's endorsement of final causality in describing their activities. It is also consistent with Aristotle's notion of a hierarchy of ends. For example, an acorn develops into a mature oak through the activation of matter by its entelechy in accordance with the acorn's final form. In such organic examples, the various functions of the constituents comprising the animal or plant may be seen as serving the *telos* and executing its natural program of development. In turn, the tree's *telos* can be viewed as a program of action consisting of numerous subprograms of action. Thus all the substructures that make up an oak tree—branches, leaves, cells, subcellular constituents, etc.—are organized by a single program and directed toward a single end. At the same time, each constituent is fully organized (and in turn organizes its sub-structures) towards the fulfillment of its function. A leaf is a unit whose function is to produce sugar, which, in turn, provides energy for the tree's growth. The leaf itself may be seen as a fully organized unit whose constituents are organized and activated in order to perform their functions (e.g., one of chlorophyll's functions is to provide color), and thereby to contribute to the function of the leaf. In turn, their constituents, such as cells, are themselves entirely organized towards the performance of their functions in the overall program of the leaf, which in turn is organized towards the performance of its function in the program of the oak. This model of a functional hierarchy with a complete individual's program informing an unending series of constituents can be taken to exemplify Leibniz's

---

[52] e.g., see GP VI, 543.

notion of nestedness. The main point is that the primary sense of nestedness is functional, rather than physical embodiment, which is why it is applicable to the domain of the living described in metaphysical terms. Thus the tree's leaf is not physically in the tree's branch or trunk; but it is nested in it.

The idea of a stratified structure of organisms is intrinsically connected to another feature of Leibniz's notion of individuality.[53] The inherent hierarchy of nested individuals is ordered by degrees of complexity that correspond to varying levels of activity. Although individuals are nested, and hence dominated by other individuals, they are nevertheless regarded as complete individuals, rather than as incomplete parts of individuals. The notion of levels of individuality does not imply that a certain individual is more or less of an individual. The question of whether x is an individual or not is decided by considering whether x has its own source of activity (which is also its source of unity and identity over time) as well as a unique complete concept. The notion of "levels of activity" implies that an individual may be more or less active and, correspondingly, more or less passive (that is, more or less dominating in the hierarchy). The degree of activity corresponds to the place the individual occupies in the hierarchy of nested individuals. Since an individual is defined by means of an inner source of activity, it can be nested within a more active individual (i.e., dominated by such an individual) without eliminating its own individuality or its unity and identity. In turn, it may also dominate other individuals nested within it. It is to be primarily understood in terms of degrees of activity (or domination and organization). The expression "degrees of activity" is only shorthand for the relative proportions of activity and passivity or the relation between active and passive forces.

Note that the essential role of activity in individuals in general, and that of a rule of activity (which prescribes a program of action) in particular, is compatible with this interpretation. Given the notion of

---

53 See Nachtomy, *Possibility, Agency, and Individuality in Leibniz's Metaphysics*, chapter 2.

activation as functional organization, it is easier to see why Leibniz held that the structure of nested individuals, which is based on activity, proceeds to infinity. Furthermore, this also explains why Leibniz thinks that artificial machines, being devoid of a single source of activity, do not possess such a structure. Given this sense of nestedness, we can also see how Leibniz reconciles his view of nested individuals and Aristotle's criteria of individuality. A nested individual may be a constituent of the dominant nesting individual. However, it is not a property or a predicate of it. A nested individual is not a universal property instantiated in many individuals, or a predicate instantiated in many individual concepts; rather, it is a unique and complete being whose unique "place" plays a constitutive role in the program of the nesting individual. Since a nested individual is not a predicate of an individual concept or a property of a real individual, it cannot be predicated on the nesting individual. It is *in* the nesting individual but not primarily in a physical sense. On the reading I advance here, the Leibnizian sense of nestedness has more to do with conceptual and functional relations than with physical and efficient causal ones. This interpretation of nestedness is in contrast to a purely mechanistic interpretation. According to this interpretation, there is an intrinsic relation between nestedness to infinity and the other characteristics of Leibnizian individuals such as being, unity, indestructibility, and life.[54] Let us not forget that, according to Leibniz, it is the nested structure to infinity that distinguishes natural machines from artificial ones—a point that is intrinsically related to the infinite nature of a complete concept of an individual.

8. Conclusion

Throughout this chapter, I used the term "nestedness" to characterize the unique feature of a Leibnizian individual substance as

---

54 Leibniz makes such explicit connections in GP VI, 543.

embedding (or involving) infinitely many other substances as essential components. As noted in my opening remarks, I do not concur with interpretations taking the Leibnizian notion of living beings to be adequately described by the term "embodiment," as I do not take Leibniz's account to be that of a substance that is embodied (i.e., that is "in" an organic or corporal body). On my view, a corporeal substance is not an embodiment of a spiritual principle; rather, the whole structure (described above) of organizing and organized substances, according to a law of order, *is* the substance—a substance whose stages are not embodiments of anything but are necessary constituents of the substance itself. The body may be considered in abstraction from the substance or the whole animal, as a corpse may be, but the substance itself is, much as in Aristotle, a hylomorphic unity rather than an embodiment of a soul or a substantial form or something analogous.

I have thus tried to substantiate the following claims: (1) An individual substance has a nested structure; (2) the unity of such a structure is given by a single (dominating) source of activity, which stresses the significance of Leibniz's notion of agency; (3) both the notion of nestedness and that of unity are to be understood primarily according to the model of active functional organization and domination rather than according to the model of physical inclusion or the logical model of entailment; (4) the notions of activation and domination are to be interpreted in terms of functional organization, explicitly related to the notion of final cause; and (5) the notion of organizing and uniting activity (which Leibniz calls domination) is interestingly related to the notions of being and life, such that aggregates and mere possibilities are neither alive nor fully exist. This is consistent with the essential role Leibniz ascribes both to passivity and to activity. Possibilities, for example, are organized but are not active while aggregates are not organized according to a single internal principle and therefore are not internally united. Thus, aggregates are seen as well-founded phenomena since they lack essential unity.

Abbreviations

A = Leibniz, G. W. *Sämtliche Schriften und Briefe*. Berlin: Edition of the German Academy of Sciences, 1923. Cited by series volume and page.

AG = Leibniz, G. W. *Philosophical Essays*. Edited and translated by R. Ariew and D. Garber. Indianapolis: Hackett, 1989.

C = Liebniz, G. W. *Opuscules et Fragments Inédits de Leibniz*. Edited by L. Couturat. Hildesheim, Germany: Olms, 1961.

DSR = Leibniz, G. W. *De Summa Rerum: Metaphysical Papers 1675–1676*. Edited and translated by G. H. R. Parkinson. New Haven, CT: Yale University Press, 1992.

GP = Leibniz, G. W. *Die Philosophichen Schriften von Leibniz*. Edited by C. I. Gerhardt. 7 vols. Berlin: [Weidmann, 1875–1890] Olms, 1978.

L = Leibniz, G. W. *Gottfried Wilhelm Leibniz: Philosophical Papers and Letters*. Translated by L. E. Loemker, 2d ed. Dordrecht, The Netherlands: Reidel, 1969.

LLC = Leibniz, G. W. *The Labyrinth of the Continuum: Writings on the Continuum Problem, 1672–1686*. Translated by R. T. W. Arthur. New Haven, CT: Yale University Press, 2001.

WFN = Leibniz, G. W. *Leibniz's "New System" and Associated Contemporary Texts*. Translated by R. S. Woolhouse and R. Francks. Oxford: Oxford University Press, 1997.

CHAPTER NINE

Descartes and Spinoza

TWO APPROACHES TO EMBODIMENT

Alison Peterman

1. Introduction

Descartes[1] (1596–1650) and Spinoza (1632–1677) each gave us interesting and influential approaches to answering what I'll call "embodiment question": what is the relationship between a mind and its body—the one that it seems to inhabit, feel, control or otherwise be uniquely involved with?[2] In Spinoza we find (at least) three different answers, the ingenuity of all of which is attested to by their long reception in the philosophical tradition. Descartes was an important influence on Spinoza, but on many others, too, ushering in the era of the "mind-body

---

[1] I am grateful to Colin Chamberlain, Michael Della Rocca, Keota Fields, Kristin Primus, and Alison Simmons for discussion, and also to the other contributors to this volume.

[2] This question is broader than one than one about the *constitutive* or *essential* relationship between a mind and its body.

problem" in the form that many philosophers still grapple with. Here, I'll by no means attempt a comprehensive treatment of their contributions. Instead I will try to uncover an unnoticed similarity between the two, and apply it to understanding the coherence of Spinoza's account of embodiment. I'll argue that Descartes and Spinoza both approach the embodiment question in two different ways: one approach starts with some metaphysical commitments about the kinds of entities, properties, and interactions there are in the world, and the other starts by attending to the experience of an embodied subject. The "third-personal" or "metaphysical" approach and the "first-personal" approach lead each to two different conclusions, which neither Descartes nor Spinoza is able fully to merge. In Section 2 I'll show this for Descartes, who makes the tension between these approaches relatively explicit. Then I'll go on in Section 3 to show this for Spinoza, who does not.

2. Descartes

As the previous contributions to this volume attest, up until around the time of Descartes, the animate soul plays an ineliminable role in accounts of embodiment. By "soul" I mean a single entity that performs (at least) three different kinds of functions: it is responsible for rational thought; for informing a body or actualizing it as an organic body; and for explaining motion, sensation, and other organic functions of living creatures. It is an egregious but useful oversimplification to say that Descartes is responsible for popularizing a philosophical research program that eschews appeals to this kind of entity.[3] Instead, Descartes argues that we can explain all of the same physical, organic, and human

---

[3] Not to say that Descartes does not invoke substantial forms, even to explain the relationship of the mental to the body; see, for example, CMK 207-208/AT III 505–506, CSM I 279/AT XI 315, CSMK 278–279/AT IV 344–346, see Paul Hoffman, "The Unity of Descartes's Man," *Philosophical Review* 95 (1986): 339–370. Descartes also continues to use the word "soul," sometimes meaning "mind" and sometimes intending something closer to the scholastic sense.

phenomena by functions that can be cleanly sorted into either mental or physical functions. An animal is a physical machine, and so is a human in respect of the functions that it shares with animals, so that "it is not necessary to conceive of this machine as having any vegetative or sensitive soul or other principle of movement and life."[4] Human mental life can be explained by the mind, whose essence is thought, where this includes "everything that is within us in such a way that we are immediately aware of it."[5] That includes not only rational thought, which was specific to the intellectual part of the Aristotelian Scholastic soul, but also conscious sense experience and imagination.

A human being involves a mind and a body, each of which is a substance distinct from and independent of the other.[6] According to Descartes, every substance has one and only one principal attribute or property "which constitutes its essence, and to which all its other properties are referred."[7] Extension is the principal attribute of any body and thought is the principal attribute of any mind. To the metaphysical claim that all the properties of a substance depend upon one of these primary attributes, Descartes adds the epistemic claim that all the properties of a substance must be "understood through" their primary attribute and that they are "unintelligible when referred to one another."[8] This suggests some affinity with his claim in correspondence that extension and thought are "primitive notions," which are "as it were the patterns on the basis of which we form all our other conceptions" and "each of which can be understood only through itself."[9]

How are this mind and this body related to one another? Descartes struggled with this question, and there are many illuminating and

---

[4] CSM I 108/AT XI 315.
[5] CSM II 113/AT VII 160.
[6] CSM II 54/AT VII 78; CSM I, 213/AT VIIIA 29.
[7] CSM I 210/AT VIIIA 23.
[8] See also CSM I 299/AT XI 351: "neither is contained in the concept of the other."
[9] CSMK 218/AT IV 665.

contrasting accounts of this struggle and its results.[10] Here, I'll argue that Descartes was led by two different approaches to two different answers, and that Descartes himself saw them as distinct.

The first approach begins with the metaphysical picture outlined in the last few paragraphs. Descartes thinks that the world is populated by finite substances, some of them thinking and some of them extended.[11] He also argues that every physical event can be explained in terms of the laws of motion, by an efficient cause. But physical and mental events are correlated in such a way that they seem to cause one another: an apple causes me to have a certain perceptual experience, and the desire that forms on the basis of that experience causes me to reach for it. But how does a mental event cause a physical event, and vice versa? For one thing, physical events are completely explained in terms of physical laws, leaving no causal role for mental events. What is more, the fundamentally different natures of minds and bodies make it difficult to see how they can influence one another. This problem is put to Descartes by Princess Elisabeth of Bohemia, and Descartes's response to her probing questions contains his most sustained discussion of the mind-body union. Elisabeth raises the problem for minds and bodies specifically: a mind, for example, is not extended and cannot make contact with a body, which properties seem to be required in something that acts on a body (Elisabeth to Descartes, 6 May 1643). But it can be generalized to any properties of any two substances with different attributes. If their properties are "unintelligible when referred" to one another, in virtue of what

---

[10] For differing accounts of Descartes's account of the mind-body union, see John Cottingham, "Cartesian Trialism," *Mind* 94, no. 374 (1985): 218–230; Hoffman, "The Unity of Descartes's Man"; Daisie Radner "Descartes's Notion of the Union of Mind and Body," *Journal of the History of Philosophy* 9, no. 2 (1971): 159–170; Rozemond, *Descartes's Dualism* (Cambridge, MA: Harvard University Press, 2002); and Wilson, "Cartesian Dualism."

[11] There's an argument to be made that Descartes thinks there is only one extended substance and that this bears on the relationship of the mind and the body; see CSM II 9/AT VII 13.

properties do the substances causally interact? Descartes does not put the problem quite this way, but Frans Burman reports Descartes to claim that "it is a common axiom and a true one that the effect is like the cause."[12]

This cluster of problems is taken up in a variety of ways by Descartes's followers and opponents like Malebranche, Gassendi, Arnauld, Elisabeth, and, of course, Spinoza. But Descartes himself is not as concerned with it as this legacy might suggest. He claims simply that the mind and the body *do* causally interact, explaining a variety of psychophysical phenomena, and that arguments against it fail to show that such interaction is impossible. Questions about the possibility of interaction

> arise simply from a supposition that is false and cannot in any way be proved, namely that, if the soul and the body are two substances whose nature is different, this prevents them from being able to act on each other.[13]

Descartes's claim that minds and bodies can interact provides him with one answer to the embodiment question: a mind is related to its body just by interacting with it, albeit more immediately than it interacts with other bodies. In the *Passions of the Soul*, the *Treatise on Man*, and the *Description of the Human Body* Descartes develops the story of this interaction in some detail: there are physical events outside the body that cause physical events inside the body, which cause events in the mind, which in turn cause events in the body. Although

---

12 CSMK 339/AT V 154. Descartes doesn't write anything quite so explicit, but he does writes things like this: "There can be nothing in an effect which was not previously present in the cause" (CSMK 192). For a recent treatment of Descartes on causation and likeness, see Gorham, "Causation and Similarity in Descartes," in *New Essays on the Rationalists*, eds. Rocco Gennaro and Charles Huenemann, 296–308. Oxford: Oxford University Press, 2002.

13 CSM II 275/AT IXA 213.

the soul can act on and be acted on by all parts of the body, its "principal seat" is in what Descartes identified as the pineal gland,[14] which is especially sensitive to the volitions of the soul and to the movements of the body's animal spirits.

Descartes does not deny that the model of efficient causation derived from body-body interaction is an awkward fit for mind-body and body-mind causation; for example, he warns against "confus[ing] the notion of the power with which the soul acts on the body with the power with which one body acts on another."[15] We should not expect that the mutual influence between mind and body conforms perfectly to this model. Nonetheless, when Descartes explains sensation and action by claiming in the *Passions* and the *Treatise* that the "most proximate cause of the passions of the soul is simply the agitation by which the spirits move the little gland in the middle of the brain,"[16] he assumes that mind-body influence shares some fundamental features of body-body interaction. For example, a body event must follow on a mind event (or vice versa) immediately in time and the two events must take place at the same point in space. Also, at the beginning of the *Passions*, Descartes posits that "what is a passion in the soul is usually an action in the body" in light of the principle that "what is a passion with regard to one subject is always an action in some other regard."[17] This principle relies on treating the body and mind as distinct subjects involved in a single interaction rather than a united subject involved in joint action, so that whenever the mind and body are involved with one another, one is the agent, and the other is the patient.

In contrast, Descartes tells Elisabeth that it is a fundamental fact that the mind, "being united to the body . . . can act and be acted upon

---

14 CSM I 340–341/AT XI 352–354.
15 CSM II 275/AT IXA 213.
16 CSM I 380/AT XI 439.
17 CSM I 328/AT XI 328.

along with it."[18] This suggests a different story about the relationship of the body and mind, in which sensations, emotions, imaginations, and volitions involve, not the action of one and the passion of the other, but their joint action and passion. And indeed, in many contexts, Descartes emphasizes not the distinction between the mind and the body, but their union.

The union approach takes as axioms not some claims about substances, attribute, and interactions, but claims about the experience of any embodied subject. To Elisabeth, Descartes writes that "people who ... use only their senses have no doubt that the soul moves the body and the body acts on the soul. They regard both of them as a single thing, that is to say, they conceive their union."[19] And in the Sixth Meditation, Descartes takes pains to emphasize that the special quality of his sensations indicates to him that the body in which he feels those sensations "more than any other, belong[s] to [him]" and can never be separated from him.[20] When Descartes is in this mood, he will write that the mind and body are "substantially " or "essentially" united,[21] or that they form an *ens* per se[22] or a "real union,"[23] and that sensory ideas like pain and heat "arise from [the soul's] union, and, as it were, intermingling with the body."[24] It's worth noting that "substantial union" in the Scholastic context refers to the kind of union that a form has with matter; this is just one place where Descartes's break with Scholastic explanations in terms of the animate soul is not entirely clean.[25]

---

18 CSMK 218/AT III 665.
19 CSMK 227/AT III 692.
20 CSM II 52/AT VII 76.
21 CSMK 209/AT III 508.
22 CSMK 200/AT III 460.
23 CSMK 206/AT III 493.
24 CSMK 190/AT III 425.
25 For a much more detailed account of the relationship between Descartes's theory of embodiment and Scholastic views, see Rozemond, *Descartes's Dualism*.

In his exchange with Elisabeth, Descartes explicitly treats these as two different perspectives, approaches, or emphases. He claims that there are actually three primitive notions: besides thought and extension, there is a third notion of the union of the soul and the body, "on which depends our notion of the soul's power to move the body, and the body's power to act on the soul and cause its sensations and passions."[26] It is a little mysterious how this notion can be a notion of a union of mind and body as such, since it is primitive and so it cannot be understood in terms of those concepts. But in any case, while the primitive notions of thought and extension can each be conceived clearly "by the pure intellect" (and extension by the imagination as well)

> what belongs to the union of the soul and the body is known only obscurely by the intellect along or even by the intellect aided by the imagination, but it is known very clearly by the senses.[27]

Descartes does not explain what it means to know something by the senses, and especially to know it clearly by the senses. But he goes on to stress the difference between these two manners of conceiving. The essence of thought is revealed to us by "metaphysical thoughts" and the nature of body by mathematics. But metaphysics will actually prevent us from learning about the union; instead we learn about it through "the ordinary course of life and conversation, and abstention from meditation."[28] In fact Descartes tells Elisabeth that she can think about the distinction between the mind and the body only in spite of having conceived their union, since

> it does not seem to me that the human mind is capable of forming a very distinct conception of both the distinction between the soul

---

26 CSMK 218/AT III 665.
27 CSMK 227/AT III 691.
28 CSMK 228/AT III 694.

and the body and their union; for to do this it is necessary to conceive them as a single thing and at the same time to conceive them as two things, and this is absurd.[29]

Descartes thinks that nothing about our "metaphysical meditations" will tell us that there is any special relationship between a mind and a particular body. When he confines himself to metaphysics, Descartes treats the relationship between the mind and its body as simply an instance of interaction, on the model of efficient causation derived from bodies. But when we attend to the primitive notion of the union that embodied experience provides us, we see that such a model is inadequate.[30] Descartes doesn't necessarily contradict himself here— although he will have to address those claims, seemingly in tension, that the mind is always agentive when the body is patient and also that the mind and body can act together. But he suggests in both cases that he has not provided, should not be expected to provide, and perhaps cannot provide an exact mechanism or account either of the interaction or of the union.[31] Leaving this philosophical black box in both accounts means that Descartes can treat these as two ways of approach an ultimately unresolved, and perhaps unresolvable, problem. [32] But it also means that there is no way for us to know that the body that the first-person account picks out is the same body as the medical or

---

[29] CSMK 227–228/AT III 695.

[30] There is admittedly an important place for "first-person" considerations in Descartes's identification of the essence of mind as conscious thought, in his claim that thought is indivisible, and in his argument for the real distinction, but I'm focusing here on such considerations with respect to claims about embodiment specifically.

[31] CSM II 275/AT IXA 213.

[32] In recent work, Alison Simmons ("Mind-body Union") has also emphasized that "we do not have a clear and distinct intellectual idea of the mind-body union" but that "our access to our humanity is not through the intellect but through the senses." Simmons's paper offers a much more detailed treatment of Descartes's arguments for these claims as well as of their implications, including a discussion of the special role of the internal senses, a defense of the epistemic value of clear sensory knowledge, and a phenomenological analysis of our experience of embodiment.

biological body of the *Treatise on Man* or the *Description of the Human Body*—the one that our souls correspond with via our pineal glands.

3. Spinoza

Spinoza makes three claims about the relationship of the mind and the body:

(1) **Parallelism**: the mind relates to other minds in the same way that the body relates to other bodies
(2) **Idea-of**: the mind is the idea of the body; or, the body is the object [*objectum*] of the mind.
(3) **One and the same**: the mind and the body are "one and the same thing, understood in two different ways" (E 2p7s).

I am going to ignore (3).[33] It is a question well beyond the scope of this paper what Spinoza thinks makes things "one and the same thing." The most natural interpretation is that it means that the mind and the body are numerically identical. If Spinoza does think that, what can we learn about the embodiment question?

Ultimately, I think, not much. Presumably an important part of what we are after when we ask the embodiment question is an understanding of the properties and functions of the mind and the body, and of how the properties and functions of one relate to the properties and functions of the other. But if Spinoza thinks the mind and body are identical, then he denies the indiscernibility of identicals for many of the properties and functions you might be interested in knowing about. For example, just because a body is in a certain place or has a certain speed doesn't mean that the mind that is identical to it does, and just because the mind can

---

33 For a recent treatment of (3), see Colin Marshall, "The Mind and the Body as 'One and the Same Thing' in Spinoza," in *British Journal for the History of Philosophy* 17, no. 5 (2009): 897–919.

represent bodies doesn't mean that the body that is identical to it can. What that means is that the claim that the mind and the body are identical just does not teach us very much about the nature of the mind and the body, and it doesn't tell us anything further about the nature of their relationship.[34] And indeed, Spinoza never really uses it to establish anything about the mind and the body—with one exception, which I'll mention later.

Focusing on (1) and (2) then, I'll try to show that Spinoza's arguments for these two claims are entirely independent of one another, starting with their initial premises. Unlike Descartes, however, Spinoza makes no suggestion that these two accounts of embodiment result from two different approaches; instead, he takes them to be compatible and even runs them together as equivalent.[35]

Spinoza follows Descartes in rejecting the existence of animate souls:

> ... those three souls they attribute to plants, the lower, animals, and men are only fictions, for we have shown that there is nothing in matter but mechanical constructions and operations.[36]

We need not posit any special stuff beyond the physical to explain animal behavior, because it can be explained in terms of the structure and motion of the physical stuff we already have:

> no one has yet determined what the Body can do (i.e., experience has not yet taught anyone what the Body can do from the laws of

---

34 In Section 2 of "Points of View," Della Rocca makes a similar point, stressing in particular that the fact that my mind and my body are identical does not explain why my mind is "peculiarly sensitive to the goings-on in that body."

35 In "Finite Subjects in the Ethics: Spinoza on Indexical Knowledge, the First Person and the Individuality of Human Minds," in *The Oxford Handbook of Spinoza*, edited by Michael Della Rocca (Oxford: Oxford University Press, 2013), Ursula Renz defends the intriguing suggestion that while Spinoza likely has Descartes in mind when he articulates his theory of the mind-body union, he is likely also arguing against the Averroist claim that there is a single intellect for all humanity.

36 KV II III, G I 259/C 325.

nature alone, insofar as nature is only considered to be corporeal) ... For no one has yet come to know the structure of the Body so accurately that he could explain all its functions—not to mention that many things are observed in the lower Animals that far surpass human ingenuity, and that sleepwalkers do a great many things in their sleep that they would not dare to awake. This shows well enough that the Body itself, simply from the laws of its own nature, can do many things which its Mind wonders at.[37]

Like Descartes, Spinoza claims that extension and thought are different attributes, each of which must be conceived through itself and not through the other, and each of which constitutes the essence of a substance.[38] But Spinoza writes that Descartes is wrong to infer from this that the mind and the body are two independent substances.[39] Spinoza goes on to prove that they are instead attributes of the same substance, God or nature,[40] which, moreover, has not just these two but infinite attributes.[41] A mind is a mode of substance conceived under the attribute of thought, and a body is a mode of substance conceived under the attribute of extension.

Spinoza proves explicitly that since extension and thought, or any two modes of different attributes, have nothing in common and cannot be conceived through one another, they cannot causally interact.[42] Spinoza marvels at what he considers the absurdity of Cartesian interactionism (as he understands it): "I would hardly have believed it had been propounded by so great a man, had it not been so subtle ... [it is] a hypothesis more occult than any occult quality" (5 Preface).

---

37 E 3p2s/C 495/G II 142.
38 E 1p10s/C 416/G II 52.
39 E 1p10s/C 416/G II 52.
40 E 2p1-2/C 448-449/G II 86.
41 E 1p11/C 417/G II 52.
42 E 1p3/C 410-411/G II 47.

How does Spinoza explain correlations between mind events and body events, then? Spinoza claims at E 3p2 that "the body cannot determine the mind to thinking, and the mind cannot determine the body to motion, to rest, or to anything else (if there is anything else)." The proof appeals to E 2p7s, which I'll quote here, along E 2p7 and its demonstration and corollary:

> 2P7: The order and connection of ideas is the same as the order and connection of things.
> Dem: This is clear from 1a4. For the idea of each thing caused depend on the knowledge of the caused of which is is the effect.
> Corr: From this it follows that God's actual power of thinking is equal to his actual power of acting (i.e., whatever follows formally from God's infinite nature follows objectively in God from his idea in the same order and with the same connection.)
> Schol.: ... the thinking substance and the extended substance are one and the same substance, which is not comprehended under this attribute, now under that. So also a mode of extension and the idea of that mode are one and the same thing, but expressed in two ways ... Therefore, *whenever we conceive nature under the attribute of Extension, or under the attribute of Thought, or under any other attribute, we shall find one and the same order, or one and the same connection of causes, i.e. that the same things follow one another.*

Note that E 2p7 and E 2p7s (in italic) are not the same. E 2p7 says that "the order and connection of ideas is the same as the order and connection of things" while E 2p7s says that we can find the same causal order and connection in any attribute. The proof of E 2p7 invokes E 1a4, which relates ideas to what they are of, while the proof of E 2p7s only shows that the causal order in all the attributes is the same, and does not mention what each idea is of. And as Yitzhak Melamed has argued at length in print, where he distinguishes carefully between E 2p7 and E 2p7s, Spinoza uses the two differently throughout the *Ethics*.[43]

Is E 2p7s proven from E 2p7? Spinoza does not suggest that it is. Instead, he starts by emphasizing that the thinking substance and the extended substance are one and the same substance, comprehended under two different attributes. Therefore, he continues, a mode of extension and the idea of that mode are one and the same thing, expressed in two ways. Then he concludes that the order and connection of causes is the same under all the attributes. This is the place that I mentioned earlier, where Spinoza seems to use mode identity to prove something important—namely, that the causal order is the same among the attributes.

I don't know if this is the proof that Spinoza had in mind. But we face the same issue here that emboldened me to dismiss identity above. Spinoza does not tell us why mode identity follows from substance identity. (For example, two different modes of thought are modes of the same substance, but that does not mean that they are identical modes.) And he does not tell us why identity of causal order follows from mode identity. (This last one might seem obvious, but Spinoza seems precisely to deny that we can validly infer from the identity of two modes that they share all of their causal properties.) So there is only so much we can learn from the fact—if it is one—that Spinoza thinks that the proof that the causal structural of the attributes is the same relies on mode identity.

Moreover, there is another plausible reconstruction of the proof that relies on considerations of the necessity that attends God's power. Spinoza establishes in Part I that the things that proceed from God "could have been produced in no other way and in no other order than they have been produced." The thought is that if this order is necessary, then it must be the same in any attribute. This version is supported by

---

[43] Yitzhak Melamed, "Spinoza's Metaphysics of Thought: Parallelisms and the Multifaceted Structure of Ideas." *Philosophy and Phenomenological Research* 86, no. 3 (2013): 636–683.

an interesting claim that Spinoza makes even before E 2p7. E 2p6 establishes that a mode follows from God only insofar as he is considered under the attribute of that mode, and its corollary infers from this that

> the objects of ideas follow and are inferred from their attributes in the same way and by the same necessity as that with which we have shown ideas to follow from the attribute of Thought.

This is offered as an explanation of the correlation between God's ideas and created things—an alternative to the claim that God's ideas are prior to the things that they are of. The explanation seems to be that ideas and things follow "in the same way and by the same necessity"—something very reminiscent of the claim that they follow with the same order.[44]

What I want to stress here is just that the proof of E 2p7s does not depend on E 2p7, and so it does not tell us whether the body that is parallel to a given idea is also what that idea is of. E 2p7s either depends on claims about the identity of modes, or it is motivated by propositions like E 1p16 and E 1p29, which establish the necessity of what follows from God's essence, considered under any attribute. In either case, the proof of E 2p7s is based on considerations about God in Part I of the *Ethics*, and certainly not on any claims about human sense experience or other kinds of mental representation. Meanwhile, 2p7's proof relies exclusively on E 1a4:

> The cognition of an effect depends upon, and involves, the cognition of its cause.

---

44 In fact, the only place where Spinoza uses E 2p6c is when he shows at E 5p1 that thoughts and bodily affections are ordered and connected in the same way. There he gives separate proofs for the claim that the thoughts are connected like body affections and the claim that body affections are connected like thoughts. He appeals to E 2p7 for both the mind-body and body-mind direction, but he adds an appeal to 2p6c for the mind-body direction. I submit that Spinoza's appeal to E 2p7 for both is carelessness on Spinoza's part—a carelessness that arises from his desire to treat E 2p7 and E 2p7s as interchangable. But his inclusion of E 2p6c for the mind-body direction only suggests that he knows very well indeed that they are distinct.

This (arguably[45]) *does* concern the relationship between an idea and what it is *of*.

Let's now look at the argument for (1): that the mind and its body are parallel modes, or are "ordered and connected" in the same way with the other modes of their respective attributes. It is actually much harder than you might expect given how large it looms in the popular conception of Spinoza's system. The strongest evidence that Spinoza accepts it is E 3p2s. There, after explaining that the mind cannot determine the body and vice versa, Spinoza writes we can understand how this could be true

> from what is said in 2p7s, viz., that the Mind and the Body are one and the same thing, which is conceived now under the attribute of Thought, now under the attribute of Extension. The result is that the order, or connection, of things is one, whether nature is conceived under this attribute or that; hence the order of actions and passions of our Body is, by nature, at one with the order of actions and passions of the Mind (E 3p2s).

So it looks from this like the mind and body are parallel in the sense that E 2p7s establishes, not (just) in the sense that E 2p7 establishes. And as we saw, E 2p7s derives from some claims about the necessity of God's essence and what follows from it, not from an appeal to first-person data.

The juxtaposition of 3p2s with Spinoza's screed against interactionism suggests that Spinoza is thinking of parallelism as a solution to the interaction problem. Compare Spinoza's claim that the mind and

---

45 Arguably, because one way to read "the idea of an effect depends upon, and involves, the idea of its cause," which Spinoza takes as equivalent to E 1a4, is just as saying that the idea that corresponds to a thing is caused by the idea that corresponds to that thing's cause. That is, it is possible to read E 1a4 without representational import.

body are parallel with Descartes's treatment of the mind and body as interacting substances. Both accounts of embodiment start with the metaphysical claims that the mind and the body are conceived under different attributes. Both are aimed at explaining the appearance of mind-body interaction in general. Both see the problem of mind-body interaction as an instance of the more general problem of interattribute interaction, and both apply their accounts of interattribute interaction to explaining mind-body interaction.

But just like Descartes, Spinoza has another answer to the embodiment question: what I called above the "idea-of" account. He asserts it at E 2p13:

> The object of the idea constituting the human Mind is the Body, or a certain mode of Extension which actually exists, and nothing else.

Spinoza claims in the scholium that from E 2p13 and its corollary, "we understand not only that the human mind is united to the body, but also what should be understood by the union of mind and body." This is the only place in the *Ethics* that Spinoza mentions a union of the mind and body.

The proof of E 2p13 is very complicated and involves many propositions, themselves contentious, so I can only make a claim here and go a little way toward justifying it. Also for the sake of space, I'm going to ignore the negative claim in 2p13, that the object of the human mind is nothing in addition to the body, and focus on the positive one, that the object of the mind is the body.

The argument that the mind is the idea of the body starts with E 2a4:

> We feel that a certain body is affected in many ways.

Like Descartes's own union account, Spinoza's starts with some first-person premises. These premises concern, in particular, the felt quality of sensations—or, in Spinoza's terms, ideas of affections, where affections are just states of the body arising from its interaction with other bodies. The indexicality of "a certain" body is preserved all the way through 2p13: there is no way of characterizing your body other than as *that* one—the one that you feel.[46]

Now I'd like to show, very briefly, that the argument from 2a4 to 2p13 is independent of the argument for the parallelism account of embodiment.

The proof of the positive claim—that my mind is the idea of my body—is this, in short:

1. I feel the affections of a certain body (E 2a4).
2. If my mind were not the idea of my body, I would not feel the affections of that body (E 2p9c and E 2p11c).

3. Therefore, my mind is the idea of my body (1 and 2).

Let's take a look at (2). E 2p9c says that the idea of an affection of some body is in God "only insofar as" the idea of that body is in God. But what does this mean—"only insofar as"—this phrase that is used for the first time in this context at 2p9c? (Spinoza uses it in many other, equally vexing, contexts.) We can try to answer this by looking at the meaning that is licensed by E 2p9 and E 2p9c. E 2p9 says that God is the cause of the (finite) idea of something only considered as affected by another (finite) idea. Spinoza justifies this by appealing to E 1p28, which is the claim that every finite thing has a finite cause. So when Spinoza says that God is the cause of an idea only insofar as he is modified (or "affected") in a certain way, his appeal to E 1p28 suggests that it's because a finite idea needs a finite cause. If that's right, then to say that one idea is caused by God "only insofar as" God has another

---

[46] Renz ("Finite Subjects") also stresses that 2a2–4 involve the subjective perspective, and that although Spinoza does not develop the first-person perspective, these axioms have "crucial argumentative functions in the *Ethics*."

idea as a mode just means that one idea is caused by God only if God has another mode to cause it. So the meaning of "only insofar as" licensed by E 2p9 is analogous to this: a window breaks only insofar as a stone is thrown.

Note that this should be true for all the partial causes of an event: a window breaks only insofar as a stone is thrown, the glass is fragile, and so on. Now Spinoza thinks that an idea of any affection is caused both by my body as well as by the external thing affecting my body.[47] That means that God should be the cause of that idea only insofar as God is modified by my body and God is modified by the external body. Spinoza goes on at E 2p7c to claim that the idea of an affection of a thing is in God only insofar as God has the idea of that thing. But note that given how Spinoza understands "only insofar as" in E 2p7, this means that the idea of an affection of a thing is in God only insofar as God has the idea of all of its partial causes.

Remember that Spinoza needs to show (2), that if my mind weren't the idea of my body, then I wouldn't feel the affections that I do. But given how I've read E 2p7c, it does not distinguish in any way between my body and the external cause.

Instead, a lot of the work of proving E 2p13 is done by E 2p11c, which is the claim that for me to have[48] an idea of a something (or, for the ideas of the affections of something to be in my mind) is just for God to have an idea of that thing insofar as he constitutes my mind. Spinoza simply provides no proof of this, no less a proof that appeals

---

47 E 2p16/C 463/G II 104.

48 For this to be true, "have" must be used here with a sense that applies only to the special way that we can be said to have the ideas of our bodily affections, and not in a sense, that might be otherwise natural, in which we can be said to have the ideas of affections of other bodies. At the same time, as I'll argue in the coming paragraphs, there is a sense in which Spinoza wants to explain our ideas of sensations in our own body and our ideas of other things in the same terms. Compare this with Descartes's, who provides a relatively careful phenomenological analysis of the difference between how I feel sensations in my body and how I represent properties and changes in other bodies (e.g., CSM II, 56/AT VII 81; CSMK, 190/AT III 424).

to parallelism. He does not suggest a proof from 2p11, which is the claim that the human mind is an idea of something that exists. But in any case, I cannot see that the proof of 2p11 sheds any light, either, on what are Spinoza's reasons for thinking that this is the only explanation of our sensations.

This should not be too surprising, since 2p11c is Spinoza's attempt to move from a claim about our awareness of certain sensations to a metaphysical claim about what sort of entities my mind and its ideas are. To do this requires solving an incredibly deep, difficult, and perennial problem: what metaphysical story underlies felt mental experience, including our experience of our own bodies and the world through those bodies? Spinoza's answer is that my feeling of a certain affection is an idea in God insofar as God constitutes the essence of my mind, but since his attempt to justify this claim comes up short, we have to look elsewhere to understand why Spinoza thinks that it is true.

Some of the intuition behind Spinoza's adoption of the "idea-of" account of embodiment is illuminated by taking a look at Spinoza's earlier work. There the parallelism account hasn't emerged yet, and a somewhat different "idea-of" account makes Spinoza's intentions in adopting it a little more explicit.

In the *Treatise on the Emendation of the Intellect*, one of his earliest works, Spinoza writes:

> after we clearly perceive that we feel such a body, and no other, then, I say, we infer clearly that the soul is united to the body, which union is the cause of such a sensation; but we cannot understand absolutely from this what that sensation and union are ... we understand nothing through that union except the sensation itself; ... concerning ... the cause, we understand nothing.[49]

---

49 TIE 21/C 14/G II 11.

This is almost exactly what Descartes thinks about the union: we perceive that the soul and body are united and that this union is the cause of our sensations. So why does Spinoza change his mind by the *Ethics*, deciding that we can learn something about the union? Why does he come to believe that the fact that we feel the sensations that we do means that a human mind is the idea of the body?

In the *Short Treatise*, written a few years after the *Treatise on the Emendation of the Intellect*, Spinoza starts by making a Cartesian point. He explains that when we consider the nature of extension or thought alone, we cannot see how it is possible for a mind to intervene in the physical world or a body in the mental world. However, he continues:

> according to what we perceive in ourselves, it can indeed happen that a body which is not moving in one direction comes to move in another direction—e.g., when I stretch out my arm, and thereby bring it about that the spirits, which previously were moving in a different direction, now however have this one . . .

Descartes says something simlar to Elizabeth: when we consider the essences of minds and bodies, we have difficulty in seeing how they can interact. Descartes contrasts this with "what we perceive in ourselves," which forces us to conclude that they do influence one another. But instead of claiming that the union is inscrutable, Spinoza writes that the cause of the union

> is, and can only be, that the soul, being an Idea of this body, is so united with it, that it and this body, so constituted, together make a whole.[50]

There are a couple of important differences between Spinoza's approach to embodiment in the *Short Treatise* and in the *Ethics*.

---

50 ST II XIX/C 131-132/G I 91.

First, in the *Short Treatise*, Spinoza classifies the object-idea relationship as a kind of dependence, so that the body affects, influences or causes changes in the mind. For example, Spinoza writes that "there is in Nature a body by whose form and actions we are affected, so that we perceive it,"[51] and that "the principal [action of the body on the soul] is that it causes the soul to perceive it, and thereby to perceive other bodies also."[52] Bodies act on the soul by "making themselves known to it as objects,"[53] and the soul is "an idea arising from an object which exists in nature."[54]

Spinoza rejects the idea that this is a dependence relationship in the *Ethics*, for the arguments outlined earlier in this section. Even further, he explicitly denies at E 2p6c that an object causally influences or otherwise explains the idea of it. So while in the *Short Treatise* Spinoza explains mind-body interaction in terms of the idea-object relation, he needs a different explanation in the *Ethics*, and that is where parallelism makes its first appearance.

Furthermore, since there is no parallelism in the *Short Treatise*, there is nothing besides the idea-object relationship anchoring a mind to its body. That means that if I think about something else, my mind literally become the mind of that thing. This is a consequence that Spinoza embraces: for our own sakes, Spinoza argues, we should turn our minds to God, seeking to unite our minds to something incorruptible rather than corruptible:

> if we once some to know God (at least with as clear a knowledge as we have of our body), we must then come to be united with him even more closely than with our body, and be, as it were, released from the body.[55]

---

51 ST II XIX/C 130/G I 89.
52 ST II XIX/C 133/G I 93.
53 ST II XIX/C 133/G I 93.
54 ST II C 155.
55 ST II XIX/C 133/G I 93.

Spinoza describes this process as being "born again."[56]

Not only is the soul the idea of the body according to the *Short Treatise*, but the soul *loves* the body, since "love is nothing but enjoying a thing and being united with it."[57] This doctrine bears a resemblance to some comments that Descartes makes in an exchange with his friend, the French diplomat Pierre Chanut. Descartes tells Chanut that intellectual or rational love "consists simply in the fact that when our soul perceives some present or absent good . . . it joins itself to it willingly, that is so say, it considers itself and the good in question as forming two parts of a single whole."[58] While both Descartes and Spinoza think that love is naturally inspired in the soul by the body and that the soul and body are brought closer by this love, only Spinoza seems to think of love as *constitutive* of the union:

> Love is a union with an object that our intellect judges to be good and magnificent; and by that we understand a union such what the lover and the loved come to be one and the same thing, or to form a whole together.[59]

The claim that love is constitutive of the union between mind and body drops out of *Ethics*, but a transformed and implicit one takes its place. According to the *Ethics*, "one who loves necessarily strives to have present and preserve the thing he loves,"[60] and the mind "strives to imagine those things that increase or aid the body's power of acting."[61]

---

56 ST II XXII/C 140/G I 102
57 ST II V/C 105/G I 62. I am grateful to Colin Chamberlain for pointing out that Descartes, too, claims that the soul loves the body.
58 CSMK 306/AT IV 602.
59 ST II V/C 105/G I 62.
60 E 3p13s/C 502/G II 151.
61 E 3p12/C 502/G II 150.

So one important difference between the *Short Treatise* account and the *Ethics* account is that in the *Short Treatise*, the mind depends on the body in virtue of being the idea of it.

A second important difference between the *Short Treatise* and *Ethics* claims that the mind is the idea of the body is that in the former, Spinoza makes very explicit that this implies that the mind is aware of the body. There has been a lot of interesting work done trying to square Spinoza's claim that the body is the object of the mind with the apparent facts that most of our ideas are about other things and that we don't have ideas of much of what goes on in our bodies. One way to do this is by distinguishing in some way or other between the relationship that my mind has with my body and the relationship that my mind has with other things, with the result that my mind doesn't have anything like the relationship to my body that it has to the things that it represents.[62] And it is true that in the *Ethics* there are many suggestions of such a distinction.[63]

But in the *Short Treatise*, it is clear that Spinoza takes the mind to represent the body in a much more robustly mentalistic sense: for example, he writes that the mind is aware of the body,[64] and that a mind's awareness of other bodies is of the same kind as the awareness of the its own body and derive from it.[65] I think that this suggests that the initial intuition behind the idea-of account of embodiment is that God, understood under the attribute of thought, is characterized by a certain kind of basic awareness or distinctively mental representation,

---

[62] For a variety of approaches to this issue, see Robert Brandom, "Adequacy and the Individuation of Ideas In Spinoza's Ethics," *Journal of the History of Philosophy* 14, no. 2 (1976): 147–162; Margaret Wilson, "Objects, Ideas, and 'Minds':Comments on Spinoza's Theory of Mind," in *Ideas and Mechanism*, ed. Margaret Wilson (Princeton, NJ: Princeton University Press, 1999), 126–140.;" Radner, "Spinoza's Theory of Ideas"; Michael Della Rocca, *Representation and the Mind-Body Problem in Spinoza* (Oxford: Oxford University Press, 1996).

[63] I myself think that the most promising way of doing this in the *Ethics* is to restrict the ideas we have to ideas of affections, distinguishing them from ideas that we are constituted by, as suggested by E 2p12.

[64] e.g., ST II Pref./C 96/G I 52; ST II XXI/C 139/G I 101.

[65] e.g., ST II XIX/C 132/G I 92.

which our ideas inherit. It makes sense to think of this on an analogy with motion in extension: just as the motion of finite bodies can be understood as partaking in God's motion, finite thoughts partake in God's representation. This is much clearer in the *Short Treatise* than in the *Ethics*, where Spinoza is trying to resolve the idea-of picture with parallelism. But I think it is what is behind 2p11c of the *Ethics*—the unproven corollary that Spinoza relies upon to prove that the mind is the idea of the body—and ultimately behind 2p13's claim that the mind is the idea of the body. It is less surprising that Spinoza's two accounts of embodiment are articulated independently when we consider that he held the idea-of account before accepting the parallelism account.

Why does Spinoza add the parallelism account? I am not sure, but it is interesting to note that the attempt to explain mind-body interaction by positing that an idea depends on the body that is its object works nicely as a model for explaining body-mind influence but not so nicely for explaining mind-body influence. It is even more interesting to note that Spinoza spends much more time explaining phenomena, like sensation and imagination, that seem to involve body-mind causation, and he never appeals to parallelism—that is, to E 2p7s—in those cases, instead relying on E 2p12. I think this shows that Spinoza still thinks of the idea-object relation as involving some kind of dependence. In contrast, he only uses E 2p7s three times and rarely makes claims that involve the mind moving the body.

4. Conclusion

I've argued that despite Spinoza's desire that they be compatible and even identical, his two accounts of embodiment derive from very different considerations. It turns out that Descartes, before Spinoza, develops two similarly distinct accounts of embodiment, but does so more explicitly. Both Descartes and Spinoza offer one account of embodiment that is aimed at addressing the apparent causal interaction of minds and bodies, and one that addresses the special quality of the relationship that a mind has with its particular body. Both start, in the former case, with a set of metaphysical commitments about the kinds of things, properties and interactions there are in the world, and in the latter case with the fact and subjective quality of embodied experience, especially sensation. In trying to square these two approaches, both Descartes and Spinoza are attempting to answer a deep, difficult and perennial question: what metaphysics gives an account of our mental experiences, especially the experience that we have of our bodies and the world through our bodies?

While Descartes acknowledges that squaring these two approaches is difficult and maybe even impossible, Spinoza does not. But there remains to be undertaken a more detailed analysis of how Spinoza explains away individual cases of apparent psycho-physical interaction to see how deeply these two approaches are intertwined and whether he can indeed eventually square them.

Abbreviations

(CSM I and II). Descartes, René. *The Philosophical Writings of Descartes, Vol. I and II*. Translated and edited by John Cottingham, Robert Stoothoff, and Dugald Murdoch. Cambridge, UK: Cambridge University Press, 1984 and 1985.

(CSMK). Descartes, René. *The Philosophical Writings of Descartes, Vol. III*. Translated and edited by John Cottingham, Robert Stoothoff, Dugald Murdoch, and Anthony Kenny. Cambridge, UK: Cambridge University Press, 1991.

(C). Spinoza, Baruch. *The Collected Works of Spinoza, Vol. 1*. Translated and edited by Edwin Curley. Princeton, NJ: Princeton University Press, 1985.

CHAPTER TEN

Man-Machines and Embodiment

FROM CARTESIAN PHYSIOLOGY TO CLAUDE BERNARD'S
"LIVING MACHINE"

Philippe Huneman and Charles T. Wolfe

1. THE PROBLEM OF POLYSEMOUS EMBODIMENT

In what follows we seek to trace and reconstruct, through a series of examples running from the early modern Cartesian context through Enlightenment materialism to mid-19th-century medicine, a revised concept of embodiment as emerging out of naturalistic, mechanism-friendly practices in the life sciences and in theoretical efforts relating to such practices. Such an approach runs directly counter to the common understanding in which "embodiment" (whether it is approached historically or from a contemporary standpoint) is precisely what the scientific study of organic life "misses." But what is embodiment? Or more precisely, when a concept of embodiment is invoked in, *inter alia*, scholarship on Descartes or Spinoza, early modern "cultures of the body," or the study of embodied cognition (to list some examples[1]) what concept is this, if there is any conceptual unity here at all? Broadly speaking, in the study of cognition, "embodied mind" perspectives reject traditional computational approaches and present our cerebral life as necessarily occurring within a body, understood both as a dynamic system and as something fundamentally *my own* in the sense of Merleau-Ponty's *corps propre*: I am not "in my body," on this view, as if I were in a merely material container; instead, I sense in a profound way that my body is my own.[2] The emphasis here usually falls on how an embodied agent inhabits the world, not as one body amongst others (atoms and asteroids and bottles) but as a *subject* in her own environment. In cultural studies, embodiment seems to connote a complex relation between historicity and gender, in which "subjectivity [is] profoundly experienced as interrelated with the physical, and societal changes or structures influenced the ways in which the body was perceived,"[3] through scientific discourses but also in many other ways.[4] Embodiment here is not the facts about our biology but, paradoxically, about our historicity:

---

[1] For example, Amelie Oksenberg Rorty, "Descartes on Thinking with the Body," in *The Cambridge Companion to Descartes*, ed. J. Cottingham (Cambridge, UK: Cambridge University Press, 1992), 371–392; Iris Marion Young, *On Female Body Experience: "Throwing Like a Girl" and Other Essays* (New York: Oxford University Press, 2005); Lawrence Shapiro, *Embodied Cognition* (London: Routledge, 2011).

[2] Maurice Merleau-Ponty, *Phenomenology of Perception*, trans. C. Smith (London: Routledge & Kegan Paul, 1962), 104.

[3] Ursula Rublack, "Fluxes: The Early Modern Body and the Emotions," *History Workshop Journal* 53 (2002), 13.

[4] Aside from the variety of works in "history of the body" that appeared at a bewildering rate during the 1980s and 1990s, in early modern studies one can mention Caroline W. Bynum, "Why All the Fuss about the Body? A Medievalist's Perspective," *Critical Inquiry* 22 (1995); T. Reiss, "Denying the Body? Memory and the Dilemmas of History in Descartes," *Journal of the History of Ideas* 57, no. 4 (1996); G. K. Paster, "Nervous Tension: Networks of Blood and Spirit in the Early Modern Body," in *The Body in Parts*, eds. D. Hillman and C. Mazzio (London: Routledge, 1997); and in embodied cognitive science, Young, *Throwing Like a Girl*; for interesting and original ways of extending and modifying their programs, combining a sense of historicized embodiment with notions in "historical cognitive science," see John Sutton, "Spongy Brains and Material Memories," in *Embodiment and Environment in Early Modern England*, eds. M. Floyd-Wilson and G. Sullivan (London: Palgrave, 2010). For a recent attempt to compensate for the total absence of "embodiment" discourse in the

There is no clear set of structures, behaviors, events, objects, experiences, words, and moments to which body currently refers. Rather, it seems to me, the term conjures up two sharply different groups of phenomena. Sometimes body, my body, or embodiedness seems to refer to limit or placement, whether biological or social. That is, it refers to natural, physical structures (such as organ systems or chromosomes), to environment or locatedness, boundary or definition, or to role (such as gender, race, class) as constraint. Sometimes on the other hand it seems to refer precisely to lack of limits, that is, to desire, potentiality, fertility, or sensuality/sexuality . . . or to person or identity as malleable representation or construct. Thus body can refer to the organs on which a physician operates or to the assumptions about race and gender implicit in a medical textbook, to the particular trajectory of one person's desire or to inheritance patterns and family structures.[5]

The "lived body" we encounter in contemporary embodiment discourse is the body in pain, or in a state of enjoyment; in a reflexive, indeed intimate relation to itself—quite different, according to embodiment theorists, from the more generic body in space. They maintain that the lived body (which is the only relevant sense of the body for them) exists at least in part "outside of physical space."[6] Thus the living body—indeed, any organism—"is an individual in a sense which is not that of modern physics" (ibid., 154). This is often presented in cultural studies as an insight countering "Cartesianism." So, Jonathan Sawday, in his otherwise impressive study of early modern anatomy, *The Body Emblazoned*, refers to the rise of a Cartesian mechanistic world-picture and states that "As a machine, the body became

---

history of science (here, early modern life science), see the essays collected in Charles T. Wolfe and Ofer Gal, eds., *The Body as Object and Instrument of Knowledge* (Dordrecht: Springer, 2010).
5 Bynum, "Why All the Fuss about the Body?" 5.
6 Maurice Merleau-Ponty, *The Structure of Behaviour*, trans. A. L. Fisher (Boston: Beacon, 1963), 209.

objectified; a focus of intense curiosity, but entirely divorced from the world of the speaking and thinking subject."[7] That this is a rather impoverished and historically unfortunate portrayal of early modern mechanism is not germane to the present paper, although it is worth exploring elsewhere.

We are faced already with one general problem: the gap between discourses of embodiment and the complexity of "body" and biological or medical terms as understood from the standpoint of the history and philosophy of the life sciences. That is, cultural discussions of early modern embodiment usually position themselves *counter* to a kind of "mainstream science," which they present as alienated and alienating, as quantitative and reductionist, and of course dehumanizing. The quantitative and reductionist part turns out to be partly true but more complicated; the rest is at best highly debatable, not least given the importance of reflections on "organism" and "organismic" approaches at least since the Leibniz-Stahl debate, and prominently part of physiological discussions in the era of Claude Bernard.[8] This complexity can be shown in a variety of cases, ranging from recent reinterpretations of Descartes on life, passions, and physiology, the role of early modern automata in modelling vital processes (and thus creating bridges in between the mechanical and the organic); vital materialism understood as a form of materialism specifically concerned with body and vitality; and lastly, vitalist

---

[7] Sawday, *The Body Emblazoned: Dissection and the Human Body in Renaissance Culture* (London: Routledge, 1995), 29. Thus present-day embodied mind theorists assert quite bluntly that "Life is not physical in the standard materialist sense of purely external structure and function. Life realizes a kind of interiority, the interiority of selfhood and sense-making. We accordingly need an expanded notion of the physical to account for the organism or living being" (Evan Thompson, *Mind in Life* [Cambridge, MA: Harvard University Press, 2007], 238). In fact, this "expanded notion of the physical" has always been present; it is rather the picture of "standard materialism" that needs to be revised.

[8] This problem of doing justice to embodiment without producing a strictly reactive historiography matches up with the problem surrounding the Scientific Revolution and the "death of Nature" (Carolyn Merchant, *The Death of Nature: Women, Ecology, and the Scientific Revolution* [San Francisco: Harper and Row, 1980]; see John Sutton and Evelyn B. Tribble, "Materialists Are Not Merchants of Vanishing," *Early Modern Culture* 9 (2011), for an inspiring critique of her view).

models of the "animal economy" in the mid-eighteenth century and their combined reprisal and rejection in nineteenth-century experimental medicine, from Bichat to Bernard. We shall discuss four cases: Descartes and medicine (section 2), embodied materialism versus the older concept of mechanistic materialism (section 3), and the emergence of organismic yet mechanism-friendly models in nineteenth-century medicine such as Bichat's physiology, leading up to Claude Bernard's notion of "machine vivante" (section 4); the status of vitalism, including its scientific pertinence, is addressed in sections 3 and 4.

2. Body and Soul in a Medical Context

Contrary to the standard picture of Descartes the substance dualist, whose understanding of nature is so purely mechanistic that no particular features of "life" or "bodies" subsist in a nonreduced form, scholars including Gaukroger, Sutton, Des Chene, and, differently, Shapiro have pointed to the presence of functional concepts in Cartesian physiology: of body-soul union (in the correspondence with Elizabeth) and of a notion of health and consequently normativity generated out of the body-machine concept.[9] This is not to say that Descartes did not influentially adopt a deflationary approach to embodiment, or that iatromechanism[10] should be confused with, say, Georg-Ernst Stahl's focus on the holistic properties of organism and the temporal character of disease, as presented for instance in his

---

9 See for instance Amélie Oksenberg Rorty, "Descartes on Thinking with the Body"; John Sutton, "The Body and the Brain," in *Descartes' Natural Philosophy,* eds. S. Gaukroger, J. A. Schuster, and J. Sutton (London: Routledge, 2000); Lisa Shapiro, "The Health of the Body-Machine? Or Seventeenth Century Mechanism and the Concept of Health," *Perspectives on Science* 11, no. 4 (2003) and, differently, Dennis Des Chene, *Spirits and Clocks: Machine and Organism in Descartes* (Ithaca, NY: Cornell University Press, 2001) (e.g., chapter 6 [on *functio* and *usus*]).

10 "Iatromechanism" designates a school of medical and physiological thought that extensively views living bodies as mechanical devices, wholly following the laws of mechanics and likely to be understood, analyzed, and cured through them.

critique of Leibniz.[11] As concerns Cartesian mechanism as apparently a denial or reduction of embodiment, passages like this one from the *Treatise on Man* are numerous (as they are in authors such as Borelli, Pitcairne, Croome, and beyond):

> Indeed one may very well compare the nerves of the machine which I am describing with the tubes of the machines of those fountains, the muscles and tendons of the machine with the other various engines and springs which serve to move these machines, and the animal spirits, the source of which is the heart and of which the ventricles of the brain are the reservoirs, with the water which puts them in motion. Moreover breathing and other like acts which are natural and usual to the machine and which depend on the flow of the spirits are like the movements of a clock or of a mill which the ordinary flow of water can keep going continually.[12]

Yet we must summarily make two observations that nuance the picture of the Cartesian body-machine as merely a "machine made of earth." The first is internal to Descartes' system and concerns the extent to which features as diverse as sensation, self-preservation, health, function, and perhaps even a "life principle" are—surprisingly—irreducible.[13] The second is more external and concerns medical mechanism as a whole.

---

[11] Georg Ernst Stahl, *Negotium otiosum, seu* Schiamaxia *adversus positiones aliquas fundamentales theoriae verae medicaea Viro quodam celeberrimo intentata sed adversis armis conversis* (Halle: Impensis Orphanotrophei, 1720).

[12] AT XI 131; CSM I, 100. Cf. also the passage in the Sixth Meditation on the "health" of a watch: "A clock constructed with wheels and weights observes all the laws of its nature just as closely when it is badly made and tells the wrong time as when it completely fulfills the wishes of the clockmaker. In the same way, I might consider the body of a man as a kind of machine equipped with and made up of bones, nerves, muscles, veins, blood, and skin in such a way that, even if there were no mind in it, it would still perform all the same movements as it now does in those cases where the movement is not under the control of the will or, consequently, of the mind" (AT VI, 84; CSM II: 58); thanks to Christoffer Basse Eriksen for discussion on this).

[13] See Fred Ablondi, "Automata, Living and Non-Living: Descartes' Mechanical Biology and His Criteria for Life," *Biology and Philosophy* 13, no. 2 (1998) and the discussion in Barnaby Hutchins, "Descartes and the Dissolution of Life," *The Southern Journal of Philosophy* 54, no. 2 (2016).

For the "body-soul" problem—arguably the immediate ancestor of the "mind-body" problem, inasmuch as it was concerned with possible relations between corporeal states and mental processes—was also a medical one. With reference to the Cartesian context alone, entire books have been written just on the specifically medical context of Cartesianism.[14] Both during Descartes' own lifetime and in the following decades, numerous physicians claimed to be carrying out a legitimate Cartesian project (e.g., eliminating final causes and explaining all of nature mechanically, including the human body, while in fact moving ever closer to an integrated view of psychosomatic processes). Thus Henricus Regius, a physician and Professor of Theoretical Medicine at the University of Utrecht, often called the "first apostle of Cartesianism" (e.g., in a review in the *Nouvelles de la république des lettres* in October 1686), asserted that the soul could be a mode of the body, with the body being understood as a machine, and that the human mind, inasmuch as it exists in a body, is organic.[15] Even Marx (borrowing from Renouvier's history of philosophy) mentioned Regius as a precursor of La Mettrie: "Descartes was still alive when Le Roy applied to the human soul the Cartesian idea of animal structure, and declared that the soul was but a *mode of the body*, and ideas were but *mechanical motions*."[16] Others have asserted that Descartes was too timid, and one should be a Cartesian in physiology while eliminating substance dualism in favor of a parallelism of physical events and mental events (Louis de La Forge[17]); or, rather tortuously, have tried to argue "from"

---

14 Most recently, Annie Bitbol-Hespériès, *Le principe de vie chez Descartes* (Paris: Vrin, 1990); Vincent Aucante, *La philosophie médicale de Descartes* (Paris: PUF, 2006); and Gideon Manning, "Out on the Limb: The Place of Medicine in Descartes' Philosophy," *Early Science and Medicine* 12, no. 2 (2007) (a useful review essay).

15 Henricus Regius, *Fundamenta physices* (Amsterdam: Elzevier, 1646), 248, 246. For more discussion of Regius see the excellent analysis in Delphine Bellis, "Empiricism Without Metaphysics: Regius' Cartesian Natural Philosophy," in *Cartesian Empiricisms*, eds. M. Dobre and T. Nyden: http://www.springer.com/la/book/9789400776890 (Dordrecht: Springer, 2014).

16 Marx, *The Holy Family*, VI, 3, d, discussed in Olivier Bloch, "Marx, Renouvier et l'histoire du matérialisme," *La Pensée* 191 (1977).

17 Louis de La Forge, *Traité de l'esprit de l'homme, de ses facultés et de ses fonctions, et de son union avec le corps, suivant les principes de René Descartes* (Paris: Théodore Girard, 1666), ch. XV.

Descartes toward a materialist account of mind-body interaction, at times seeking to integrate Cartesianism and Epicureanism.[18] Such thinkers tried to collapse their ideas into Descartes' own, but others—perhaps tellingly, outside of France—were quicker to dispense with any monopoly Descartes might have had over the prestige of mechanism in medicine, like Herman Boerhaave (1668–1738) or Hieronymus Gaub (1705–1780).

Boerhaave's 1690 doctoral thesis in philosophy at Leiden, where he was later Professor of Medicine, Botany, and Chemistry (he was widely viewed as the most influential lecturer in medicine in Europe, and taught figures including La Mettrie, Gaub and Haller) was entitled *De distinctione mentis a corpora*, and there he argued for a distinction between mind and body. But in his later *Praelectiones academicae* (1739), he denied any medical or physiological pertinence to the distinction between body and soul or mind understood as a form of substance dualism (§ 27). Body and mind are united and communicate with and mutually affect one another, and a change occurring in the one produces a change in the other; this view may explain the unfair accusations of Spinozism that were laid against him. Boerhaave admits that he has no way of explaining the interaction between body and mind experimentally.[19] He considers three hypotheses: "physical influx," occasional causes, and divine harmony, and opts for the last (§ 27.7). He adds a remark that was repeated, with or without attribution, many times during this period (similar comments can be found in Galen): physicians should only concern themselves with the body, *even when dealing with mental illness* (or "diseases of the soul"), for once the body is working correctly, the mind will return to its proper "officium"

---

18   Henri Busson, *La religion des classiques* (Paris: PUF, 1948).
19   La Mettrie was quick to fill in the descriptive gaps in Boerhaave's psychophysiology, both in his edition and translation of Boerhaave's lectures (*Institutions de médecine de M. Hermann Boerhaave*, trans. with commentary by La Mettrie, 2nd ed., vol. 5 out of 8. Paris: Huart & Cie, 1747), and in his own writings.

(§ 27.8)—the ancient Stoic term for the role we are destined to play, which in this context can be rendered as "function."[20]

Boerhaave's student Gaub, who took over his Chair in Leiden, gave a lecture there in 1747 which La Mettrie claimed to have attended (some months prior to finishing *L'Homme-Machine*), entitled *De regimine mentis*. This text is important for us because there Gaub suggests a clinical perspective on the problem of mind-body interaction (for he is speaking of *mens* rather than *anima*, reflecting a process of naturalization which is underway in this period).[21] La Mettrie spoke favorably about the ideas he heard, and his enthusiasm[22] makes sense, for Gaub had defended the view that for the physician, the metaphysical distinction between mind and body is irrelevant. "Although the healing aspect of medicine properly looks toward the human body only, rather than the whole man, it does refer to a *body closely united to a mind* and, by virtue of *their union*, almost continually acting on its companion as well as being itself affected in turn."[23] Gaub refers to the authority of Descartes, "the most ingenious philosopher of his age," who "yielded to physicians" regarding the priority of medicine in these matters (74)[24], and states that due to the variability of temperaments, itself explainable in humoral (and hence medical) terms, the

---

20 On "officio" or "office" as a functional, teleological, or "teleomechanical" concept in early modern medicine, see Charles T. Wolfe, "Teleomechanism Redux? Functional Physiology and Hybrid Models of Life in Early Modern Natural Philosophy," *Gesnerus* 71, no. 2 (2014): 290–307.

21 John P. Wright, "Substance vs. Function Dualism in Eighteenth-Century Medicine," in *Psyche and Soma. Physicians and Metaphysicians on the Mind–Body Problem from Antiquity to the Enlightenment*, eds. J. P. Wright and P. Potter (Oxford: Clarendon, 2003), 249. Gaub, like Haller, did not appreciate La Mettrie's materialist appropriation of his ideas, and in 1763 included a short essay against La Mettrie in his new edition of *De regimine mentis*, calling him "a little Frenchman" who produced a "repulsive offspring . . . his mechanical man" (in L. J. Rather, *Mind and Body in Eighteenth-Century Medicine. A Study Based on J. Gaub's* De regimine mentis [Berkeley: University of California Press, 1965], 115).

22 More on which in our penultimate section.

23 Gaub, *De regimine mentis* (1747), in Rather, *Mind and Body in Eighteenth-Century Medicine,* 70, emphasis ours.

24 Gaub has in mind the passage from Part VI of Descartes' *Discours de la méthode* where Descartes notes the interpenetration of mind and the organs of the body, so that medicine is the best way to render people wiser than they have hitherto been (AT VI, 62).

philosopher "cannot dispense with the aid of the physician" where the mind is concerned (86).

So whereas some of the Cartesians, Boerhaave, and Gaub thought that the body-soul union (or relation, depending on their convictions) fell under the medical purview, but that it was perhaps best to focus on the body, others were more aggressively materialist in asserting the autonomy of medicine with respect to theology or other disciplines. Thus Boerhaave's advice to physicians ("only concern yourself with the body") becomes, in the Montpellier physician Ménuret de Chambaud's entry "Mort" in the *Encyclopédie*, more radical:

> The separation of the soul from the body, a mystery which may be even more incomprehensible than its union, is a theological dogma certified by religion, and consequently is uncontestable. But it is in no way in agreement with the lights of reason, nor is it based on any medical observation; hence we will not mention it in this purely medical article, in which we will restrict ourselves to describing the changes of the body, which, as they alone fall under the senses, can be grasped by the physicians, those sensual artists, *sensuales artifices*.[25]

Here the medicalization is administered in such strong doses that the concept of soul falls out altogether.

But these attempts to articulate and justify a specifically medical approach to body-soul relations (which will gradually be termed "body-*mind*" relations by the later eighteenth century) can also accept substance dualism, albeit idiosyncratically. William Cullen, in physiological lectures given at the Royal College of Physicians of Edinburgh in the mid-1760s, reflected on substance dualism, not in order to reject it, but to give it a peculiarly medical cast. For Cullen, we can

---

25 Ménuret de Chambaud, "Mort," *Encyclopédie ou Dictionnaire raisonné des sciences, des arts et des métiers*, eds. D. Diderot and J. D'Alembert (Paris: Briasson, 1765), X, 718b.

know the mechanism(s) governing our bodies, not that which governs our minds. Yet, like Boerhaave, he also thinks that our mental states are inseparable from "some conditions in the body."[26] But—perhaps on ideological grounds—Cullen immediately appealed to the good reputation of Boerhaave and Haller, who were never "suspected of Irreligion." However, he also recognizes that the mind-body problem remains problematic for physicians as well; but the specifically medical version of the problem as he states it sounds much like an *embodied* materialist statement from Diderot or La Mettrie, as we shall discuss below: it reduces "the problem of the action of the mind upon the body" to the problem: "how one State of the body or of one part can affect another part of it." Such reduction is a reduction *to states of the body, in accordance with explanations of bodily processes*; it is not a reduction to some "fundamental physics" or to the properties of matter as a whole.

Similar (although not in medical-historical terms) to Cullen's way of defending substance dualism while insisting on a *specifically medical* variant, the Paris physician Antoine Le Camus, in his *Médecine de l'esprit* (1753), put forth the program that medicine should know both minds and bodies, so that it can perfect the mind by acting on the body. Le Camus notes that most people would not deny medicine's expertise when it comes to the body, but they would be reluctant to grant it authority over the mind, and he wants to remedy this situation: "to remedy to the vices of the mind is nothing other than to remedy the vices of the body."[27] Although phrased in terms of Cartesian dualism, Le Camus' conception of medicine and of therapeutics is a different creature, for it belongs to the conceptual scheme of the

---

26 Cullen, notes added to "Lectures on the Institutes of Medicine," cit. in Wright, "Substance vs. Function Dualism in Eighteenth-Century Medicine," 244.

27 Antoine Le Camus, *Médecine de l'esprit, où l'on traite des dispositions et des causes physiques qui sont des conséquences de l'union de l'âme avec le corps, influant sur les opérations de l'esprit; et des moyens de maîtriser ses opérations dans un bon état ou de les corriger quand elles sont viciées* (Paris: Ganeau, 1753), I, 7; "God only excites ideas in our souls relative to the dispositions in our bodies" (ibid., ch. III, section 2, 49).

"animal economy"—a more integrated, organizational approach,[28] as we discuss below. Although his title suggests that Le Camus is a sort of Cartesian (since the Cartesian thesis is that passions are effects of the mind-body union on the mind), he has a more expansive conception of medicine. Similarly, Le Camus gestures initially in a Cartesian direction, saying he knows the soul is rational and immortal, but he immediately adds that it is also true that the soul is "aided in its operations" by "genuinely mechanical causes."[29] Le Camus's program for medicine holds that it is the science which has equal knowledge of mind and body, and hence can treat their "abstract combinations" and their "relations" (*commerce*). While he still refers to these as two substances in his terminology, in practice he gives an integrated account of "virtues" and "passions" as being as much part of the body as of the soul.[30]

3. Mechanistic Materialism or Materialist Embodiment? Vitalist Intimations

The medical outlook here allows for a particular kind of materialism, in which embodiment is not reducible to more general claims about how what is real is (a) body. Contrast this more integrated sense of "the body" with Hobbes's "That which is not body is no part of the universe...there is no motion save of corporeal substance"[31] or the assertion that Nature in its entirety is a "weave of bodies" (*tissure de corps*), in an intriguing, then-anonymous work of medical materialism known as the *Parity of Life and Death* (1714) by the eighteenth-century

---

28 Huneman, "'Animal Economy': Anthropology and the Rise of Psychiatry from the *Encyclopédie* to the Alienists," in *The Anthropology of the Enlightenment*, eds. Larry Wolff and Marco Cipolloni (Stanford, CA: Stanford University Press, 2007), 266.

29 Le Camus, *Médecine de l'esprit*, I, xviii.

30 Le Camus, *Médecine de l'esprit*, I, 111f.; II, 239.

31 Hobbes, *Leviathan*, IV, § xlvi, ed. E. Curley with selected Latin variants (Indianapolis: Hackett, 1994), 459; Hobbes, *Thomas White's "De Mundo" Examined* (approx. 1642–1643), trans. H. W. Jones (London: Bradford University Press, 1976), ch. 37, § 4, 447.

physician and materialist Abraham Gaultier.[32] Diderot gives a more explicitly reductionist cast to the claim that "all is body," when, in a major unpublished work which occupied him during the last two decades of his life, the *Elements of Physiology*, he explains that "the action of the soul on the body is the action of one part of the body on another, and the action of the body on the soul is again that of one part of the body on another" and, in his marginal commentary on Franz Hemsterhuis' 1772 *Lettre sur l'homme*, "wherever I read *soul* I replace it with *man* or *animal*."[33] Similarly, La Mettrie in his first philosophical work, the *Natural History of the Soul* (1745, later revised under the title *Treatise on the Soul*), declares that "he who wishes to know the properties of the soul must first search for those which manifest themselves clearly in the body," and a few years later, in *Man a Machine*: "But since all the faculties of the soul depend to such a degree on the brain and the whole body's own organization that they visibly are nothing but this organization itself—here is a *machine bien éclairée*! (really, a sophisticated machine; Eds)."[34]

That the historian of philosophy concerned with mind-body relations, mechanism and the status of the soul in a context of "naturalization" ignores the medical context at her peril, is one lesson emerging from the above. The same applies to the specific case of materialism, with an additional "moral" regarding its well-known assimilation to the position known as "mechanistic materialism." For one often hears that proper materialism—that of Hobbes, d'Holbach, and also what will become "physicalism" in the twentieth century—reduces all causes to physical causes, and all matter to a kind of mechanistically (and by

---

32 Abraham Gaultier, *Parité de la vie et de la mort. La Réponse du médecin Gaultier* (1714), ed. O. Bloch (Paris: Voltaire Foundation, 1993), 167; he is actually discussing Spinoza's views.

33 Diderot, *Éléments de physiologie* (a work which on every page seeks to explore connections between "physiological" ideas of living bodies and philosophical materialism), in Diderot, DPV XVII, 334–335; Diderot, in François Hemsterhuis, *Lettre sur l'homme et ses rapports* (1772), *avec le commentaire inédit de Diderot*, ed. G. May (New Haven, CT: Yale University Press/Paris: PUF, 1964), 277.

34 *Traité de l'âme*, I, in La Mettrie, *Œuvres philosophiques*, ed. F. Markovits (Paris: Fayard-"Corpus," 1987), I, 125; *L'Homme-Machine*, ibid., I, 73.

extension mathematically) specifiable matter. This view was prominently expressed by a thinker not so frequently cited in scholarly contexts, Friedrich Engels, in a statement as rewarding of study as it is rife with mistakes:

> The materialism of the past century was predominantly mechanistic, because at that time ... only the science of mechanics ... had reached any sort of completion. .... For the materialists of the eighteenth century, man was a machine. This exclusive application of the standards of mechanics to processes of a chemical and organic nature—in which the laws of mechanics are also valid, but are pushed into the background by other, higher laws—constitutes the specific (and at that time, inevitable) limitation of classical French materialism.[35]

There are two major mistakes here.

One is the belief that chemistry emerged suddenly in the nineteenth century. On the contrary, matter theory, materialism, and "philosophies of nature" in the eighteenth century, from Stahl to Rouelle and Venel, including individuals attending Rouelle's lectures at the Jardin du Roi (like Diderot who was an active participant for three years in the 1750s) were chemically obsessed.[36] Diderot's metaphysics of a universally sensing matter (i.e., his enhanced materialism in which sensitivity [*sensibilité*, typically translated "sensibility"] is an irreducible property of matter), is laden with chemical concepts and vocabulary, in a usage (not unique to him) of the image of the chemical laboratory

---

35 Engels, *Ludwig Feuerbach und der Ausgang der klassischen deutschen Philosophie*, in Marx and Engels, *Werke*, vol. 21 (Berlin: Dietz Verlag, [1888] 1982), 278; Karl Marx and Friedrich Engels, *Basic Writings on Politics and Philosophy*, ed. L. S. Feuer (New York: Doubleday/Anchor Books, 1959), 211.
36 On chemistry in this context see François Pépin, *La Philosophie expérimentale de Diderot et la chimie* (Paris: Garnier, 2012). Diderot criticized physics for its abstraction and insisted that "it is from chemistry that it learns or will learn the real causes" of natural phenomena (Diderot, DPV IX, 209). His lecture notes were first published in 1887, and are now available in the standard edition of his works: *Cours de chimie de Mr Rouelle* (1756), in Diderot, DPV IX. Note that this criticism of physics

or the distillation still as a way to describe the body: "The animal is the laboratory in which sensitivity shifts from being inert to being active."[37]

The other mistake is to take the man-machine model so literally, while it is really, primarily, an organic model, that is, an organism-centered model.[38] Even when La Mettrie uses the celebrated mechanistic image of the watch or clock as an analogy for the brain's capacity to think, in the opening paragraphs of *L'Homme-Machine*, when he states that the question, "can matter think?" is tantamount to asking "can matter tell time?" he is not literally saying that brains are like clocks, but rather putting forth a functional analogy between different arrangements of matter and their correspondingly different functional properties.[39] Again, La Mettrie is not asserting that the processes and properties of the specific material organization of the brain are *the same* as the processes and properties of the specific material organization of a clock.

But also, Engels can be rebutted by showing that materialism had a more constitutive relation to the emerging life sciences and their ontology (as in the case of Diderot's "Spinozism" mentioned below) as well as to vitalism.[40] Thinkers such as La Mettrie and Diderot articulated their form(s) of materialism, not just in direct dialogue with the emerging and evolving life sciences, particularly disciplines such as medicine, physiology and natural history (for Diderot: "there are no works

---

is more or less identical with his criticism of mathematics in the name of a kind of irreducible embodiment: "of all the physical sciences to which one has attempted to apply geometry, it appears that there are none in which it penetrates less than in Medicine" (Diderot, "Méchanicien," 221). A variety of kindred spirits such as Buffon, Maupertuis, La Mettrie and Bonnet (who rejected materialism as a metaphysics) concurred in *denying* that the body is something that could be *mathematized*.

37 Diderot "Lettre à Duclos," October 10 1765, *Corr.*, vol. 5, 141.

38 Ann Thomson, "Mechanistic Materialism versus Vitalistic Materialism," in *Mécanisme et vitalisme*, special issue of *La Lettre de la Maison française d'Oxford*, ed. M. Saad, 14 (2001).

39 Timo Kaitaro, "'Man is an admirable machine'—a dangerous idea?" In *Mécanisme et vitalisme*, special issue of *La lettre de la Maison française d'Oxford*, ed. M. Saad, 14 (2001).

40 Charles T. Wolfe and Motoichi Terada. "The 'Animal Economy' as Object and Program in Montpellier Vitalism," *Science in Context* 21, no. 4 (2008): 537–579; Thomson, "Mechanistic Materialism versus Vitalistic Materialism."

I read with more pleasure than medical works"[41]), but more strongly, in such a way that the ontological implications of these sciences have a direct impact on the core philosophical commitments. This relation between core materialist commitments and new life science developments (here, generation/development rather than medicine) is explicit in a particularly fascinating if brief text, Diderot's article "Spinosiste" in the *Encyclopédie*.[42] What is striking in this short article is that so-called "modern Spinozists" are presented as agreeing with the basic tenets of a metaphysics of substance and modes, *and in addition* as defenders of the biological theory of epigenesis, according to which the embryo is formed by successive addition of layers of material substance, without addition of any purely "informational" entity, as in preformationism.

The relation to vitalism deserves more analysis than can be provided here, not least because in this case, it consists of not one but two major misconceptions that are still common, including in major survey works like the *Oxford Companion to the History of Modern Science*: that materialism reduces everything to matter and motion, while vitalism has as its basic principle an immaterial vital force or principle. The present essay builds on work we have done earlier on the eighteenth-century Montpellier vitalists, and nineteenth-century physiology and medicine (from Bichat onwards), respectively.

Since our "Leitfaden" in this essay is the nonoppositional relation between machine models and embodiment, and thus between mechanistic and organismic explanations (if the latter are understood structurally rather than "foundationally," i.e., as attempts to model organizational complexity rather than as a strong distinction between a foundational principle of order, unity, or individuality and the aforementioned complexity), we will simply indicate for now that the case

---

41 *Éléments*, in Diderot, DPV XVII, 510.

42 *Enc.* XV, 474. It is not signed by him but strongly resembles passages in his other works and is included in most editions of his complete works. For full discussion of this text see Charles T. Wolfe, "Epigenesis as Spinozism in Diderot's Biological Project," in *The Life Sciences in Early Modern Philosophy*, eds. O. Nachtomy and J. E. H. Smith (Oxford: Oxford University Press, 2014).

of vitalism, at least in some of its Enlightenment forms, can be shown to be much the same. That is, just as the reductionist potential of materialist explanations did not mean a denial of embodiment but rather a response to the (simultaneously ontological and explanatory) challenge of its existence, similarly, the vitalist insistence on the specific organizational complexity of living systems is not an insistence on ontological "otherness" with respect to mechanical models. Ménuret de Chambaud, one of the more intriguing of the physicians associated with the Montpellier School of Medicine, commonly referred to today as "Montpellier vitalists" (not least since they were the first to use the term and apply it to themselves), speaks of the "human machine," playing on classic mechanistic language while adding on higher-level, chemical properties:

> What is man? Or to avoid any misunderstanding ... what is the human machine? It appears at first sight to be a harmonious composite of various springs, each of which is impelled by its own motion but (which) all concur in the general motion; a general property especially restricted to organic composites, known as irritability and sensibility spreads through all springs, animates them, vivifies them and excites their motions. But, modified in each organ, it infinitely varies their actions and motions: it leads the various springs to tighten against one another, to resist, to press, act and mutually influence one another. This reciprocal commixture sustains motions, no action without reaction. From this continuous antagonism of actions, life and health result.[43]

There is a kind of equilibrium here—for if we no longer have an autonomous, immaterial soul controlling the motions of a mechanically defined body, a more unified, more immanent picture of vital

---

43 Ménuret de Chambaud, "Spasme," *Enc.* XV, 435b.

activity is needed. Ménuret observed this quite sharply, in his ambitious and programmatic article for the *Encyclopédie* on the "animal economy":

> This idea that the soul is the efficient cause of phenomena because it is the origin (*principe*) of vital motions is not an undeniable truth. It is true that if our body was a brute, inorganic machine, it would necessarily have to be directed by some other agent, maintaining and powering its motions. And I do not think the errors of the mechanists stem from anything else than the fact that they do not hold animals to be living, organized composites.[44]

The human machine or organic machine is thus not literally the same as another "brute" machine; but the difference lies neither in a "soul" nor in a "vital principle." Rather, it is one of organizational complexity.[45] These models of biological "organization," including the "animal economy," which in many respects is a direct predecessor of the organism concept, as when its practitioners oppose it to merely mechanical explanations of the living body (in Wolfe and Terada's, "Animal Economy"), open up a conceptual space which sometimes resembles a kind of "expanded mechanism," sometimes a heuristic vitalism which would remain compatible with mechanistic accounts of specific lower-level organs and functions (in Bordeu and Ménuret de Chambaud notably[46]), in the sense that these models would seek to understand higher-level functions—from digestion and fevers to sleep and perhaps Life itself—while not losing sight of lower-level entities and processes enabling the higher functions.

---

44 Ménuret de Chambaud, "Œconomie Animale (Méd.)," *Enc.* XI, 364b.
45 We leave open here the possible comparison with Leibnizian "machines of nature," which are also defined by a specific organizational complexity, as discussed in the chapter by Ohad Nachtomy in the present volume, "Leibniz's view of Living Beings: Embodied or Nested Individuals."
46 See E. Williams' helpful comment particularly regarding Bordeu: "Mechanists had long attributed glandular action to the compression of glandular bodies by surrounding muscle and bone, but by 1750

What then of nineteenth-century medicine in the wake of vitalism and newer, more sophisticated mechanistic models?

4. From Bichat to Bernard (Embodiment in Physiology after 1800: The "French Connection")

Late eighteenth-century physiologists inherited from the medicine of the animal economy—whether that of Montpellier vitalists, or Scottish and English physiologists like the school of Munro and Cullen[47]—a concern with specifying the proper vital properties likely to support the functioning of the "machine":sensibility, contractility, irritability, and elasticity. Some carried on experiments on frogs to capture the role of electricity within the nervous system (so-called Galvanism). Haller's milestone textbook, the *Principles of Physiology*, was very influential and his experiments to isolate the properties of sensitivity and irritability[48] triggered a trend towards experiments in physiology—even though the scope and use of experimentation and especially vivisection were also critically discussed at the time and opposed the value of observation, as Ménuret did in his "Observation" entry in the *Encyclopédie*.[49] At the same time, medicine initiated its turn towards

---

it was widely recognized that this approach did nothing to explain why particular glands secreted particular fluids. Indeed it was in regard to this problem that vitalists first made inroads against mechanists, denying the explanatory power of such a model for glandular action and substituting for it a view based on the 'internal sensations' alluded to earlier, specifically the 'taste' or 'desire' of the gland that determined which components of blood it drew to itself and acted upon in furtherance of its specific function"; see "Sciences of Appetite in the Enlightenment, 1750-1800," *Studies in History and Philosophy of Science Part C: Studies in History and Philosophy of Biological and Biomedical Sciences* 43, no. 2 (2012), 398.

47 John P. Wright, "Metaphysics and Physiology. Mind, Body, and the Animal Economy in Eighteenth-Century Scotland," in *Studies in the Philosophy of the Scottish Enlightenment*, ed. Michael A. Stewart (Oxford: Clarendon, 1990).

48 Albrecht von Haller, *A Dissertation on the Sensible and Irritable Parts of Animals* (London, J. Nourse: 1755; reprint, Baltimore, John Hopkins University Press: 1936).

49 On experimentation in physiology in the earlier vitalist context see Charles T. Wolfe, "Vitalism and the Resistance to Experimentation on Life in the Eighteenth Century," *Journal of the History*

clinical medicine, with the idea that disease is a (possibly local) alteration of a functional organism rather than a "species" which would be instantiated by the diseased body. Bichat's work, spanning medicine and physiology, was elaborated around 1800 at the crossroads of those trends. As has been extensively studied, he instituted foundations for anatomo-clinical medicine by showing that diseases should ultimately be traced back to the altered tissues,[50] the basic building-bricks of an organism, while his Anatomy (*Anatomie générale*, 1798; *Anatomie descriptive*, 1802) inventoried the twenty-one various types of tissue in detail.[51] His physiology undertook, in the wake of Haller, a systematic experimental investigation of the functioning and death of the organism's main organs. We take this physiology as a major locus for elaborating an embodiment concept in the life sciences, along the lines described below.

i. *The general argument. Making embodiment into an object of experimental science*

Bichat's physiology put forth three types of principles: a definition of life as the set of functions that resist death;[52] a specification of tissues in terms of their elementary properties of sensitivity and contractility in his anatomical works; and a division between what he called the two lives (i. e., the organic life and the animal life).[53] The first life—universal

---

of Biology 46, no. 2 (2013) and for Bichat and the nineteenth-century context, Philippe Huneman, *Bichat: La vie et la mort* (Paris: PUF, 1998).

50 Michel Foucault, *Naissance de la clinique* (Paris: PUF, 1963); Toby Gelfand, *Professionalizing Modern Medicine: Paris Surgeons and Medical Science and Institutions in the 18th Century* (Westport, CT: Greenwood, 1980).

51 James E. Lesch, *Science and Medicine in France: The Emergence of Experimental Physiology, 1790–1855* (Cambridge, MA: Harvard University Press, 1984). For Auguste Comte, this was one major foundation of biology as a science (*Cours de philosophie positive* [Paris: Hermann, 1982], 41ème leçon, p. 752).

52 Bichat, *Recherches physiologiques sur la vie et la mort* [1800], second edition. Paris: Brosson & Gabon, 1802), 1.

53 Bichat, *Recherches*, Book I, chapter 2.

among living things—is described as a "relation between the organism and itself"; the second—proper to animals—is described as its relationship to the external environment. Interestingly, it is a new way of conceiving of the traditional distinction between "vital functions" and "animal functions"—here, in terms of distinct logical kinds of relationship, namely reflexive or correlational. It is here that the notion of embodiment seems to find its way into physiology: organisms include a sort of inner space through which they can be related to themselves.[54] This basic duplication or reflexivity supports the very idea of functionality and functions in Bichat's physiology.

In other words, what ontologically characterizes the animal are those two "lives" and their relations. Within each *life*, one finds "functions" in the sense of "major biological functions"—respiration, digestion, motion, perception. And then, each of these functions is achieved through the "functions of several organs"—the eyes see, the stomach decomposes nutriments, etc. Those are the functions in a second sense, "local functions," functions that the physiologist first tries to identify ("what's the function of this organ?") and then, analyze ("through which mechanism is this function achieved?") and more precisely for Bichat, "which specific combination of tissues, endowed with their specific properties, is required for this function to be carried on?").[55] Functions, in both senses, are the elementary units required to analyze and understand the existence of lives and their essential relations. Thus, the bipartition of lives defines the territory of *functional analysis*

---

54 This conceptual distinction between organic and animal life was highly praised by nineteenth-century post-Kantian philosophers. Hegel appreciated it greatly in his lectures on the philosophy of nature and turned it into a dialectical opposition between merely organic life and a life in which the animal "lives outside of its body" (in Bichat's own terms). (Georg Wilhelm Friedrich Hegel, *Enzyklopädie der philosophischen Wissenschaften,* eds. E. Moldenhauer and K. M. Michel (Frankfurt am Main: Suhrkamp, 1970). II: Naturphilosophie, 3: Organische Physik, C. Der tierische Organismus, § 355). His opponent Schopenhauer saw it as a massive proof, through empirical science, of his own distinction between representation and will: the organic life is the will, the animal life is representation, and Bichat's thesis, according to which passions originate from the epigastrum—namely the center of organic life (hence the life related to itself and not to any object)—confirms the philosopher's thesis about the originality of the will (Schopenhauer, *World as Will and Representation*, Suppl. X).

55 Bichat, *Recherches* I, chapter 1, "Division générale de la vie."

for physiology, which is classically indeed oriented toward functions, while anatomy is oriented towards structures and can therefore rely on mere observations.

"Embodiment" here refers first of all to organic life as—in phenomenological terms—what differentiates any living body (including plants) from mere bodies (a space of reflexivity so to speak); and second, the articulation between organic and animal life, which makes it possible for the animal to be an embodied agent behaving in the world. Before examining the move from Bichat's inaugural experimental physiology to Claude Bernard's ambiguous position regarding embodiment and vitalism, it is worth mentioning that the latter's most famous idea, that of the *milieu intérieur* or "internal environment," could be seen as an additional extension of Bichat's idea of *vie organique*. The *milieu intérieur*, as is well known, is the set of liquids (mostly) in which each organ of the organism lies, and which mediates the communications between organs, and, above all, between each organ and the external environment.[56] The conceptual divide between an external and an internal "milieu" allows Bernard to account for the fact that organisms are not directly determined by changes in their milieu (e.g., their temperature does not covary with external temperature; their glucose rate is not immediately affected by glucose intake from the external environment etc.) *without giving up on general determinism*—that is, the idea that in a given set of conditions, the same effect will always happen. The exact mechanism (in Bernardian terms, *le déterminisme*) that governs animal functioning and behavior is not a strict relation between organism and the external milieu, but a double relationship, between organs and their *milieu intérieur*, and then between this *milieu intérieur* and the external environment. To this extent, the state variables that describe the trajectories of each organ are not directly affected by the

---

56 Claude Bernard, *Introduction à l'étude de la médecine expérimentale* (Paris: J.B. Baillière & Fils, 1865), 115; *Principes de médecine expérimentale* (Paris: J.B. Baillière & Fils, 1882), 25.

modification of environmental variables; the *milieu intérieur* somehow buffers them against external extreme and rapid changes likely to be met by the organism.

Claude Bernard's *milieu intérieur* can then easily be understood as an operationalizable way to understand what Bichat called the "lives" of the animal: it is the *medium* of the relation between the animal and itself, which Bichat termed "*vie organique*." In this sense, the "*milieu intérieur*" can be seen as a figure of animal embodiment, inherited from Bichat's physiological bipartitioning of lives, which can be can be analyzed regarding its composition and potential alteration as a specified mix of liquids, and thus addressed by the tools of chemistry (toxicological analysis, etc.), which is the way through which Bernard intends to make experimental physiology more rigorously scientific, and therefore overcome vitalism.[57]

ii. Embodiment in experimental physiology, from Bichat to Bernard—or how determinism and vitalism come into play

It is impossible to account for this conceptual history without highlighting the fact that in Bichat's concepts in anatomy (e.g., tissue [*Anatomie générale*] and physiology [*Recherches physiologiques*]) these two "lives" were systematically related, and both were embedded in a specific physiological experimental device for producing knowledge. Bichat was clearly a vitalist, in the sense that he acknowledged a principled opposition between living and brute matter, and insisted on the fact that living matter could not display the same regularity and generality that characterizes brute matter.[58] Epistemologically, this means that whereas physicists unveil laws of nature, under the form of what philosophers would now call a set of general counterfactual-supporting

---

57 See Mirko Drazen Grmek, *Raisonnement expérimental et recherches toxicologiques chez Claude Bernard* (Geneva: Droz, 1973).
58 Bichat, *Anatomie générale*, 37.

statements, physiologists can neither access robust counterfactuals such as: "if organism A were heated it would do such and such," nor claim general statements such as "swans like to eat eels." The former impossibility Bichat understands as, somehow, the *plasticity* of the living (i.e., answers to stimulation are variable);[59] the latter is the "*idiosyncrasy*" of the living. This conceptual opposition is neatly stated in physiology under the form of a famous metaphysical opposition: "*la vie c'est l'ensemble des fonctions qui résistent à la mort*" that cannot but remind us of Stahl's *Theoria medica vera*, in which chemical forces conspire towards the death of living animated bodies. However, elsewhere Bichat curiously acknowledges that this quite classical formulation of the singularity of life is somehow contingent and hinges upon the historical sequence of the invention of scientific theories: had humans invented physiology and not physics first, he said, instead of talking of forces and weight when we try to understand the living they would talk in terms of pulses, sympathies, secretions, etc. when they would describe motions of bodies, flowing of rivers, etc.[60]

The second part of *Recherches physiologiques sur la vie et la mort*, "Recherches sur la mort," is crucial in the articulation between physiology and anatomy because it somehow legitimizes the scientificity of physiology, even though one should acknowledge the strong vitalism to which Bichat was committed, as indicated by his ideas about plasticity and idiosyncrasy. We will not enter into the details of this epistemological structure.[61] Suffice it to say that in this work Bichat investigates the way each of the three major organs (in the physiological tradition he inherits)—namely brain, lung, and heart—conditions

---

59 Bichat, *Recherches* I, chapter 4.
60 *Recherches*, 77-78. This interesting remark about the contingency of some of the most deeply entrenched ingredients of our conceptual scheme is recalled here in order to indicate that the conceptual and metaphysical opposition between the brute and the living should not be taken as a proof of the epistemic inferiority of physiology as compared to physics. It is an anticipated rebuttal of any physics envy, so to speak.
61 For more details see Huneman, *Bichat: La vie et la mort*.

the death of the two others (e.g., how does the death of the brain cause the death of the lungs?) Is it direct or happening through the death of the heart? Each question is answered by the construction of a sophisticated device that neutralizes one organ in an organism slowly enough to make manifest all the downstream effects. To this extent, what these physiological researches about death show are the sets of necessities required to sustain life in a healthy organism. Even though life is plastic and idiosyncratic, so that no gathering of observations would let us know anything about life in general and its manifestations, we can still, through these experimental devices, understand which set of necessary conditionings yields in general all the various manifestations of physiological functioning and therefore life.

One especially important object for Bichat in this framework of study is constituted by the relationship between the two *lives*—since the brain is the major organ for the *vie animale* and the heart is the crucial organ for the *vie organique*. Therefore, the physiological apparatus that explores the sets of necessary conditionings proper to sustain life—conditionings which involve primarily the heart and the brain—is capable of showing us how the two lives relate to one another.

We earlier hypothesized that Bichat grasped embodiment as *vie organique*, conceptualized it in the complex structure of knowledge that articulates *vie organique* and *vie animale*, and then related both of them into a rich anatomical structure implementing them and decomposable at the level of tissues rather than organs. If this hypothesis is correct, we also understand now that a new path taken by the history of embodiment in the nineteenth century goes through the novel structure of physiology that Bichat elaborated, which centered around the figure of the dying animal, whose death is monitored and grasped by complex experimental apparatuses.

As indicated, the next step in this sketch of a history of "clinical embodiment" was taken by Claude Bernard. But before that, however, it is important to consider the work of Bichat's major disciple, who was the teacher of Claude Bernard (a *préparateur* for his lectures from 1841 on): François Magendie, himself a famous physician and physiologist at the College de France (1831–1855), even though the fame of his disciple finally eclipsed his own. Magendie indeed pursued Bichat's project of establishing experimental physiology as a science, as it is clear from reading his *Précis élémentaire de physiologie* (1816–1817). However, in contemporary terms one could say that deflationism and minimalism were crucial in his approach, in medicine as well as in physiology.

Magendie was a supporter of what is called "expectant medicine," which means the preference for not intervening on a diseased patient, and letting nature naturally bring recovery. This attitude stems from two ideas, one which concerns philosophy of nature and consists in an Aristotelian or Hippocratic confidence in the healing power of nature itself, the other an epistemic skepticism regarding all human ways of intervening in the complex working of pathological conditions. Here the old slogan *"primum non nocere"* is pushed to its limits: since any intervention is potentially harmful, and we subscribe to a principle of not being harmful, it's better not to intervene at all.

In physiology too, Magendie was somehow deflationist, for he was precisely deflating Bichat's vitalism, in a very interesting way. For Magendie, the idea that unknown forces lead organisms and organismic tissues to behave in an unpredictable, plastic, and idiosyncratic way is absurd: since these forces are unknown, we cannot even ascribe these properties to them. There is a *roman* of the vital properties which basically is "the philosophers' anthropomorphism applied to molecules."[62] It is therefore more rational to say that we don't know anything about the substance of what behaves in physiological and biological ways, and be content with describing these behaviors as well as all the regularities we can observe, then relating them to chemical and physical regularities involved in them that our physiological devices can make manifest. Science is about detecting regular correlations rather than unraveling

---

[62] François Magendie, *Précis élémentaire de physiologie* [1816], 2d rev. ed. (Paris: Méquignon-Marvis, 1825), 30.

hidden natures: paradigmatically, the glory of Newton does not consist in having "discovered attraction," but in having "established that it acts as a direct function of the mass, and inverse of the squared distance."[63]

Magendie therefore gives up Bichat's commitment to a metaphysical opposition between the living and the nonliving; according to him, this statement would go far beyond what our observations and experiments allow us to claim. Nothing authorizes us to draw any principled differences between the metaphysical forces that support physiological properties and behavior and the physical forces that explain the natural phenomena investigated by physicists. Actually, the apparent irregularities, variations, and unpredictability that we see in the case of physiology and pathology could perfectly be ascribed to a lack of understanding, observation, and information on our part, with no need to attribute these properties to the natural forces themselves. We could only hope that progress in our observations and experiments would ultimately bridge the gap between the degree of completeness of our knowledge in physics and the then-current state of physiology.

Magendie's skepticism as such is not especially telling for the history of embodiment. In this regard, one could even argue that whereas Bichat's vitalism allowed him to conceptualize the two lives and make "embodiment" into a concept which can be encompassed in the project of an experimental physiology, Magendie's denial of vitalism, epistemological skepticism, and almost phenomenalist philosophy of scientific method[64] is extraneous to the history of the avatars of embodiment. However, this skepticism plays an important logical role in our story, because it provides the grounds on which Claude Bernard will elaborate some of its most crucial concepts, including the elements

---

63 Magendie, *Précis*, 15.
64 "All phenomena of life can be traced back to nutrition and vital action ultimately; but the hidden motions constituting those two phenomena being out of scope of our senses, it's not to them that we should pay attention: we limit ourselves to studying their results, that is in the physical properties of the organs, and search for the content with the physical properties of the organs, and search for the way the ones and the others concur to the general life" (*Précis*, 37).

TABLE 10.1 Magendie—classification of bodies: "Difference between between brute bodies ("corps bruts") and living bodies ("corps vivants")

	Form	
Brute bodies	Angular shape.	Round shape. **Living bodies**
	Undetermined volume.	Determinate volume.
	Composition	
Brute bodies	Sometimes simple.	Never simple. **Living bodies**
	Seldom constituted by more than three elements.	At least four elements.
		Often eight or ten.
		Variables.
	Each part can exist independently from the others.	Each part more or less dependent upon the others.
	Can be compounded and decomposed	Can be decomposed, but no more recomposed
	Laws that rule them	
Brute bodies	Entirely subject to attraction and chemical affinities.	Partly subject to attraction and chemical affinities **Living bodies**
		Partly *subject to an unknown force*

of a theory of *milieu intérieur* in various general publications, from the *Introduction à l'étude de la médecine expérimentale* (1855) to the *Leçons sur les phénomènes de la vie communs aux végétaux et aux animaux,* the published version of his lectures at the Collège de France in 1873.

Magendie was not exactly a pure behaviorist or phenomenalist. He admits some "forces" that are involved in living phenomena, and that are manifested each time a biological phenomenon occurs, since he acknowledges that there may be an unknown force acting within living bodies (see Table 10.1). However, he refuses, against what he sees as vitalism, to ascribe to them some distinct properties (such as plasticity, etc.) that would make them proper to the living realm (i.e., treating them as ontological entities that instantiate a specific and independent ontological realm). Instead, he conceives of these forces as pure unknown references or designations that we make in specific contexts of scientific descriptions. We just label "vital force," he says, "an unknown cause of the phenomenon of life." We have to recognize these forces, because they are supporting the constant connections between phenomena that we can identify through experiments and observations, and because we need them to turn the mere establishment of connections into useful relationships of causality.

Actually, even though he applies Bichat's ideal of experimental physiology, Magendie's metaphysical views are not so far from Barthez's vitalism, in which a vital "principle" was understood as a sort of unknown, and physiology is an effort to grasp the systematic manifestations of this principle through organized machines. Therefore, Magendie could be seen as a vitalist *in the sense of those embodied vitalist thinkers*, or "materialist vitalists" discussed in section 3, rather than in the sense of Bichat, whose vitalism is more exclusive vis-à-vis ordinary materialism. Yet one needs just one more step to definitively get rid of these vital forces and the meager commitments to vitalism that could therefore be found in Magendie's writings, notwithstanding his own wording.

Claude Bernard's idea of "determinism"—as it is explicated carefully in his two books on the methodology of experimental physiology or medicine[65]—takes this step. Since what physiology establishes is in many cases a regular succession of physiological events, such as for example, the secretion of sugar when the liver is left alone, or the neutralization of the parasympathetic nervous system when curare touches it, it is unnecessary to stipulate an unknown force which, so to say, makes this connection. What exists is this mere connection, whose existence has to be attested and demonstrated through careful and methodical investigation. Physiology aims at unraveling all these connections. These are what we now call the *mechanisms* implementing some specific functions: for instance, the mechanism of the gluconeogenic function of the liver, which allows animals to produce their own glucose and therefore not rely on consuming plants to gather one of the crucial constituents they need (glucose). Experimental physiology thereby does two things: identifying functions (e.g., the gluconeogenic function, etc.)and finding the mechanisms that implement such functions.

A Bernardian function is actually a more fine-grained instantiation of the sets of necessary conditioning that Bichat intended to explicate through his researches *sur la mort*. A mechanism implementing a function is often established through the same method Bichat systematically elaborated: disturbing or killing some of the tissue putatively involved in the realization of the function, identifying the subsequent effects of the intervention, and finally summing up this information about the effects of the controlled disturbances and reconstituting the mechanism.[66]

---

65 See Jean Gayon, "Déterminisme génétique, déterminisme bernardien, déterminisme laplacien," in *Le hasard au cœur de la cellule: Probabilités, déterminisme, génétique*, ed. J.-J. Kupiec (Paris: Editions Syllepse, 2009), on Bernadian and Laplacian determinism.
66 Grmek, *Raisonnement toxicologique*.

Bernard calls "a determinism" the "mechanism" that the research unravels. This "determinism" should not be confused with another meaning of determinism, which is nevertheless bound to it—namely, the metaphysical principle of determinism, stating that any effect produced in a given set of circumstances, will reoccur once the same set of circumstance is reactivated. This principle, obviously not falsifiable—since any putative falsification could in fact be traced back to a fine-grained undetected break-up of the identity of conditions—is necessary for science to be possible, and especially, for any experimental physiology[67], such as the science which was modeled by Bichat's devices of animal experimentation.

According to this viewpoint, no vital forces of any kind are therefore necessary to account for the regular and necessary connections established by experimental physiology. "Vital phenomena are not manifestations of a free and independent principle. One cannot grasp this inner living principle, isolate it and act on it. On the contrary one sees vital acts having constantly as conditions some external physicochemical circumstances, perfectly determined and capable of hindering or allowing their appearance."[68] Bernard's determinism succeeds in getting rid of Magendie's deflated vitalism. Interestingly, the arguably metaphysical principle of general determinism—and its connection to the idea of "*le déterminisme de*," as a target of experimental research— permits the elimination of this other metaphysical idea: the "unknown forces" or the vital forces that a whole tradition of physiologists postulated, from Bordeu to Magendie through Barthez or Bichat. Moreover Bernard does not hesitate to explicitly reject Bichat's famous dualistic and conflict-centered definition of life: "Science, one must say, has debunked this definition, according to which there would be two kinds of properties within living bodies: physical properties, and vital

---

67 Bernard, *Introduction*.
68 Claude Bernard, *Leçons sur les phénomènes de la vie communs aux animaux et aux végétaux*, vol. II (Paris: Germer Baillière, 1879).

properties, constantly fighting, and tending to predominate the ones over the others."[69]

Such is the logic governing the construction of the concept of *"milieu intérieur."* Organisms *seem* to be plastic and idiosyncratic, as Bichat initially recalled; however, no vital forces govern them. There are just sets of determinisms to be investigated. What is therefore the reason for the seemingly unconnectedness between environmental events such as cold, increase in temperature, etc., and the organismic behavior—an unconnectedness that seems to challenge the idea of a general and predictable (nomothetic) connectedness between all events and things in physical nature? This "unconnectedness" would, in our terms, relate to the acknowledgement of this "embodiment" which is the focus of our story. And it can be accounted for in terms of a specific kind of determinism, which would explain the apparent disconnection by mediating the relation between the organs of the organisms and the external environment. What Claude Bernard achieves here is a way of allowing for a scientific conceptualization of embodiment.

To put it bluntly, the *"milieu intérieur"* is a privileged *object* for Bernardian physiology—but it is also a *tool*, because any modification of the organism that can be controlled and measured, in order to understand an organism's proper patterns of causality, should either initially modify some parameters of this milieu, or influence its composition. More generally, experimental physiology uses the tools of toxicology in order to show how the tiny alterations of some liquids constituting the *milieu intérieur* entail major disturbances of some organs—or how perturbations of these organs (e.g., the curare neutralizing neurotransmission in the parasympathetic nervous system) are diffracted through various layers of the *milieu intérieur*.

---

[69] Bernard, *Leçons sur les phénomènes communs.*

Embodiment therefore appears as epistemologically crucial in the deterministic science of living things. This would be the last twist given to the idea of embodiment, once it took the path of experimental physiology, under the mode of a *vie organique* as understood by Bichat.

5. Conclusion

Common perceptions of early modern mechanism, of Enlightenment materialism, and of the genesis of nineteenth-century experimental medicine (and biochemistry), all share a tacit, sometimes explicit supposition that these must rule out the richness, the experiential texture, the significance of "embodiment." Thus Ian Hacking recently spoke in rather mournful tones of our current "Cartesian bodies": no longer machines governed by immaterial souls, but nevertheless fully mechanical assemblages of replaceable parts, whether prostheses or artificially grown biological parts.[70] Similarly, Terry Eagleton warned that the body of embodiment discourse was quite remote from biology—"the plastic, remouldable, socially constructed body, not the piece of matter that sickens and dies."[71] But if Descartes already warned (thus defusing one giant phenomenological objection against him in advance) that we should not conceive of the mind in the body like a sailor (or pilot) in a ship[72]—and if in some moments in Cartesian physiology,

---

70 Ian Hacking, "The Cartesian Body," *BioSocieties* 1, no. 1 (2006): 13–15. Notice that an entire mini-generation of prominent Descartes scholars has rejected this reading, emphasizing instead an "embodied Descartes," as we noted in Section 2. But that doesn't affect the prevalence of our common concept of the "Cartesian body," often associated with a "scientific" image of the body.

71 "Postmodernism is obsessed by the body and terrified of biology. The body is a wildly popular topic in US cultural studies—but this is the plastic, remouldable, socially constructed body, not the piece of matter that sickens and dies. The creature who emerges from postmodern thought is centreless, hedonistic, self-inventing, ceaselessly adaptive. He sounds more like a Los Angeles media executive than an Indonesian fisherman" (Terry Eagleton, *After Theory* [London: Allen Lane, 2003], 186).

72 "It is not sufficient for [the rational soul] to be lodged in the human body like a helmsman in his ship ... but that it must be more closely joined and united with the body in order to ... constitute a real human being" (AT VI 59; CSM I 141), cf. Geir Kirkebøen, "Descartes' Embodied Psychology: Descartes or Damasio's Error?" *Journal of the History of the Neurosciences* 10, no. 2 (2001), 181.

La Mettrie and eighteenth-century vitalist medicine and on to Claude Bernard, we are faced with different rearrangements of the conceptual landscape in which mechanism, body and the concept we here term "embodiment" are constantly overlapping, modifying and overdetermining one another—the status of embodiment in relation to life science requires some fresh consideration.

Where certain discussions of embodiment tend to emphasize its cultural embeddedness or its presence in literary texts of the period at the expense of so-called scientific works, we would instead point to the series of "negotiations" or displacements in which, from early modern automata to scientific physiology in the nineteenth century, and in theoretical constellations we could term "vitalism" but also "vital materialism," the idea of "organism as individuality" (as Bernard put it), of the body-machine as necessarily *my own*, given that it is an affective, desiring, hedonistic entity,[73] come to the fore.

Among these negotiations, we insisted on the last one, which culminated with Claude Bernard's idea of physiology—wherein the *milieu intérieur* appeared not only as a crucial concept, but also as an organizing principle. Now assuming that embodiment of the living is at least partly about the way living beings can relate to themselves in a way which mediates their relation to their environment and ultimately specifies their specific patterns of behavior, the construction of the concept of *milieu intérieur*, together with its embedding within a specific experimental set of practices inaugurated by Bichat's *Recherches physiologiques*, is a crucial moment in the history of embodiment: it becomes the correlate of an operational scientific practice. Bernard inherits some of the strictures Bichat imposed onto physiological knowledge: pervasiveness of an apparatus that displays, through the

---

[73] "To be a machine, to feel, to think, to know how to distinguish good from evil, as well as blue from yellow, in a word, to be born with an intelligence and a sure moral instinct, and to be but an animal, is thus no more contradictory, than to be an ape or a parrot and to know how to give oneself pleasure" (La Mettrie, *L'Homme-Machine*, in *Œuvres philosophiques*, I, 192).

making of regular sequences of dying (and here, Bernard replaces Bichat's mechanical death with mostly chemical ways of killing organisms or organs, via toxic substances) the essential organic relationships of causality or conditioning.

Now whereas Bichat understood embodiment under the mode of a specific *life* and tied it to a vitalism that accepts contingent and unpredictable changes of regime—which oppose any nomothetic understanding and possibly scientificity—Claude Bernard invests the Bichatian structures of physiological knowledge into a *milieu intérieur*, which is less directly laden with the idea of "life" and the notion of vitalism, and which allows for determinism and scientific manipulation.[74] In concluding the last section, we pinpointed a logical link between giving up the notion of vital forces—even the deflationary forces postulated by Magendie—elaborating the idea of determinism and the many determinisms as objects of experimental knowledge in physiology, and finally, elaborating the notion of *milieu intérieur* as a set of determinisms that mediate between organs (on which physiology either intervenes, or notices the effects of interventions) and physical and chemical variables describing the environment. This logic supported the constitution of perhaps the last figure of "embodiment," taken in the context of the story of its progressive acculturation within a physiology that progressively turned into "experimental physiology" during the nineteenth century.

From Cartesian mechanism and automata (a case not discussed here) as engagements with the organizational complexities of living being, through a kind of historico-scientific dialectic of materialism and vitalism in philosophy, medicine, and physiology in the eighteenth

---

[74] Bernard spoke of "le vrai vitalisme de B(ichat)" in his *Carnet de notes*—an expression he crossed out. The letter "B" referred to Bichat (G. Canguilhem, "Claude Bernard et Bichat," in *Études d'Histoire et de philosophie des sciences* [Paris: Vrin, 1968], 157). This is not an essay on the dialectics of the figures of vitalism in nineteenth-century medicine and philosophy but it is worth noting that a series of these figures engaging both in new articulations of experimental, laboratory-driven life science *and in* reflections on the nature of life shift and negotiate positions in an uneasy ballet with the notion of "vitalism."

and nineteenth centuries, we arrived at Bichat, Magendie, and Claude Bernard. Rather than a linear progression from "blind mechanism" to the complexities of embodiment, with the discovery of the *milieu intérieur*, we are faced instead with a perpetual elaboration of mechanisms or organizational wholes in which a "vitalistic" component is never entirely eliminated, nor entirely acknowledged. As Bernard puts it, "The final component of the phenomenon is physical, but the arrangement is vital."[75] Or, in La Mettrie's terms, "That the mind possesses such a corporeal nature need not be feared as a blow to our self-esteem."[76]

---

[75] Bernard, *Leçons sur les phénomènes communs*, 524.
[76] Julien Offray de La Mettrie and Hermann Boerhaave. *Institutions de médecine de M. Hermann Boerhaave*. Vol. 5, trans. with commentary by La Mettrie (Paris: Huart & Cie, 1747), 111.

CHAPTER ELEVEN

The Embodiment of Virtue

TOWARD A CROSS-CULTURAL COGNITIVE SCIENCE

Jake H. Davis

1. Introduction

The well-known Stanford Prison Experiment has recently become even more famous as a result of its Hollywood dramatization and its connections to incidents at the forefront of contemporary discussion in the United States, such as Abu Ghraib. Randomly assigned to roles as guards and prisoners, volunteers in the Prison Experiment quickly took on these social and emotional roles, and some guards became inventively sadistic.[1] Though this work by Zimbardo and colleagues has sometimes been taken to show that people with an ostensibly good character will act in evil ways depending on arbitrary external conditions, this is not quite what the evidence shows; even under the

---

1   Craig Haney, Curtis Banks, and Philip Zimbardo, "Interpersonal Dynamics in a Simulated Prison," *International Journal of Criminology and Penology*, no. 1 (1973): 69–97.

experimental conditions, not all of the guards took on an active role in perpetrating abuse. However, supported by the authority of the experimenters as well as the solidarity with their assigned group, what all of the other guards did do was to stand by as others committed dehumanizing abuse.

To begin our examination of the relation between embodiment and virtue, then, imagine how it would be for you to find yourself standing in the shoes of one of the "good" guards. One might stand by as members of one's group treat others inhumanely, as the subjects in the Prison Experiment did. Alternatively, certain individuals in certain conditions might stand up against perceived wrongdoing. What is important to notice here is the emotional conflict one would feel, whichever direction one ultimately chose. On the one hand, there is the empathic motivation to relieve the suffering of the victims. Yet there is equally the pull of emotional solidarity with one's group as well as—in real life cases—the motivation to protect not just oneself, but perhaps also family and friends, from the social, financial, and physical consequences of speaking out.

Although the course of action one ultimately chooses in such a situation is of course of great import, the experimental evidence suggests that individuals imagining ahead of time how they would conduct themselves are often mistaken. So consider what your bodily behavior and experience might be in the moments before you ultimately chose to speak out or to remain silent. How would the emotional conflict feel in your body? How would you direct your outward gaze, and how would you direct your mental attention? What action would feel most natural? Which actions would you find yourself inhibiting, holding yourself back from? Would you find yourself holding your tongue in order not to speak out, or resisting the impulse to respond forcefully to rebellious prisoners?

In this chapter, I will survey some specific ways in which virtue can be, and can fail to be, embodied by human beings. Much of the discussion of ethics in modern western philosophy has focused on applying abstract principles of right and wrong to outward actions. Even within such approaches to ethics, there are some obvious ways in which virtue and vice depend on embodiment. In physically abusing prisoners, guards use their bodies. And which types of actions will inflict suffering depend crucially on features of the prisoners' human bodies; the fact that turning on lights every few hours will cause sleep deprivation or that prolonged confinement in a dark space will cause psychological suffering both depend on features of human neurophysiological systems. We share many of the same conditions for pleasure and pain with other mammals, and a more minimal set of conditions perhaps even more broadly. So if we assume that the pain and pleasure caused to others is relevant to how we should act, then which traits count as virtuous depends at least in this minimal way on features of our embodiment, on what kinds of bodies we inhabit.

Adopting a cross-cultural and empirically based approach to ethics opens up a range of less obvious and perhaps philosophically more interesting ways in which virtue depends on, and can be supported by, our human embodiment. In this chapter, I survey three areas in particular. In section 2, I focus on the training of virtuous habits of body and brain, through habituation. Here inspiration from early Chinese philosophical sources is of particular importance in moving forward some contemporary debates over the stability of ethical virtue. In section 3, I focus more specifically on habits of internal attention to emotional motivations. This leads us to a discussion, in section 4, of ethical conflict as embodied in emotional conflict.

2. Situating and Training Virtuous Habits

One response to the perceived overemphasis in modern philosophical ethics on application of abstract principles to ethical decision making was to shift toward earlier Greek approaches, particularly virtue-theoretic models inspired by Aristotle. We can give a general characterization of such an approach as focusing on the question

"What kind of person should I be?" as the central question of ethics, rather than the question "How should I act?"[2] One should not be the kind of person who would turn sadistic in the role of prison guard, for instance, or even the kind of person who would stand by while others do so. In emphasizing being a certain kind of person, with certain virtuous habits and tendencies, this approach to ethics is dependent on human embodiment in a different way. In particular, it requires a certain stability in the behavioral dispositions of an individual organism over time and across different environmental contexts. Yet more recent theorists including Gil Harman and John Doris have charged that simulations such as the Stanford Prison Experiment, as well as a number of more controlled demonstrations by Milgram and others,[3] show that the behavioral tendencies of human beings are not of the right kind to make virtue ethics empirically plausible. The empirical evidence seems to show that in many cases the correlation across situations may be, in general, no better than .30. That is, putting an individual brain-body system in different social and environmental contexts elicits very different behavioral tendencies. Simply put, human behavioral dispositions are narrow and unreliable, not global and stable.[4]

Edward Slingerland argues that these low correlations are actually strong relative to other psychological results and also perfectly

---

[2] If incomplete; see, for example, Rosalind Hursthouse, *On Virtue Ethics* (Oxford: Oxford University Press, 1999).

[3] See, for example, Alice M. Isen and Paula F. Levin, "Effect of Feeling Good on Helping: Cookies and Kindness," *Journal of Personality and Social Psychology* 21, no. 3 (1972): 384; John M. Darley and C. Daniel Batson, "'From Jerusalem to Jericho': A Study of Situational and Dispositional Variables in Helping Behavior," *Journal of Personality and Social Psychology* 27, no. 1 (1973): 100; Stanley Milgram, *Obedience to Authority* (Harper & Row, 1974).

[4] See, for example, Owen J. Flanagan, *Varieties of Moral Personality: Ethics and Psychological Realism* (Cambridge, MA: Harvard University Press, 1991); John M. Doris, "Persons, Situations, and Virtue Ethics," *Nous* 32, no. 4 (1998): 504–530; John M. Doris, *Lack of Character: Personality and Moral Behavior* (Cambridge, MA: Cambridge University Press, 2002); Gilbert Harman, "Moral Philosophy Meets Social Psychology: Virtue Ethics and the Fundamental Attribution Error," in *Proceedings of the Aristotelian Society* 99 (139): 315–331.

admissible for many of our practical concerns.[5] For instance, in choosing a student to guard a donation box, we are justified in choosing someone who has not cheated on tests in the past over someone who has, even if past tendencies are not perfectly reliable predictors of future actions. Similarly, we might well recommend to our friends a mechanic who performs his services in a trustworthy fashion, even if he cheats on his taxes—that is, even though the mechanic's trustworthiness is less than completely global. In many cases we can settle for virtues that are less than perfectly reliable and less than completely global.

Nonetheless, being faithful to one's spouse one third of the time will hardly qualify as a virtue. For certain virtues, we expect, at least in moral exemplars, 100% reliability. And some moral exemplars in Chinese moral discourse do claim this kind of reliability. Slingerland notes, for one, "Confucius's famous declaration that he could go and live among the Eastern barbarians and not only maintain his moral perfection but in fact transform his social environment through his moral influence (*Analects* 9.14)." Early Confucian philosophy proposes to achieve something like this kind of stability through two complementary means.

For one, Confucian moral culture prescribes a fine-grained manipulation of the social context. As Slingerland puts it, "the early Chinese Confucians paid a great deal of attention to the power of the embodied situation—social role, dress, ambient color, and sound—to effect human dispositions and behavior."[6] According to Slingerland, this focus strengthens the empirical plausibility of virtue ethics, or at least this early Confucian version of the approach. To be fair, the empirical literature cited by Harman and Doris is intended precisely to show the power of social situations; it is just this power of such social context in

---

5 Edward Slingerland, "The Situationist Critique and Early Confucian Virtue Ethics," *Ethics* 121, no. 2 (January 2011): 390–419.
6 Ibid., 418.

determining behavior that critics take to show a lack of stable, global ethical dispositions in individuals. Still, perhaps the point here is that this very emphasis on the individual as the focus of ethical theorizing is problematic, and a problem implicit in the situationist critique of virtue ethics as much as in the modern theoretical alternatives to virtue ethics. Virtue ethics done properly is based on the idea that virtue can be embodied only in certain kinds of social situations as much as only in certain sorts of dispositions; the contention is that this is not a weakness but a strength of such an approach to answering the question of how we ought to be.

Perhaps more importantly for our purposes, manipulating the social environment can be seen, as in the Confucian context, as a means to enable the cultivation of stable dispositions towards certain types of behavior. These are ultimately intended to be dispositions stable enough to be maintained "even among the Eastern Barbarians," as we have seen. They are presumably also intended to be stable enough to be maintained by individuals cast in the role of a prison guard, or a supreme ruler. Slingerland describes in detail the method of cultivation employed by the teacher Mencius with an oppressive king who displays a profound lack of the virtue of benevolence (*ren*) in his dealings with his subjects. Mencius notes a story of the king's own display of compassion towards an ox being lead to ritual sacrifice—a narrow context. By means of creating emotional resonance between that narrow situation and the the broader set of situations in which the king relates to his human subjects, the teacher works towards a gradual strengthening and "extension" (*tui*) of the disposition toward benevolence in the king. In short, Mencius aims at fostering in the king benevolence as a global virtue.

The empirical literature cited by situationist critics of virtue ethics focuses on "untutored" dispositions, as Slingerland points out. Indeed, the interest of studies such as the Stanford Prison Experiment to critics such as Harman and Doris is that they challenge our own self-conception, by showing that untutored folks like us wrongly attribute stable virtues to ourselves.[7] This point is crucial. The viability of virtue ethics may yet be vindicated by new studies on the ability of human dispositions in general, and ethically relevant dispositions in particular, to become more stable and more global through training.

As Slingerland notes, the Confucian emphasis on ritual (*li*) involves training bodily habits of behaving in prescribed ways. This emphasis on training bodily habits helps to explain how some of these might achieve stability across contexts. Perhaps stable, reliable, ethically relevant dispositions can be trained through the use of logical reasoning and emotional analogy alone. But, on the other hand, perhaps this stability can only be achieved through the training of bodily habits. Perhaps both are required, or perhaps neither is effective enough, even in conjunction with one another. Ultimately, this is an empirical question, though one that is largely yet to be explored. There is some preliminary evidence that academic training in ethical reasoning is not sufficient; ethics professors apparently do not in general display more consistency between their expressed attitudes and their behavior than others, nor do they show consistently better behavior in general, and their reasoning about ethical questions is affected by irrelevant factors such as the order of question presentation, just as it is for the rest of us.[8] In advance of other evidence, it seems likely that whereas ethical reasoning is fickle and subject to rationalization, bodily habits of perceiving suffering and reacting with kindness may be more ingrained and

---

7 There is a side issue here in that virtue ethics was revived in recent philosophy in part as an antidote to the perceived impracticality of utilitarianism and deontology, and to return to a more humanly practicable ideal. Still this selling point for virtue theories may yet be vindicated to the degree empirical work shows a viable method for training the mind and body so as to achieve more stable and more global ethical dispositions.

8 Eric Schwitzgebel and Joshua Rust, "The Moral Behavior of Ethics Professors: Relationships among Self-Reported Behavior, Expressed Normative Attitude, and Directly Observed Behavior," *Philosophical Psychology* 27, no. 3 (2014): 293–327; Eric Schwitzgebel and Joshua Rust, "The Moral Behaviour of Ethicists: Peer Opinion," *Mind* 118, no. 472 (2009): 1043–1059; Eric Schwitzgebel, "Do Ethicists Steal More Books?" *Philosophical Psychology* 22, no. 6 (2009): 711–725; Eric Schwitzgebel and Fiery Cushman, "Expertise in Moral Reasoning? Order Effects on Moral Judgment in Professional Philosophers and Non-Philosophers," *Mind & Language* 27, no. 2 (2012): 135–153.

less subject to situational factors. If so, this would be a further sense in which virtue depends on embodiment.

3. Embodying Attentiveness

In the previous section, we raised the question of whether training in certain external behavioral routines or, alternately, training in ethical reasoning would be more effective in cultivating the sort of stable global dispositions worthy of being called virtues. However, there is a third option: the training of attention. Perceptual habits of attending to certain aspects of the external environment and certain aspects of one's internal states may in fact structure many responses to ethically charged situations. Indeed, attentional habits may help in determining both the trajectory of an individual's ethical reasoning and also the trajectory of behavioral response.

In offering an empirically grounded analysis of the situationist challenge to virtue ethics, Merrit, Doris, and Harman emphasize the importance of other-directed attention.[9] In Milgram's obedience studies, subjects were instructed by an authority figure in a lab coat to administer increasing levels of electric shock to a "learner," a confederate of the experimenters who acted out intense physical pain, protested, and finally collapsed. What is shocking about the results is the evidence of how far apparently normal individuals will go to follow the directions of an authority figure. Merritt and colleagues note, however, that variations of the Milgram experiment showed that when the authority figure was physically more distant, subjects' tendency to continue to inflict shocks to the "victim" was drastically lower. This and related evidence they take to show the crucial role in which external situations can structure attention to the embodied presence of authority figures and thus attention and deference to their suggestions. They

---

[9] Maria Merritt, John Doris, and Gilbert Harman, "Character," in *The Moral Psychology Handbook*, ed. John M. Doris (Oxford University Press, 2010), 355–401.

thus echo the point relayed by Slingerland from the early Confucian tradition of the ethical importance of the external social situations we create and situate ourselves in.

A second relevant aspect of other-directed attention is attending toward victims. Merritt et al. note that in the Milgram obedience studies subjects were "viscerally" affected by the victim's cries and exhibited signs of affective and physiological arousal indicating stress. Interestingly, some subjects turn their heads "to avoid seeing the victim suffer," mask the victim's cries with their own vocalizations, or turn their attention away from the victim and confine it to the mechanics of the procedure.[10] This human impulse to turn away is familiar to us, for instance from the good guards' actions in dramatizations of the Stanford Prison Experiment, and—perhaps in less extreme circumstances—from our own lives. There are two points here of special importance for our purposes. First, the virtue of care for others in such situations can be embodied in whether or not we turn our eyes away, or move away. Secondly, the disposition to turn away serves at least in part as a method of emotional regulation, a means to decrease the stress of seeing another suffer. We return to this point in more detail in section 4. For now, however, note that some measure of this kind of distraction from others' suffering can be achieved through mental distraction, even when we do not physically turn away. Conversely, perhaps part of what is required in order to embody virtue is the disposition not to distract ourselves from the stress of seeing others suffer, not to become overwhelmed by it, but rather to feel our own emotional suffering in a full and balanced way.

Buddhist ethical texts claim that this kind of mindful awareness of the body, affective reactions, and other internal states facilitates wise judgment and virtuous behavior. They are not alone in emphasizing the connection between attention and virtue. William James asserted

---

10 Milgram, *Obedience to Authority*, 155, 161, quoted in Merritt, Doris, and Harman, "Character," 382–383.

that "the faculty of voluntarily bringing back a wandering attention, over and over again, is the very root of judgment, character, and will."[11] More recently, a small number of theorists including Goldie and, separately, Brady, have debated the role of "virtuous habits of attention" in facilitating the kinds of understanding required for moral development and ethical behavior: understanding of what is dangerous, what is shameful, what is praiseworthy, and so on.[12] Yet despite agreeing on the ethical importance of habits of attention, these western theorists have not offered anything like the detailed practical guidance for, and philosophical analysis of, training programs aimed at developing virtuous habits of attention that is offered in Buddhist traditions.

The recent upsurge in research on attention training programs derived from Buddhist traditions, particularly mindfulness meditation, offers an opportunity to test the ethical relevance of training embodied awareness. Research has shown that mindfulness practice not only improves attention, perception, and metacognition,[13] and is associated with decreased mind wandering,[14] but also predicts introspective accuracy in bodily awareness,[15] and is correlated with more accurate first-person reports about emotional response.[16] These

---

11 William James, *The Principles of Psychology* (New York: Holt), 1890, Chapter 11.

12 Peter Goldie, "Emotion, Reason, and Virtue," in *Emotion, Evolution, and Rationality*, eds. Dylan Evans and Pierre Cruse (Oxford: Oxford University Press, 2004), 249–267; Michael S. Brady, "Virtue, Emotion, and Attention," *Metaphilosophy* 41, no. 1–2 (2010): 115–131; Michael S. Brady, *Emotional Insight: The Epistemic Role of Emotional Experience* (Oxford: Oxford University Press, 2013).

13 Antoine Lutz et al., "Mental Training Enhances Attentional Stability: Neural and Behavioral Evidence," *The Journal of Neuroscience* 29, no. 42 (October 21, 2009): 13418–13427; K. A. MacLean et al., "Intensive Meditation Training Improves Perceptual Discrimination and Sustained Attention," *Psychological Science* 21, no. 6 (May 11, 2010): 829–839; Benjamin Baird et al., "Domain-Specific Enhancement of Metacognitive Ability Following Meditation Training," *Journal of Experimental Psychology: General* 143, no. 5 (2014): 1972.

14 Judson A. Brewer et al., "Meditation Experience Is Associated with Differences in Default Mode Network Activity and Connectivity," *Proceedings of the National Academy of Sciences* 108, no. 50 (December 13, 2011): 2054–2059.

15 Kieran C. R. Fox et al., "Meditation Experience Predicts Introspective Accuracy," *PloS One* 7, no. 9 (2012): e45370.

16 Jocelyn A. Sze et al., "Coherence between Emotional Experience and Physiology: Does Body Awareness Training Have an Impact?" *Emotion* 10, no. 6 (2010): 803–814.

abilities may derive in part from temporary increases in neural activity in somatosensory areas,[17] as well as longer-term structural changes in the brain.[18]

If the psychological and neuroscientific exploration of how mindfulness practice works to train embodied awareness is still in its early years, testing of the Buddhist claims for a relation between mindfulness practice and ethical understanding is barely in its infancy. Condon and collaborators recently found that individuals training in either mindfulness practice or in compassion meditation were more likely than controls to help a bystander in need. Interestingly, there was no significant different between the two meditation types in helping behavior.[19] Kirk and colleagues drew a closer tie to embodiment with a study showing associations between mindfulness training, neural activity consistent with increased interoceptive awareness, and more altruistic and less punishing responses in the Ultimatum Game.[20] The Ultimatum Game is a simulation of economic behavior, in which one party, the proposer, is given the decision of how to split $10, say, with a second party, the responder, with the caveat that if the responder rejects the offer, neither gets any. Most equal offers are accepted. But as offers become increasingly less equal, they are more likely to

---

17 Catherine E. Kerr et al., "Mindfulness Starts with the Body: Somatosensory Attention and Top-down Modulation of Cortical Alpha Rhythms in Mindfulness Meditation," *Frontiers in Human Neuroscience* 7 (2013), http://www.frontiersin.org/Human_Neuroscience/10.3389/fnhum.2013.00012/abstract; Catherine E. Kerr et al., "Effects of Mindfulness Meditation Training on Anticipatory Alpha Modulation in Primary Somatosensory Cortex," *Brain Research Bulletin* 85, no. 3–4 (May 2011): 96–103.

18 S. W. Lazar et al., "Meditation Experience Is Associated with Increased Cortical Thickness," *Neuroreport* 16, no. 17 (2005): 1893; B. K Hölzel et al., "Stress Reduction Correlates with Structural Changes in the Amygdala," *Social Cognitive and Affective Neuroscience* 5, no. 1 (2010): 11–17; B. K Hölzel et al., "Mindfulness Practice Leads to Increases in Regional Brain Gray Matter Density," *Psychiatry Research: Neuroimaging* 191, no. 1 (2011): 36–43.

19 P. Condon et al., "Meditation Increases Compassionate Responses to Suffering," *Psychological Science*, August 21, 2013.

20 Ulrich Kirk, J. Downar, and P.R. Montangue, "Interoception Drives Increased Rational Decision-Making in Meditators Playing the Ultimatum Game," *Frontiers in Decision Neuroscience* 5 (2011): 49.

be rejected. Chapman et al. investigated the emotional basis of these decisions by asking participants in an Ultimatum Game to indicate how well their feelings about the preceding offer were represented by photographs of faces displaying disgust, anger, contempt, fear, sadness, surprise, or happiness.[21] Not surprisingly, ratings of happiness dropped rapidly from a high when offers were equal (5:5) as the offers became less equal, with the proposer offering to keep $7 and give the responder $3, or to keep $9 and give the proposer $1. In contrast, ratings of disgust and anger increased dramatically as the offers became more unequal. Moreover, the researchers found that changes in facial muscles associated with disgust were correlated with subjective identification with disgust faces. This suggests that emotions such as anger and disgust drive the behavioral response of rejecting unfair offers in economic games.

Kirk et al.'s investigation suggests that individuals with increased interoceptive awareness were more willing to accept unfair offers, and thus that their actions were not driven to the same extent as controls by sentiments of anger and disgust. The authors characterize their results as showing that mindfulness serves to cultivate "rational" responses to economic exchanges in the Ultimatum Game. However, a note of caution is necessary. On the individual level, the costs of retributive response may indeed outweigh the benefits, both in these laboratory-based economic games and also in daily human interactions. Nonetheless, the enforcement of fairness norms serves an important communal function. And more generally, sentiments such as outrage or guilt driving outcome-based moral judgment may be adaptive in terms of reproductive fitness.[22] In his classic paper on the emergence of altruistic behavior, Trivers notes that moralistic aggression and indignation

---

[21] H. A. Chapman et al., "In Bad Taste: Evidence for the Oral Origins of Moral Disgust," *Science* 323, no. 5918 (2009): 1222–1226.

[22] Ernst Fehr and Simon Gächter, "Altruistic Punishment in Humans," *Nature* 415, no. 6868 (January 10, 2002): 137–140.

might have been selected for as a means to counteract the tendency of the emotional rewards of altruism to drive continual altruistic acts in the absence of reciprocity.[23] This gives rise to a possible explanation of Kirk et al.'s result: if feeling altruistic is emotionally more rewarding than feeling anger or disgust, individuals who are for whatever reason more fully and accurately aware of which emotional motivations are intrinsically punishing and which are not might be less motivated to engage in retributive emotional reactions and more motivated to cultivate altruistic ones. We turn to this further aspect of the embodiment of virtue, in the emotional reward of certain motivations over others, in the next section.

4. Ethical Conflict in the Body

There is considerable controversy about the about the role of embodied emotion in ethical concepts and ethical judgment,[24] and about the role of emotion in ethical motivation.[25] Nonetheless, as Hollywood dramatizations and first-person reflection help to illustrate, to face an ethical dilemma is often to face an emotional conflict, one that is expressed bodily and that we can feel in our bodies. To take one extreme example, Jonathan Bennett reads Heinrich Himmler's remarks in a 1943 speech as indicating that the principles the architect of the Final Solution held

---

[23] Robert Trivers, "The Evolution of Reciprocal Altruism," *The Quarterly Review of Biology* 46, no. 1 (1971): 49.

[24] Jesse Prinz and Shaun Nichols, "Moral Emotions," *The Moral Psychology Handbook*, ed. John M. Doris, (Oxford: Oxford University Press, 2010), 111–147; Jesse J. Prinz, *The Emotional Construction of Morals* (New York: Oxford University Press, 2007); B. Huebner, S. Dwyer, and M. Hauser, "The Role of Emotion in Moral Psychology," *Trends in Cognitive Sciences* 13, no. 1 (2009): 1–6; Bryce Huebner, "Do Emotions Play a Constitutive Role in Moral Cognition?" *Topoi* 34, no. 2 (2015): 427–440; J. Greene, "Emotion and Cognition in Moral Judgment: Evidence from Neuroimaging," in *Neurobiology of Human Values,* edited by J.P. Changeux, et al., 57–66 (New York: Springer, 2005); Mark Johnson, *Morality for Humans: Ethical Understanding from the Perspective of Cognitive Science* (Chicago: University of Chicago Press, 2015).

[25] Timothy Schroeder, Adina Roskies, and Shaun Nichols, "Moral Motivation," in *The Moral Psychology Handbook*, ed. John M. Doris (Oxford: Oxford University Press, 2010), 72–110.

to be moral ones forced him to overcome emotional reactions of sympathy that he did nonetheless feel for the living beings he was responsible for exterminating. Himmler apparently suffered from nausea, stomach-convulsions, and various other complaints; Bennett quotes and endorses the characterization by Kersten, Himmler's physician, of these ailments of Himmler's as "the expression of a psychic division which extended over his whole life."[26]

The motivation to avoid cognitive dissonance seems likely to be a widely shared aspect of animal psychology. Although Festinger's theory of cognitive dissonance as a core drive has been controversial, a recent review by Gawronski argues that this core drive imposes a universal constraint on belief systems across cultures and species.[27] He notes, for instance, that the motivation to avoid cognitive dissonance seems to be present even in rats.[28] These sorts of results, in contrast to some of the earlier research, seem to suggest a kind of dissonance that is not dependent on language, but is instead a more embodied and broadly shared animal motivation. In light of such evidence, we can see part of the motivation to act virtuously as a motivation to avoid conflict within ourselves, an emotional conflict that is as much physiological as rational.

If the emotionally painful social consequences that encourage even "good" guards not to speak out are abundantly clear, it is less clear the nature of the forces on the opposite side of the emotional conflict. Aristotle emphasizes the role of emotion and of pain and pleasure in virtue (*NE*, Book II, Chapter 3). While agreeing with this broad emphasis, Buddhist traditions make a further claim that is interesting

---

26 Jonathan Bennett, "The Conscience of Huckleberry Finn," *Philosophy* 49, no. 188 (1974): 129.

27 Leon Festinger, *A Theory of Cognitive Dissonance* (Evanston, IL: Row, Peterson, 1957); Bertram Gawronski, "Back to the Future of Dissonance Theory: Cognitive Consistency as a Core Motive," *Social Cognition* 30, no. 6 (2012): 652–668.

28 Emma S. Lydall, Gary Gilmour, and Dominic M. Dwyer, "Rats Place Greater Value on Rewards Produced by High Effort: An Animal Analogue of the 'Effort Justification' Effect," *Journal of Experimental Social Psychology* 46, no. 6 (November 2010): 1134–1137.

in light of recent research: that ethically wholesome emotional motivations actually feel good, while ethically unwholesome emotional motivations feel bad.[29] To be at all plausible, this sort of claim has to be bolstered, as the Buddhist account is, by a proposal for how we can come to see more clearly which of our own emotional motivations are pleasurable and painful, and thus by a corresponding account of how we might (many of us, much of the time) be mistaken about this. The essential idea as that, when we train a more fully embodied awareness in the way sketched in the previous section, altruistic motivations are revealed as being more pleasurable than their opposites.

Altruistic behavior can be rewarding in various ways, and in many cases helping others may be merely an instrumental goal in service of getting social or other emotional rewards for oneself. In a series of classic studies, Batson and colleagues tested a range of such egoistic explanations of helping behavior against their own empathy-altruism hypothesis that egoistic concerns are not the only motivation for altruistic behavior. Put another way, Batson's hypothesis is that some motivations for some altruistic acts do take as their ultimate goal the welfare of the other, rather than the motivation to help another always being proximate, in the sense of being merely a means to some other self-interested ultimate goal. The power of Batson's work lies in the groundbreaking experimental paradigms he used to isolate and test cases in which the posited egoistic concerns could be satisfied without altruistic action to relieve another's suffering. In some experiments, Batson and colleagues manipulated feelings of empathy in subjects by using similarity manipulations, such as providing a filled-out questionnaire indicating that the suffering person's values were similar or dissimilar to those indicated by the subject; in others they induced emotion-specific misattribution, by providing a placebo pill and information either that the pill had the side effect of

---

29 Maria Heim, *The Forerunner of All Things: Buddhaghosa on Mind, Intention, and Agency* (New York: Oxford University Press, 2014).

inducing feelings of personal distress, or else that the that the pill had the side effect of inducing feelings of concern.[30] These manipulations allow a test of the empathy-altruism hypothesis against the competing view that all helping behavior is motivated by egoistic concerns, such as the motivation to reduce the empathic distress brought on by seeing another suffering noted above in Milgram's subjects. In high-empathy conditions in Batson's experiements, individuals provided with an easy possibility for removing themselves from a situation in which they observed another suffering were less likely to choose to escape than in low-empathy conditions. This counts against the idea that altruistic helping is driven by a simple goal of reducing aversive arousal. With similar manipulations, Batson and colleagues provided powerful experimental evidence against a range of more sophisticated egoistic explanations of altruistic behavior, including social evaluation and self-criticism.[31] Using a reaction time task, for instance, individuals in the high-empathy condition in one study showed no increases in cognitive association with concepts of social reward such as PROUD, HONOR, PRAISE, but did show a positive association with victim-related words. In another study, Batson and colleagues found positive changes in self-reported mood when the suffering of the other was ended, even when the possibility to help was taken away. One especially interesting study addressed a proposed egoistic motivation to gain vicarious or contagious good feelings when the suffering of another is relieved.[32] Contradicting the conclusions of a previous study, Batson and colleagues again found support for the empathy-altruism hypothesis. Although there was some evidence for motivation to experience vicarious relief in

---

30 C. D. Batson et al., "Is Empathic Emotion a Source of Altruistic Motivation?" *Journal of Personality and Social Psychology* 40, no. 2 (1981): 290.

31 C. D. Batson and L. L. Shaw, "Evidence for Altruism: Toward a Pluralism of Prosocial Motives," *Psychological Inquiry* 2, no. 2 (1991): 107–122.

32 C. D. Batson et al., "Empathic Joy and the Empathy-Altruism Hypothesis," *Journal of Personality and Social Psychology* 61, no. 3 (1991): 413.

the low-empathy conditions, individuals in the high-empathy condition did not increase their helping behavior when expecting to receive feedback from the person helped, and did not increase their interest in hearing about the suffering person's status dependent on the likelihood that the person's condition would in fact improve.

Batson's results, if correct, show that we cannot explain altruistic behavior in terms of expected future rewards, even internal ones. They explicitly rule out the hypothesis that subjects "learn through prior reinforcement that, *after* helping those for whom we feel empathy, we can expect a special mood-enhancing pat on the back," for instance.[33] Nonetheless, it is consistent with Batson's results, and perhaps also with the spirit of his proposal, to suggest that people are motivated to act altruistically because feeling altruistic feels good—that is, making another's welfare one's ultimate goal could be motivated by the hedonic reward of present altruistic emotional motivations themselves. It is important to note that emotional motivations can be seen as distinct from the external stimulation they arise with. When one encounters others suffering, such an experience may be painful, as it seems to have been for some subjects in the Stanford Prison experiment and Milgram's obedience studies. But the negative affective valence of such external stimuli can be met and held by an internal emotional motivation of friendliness. One way of reading the Buddhist claim is that this basic friendliness, just as it arises and before it can manifest in helping behavior, may itself be more pleasurable than the alternative ways of reacting to suffering. When this sort of basic friendliness comes into contact with another's success, on this account, it protects one against feeling envy, and manifests instead as what Buddhist translators have termed sympathetic joy. Equally, when this same internal quality of heart of basic friendliness and care comes in contact with suffering, it manifests as compassion, a desire to help.

---

33 Batson and Shaw, "Evidence for Altruism," 117, my emphasis.

It is conceivable that individuals could be motivated to cultivate an altruistic state just because it feels better to feel that way toward others than the relevant alternative emotional options. On one construal we could take this as just another sort of proximate motivation: one is only motivated to be motivated to help because that desire to help feels good. On the other hand, one could also take this as a claim about the nature of motivation: what it is to be motivated in a certain way is that it feels pleasurable to move oneself towards that goal. On this construal, what makes it the case that helping another is one's ultimate goal is just the fact that the physiological state that results in such actions is experienced as pleasurable. And if individuals are motivated to cultivate this basic friendliness because of its relative ease, simply by being more often in this emotional state rather than its opposites, they would more often be disposed to act for other's welfare in cases of need.

This is of course an empirical claim that we are deriving from Buddhist tradition, and as such subject to empirical refutation. Nonetheless, anecdotal evidence from a few recent investigations provides initial support for the idea that there can be a pleasurable internal response to suffering, or at least helps to clarify the notion for further testing. In a recent pilot investigation of the neural basis of compassion, Tania Singer asked the Buddhist monk Matthieu Ricard to help differentiate compassion from empathic distress by directing his mind for one hour in the fMRI scanner just toward images of suffering, feeling the distress that brings on, without allowing this to move into the emotions of well-wishing that the Buddhist tradition suggests are so important to train. According to recent comments by both Ricard and Singer, Ricard found this one hour nearly unbearable, and practically begged Singer to allow him to switch to his highly trained manner of responding to suffering with what he describes as "human warmth ... love and compassion."[34] What this

---

34 Comments by Tania Singer at Mind and Life XXV, 2012.

suggests is that it is possible to train a more fully embodied awareness that feels the relief of altruistic motivations, and thereby can help to strengthen the power of these forces over others in cases such as the "good" guards' internal struggle. If this proves right, it provides a yet a further way in which virtue depends on embodiment.

5. Conclusion

In this chapter I have brought together recent empirical research with Confucian and Buddhist philosophical proposals, in order to sketch specific avenues for further investigation of the embodiment of virtue. The aim of such a cross-cultural approach is to ensure that our explorations of embodiment and of virtue do not become—or remain—overly beholden to any one particular conceptual framework for understanding the human mind and human life.[35] On the topics of embodiment and of ethics this need is especially pressing—for the rationalism of modern western philosophy and the cognitivism of recent empirical investigations of the mind, for all their achievements, have equally left of us blind to important aspects of lived experience, and of ourselves. Buddhism and Confucianism have their own blindspots, of course, and this is why dialogue is so valuable to all parties. I have sketched three areas where integrating cross-cultural reflection with recent empirical research may prove particularly useful in pushing our investigation into virtue beyond its current confines: the training of ethical dispositions in social contexts; the training of attentional habits in relation to embodied emotion; and finally the topic of conflict as well as resolution between embodied ethical motivations.

---

35 Jonardon Ganeri, *Attention and Consciousness: The Metaphysics of Autonomous Shadows.*, forthcoming; J. Garfield, *Engaging Buddhism: Why It Matters to Philosophy.* 1st ed. (Oxford: Oxford University Press, 2015); Jake H. Davis and Evan Thompson, "From the Five Aggregates to Phenomenal Consciousness: Towards a Cross-Cultural Cognitive Science," in *A Companion to Buddhist Philosophy*, ed. Steven M. Emmanuel (John Wiley & Sons, 2013), 585–597.

Reflections

The Devil in the Flesh
ON WITCHCRAFT AND POSSESSION
Véronique Decaix

The large-scale witch-hunt in Europe, beginning in the fourteenth century and ending in the seventeenth (with a peak during the sixteenth when thousands of witches, mostly women, but including some male wizards were burned at the stake) reveals the dark side of the Renaissance. Witches, together with lepers and wanderings Jews, are constructed as figures of otherness in a normalizing process. During the humanist period, characterized by rationality and enlightenment, the authorities needed to provide a theoretical basis for the persecution of witches. In the *Malleus Malleficarum* (1484), Jacob Sprenger and Henrich Krammer provide a conceptual arsenal for the identification and punishment of witches. Although the *mallefici* could also be male (i.e., wizards or sorcerers) the arguments in most of the cases targeted women; the Inquisitors reasoned that women, due to their constitutive weakness, were more inclined to fall into witchcraft. In their thorough descriptions, Sprenger and Krammer give a rational foundation for a typically female form of evil. As the witch defies natural laws, this handbook for the Inquisition, reprinted thirty-four times between 1487 and 1669, conceptualizes an alternative anthropology, based upon scholastic ideas, such as a demonology inherited from Augustine and an Aristotelian definition of man as a compound of matter and form, in order to give an account of the abnormality incarnated by the witch. In this account, the body of witches, being their bond to the Devil, stands at the core of the process to eradicate them.

Witches were depicted as wild women (*mulieres sylvestris*) living at the margin of human community. Inhabiting the woods or the countryside, secluded from society, witches personify a certain relationship to the hidden powers of nature, resistant to civilization. Outsiders in the literal sense, witches are antisocial beings, existing at the boundary between humanity and animality. This asocial feature of witchcraft must be balanced with the fact that witches substitute for the natural link to God and human society an unnatural one: the pact with the Devil. This diabolic contract is understood as the exact opposite of baptism, where the infant is both introduced into the realm of God and as a member of the human society. In opposition to the performative act of language "*Ego te baptismo*," the pact with the Devil is concluded by an action that breaks the law and order of nature. In accomplishing a perverse act (for example: to fornicate with Satan, or to "kiss a goat's anus"), the witch renounces her relation to God and Christian society while establishing an effective bond to Satan. As a symbol of this malefic pact, the witch bears a mark in her flesh. By a scratch or a bite during copulation, the devil leaves an imprint on the witch's skin, like his signature on a parchment. Such an evil mark (which could also be a birthmark in the shape of an animal symbolizing the Devil, such as a toad) was often placed on the left side of the body, for example on the left shoulder, or else in hidden places like inside the eye or the mouth, or in the hair, pubic hairs, or in the pudenda (i.e., the vulva or vagina). This bodily sign was seen as a piece of evidence of the witch's guilt, so that the Inquisitors developed a semiotic test, which was to reveal its occult origin: the mark is invisible to one's eyes and insensible. In order to confound the witch, the Inquisitors had the duty to locate the evil seal by sticking a needle though every part of her shaved body: any spot that sheds no blood was considered as a direct proof of her unnatural relation to Satan.

One can wonder about the function of the witch's mark: several interpretations were given at the time. First, the witches and wizards could thereby recognize each other as members of the same occult society. The mark indicated their membership in an alternative community, modeled upon the animal pack and gathering at the nocturnal Sabbath. Moreover, the Inquisitors give another explanation for the witch's mark, based upon demonology. One of the most striking differences between pagan and Christian demonology lies in the fact that, in the latter, demons do not possess a proper body. According to the Augustinian principle, evil is nothing in itself (a simple privation of being), so that the Devil does not hold any real existence in the world (merely a negative one). Conceived as an incorporeal shapeless breath made of thin air, the Devil cannot consequently act on his own and exercise his malice. However, Christians had to give an account for the real existence of evil: this is where the witch comes in. She is an intermediary through which Satan infuses his evil ways into the world. In this regard, the witch's body is the instrument of Satan's will. The mark in her flesh is not just a seal of a past pact; it is rather an active principle through which Satan operates in the theatre of the world. The mark of the witch is a point of contact between the underworld and the mundane world.[1] Evil is described in the *Malleus* as an epidemic, a spread of disease.[2] The death of flocks and children, sickness, and infertility of people or of animals were

---

[1] *Malleus Malleficarum*, trans. and ed. Christopher S. Mackay (Cambridge, UK: Cambridge University Press, 2006).
1st Part, q. 2 and q. 3.
[2] *Malleus Malleficarum*, 1st Part, q. 15.

typical signs of witchcraft. The witch's body opens a gate, a channel, though which the demonic forces may infect our world. The malice lying in her body could also be an efficient mediator without the witch actively interceding for Satan, as shown in a story reported in the *Malleus*. After the death of an old woman, a village suffered from a propagation of plague, which people said was caused by sorcery. The mayor ordered her tomb reopened and found her corpse chewing her shroud, rotten and partly ingested in her stomach. Immediately upon the corpse's decapitation, the plague stopped. The body of the witch remains active even after her death, so that it can still poison the world. Therefore, the traditional punishment of the witch was the total annihilation of her body at the stake in a purification by fire.

If evil lies in the flesh of the witch and if humans are a compound of body and soul, what remains of the woman after she becomes a witch? This question was crucial to the Inquisitors. Indeed, they could not accept that the soul of the witch simply vanishes after the pact passed with the Devil because (if it were so) she would remain matter without form, and as a consequence, she would no longer be a living being able to perform in the world, and therefore the evil would be merely inefficient. Second, and more importantly, if the woman did not in a way remain herself in the witch she became, she could not be held responsible for her maleficent deeds. In order to sustain the juridical basis of witch-hunt, the Inquisitors provide a counteranthropology to explain the persistence of free will in the phenomenon of body-possession.

If witchcraft is conceived as a legal pact between the witch and the Devil, we must distinguish between three frameworks: 1) donation, 2) subjection, 3) bewitchment. According to the first model, the witch bestows her body to the Devil. This donation is conceived as a death ("the kiss of the devil") in which the witch totally renounces the realm of the living and abandons herself to darkness. Based on the Aristotelian theory of life, the witch loses her soul, which is the actuality organizing her body as a whole. As a result, only pure matter deprived of any principle of movement persists; whereupon the Devil implants a new maleficent soul in her body (the question whether he inserts a new personal soul or if he incarnates himself in the witch remains unclear). Witchcraft blurs the line between life and death, allowing for continuous activity after death. In this regard, the witch does not remain her previous self any longer and is turned into a mere henchwoman of Satan. She personifies the Devil in giving him a *substratum*, a bodily subject by means of which he operates in the mundane world. One could claim that, in this case, the witch cannot be held accountable for her demonic deeds. On the contrary, the Inquisitors pointed out that the donation of her body was decided according to the witch's absolute free choice, so that this first decision led to her responsibility for her future acts.[3]

The second blueprint for witchcraft, subjection, is framed upon the feudal bond between a sovereign and his subjects. Bodily possession is conceived as a political contract through which the witch renounces God and swears obedience to Satan as her sole master. This contract is based on an exchange: the witch lends herself to the Devil and is invested with supernatural skills in return (for example: the ability to fly, to kill, to shift shape or to take an animal form). To this extent, witchcraft is a transfer of power; witches and wizards are the vassals of Satan and the ministers of his domination on earth. They are enrolled in the army of Satan

---

[3] *Malleus Maleficarum*, Part I, qu. 2, a. 4: "With regards to the fourth argument, it is certainly true that the Devil only employs witches to bring about their bale and destruction. But when it is deduced that they are not to be punished, because they only act as instruments which are moved not by their own volition but at the will and pleasure of the principal and agent, there is a ready answer: For they are human instruments and free agents, and although they have made a compact and a contract with the devil, nevertheless they do enjoy absolute liberty [...] these women co-operate with the Devil although they are bound to him by that profession by which at first they freely and willingly gave themselves over this power."

(a typical alternative image to the animal pack mentioned above) where they act on behalf of the Devil.

The last model of witchcraft is possession or bewitchment. In opposition to donation and subjection, possession is understood as an invasion of the Devil. The Master of Lies seduces the woman and casts a spell on her, so that she becomes totally fascinated by him. In opposition to the other models of witchcraft, bewitchment seems to be operating on a woman's soul, rather than on her body. Yet this enchantment relies upon the bodily functions of the soul, such as imagination through fantasies or dreams, in which the devil deludes his victims and violates their free judgement. In the seventeenth century, a wave of possession cases occurred in Europe: in Aix-en-Provence (1609–1611), Pendle Hills (1612), Louviers (1642–1647). The most well known example remains the Loudun possessions, studied by Michel de Certeau.[4] Possessed women should nevertheless not be confused with witches.[5] While witchcraft affected country-dwelling women isolated in the forest, possessions affected nuns living in a religious community in a convent that belongs to a city. There is a shift from a juridical framework to a pastoral one: the possessed woman did not consciously make a deal with Satan, she is seen rather as a lost sheep infected against her will by malefic forces. Symptoms of her inner struggle against the Devil taking over are the bodily seizures she endures. Her convulsive body illustrates the conflict between soul and body in the mechanism of possession. According to Michel Foucault, those convulsions are a testimony of the resistance of the flesh to the normalization process of the Church on individuals through Christian penance: "It is a fortress body surrounded and besieged. It is a citadel body, at stake in a battle between the demon

---

[4] Michel de Certeau, *The Possession at Loudun* (University of Chicago Press, 2000).
[5] Michel Foucault, *Abnormal: Lectures at the Collège de France: 1974–1975* (London: Verso, 2003).

and the possessed body that resists, between the part of the person that resists and the part of herself that gives way and betrays her [. . .] All this constitutes the somatic theatre of possession."[6] In Foucault's view, possession reflects the inner conflict of women who endeavour to domesticate their desiring flesh. The unruly sexual impulses mirrored in convulsions are the confession of the flesh, struggling against the normalization process. The body is no longer interpreted as matter, but as a compound of libidinal forces, which the confessor, the bishop, and the Church try to control trough the normalizing practice of avowal and confession.

The change of paradigm between witchcraft and possession displays a shift from a juridical-theological framework, based on the holomorphic conception of the individual as a compound of soul and matter, to a medical-theological power that conceives the body as a compound of contradictory forces. The alienated person replaces the figure of otherness incarnated by the witch. The possessed woman suffers from a form of depersonalization that she can overcome to regain her true self with techniques of confession. The battlefield is relocated from the outside (between countryside and cities, darkness and light, evil and good) to the inside of one's person. This shift from witch to possessed reflects the sixteenth–seventeenth centuries' changes from a feudal society based on agriculture to a patriarchal economy based on employment defined by a normalization of model docile workers through the imposition of control on their sexual impulses.

---

6 Foucault, *Abnormal*, 206.

Phantom Limbs
Stephen Gaukroger

The phenomenon of phantom limbs, the experience of sensations where a limb has been amputated or is missing, has been known since antiquity, but it was first used to make a fundamental philosophical point about the nature of pain, and sensation more generally, in Descartes. He notes that one of his critics "expresses surprise" that he recognizes "no sensation save that which takes place in the brain." Yet such a view is, he urges, the only one compatible with medical observation. He relates the case of a girl who had to have her arm amputated by a surgeon. Kept blindfolded temporarily to ease her distress, she was unaware that her arm was gone, and reported experiencing pains in her fingers, wrist, and forearm. This, Descartes concludes, is obviously due to the condition of the nerves in her arm which formerly led from her brain to those parts of her body, and could not have occured if the sensation of pain occurred outside the brain.[1]

The way in which the phenomenon of phantom limbs has typically been described in both the philosophical and the psychological/neurological literature offers one a choice between accounts of the pain experienced as mental or as physical. Is the

---

[1] Descartes to Plempius for Fromondus, 3 October 1637: *The Philosophical Writings of Descartes, Volume III*, trans. J. Cottingham et al (Cambridge, UK: Cambridge University Press, 1991), 64.

pain in the person's brain or in their body? The question seems to have a straightforward but initially surprising answer, for if the question is rephrased in terms of what is necessary for the experience of pain, while there would be general agreement that a mind/brain was necessary, the phantom limb phenomenon seems to show that a body is not necessary. The importance of the phantom limb case is that it confounds our normal untutored assumptions about the location of pains, namely that they are in the limbs in which we experience the pain.

Descartes offered the traditional medical explanation for the phantom limb phenomenon, namely that the remaining nerves in the stump of the limb, which grow at the cut end into nodules, continue to generate impulses. Modern neurological accounts, by contrast, distinguish sharply between the brain and the nerve ending accounts, treating the latter as an alternative to the view that pains reside in the brain. Cutting off such nodules, or pathways within the spinal chord, can provide relief for pain for months or years, but this is the best case that can be made for a bodily source of pain, and it is far from conclusive since the sensation of the limb itself remains. Other kinds of cases, such as severe leg pain in paraplegics who have suffered a complete break of the spinal chord high in the upper body, where nerve impulses from the limb could not possibly traverse the break, indicate that such pains cannot originate in impulses in the remaining nerve endings as a general rule.

The move to understanding the phenomenon of phantom limbs in terms of brain activity does not in itself resolve the issue, however, and recent work suggests that such activity is far more complex than has traditionally been thought. Information from nerve endings is processed in the somatosensory cortex, and it is quite easy to explain how, in cases of limb amputation and breaking of the spinal chord, the normal processes of neural inhibition can be overridden, with the result that sensory excitations arise. The trouble is that the sensory excitation that results from such neural activity alone would be relatively random. There is no explanation here of phantom limbs and their associated sensations, such as pains.

In accounting for the more specific aspects of phantom limbs, Ronald Melzack has stressed the involvement of the limbic system, as well as the somatosensory cortex. He postulates "that the brain contains a neuromatrix, or network of neurones, that, in addition to responding to sensory stimulation, continuously generates a characteristic pattern of impulses indicating that the body is intact and unequivocally one's own. . . a neurosignature. If such a matrix operated in the absence of sensory inputs from the periphery of the body, it would create the impression of having a limb even after that limb has been removed."[2] Such a neuromatrix involves both the limbic system, which is concerned with emotion and motivation, and those cortical regions which are "important to recognition of the self and to the evaluation of sensory signals." Some of the peculiarities of phantom limb behavior make a good deal more sense once we appeciate the involvement of such areas of the brain. Phantom limbs can exist in people born without a limb, for example: one patient reported in the literature, an eleven-year-old girl born without hands or forearms, did arithmetic by counting on her phantom fingers. Moreover an itch in a phantom limb can sometimes be relieved by physically "scratching" in the affected area of the phantom limb (which usually adopts a habitual position).

One part of the system that seems to be centrally involved is the parietal cortex. Patients with phantom limbs have a strong sense of the reality of and ownership of the limb, and the limbs are not experienced as at all imaginary, even in cases where a foot, for example, might be experienced as dangling several inches beneath

---

[2] Ronald Melzack, "Phantom Limbs," *Scientific American*. Special Edition: "Secrets of the Senses" 16, no. 3 (2006), 52–59.

the stump to which the original foot was connected. Indeed, prosthetic limbs can only be fitted successfully where the patient has a phantom limb, which typically is felt to fit neatly over the phantom limb.

A crucial part of what is involved—a necessary condition for phantom limbs—is the establishment of bodily integrity, and in particular, the existence of a faculty which acts to constantly check our bodily integrity. It is something amiss in this faculty that gives rise to the peculiar phenomenology of phantom limbs, a phenomenology which exhibits an emotionally charged sense of the reality of the pathological limb.

Far from being simply the result of malfunctioning nerve endings, phantom limbs are body image disorders. They have to do with the psychological establishment of bodily integrity—"psychological" by contrast with "mental" or "cerebral"—because body images are not simply a combination of a mental/cerebral mapping and a bodily configuration but are no longer capturable if we try to break down the person into mental and physical components, or just into physical components. The appropriate treatment for pain in phantom limbs may have to do with the body, such as cutting the nerves just above the nodules or in the spinal chord, or may act on the brain, such as combinations of antidepressants and narcotics, or may be more psychological in character, such as relaxation and hypnosis. But we are dealing with something that involves cognitive and affective states, and necessarily, not contingently, involves not just embodiment, but embodiment in bodies of the kind that we have—that is, bodies having the kinds of limbs and organs we have, connected in the way they are.

Embodied Geometry in Early Modern Theatre

Yelda Nasifoglu

> *... yet how can my passions stint*
>
> *To see the heauens all orbicular*
>
> *The planets, stars & hierarchyes [a]bove*
>
> *All circular and Quadro quadro still[?]*
>
> *...*
>
> *No no it cannot bee thee'l' neuer change*
>
> *Mortalls may change but they unchanged bee*
>
> *Ile change my forme & that's the remedy*[1]

What can a set of two-dimensional mathematical shapes say about early modern attitudes towards embodiment? It appears to offer a number of clues when placed in an academic play written during the Counter-reformation.

Blame Not Our Author, editorially named from its opening lines, is a comedy that has survived in manuscript form in the Archives of the Venerable English College in Rome. Missing its

---

1 Suzanne Gossett, ed., "Blame Not Our Author," in *Collections, Volume XII* (Oxford: The Malone Society, 1983), 94–132 at 96; lines 30–33, 38–40; hereafter only line numbers will be indicated.

title page, its author and precise date remain unknown, though it is presumed to have been written sometime between 1613 and 1635 by a mathematics instructor.[2] The main protagonist is Quadro, a melancholic square who wants to become a circle. With the heavens deaf to his pleas, he decides to solicit the help of Compass, "the architecte of humain wonder" (137), imagining perhaps the dignified instrument of God illustrated in the medieval *Bibles moralisées*. Instead, he gets a Daedalian trickster. Quadro's duplicitous servant Rectangulum convinces Compass that he is being played; not wanting to be outdone, the latter gives Quadro all sorts of quack medicines and purgatives to weaken his joints, binds him with hoops, and abandons him. Realizing the trickery, Quadro vows revenge on the "base and grosse mecanicke Cumpasse" (311) who has almost slained him by "false surquadrie" (312), and with this the play quickly disintegrates into geometric revenge plots with various other shapes threatening one another with two-dimensional violence. Soon it is revealed that Line too has grievances against Compass who has tortured him with punctures and joints, and has made him divisible in *infinitum*; and Circulum is indignant at having been manhandled by such a promiscuous instrument "[t]urned and tossed by each Carpenter" (405). Line, in turn, has designs against Circulum, swearing to slice him into triangles, while Semicirculum warns Rhombus that Regulus will crack his legs and turn him into a trapezium. Eventually, order is restored by Regulus, the rule; punishment is meted out and the play ends with the warning "Let him that squars from rule and compasse bee/Vasaile to feare and base seruility" (1076–1077).

---

[2] Suzanne Gossett, "Drama in the English College, Rome, 1591–1660," *English Literary Renaissance* 3, no. 1 (1973): 60–93. For previous scholarship on this play, see also Carla Mazzio, "The Three-Dimensional Self: Geometry, Melancholy, Drama," in *Arts of Calculation: Quantifying Thought in Early Modern Europe*, eds. David Glimp and Michelle R. Warren (New York: Palgrave Macmillan, 2004), 39–65.

The 1613–1635 period in which the play was written predated the more radical inventions in mathematics such as the algebraization of geometry or calculus, but coincided with the debates on the nature of mathematical shapes, axioms, postulates, theorems, and proofs. The author of the play would certainly have been familiar with these. Founded in 1579, the English College was part of a network of institutions established on the continent after the Elizabethan Religious Settlement of 1559. Mostly run by the Jesuits, the College took on students for the study of philosophy and theology, preparing them for their mission to convert England back to Catholicism. The author would have attended lectures at the Collegio Romano, and judging from the abundant references in the play, had access to the authoritative commentaries on Euclid by the famed Jesuit professor of mathematics, Christoph Clavius (1538–1612).

One of the debates performed in the play is on the ontology of mathematical shapes. In Euclidean geometry definitions played the key role (a triangle was defined by its three sides, a square by its four equal sides, etc.) and thus any alteration of a form would irreversibly change its identity at a fundamental level, a cause of serious concern for the characters. For instance, reveling in the excesses of the Carnivale, gluttonous Line is concerned he has eaten so much that he is about to add some breadth to his length, pushing himself out of his own Euclidean definition. And would Quadro, defined by and named after its very four sides, still be *quadro* if indeed Compass helped it become a circle? Such a metamorphosis would alter the definition of a quadrangle: Rectangulum is anxious that should his master reach his goal, all their square plates would turn into round dishes and their four-cornered meat pies into Norfolk dumplings, or worse, into round fruits. This close alignment between form and its definition makes the threats of violence, of cutting shapes or breaking their legs, into threats of annihilation. However, apart from a bruise or two, no mathematical shape is seriously hurt during the course of the play, nor is Quadro converted into a circle.

Of course in this particular case Compass could not have helped Quadro perfect its shape even if he had wanted to. Compass and rule, the mathematical instruments featured in the play, were often factored into Euclidean constructions; for example Book 1, Postulate 1 explained that a straight line from any point to any point can be drawn with a rule, and Proposition 1 described how to draw an equilateral triangle with the use of a rule and compass. As powerful as these instruments may have been in terms of constructing mathematical bodies, they were ineffective when it came to the squaring of the circle, one of the three classical problems that cannot be solved using a rule and compass. The problem refers to defining a square with the exact area of a circle or vice versa, but π being an irrational number that cannot be expressed as a fraction (a fact that eluded mathematicians until the eighteenth century), this is not possible to accomplish using Euclidean geometry.

The "false surgery" Compass performs on Quadro, loosening his joints and pairing off his corners, seemingly prepares him for Archimedes' method of approximation of π by breaking the sides of a polygon inscribed within a circle into smaller and smaller units. Yet we soon find another operation being performed on stage here, one that takes us outside of the realm of pure mathematics. With Quadro so eager to be rounded off into a *punctum*, Compass easily lures him into an instrument he calls the "Squarenighers daughter," or Scavenger's daughter named after its inventor Skevington, a lieutenant of the Tower of London during the reign of Henry VIII. Rather than stretching on the rack, this device worked by severely contracting the body into a circle: the prisoner would be forced to kneel on the floor, the hoop would be placed over him and compressed until the abdomen, thighs, and lower legs were pressed into one another. Thomas Cottam (1549–1582), who had taught at the English Catholic College in Douai, was one of the victims of this instrument.

For a play featuring abstract mathematical shapes, there is an unexpected amount of violence, no doubt a reflection of the world surrounding the stage. The main goal of the College, of reconverting England to Catholicism, was considered an act of sedition punishable by the cruel mathematics of hanging, drawing and quartering, and indeed between 1581 and 1679, the College saw forty-one of its alumni martyred for their attempts, thirty-two of these before 1616. Rather than a fate to be avoided, martyrdom was celebrated if not glorified; in 1583, Niccolò Circignani (1520–1596) was commissioned to paint a cycle of thirty-four frescoes in the College chapel, featuring images of hangings and violent mutilations of victims from early Christianity to the English Mission, depicting the demise of at least one alumnus of the College. The students were encouraged to contemplate these images and even self-flagellate, perhaps in preparation of their possible fate in England. Martyrdom was a necessity for the survival of the church; the spectacle of public torture and execution of Catholic priests was expected to convert viewers impressed with the courage and intense faith of the victims. There are additional martyrology references in the play, such as the surprisingly irreverent ones by Line and Rectangulum regarding the hanging of "Papists." Furthermore, the "presse" Rectangulum tricks some of the other mathematical forms to hide in may well have been the type of large grape or olive press used in the martyrdom of Saint Jonas as illustrated in Antonio Gallonio's *Trattato de gli instrumenti di martirio*, "Treatise of the instruments of martyrdom" (1591 in Italian, 1594 in Latin).

Though he ultimately fails in his quest, Quadro longs to attain perfection by changing his form into a circle, willing to endure even torture in the process. And there are stories about self-discipline, of following strict daily regiments, being lauded at the College, hinting at a perceived relationship between changes to the body and their positive effect on the soul. Yet there is an underlying anxiety about such a close relationship, especially when the transformations are not self-inflicted or desired: if a rhombus with broken legs is a trapezium, what happens to the martyr whose body is drastically reconfigured in the hands of his or her torturer? No clear answer to this is offered in the play of course, but the theatres of cruelty illustrated by the martyrdom cycle in the chapel or in treatises like Gallonio's seem to downplay the effectiveness of worldly instruments against the fortitude of their victims; just as they are unable to square the circle, despite all the pain they can inflict, instruments appear to be powerless against the resolve of the faithful.

[Many thanks to Simon Ditchfield for his comments and suggestions on an earlier version of this text.]

Ghosts in the Celestial Machine
A REFLECTION ON LATE RENAISSANCE EMBODIMENT

Jonathan Regier[1]

The nature of celestial life was hotly debated in the long history of Aristotelian philosophy. Even if Aristotle and important commentators like Averroes said the heavens were alive, the Scholastics generally had nonliving spheres guided by angels.[2] The very regularity of celestial movement showed that celestial being, whatever it was, was superior to the flux and impermanence down here on what Dante, from his vantage point among the fixed stars, called "the little threshing-floor that makes us so fierce."[3] The attribution of life or angelic influence to celestial spheres did not hinder a mechanical interpretation of their movement, however. Quite the opposite was the case. After all, Aristotle had his God-like motors working in a give-and-take system of contact force. The benefit of using orbs and spheres, to which the luminous bodies attached, was that they behaved

---

1 Ghent University, Department of Philosophy and Moral Sciences, Sarton Centre for History of Science. I would like to thank Justin Smith for his invitation to contribute a reflection to the present volume, as well as Patrick Boner for his comments.

2 Edward Grant, *Planets, Stars, & Orbs: The Medieval Cosmos, 1200–1687* (Cambridge, UK: Cambridge University Press, 1994), 469–487.

3 Dante, *The Divine Comedy*, trans. John D. Sinclair (Oxford: Oxford University Press, 1961), 325.

in ways resembling machines, calculating instruments, and mathematical diagrams. It is often said that Nicole Oresme (*c*. 1320–1382), professor at the medieval University of Paris, was among the first to compare the skies to a mechanical clock.[4] But he also considered angelic will responsible for the impulsion and resistance within the mechanism. This is a reasonable position vis-a-vis Scholastic theology, in which angelic power was precisely calibrated by God. Shortly before Oresme's birth, Dante (1265–1321) had written of his voyage to the sphere of the sun. There, he had met past theologians, their fiery souls arranged in a "glorious wheel" that spun *come orologio*, "like a clock . . . when one part draws or drives another, sounding the chime with notes so sweet that the well-ordered spirit swells with love . . . "[5]

The history of the skies is a history of embodiment. What is embodied is some formal principle or influence that can generate orderly movement. From the late seventeenth century onward, the skies would manifest the mathematical perfection of Newtonian law. Celestial objects, like all objects, embodied a cohesive force operating instantaneously across a passive space: gravity. It might be said that in modern physics space-time itself embodies gravity, curving and swirling according to the field equations of general relativity. Celestial embodiment provides, and has provided since the Greeks, an assurance and explanation of mathematical order. This fact disproves what is still a commonplace in the history of science: that the mathematization of the world went hand in hand with its sterilization. Instead, until the seventeenth century, celestial regularity was usually the sign of embodied intelligence, soul, and knowledge. As solid sphere mechanisms became more

---

[4] Nicole Oresme, *Le livre du ciel et du monde*, ed. Albert D. Menut and Alexander J. Denomy, trans. Albert D. Menut (Madison: University of Wisconsin Press, 1968), 288, 71a.

[5] Dante, *The Divine Comedy*, 153–155.

and more untenable in the sixteenth century, celestial souls filled the explanatory void.[6] In the absence of spheres, a living planet could propel itself with sufficient neatness. The innovators of sixteenth-century cosmology— Julius Caesar Scaliger (1484–1558), Girolamo Cardano (1501–1576), Bernardino Telesio (1509–1588), Francesco Patrizi (1529–1597), William Gilbert (1544–1603), Tycho Brahe (1546–1601), Giordano Bruno (1548–1600), and Johannes Kepler (1571–1630)—were almost all in agreement that planetary movement was a kind of animal movement (whether or not they held to solid spheres). Planetary souls were frequently cast as intelligent—they had to be, in order to follow their invisible courses through the wide celestial plains.[7] Both Brahe and Gilbert suggest that planets have an inborn *"scientia."*[8]

The role of medical ideas in the sixteenth-century vision of the world is particularly fascinating. Physicians were behind many of the century's most widely read works of natural philosophy. Humanist medicine was likewise a point of convergence for non-Aristotelian currents—Stoic, Paracelsian, and Platonic in the mold of Marsilio Ficino (1433–1499).[9] As planets became animal, they

---

[6] For an introduction to sixteenth-century cosmological innovation, see Miguel A. Granada, "New Visions of the Cosmos," in *The Cambridge Companion to Renaissance Philosophy* (Cambridge, UK: Cambridge University Press, 2007), 270–286.

[7] "[...] that heaven and earth and the watery plains [...] a spirit within sustains; in all the limbs mind moves the mass and mingles with the mighty frame." Virgil, *Ecologues, Georgics, Aeneid I-VI*, trans. H. Rushton Fairclough, Loeb Classical Library (London: William Heinemann, 1916), 556–557 (bk. 6, ln. 724–752).

[8] See William Gilbert, *De magnete* ... (London: Peter Short, 1600), 210. As Brahe writes in the *De mundi aetherei recentioribus phaenomenis liber secundus* (Uraniborg, 1588), "The celestial machine is not a hard and impenetrable body, crammed full of various real orbs, as was heretofore believed by most people. On the contrary, very fluid and quite simple, it lies open everywhere, without exertion or transportation by any real spheres, to the unimpeded revolutions of the planets, governed by divinely implanted knowledge [*iuxta diuinitus inditam Scientiam administratis*], while heaven offers absolutely no obstacle." Translation in Edward Rosen, "The Dissolution of the Solid Celestial Spheres," *Journal of the History of Ideas* 46, no. 1 (March 1985): 13–31, 22.

[9] For the medical humanists of the sixteenth century, see Hiro Hirai, *Medical Humanism and Natural Philosophy: Renaissance Debates on Matter, Life and the Soul*, Medieval and Early Modern Science 17 (Leiden, The Netherlands: Brill, 2011).

became subject to medical and physiological considerations. The outstanding astronomers and celestial theorists were trained or at least well read in medicine, and sensitive to new causalities of body. Gilbert, for example, was a *medicus* by profession. He was physician to Queen Elizabeth when his seminal work on magnets, the *De magnete*, was published in 1600. It is not surprising that he describes the earth's diurnal rotation as an affair of health. If the earth were immobile, it would suffer burns on one side and frigidity on the other: "[Earth] would not choose to endure this so miserable and horrid appearance on both her faces," he writes.[10] For Gilbert, as for his Copernican contemporaries Bruno and Kepler, the planetary body is clearly a physiological body, caring for itself and avoiding pain. Gilbert's metallurgy relies on an important late-Renaissance motif: the earth as a womb or matrix for seeds. Metal formation in the *De magnete* is explained, in detail, by humors flowing through the body of the earth. These humors are the proximate cause of metals, "like the blood and semen in the generation of animals."[11] It should also be noted, given the humanist environment in which new cosmologies flourished, that Gilbert's theory of the earth has strong classical roots in Cicero and Seneca.[12]

For Kepler, who carefully studied the *De magnete*, celestial bodies are very large animals.[13] The philosophical astronomer is tasked

---

10 William Gilbert, *On the Magnet (De magnete)*, trans. Silvanus Phillips Thompson (New York: Basic Books, 1958), 224.

11 Ibid., 20–21.

12 See Cicero in *De natura deorum*, II.33, where he writes of the earth's womb and formative powers, or Seneca in *Naturales quaestiones*, III.15: "Now, in us there is not just blood but many kinds of fluid, some essential, some corrupted and rather too thick; in the head there is the brain, mucus, saliva, and tears; in the bones, marrow and something added to the joints as a lubricant so that they can bend more readily. In just the same way in the earth as well there are several kinds of fluid: some that harden when fully developed (from them comes the entire harvest of metals—from which greed seeks out gold and silver—and substances that turn from liquid to stone), and some that are formed from the decay of earth and moisture (such as bitumen and other things of that sort)." Seneca, *Natural Questions*, trans. Harry M. Hine (Chicago: University of Chicago Press, 2010), 34.

13 For Kepler's vitalism, see Patrick J. Boner, *Kepler's Cosmological Synthesis: Astrology, Mechanism and the Soul*. History of Science and Medicine Library 39 (Leiden, The Netherlands: Brill, 2013).

with studying their faculties—that is, their forces and productions. It helps that all created souls are essentially geometrical, because they can be assured to behave according to certain special proportions. In that sense, Kepler uses the celestial soul as most natural philosophers before him had used it, as a motor of force and mathematical order.[14] However, his celestial bodies possess a startling vitality. The earth puts out hair, perspires, gets angry, suffers digestive problems, breathes, imagines, and enjoys an intense sexual relationship with the sun (following an astrological-humanist motif present in Copernicus). For Kepler, this relationship is marked by an actual collaboration of penetration and reception mediated by light. Celestial sex is not only good and useful in Kepler's description, but deeply pleasurable.[15] It is, he says, another sign that the earth must possess a sensitive soul. The celestial plains also teem with generation. When pockets of celestial aether become dense and cloudy, the world soul triggers a natural process of purification. From this process, celestial novelties are born: new stars, comets, blood-red fogs. Kepler explains comets as the body's treatment of diseased matter: "Thus from this collected fatness of aether, as from excrement in a sort of abscess, [a comet] is made from the nature of its location . . . "[16] Indeed, the putrid vapor sprayed from a comet's tail can strike our terrestrial air, causing pestilence.[17] This circulation of bodily causes and the penetrability of boundaries are the hallmarks of Kepler's account of celestial generation, and here he echoes dominant

---

[14] See Jonathan Regier, "Kepler's Theory of Force and His Medical Sources," *Early Science and Medicine* 19, no. 1 (March 26, 2014): 1–27.

[15] Kepler, *Gesammelte Werke*, vi, 266. Johannes Kepler, *Harmony of the World*, trans. E. J. Aiton, A. M. Duncan, and J. V. Field (Philadelphia: American Philosophical Society, 1997), 360.

[16] "Coacta igitur illa crassa pinguedine aetheris quasi quodam excremento, velut in quoddam Apostema: fit ex natura loci [. . .]" Johannes Kepler, *Gesammelte Werke*, ed. Walther von Dyck et al. (Munich: C.H. Beck, 1937–), viii, 225.

[17] "But what if we mingle the Aristotelian opinion of the tail with the more recent one, so that some luminous matter really does exhale from the head [. . .]? Then if the tail were to touch the

sixteenth-century views on health, sickness and living bodies. Michael Stolberg has written that the early modern body was characterized by permeability, determined by the flow of fluid and humor instead of behavior in its solid parts.[18] Health and disease became an affair of "fluids, wind, and vapors" moving within a body "virtually uninhibited by any anatomical boundaries."[19]

Although it is frequently written that the sublunar and supralunar regions were utterly distinct in Aristotelian philosophy, this was never completely true. The medieval period was in general agreement about generative (and sometimes destructive) virtues being transmitted from the heavens to the sublunar realm. This attitude was largely the result of Greek and Arabic commentators trying to patch up Aristotle's theory of celestial-terrestrial causality. As the ontological gap between celestial and terrestrial was closed in the sixteenth century, the skies maintained their generative function. For most celestial innovators, space was filled with an informing *pneuma, spiritus*, light, or heat. Which brings us to a fascinating historical observation: uniform space, in its late-Renaissance incarnation, was a nourishing and formative entity. In other words, the ambient served as an incubator and instigator of local, determined bodies, rather as the flow of bodily spirits and humors fed diverse organs and faculties.

In guise of a conclusion, we might offer that it became philosophically useful in the sixteenth century to think of the celestial region not only as animate but as animal. Celestial phenomena could be explained by way of physiological processes observed in animal bodies. This shift put the focus on the faculties

---

earth, no wonder that the air be infected by a poisonous influence." Kepler, *Gesammelte Werke*, ii, 233. Translation in Johannes Kepler, *Optics: Paralipomena to Witelo, & Optical Part of Astronomy*, trans. William H. Donahue (Sante Fe, NM: Green Lion Press, 2000), 278.

18 Michael Stolberg, *Experiencing Illness and the Sick Body in Early Modern Europe*, trans. Leonhard Unglaub and Logan Kennedy (New York: Palgrave Macmillan, 2011), 83.

19 Ibid., 126.

and forces exhibited by these bodies, which could be thought of as composed of uniform matter organized by similar vital causes. It is very likely that those principles foundational to classical physics—uniformity of space, matter, force—owe a tremendous debt to vital natural philosophies of the late Renaissance. Well before mechanist philosophies dominated, nature had in some instances already become uniform. Uniform but not sterilized: because if the Baroque is marked by the *pli*, as Deleuze thought it was,[20] the sixteenth and early seventeenth centuries are marked by fluids of quarry, crucible, butcher, hospital, by what flows, by what folds in on itself in rivulets of varied density, by what expands flame-like, by what coagulates and clumps, by what boils and cools.

---

20 Gilles Deleuze, *Le pli: Leibniz et le baroque* (Paris: Les Éditions de Minuit, 1988).

The Genotype/Phenotype Distinction
Emily Herring

It was Wilhelm Johannsen who first used the terms "genotype" and "phenotype," in two separate texts dating from 1909 and 1911,[1] to distinguish between the hidden hereditary make-up of organisms (the genotype) and the ways in which it manifests itself on a macroscopic level (the phenotype). His experiments on pure lines of self-fertilized bean plants had convinced him that the development of individual organisms and the passing on of hereditary material from generation to generation were to be distinguished. Johannsen also coined the term "gene" but refused to speculate about what this denoted.

Before the chemical composition of genes was discovered or the concept of information was applied to theories of heredity, the genotype/phenotype distinction emerged out of a particulate view of living organisms (i.e., the idea that organisms can be explained, in one way or another, by the particles [in a broad sense] that compose them, and by the way these particles interact). In the 18th and 19th centuries, theories postulating invisible internal particles or entities meant to account for the external

---

1 Wilhelm Johannsen, *Elemente der exakten Erblichkeitslehre* (Jena, Germany: G. Fischer, 1909); Wilhelm Johannsen, "The Genotype Conception of Heredity," *The American Naturalist* 45, no. 531 (1911): 129–159.

appearance of living organisms were devised not just as solutions to the problems of inheritance and generation, but also as a way of addressing the intimate nature of the bodies of living beings. The problem of embodiment became for many scientists the problem of understanding how the macroscopic level could be explained by the activity of the microscopic particular level.

Georges Canguilhem argues that the birth of the cell theory in the 19th century tipped the scales in favor of a particulate, or discontinuous, view of living organisms. Faithful to his claim that "theories only proceed from older theories,"[2] Canguilhem sees the triumph of the discontinuous view partly as a biological reappropriation (and misinterpretation) of Leibniz's metaphysical theory of monads. In Germany, he notes, the Leibnizian heritage went through Schelling and Oken to Nägelli's theory of "micelles." In France, it was Buffon's theory of generation which distorted yet imported monads as elementary constituents of living beings into natural history, through the influence of Maupertuis. Buffon argued that all living beings are made of the same "organic molecules," organised by Newtonian-type forces in the form of an "internal mould," thus ridding Maupertuis' particles of their psychological component. For Maupertuis these particles could correctly form the embryo because they were able to "remember" which position they needed to adopt. For Buffon by contrast, the parents' excess organic molecules blended and organized themselves during reproduction providing the offspring with its own internal mold. The external appearance of any given animal was the result of this "internal mold" which in a non-transformist framework represented an initial type from which each organism might deviate more or less (in Buffon's mind, such deviation was always understood as degeneration).

---

[2] Georges Canguilhem, "La théorie cellulaire," in *La Connaissance de la Vie* (Paris: Vrin, 2009), 62.

In 1868 Darwin proposed his own particulate view of inheritance. He concluded *On the Variation of Animals and Plants Under Domestication* with a chapter entitled "The Provisional Hypothesis of Pangenesis." According to the pangenetic account of heredity, new organisms are not generated solely by the reproductive organs, but by the whole body. Each cell of the body is constantly "throw[ing] off minute granules or atoms," which Darwin also calls "gemmules." These gemmules circulate through the body and when they are properly nourished, self-divide and develop "into cells like those from which they were derived." The gemmules coalesce via a sort of "elective affinity" in the reproductive organs during reproduction and are transmitted from parent to offspring. This means that what is being transmitted is a "snapshot" of the parents' bodies at the moment of the act of reproduction. The offspring's appearance could be accounted for by the way in which the gemmules arranged themselves, but the state of the body itself could modify the attributes of the gemmules transmitted. The organism embodies the assembled gemmules by making them visible through growth, but each part of the body would be in turn be represented by the gemmules (even though Darwin doesn't talk about this process in these terms).

It was pointed out to Darwin that his theory of pangenesis was similar to the theories of some of his predecessors such as Hippocrates or Buffon, and it was in fact rather similar to Maupertuis' account of development in *La Vénus physique* in 1745. Darwin therefore adds a footnote to the second edition of *On the Variation of Animals and Plants under Domestication* explaining that "[t]he 'organic molecules' of Buffon appear at first sight to be the same as the gemmules of my hypothesis, but they are essentially different."[3] Darwin was indeed correct: Buffon's organic molecules

---

3 Charles Darwin, *The Variation of Animals and Plants under Domestication*, vol. 2 (London: J. Murray 1868), 350.

are elementary constituents of living matter, whereas organisms are not composed of gemmules. Rather, the gemmules are produced by the cells, though how a gemmule comes to grow into the cell it represents is unclear. What is more, Buffon's theory, unlike Darwin's, was not meant to explain inheritance in a transformist framework, but rather sought to make a case against preformationist theories of generation, which stated that new organisms grew from miniature versions contained, or *preformed*, entirely in either the male or female gametes, thus avoiding entirely the difficult problem of development. However, in both Buffon and Darwin's case, the visible features of organisms were taken to be the after-effect of the activity of invisible particles, organic molecules or gemmules, within. If embodiment is understood as the process of becoming a body, individual organisms embody their organic molecules or gemmules through growth, by making their configuration accessible to the senses.

Darwin's hypothesis of pangenesis didn't convince many of his contemporaries, mainly because it didn't take into account the findings of the newly established cell theory. A few decades later, August Weismann did take these findings into account, as well as the recent observations of what was contained in the nucleus of the cell (which would later come to be called chromosomes). Opposed to Darwin's pangenesis theory, but very much in favor of his theory of transformism by means of natural selection, he claimed that "all the phenomena of heredity depend on minute vital units . . . called 'biophores,' and of which living matter is composed."[4] In his *Histoire de la notion de gène* André Pichot links Weismann's theory of biophores back to Buffon's theory of organic molecules which was consistent with a common eighteenth-century view of the nature of organisms: "a kind of hylozoism,"[5] according to which

---

[4] August Weismann, *The Germ-Plasm. A Theory Of Heredity* (New York: Charles Scribner's Sons, 1893), 450.

[5] André Pichot, *Histoire de la notion de gène* (Paris: Flammarion, 1999), 54

living matter's property of "being alive" could be explained by the "alive" nature of the particles that composed it. These theories were probably, says Pichot, inspired by Leibniz's monads.

Instead of being produced by the whole body, the biophores were conceived as the elementary components of the "germ-plasm" located in the cells' nuclei. Weismann named his theory "the continuity of the germ-plasm" (or "blasto-genesis" meaning "origin from a germ-plasm") which involved the separation of the cells of the body, the somatic cells, and the gametes, the germ-line. In Weismann's mind, through cell division, certain cells (the somatic cells) receive part of the germ-plasm (biophores organized into "determinants"). This explains cell specialization. The cells of the germ-line conserve the whole germ-plasm in the nucleus and this is what is transmitted from parent to offspring throughout the history (and evolution) of life. This was Weismann's famous distinction between the soma and the germ-line, by which he ruled out the possibility of the inheritance of acquired characters, meaning the influence of the body on the gametes. Individual organisms, in Weismann's theory, could be seen as mortal bodies sprouting up from the immortal germ-plasm carrying them. Therefore, the germ-plasm could be said to be embodied by individual organisms in the sense that, for Weismann, each organism is a possible occurrence, or expression, of the germ-plasm.

Johannsen's genotype conception of heredity was developed explicitly to counter what he called the "transmission conception of heredity" stating that inheritance is "the transmission of the parents' (or ancestors') personal qualities to the progeny"[6] which Darwin's pangenesis exemplified. He was closer to Weismann's distinction between the soma and the germ-line: for Johannsen the genotype is not affected by environmental causes which occur

---

6 Johannsen, "The Genotype Conception of Heredity," 129

during the organism's development at the phenotypic level. This distinction would prove to be highly important for the developing science of genetics. Johannsen distanced himself, however, from what he considered to be unnecessary speculation on Weismann's part about the nature of the hereditary unit, which Johannsen was now calling "genes." At the beginning of the 20th century, incipient genetics abandoned all considerations of hylozoism (which claimed that hereditary particles were inherently "alive") and tended to strip the gene of all material reality, as Johannsen did, largely transforming it into a conceptual tool.

The refusal to engage in speculations about the nature of genes meant that ideas about inheritance would come from observation and experiments (and the revival of Mendel's laws): the phenotype was to become a clue towards the workings of the hidden mysterious entities that organisms embodied. In the period between the birth of genetics as a discipline and Watson and Crick's discovery of the structure of DNA, the embodiment problem shifted from the question, "How can the internal particulate structure of the organism explain its external features?"—this was a problem that Buffon, Darwin and Weismann all addressed in their own fashion—to the question "How can a body's external appearance offer hints about the unknown structure that lies within?" We thus see a transition from the question of the ultimate causes of embodiment, to a perception of bodies as sources of insight about the ultimate causes of life.

Bibliography

PRIMARY

Aquinas, Thomas. *Sancti Thomae Aquinatis Doctors Angelici: Opera Omnia.* Iussu Leonis XIII. Rome: Vatican Polyglot Press, 1882.

Aquinas, Thomas. *The Treatise on Human Nature: Summa Theologiae 1a 75-89.* Translated by Robert Pasnau. Indianapolis: Hackett, 2002.

Aristotle. *Nicomachean Ethics [Ethica nicomachea].* Edited by I. Bywater. Oxford: Oxford University Press, 1890.

Aristotle. *On Coming-to-Be & Passing-Away [De Generatione et corruptione].* Edited with commentary by Harold H. Joachim. Oxford: Clarendon Press, 1922.

Aristotle. *Metaphysics [Metaphysica].* Edited with commentary by W. D. Ross. Oxford: Oxford University Press, 1924.

Aristotle. *Physics [Physica].* Edited with commentary by W. D. Ross. Oxford: Oxford University Press, 1936.

Aristotle. *On the Soul [De Anima].* Edited by W. D. Ross. Oxford: Oxford University Press, 1956.

Augustine. *On the Trinity: Books 8–15.* Edited by Gareth B. Matthews. Translated by Stephen McKenna. Cambridge, MA: Cambridge University Press, 2002.

Ayache, L. "Hippocrate laissait-t-il la nature agir?" In *Tratados Hipocráticos: Actas del VIIe colloque international hippocratique, Madrid, 24-29 de Septiembre de 1990*, edited by J. A. López Férez, 19–35. Madrid: Universidad Nacional de Educación a Distancia, 1992.

Baird, Benjamin, et al. "Domain-Specific Enhancement of Metacognitive Ability Following Meditation Training." *Journal of Experimental Psychology: General* 143, no. 5 (2014): 1972–79.

Bar-Hayya, Abraham. *Hegyon Ha-Nephesch Ha-Atzuvah [The Meditation of the Sorrowful Soul]*. Edited by Geoffrey Wigoder. Jerusalem: Bialik Institute, 1971.

Barnes, J., ed. *Complete Works of Aristotle*. 2 Vols. Princeton, NJ: Princeton University Press, 1971.

Batson, C. D., J. G. Batson, J. K. Slingsby, K. L. Harrell, H. M. Peekna, and R. M. Todd. "Empathic Joy and the Empathy-Altruism Hypothesis." *Journal of Personality and Social Psychology* 61, no. 3 (1991): 413–26.

Batson, C. D., B. D. Duncan, P. Ackerman, T. Buckley, and K. Birch. "Is Empathic Emotion a Source of Altruistic Motivation?" *Journal of Personality and Social Psychology* 40, no. 2 (1981): 290–302.

Batson, C. D., and L. L. Shaw. "Evidence for Altruism: Toward a Pluralism of Prosocial Motives." *Psychological Inquiry* 2, no. 2 (1991): 107–22.

Bennett, Jonathan. "The Conscience of Huckleberry Finn." *Philosophy* 49, no. 188 (1974): 129.

Bernard, Claude. *Introduction à l'étude de la médecine expérimentale*. Paris: J.B. Baillière & Fils, 1865.

Bernard, Claude. *Leçons sur les phénomènes de la vie communs aux animaux et aux végétaux*, tome II. Paris: J.B. Baillière, 1879.

Bichat, Xavier. *Recherches physiologiques sur la vie et la mort* [1800], second edition. Paris: Gabon, 1802.

Bloom, Paul. *Descartes' Baby: How the Science of Child Development Explains What Makes Us Human*. New York: Basic Books, 2004.

Boerhaave, Herman. *Dr. Boerhaave's Academical Lectures on the Theory of Physic: Being a Translation of his Institutes and Explanatory Comments*, vol. 1 of 6. London: W. Innys, 1752.

Boerhaave, Herman. *De usu ratiocinii mechanici in medicina* [1703]. In *Opuscula selecta Neerlandicorum de arte medica*. Amsterdam: F. van Rossen, 1907.

Boerhaave, Herman. *Boerhaave's Orations*. Translated and edited by E. Kegel-Brinkgreve and A. M. Luyendijk-Elshout. Leiden, The Netherlands: E.J. Brill, 1983.

Bolens, G. "Homeric Joints and the Marrow in Plato's *Timaeus*: Two Logics of the Body." *Multilingua* 18, no. 2–3 (1999): 149–57.

Bolens, G. *La logique du corps articulaire: Les articulations du corps humain dans la littérature occidentale*. Rennes, France: Presses Universitaires de Rennes, 2000.
Brady, Michael S. "Virtue, Emotion, and Attention." *Metaphilosophy* 41, no. 1–2 (2010): 115–31.
Brady, Michael S. *Emotional Insight: The Epistemic Role of Emotional Experience*. Oxford: Oxford University Press, 2013.
Brahe, Tycho. *De mundi aetherei recentioribus phaenomenis liber secundus*. Uraniborg, 1588.
Bramhall, J. *Works of John Bramhall*. 4 Vols. Oxford: John Henry Parker, 1842–1844.
Brewer, Judson A., et al. "Meditation Experience Is Associated with Differences in Default Mode Network Activity and Connectivity." *Proceedings of the National Academy of Sciences* 108, no. 50 (December 13, 2011): 20254–9.
Brill, Sara. *Plato on the Limits of Human Life*. Bloomington: Indiana University Press, 2013.
Broadie, Sarah. "Soul and Body in Plato and Descartes." *Proceedings of the Aristotelian Society* 101, no. 1 (2001): 295–308.
Buffon, Georges Louis Leclerc Comte de. *Histoire naturelle, générale et particulière, avec la description du Cabinet du Roy*, t. 2 *Histoire générale des animaux;— Histoire naturelle de l'homme*. Paris: Imprimerie Royale, 1749.
Carone, G. R. "Mind and Body in Late Plato." *Archiv für Geschichte der Philosophie* 87, no. 3 (2005): 227–69.
Chadwick, Henry, trans. *Confessions* by Augustine. New York: Oxford University Press, 1991.
Chapman, H. A., et al. "In Bad Taste: Evidence for the Oral Origins of Moral Disgust." *Science* 323, no. 5918 (2009): 1222–6.
Cicero. *De natura deorum. Academica*. Translated by H. Rackham. Loeb Classical Library. Cambridge, MA: Harvard University Press, 1933.
Clarke, Michael. *Flesh and Spirit in the Songs of Homer*. New York: Oxford University Press, 1999.
Claus, David B. *Toward the Soul: An Inquiry into the Meaning of ψυχή before Plato*. New Haven, CT: Yale University Press, 1981.
Comte, Auguste. *Cours de philosophie positive*. Paris: Hermann, 1982.
Condon, P., et al. "Meditation Increases Compassionate Responses to Suffering." *Psychological Science* 24, no. 10 (2013): 2125–7.
Conway, Anne. *The Principles of the Most Ancient and Modern Philosophy*. Edited by Allison P. Coudert and Taylor Corse. Cambridge, UK: Cambridge University Press, 1996.
Coward, W. *Second Thoughts Concerning Human Soul*. London: R. Bassett, 1704.

Coward, W. *The Grand Essay*. London: John Chantry, 1704.
Craik, Elizabeth. *The "Hippocratic" Corpus: Content and Context.* London: Routledge, 2014.
Crescas, Hasdai. *Or Ha-Shem (The Light of the Lord)*. Edited by S. Fisher. Jerusalem: Ramot, 1990.
Csordas, T. "Somatic Modes of Attention." *Cultural Anthropology* 8, no. 2 (1993): 135–56.
Cudworth, R. *True Intellectual System of the Universe*. 3 vols. London: Thomas Tegg, 1845.
Dante. *The Divine Comedy*. Translated by John D. Sinclair. Oxford: Oxford University Press, 1961.
Darley, John M., and C. Daniel Batson. "'From Jerusalem to Jericho': A Study of Situational and Dispositional Variables in Helping Behavior." *Journal of Personality and Social Psychology* 27, no. 1 (1973): 100–8.
Darwin, Charles. *The Variation of Animals and Plants under Domestication*. Vol. 2. London: J. Murray, 1868.
Davis, Jake H., and Evan Thompson. "From the Five Aggregates to Phenomenal Consciousness: Towards a Cross-Cultural Cognitive Science." In *A Companion to Buddhist Philosophy*, edited by Steven M. Emmanuel, 585–97. Hoboken, NJ: John Wiley & Sons, 2013.
Dean-Jones, Lesley. "The Politics of Pleasure: Female Sexual Appetite in the Hippocratic Corpus." *Helios* 19 (1992): 72–91.
Dean-Jones, Lesley. "Autopsia, Historia and What Women Know: The Authority of Women in Hippocratic Gynaecology." In *Knowledge and the Scholarly Medical Tradition*, edited by D. Bates, 41–59. Cambridge, UK: Cambridge University Press, 1995.
de Certeau, Michel. *The Possession at Loudun*. Chicago: University of Chicago Press, 2000.
De Hart, S. "Hippocratic Medicine and the Greek Body Image." *Perspectives on Science* 7, no. 3 (1999): 349–82.
de La Forge, Louis. *Traité de l'esprit de l'homme, de ses facultés et de ses fonctions, et de son union avec le corps, suivant les principes de René Descartes*. Paris: Théodore Girard, 1666.
de Maupertuis, Pierre-Louis Moreau. *Vénus physique.* Paris: n.p., 1745.
Descartes, René. *Œuvres*. Edited by C. Adam and P. Tannery, 11 vols. Paris: Vrin, 1964–1974.
Descartes, René. *The Philosophical Writings of Descartes*. Edited by J. Cottingham, R. Stoothoff, and D. Murdoch. Cambridge, UK: Cambridge University Press, 1985.

Descartes, René. *The Philosophical Writings of Descartes, Vol. III*. Translated and edited by John Cottingham, Robert Stoothoff, Dugald Murdoch, and Anthony Kenny. Cambridge, UK: Cambridge University Press, 1991.

Descola, Philippe. *Beyond Nature and Culture*. Translated by Janet Lloyd. Chicago: University of Chicago Press, 2013.

Diderot, Denis. "Méchanicien." In *Encyclopédie ou Dictionnaire raisonné des sciences, des arts et des métiers*. Vol. 10. Edited by D. Diderot and J. D'Alembert, 220–2. Paris: Briasson, 1765.

Diderot, Denis. *Correspondance*. Edited by G. Roth. 9 vols. Paris: Éditions de Minuit, 1955–1970.

Diderot, Denis. *Œuvres complètes*. Edited by H. Dieckmann, J. Proust, and J. Varloot. Paris: Hermann, 1975–.

Diderot, Denis. *Œuvres*. Vol. 1, *Philosophie*. Edited by L. Versini. Paris: Laffont-"Bouquins," 1994.

Diderot, Denis, and Jean le Rond D'Alembert, eds. *Encyclopédie ou Dictionnaire raisonné des sciences, des arts et des métiers*. 35 vols. [Paris: Briasson, 1751–1780] Stuttgart/Bad Cannstatt, Germany: Frommann, 1966.

Dillon, John. "How Does the Soul Direct the Body, After All? Traces of a Dispute on Mind-Body Relations in the Old Academy." In *Body and Soul in Ancient Philosophy*, edited by Dorothea Frede and Burkhard Reis, 349–58. Berlin: Walter de Gruyter, 2009.

Doris, John M. "Persons, Situations, and Virtue Ethics." *Nous* 32, no. 4 (1998): 504–30.

Doris, John M. *Lack of Character: Personality and Moral Behavior*. Cambridge, UK: Cambridge University Press, 2002.

Duden, Barbara. *The Woman Beneath the Skin*. Translated by Thomas Dunlap. Cambridge, MA: Harvard University Press, 1991.

Equiano, Olaudah. *The Interesting Narrative of the Life of Olaudah Equiano, or Gustavus Vassa, The African, Written by Himself*. Edited by Werner Sollors. New York: Norton, 2001 (1789).

Fehr, Ernst, and Simon Gächter. "Altruistic Punishment in Humans." *Nature* 415, no. 6868 (January 10, 2002): 137–40.

Festinger, Leon. *A Theory of Cognitive Dissonance*. Evanston, IL: Row, Peterson, 1957.

Flanagan, Owen J. *Varieties of Moral Personality: Ethics and Psychological Realism*. Cambridge, MA: Harvard University Press, 1991.

Foucault, Michel. *The History of Sexuality, Volume II: The Use of Pleasure*. Translated by Robert Hurley. New York: Pantheon, 1985.

Foucault, Michel. *The History of Sexuality, Volume III: The Care of the Self*. Translated by Robert Hurley. New York: Pantheon, 1986.

Foucault, Michel. *Abnormal: Lectures at the Collège de France: 1974-1975*. London: Verso, 2003.
Fox, Kieran C. R., et al. "Meditation Experience Predicts Introspective Accuracy." *PloS One* 7, no. 9 (2012): e45370.
Frede, Dorothea. "Disintegration and Restoration: Pleasure and Pain in Plato's *Philebus*." In *The Cambridge Companion to Plato*, edited by Richard Kraut, 425-63. Cambridge, UK: Cambridge University Press, 1992.
Ganeri, Jonardon. *Attention and Consciousness: The Metaphysics of Autonomous Shadows*. forthcoming.
Garfield, J. *Engaging Buddhism: Why It Matters to Philosophy*. 1st ed. Oxford: Oxford University Press, 2015.
Gaultier, Abraham. *Parité de la vie et de la mort: La Réponse du médecin Gaultier* (1714). Edited by O. Bloch. Paris: Voltaire Foundation, 1993.
Gavrylenko, Valeria. "The Body without Skin in the Homeric Poems." In *Blood, Sweat, and Tears: The Changing Concepts of Physiology from Antiquity to Early Modern Europe*, edited by H. F. J. Horstmanshoff, Helen King, and Claus Zittel, 479-502. Leiden, The Netherlands: Brill, 2013.
Gawronski, Bertram. "Back to the Future of Dissonance Theory: Cognitive Consistency as a Core Motive." *Social Cognition* 30, no. 6 (2012): 652-68.
Gell, Alfred. *Art and Agency*. Oxford: Clarendon, 1998.
Gersonides. *The Wars of the Lord*. Translated by S. Feldman. Vol. 2. Philadelphia: Jewish Publication Society, 1987.
Gilbert, William. *De Magnete*. London: Peter Short, 1600.
Gilbert, William. *On the Magnet (De magnete)*. Translated by Silvanus Phillips Thompson. New York: Basic Books, 1958.
Gill, Christopher. *Personality in Greek Epic, Tragedy, and Philosophy: The Self in Dialogue*. Oxford: Oxford University Press, 1996.
Gill, Christopher. "The Body's Fault? Plato's *Timaeus* on Psychic Illness." In *Reason and Necessity: Essays on Plato's "Timaeus,"* edited by M. R. Wright, 59-84. Swansea, UK: Duckworth, 2000.
Ginzburg, Carlo. *Ecstasies: Deciphering the Witches' Sabbath*. Chicago: University of Chicago Press, 1991.
Goldie, Peter. "Emotion, Reason, and Virtue." In *Emotion, Evolution, and Rationality*, edited by Dylan Evans and Pierre Cruse, 249-67. Oxford: Oxford University Press, 2004.
Gossett, Suzanne, ed. "Blame Not Our Author." In *Collections, Volume XII*, edited by Suzanne Gossett, 94-132. Oxford: The Malone Society, 1983.
Greene, J. "Emotion and Cognition in Moral Judgment: Evidence from Neuroimaging." In *Neurobiology of Human Values*, edited by J. P. Changeux et al., 57-66. New York: Springer, 2005.

Gundert, Beate. "Soma and Psyche in Hippocratic Medicine." In *Psyche and Soma: Physicians and Metaphysicians on the Mind-Body Problem from Antiquity to Enlightenment*, 14–35. Oxford: Oxford University Press, 2000.

Hadot, Pierre. *Exercices spirituels et philosophie antique*. 2nd ed. Paris: Études Augustiniennes, 1987.

Hadot, Pierre. *Philosophy as a Way of Life: Spiritual Exercises from Socrates to Foucault*. Translated by M. Chase. Cambridge, MA: Wiley-Blackwell, 1995.

Haney, Craig, Curtis Banks, and Philip Zimbardo. "Interpersonal Dynamics in a Simulated Prison." *International Journal of Criminology and Penology* 1 (1973): 69–97.

Hanson, A. E. "The Medical Writers' Woman." In *Before Sexuality: The Construction of Erotic Experience in the Ancient Greek World*, edited by D. Halperin, J. Winkler, and F. I. Zeitlin, 309–37. Princeton, NJ: Princeton University Press, 1990.

Harman, Gilbert M. "Moral Philosophy Meets Social Psychology: Virtue Ethics and the Fundamental Attribution Error." *Proceedings of the Aristotelian Society* 99, no. 139: 315–31.

Havelock, Eric. "The Socratic Self As It Is Parodied in Aristophanes' *Clouds*." *Yale Classical Studies* 22 (1972): 1–18.

Hegel, Georg Wilhelm Friedrich. *Enzyklopädie der philosophischen Wissenschaften*. Edited by Eva Moldenhauer and Karl Markus Michel. Frankfurt am Main: Suhrkamp, 1970.

Heim, Maria. *The Forerunner of All Things: Buddhaghosa on Mind, Intention, and Agency*. New York: Oxford University Press, 2014.

Hemsterhuis, François. *Lettre sur l'homme et ses rapports (1772), avec le commentaire inédit de Diderot*. Edited by G. May. New Haven, CT: Yale University Press, 1964.

Hill, Edmund, trans. *The Literal Meaning of Genesis* by Augustine. In *The Works of St. Augustine: On Genesis*, 155–506. Hyde Park, NY: New City Press, 2002.

Hobbes, Thomas. *An Answer to a Book Published by Dr. Bramhall*. London: Crooke, 1682.

Hobbes, Thomas. *Opera philosophica quae latine scripsit omnia*. 5 vols. Edited by W. Molesworth. London: Joannem Bohn, 1839–1845.

Hobbes, Thomas. *English Works*. 11 vols. Edited by W. Molesworth. London, 1839–1845.

Hobbes, Thomas. *Elements of Law*. Edited by F. Tönnies. Cambridge, UK: Cambridge University Press, 1928.

Hobbes, Thomas. *Critique du* De Mundo *de Thomas White*. Edited by J. Jaquot and H. Jones. Paris: Vrin, 1973.

Hobbes, Thomas. *Thomas White's "De Mundo" Examined* (approx. 1642–1643). Translated by H. W. Jones. London: Bradford University Press, 1976.

Hobbes, Thomas. *Leviathan or The Matter, Forme and Power of A Commonwealth Ecclesiastical and Civil* (1651). Edited by E. Curley with selected Latin variants. Indianapolis: Hackett, 1994.

Hobbes, Thomas. *Elementorum Philosophiae, Sectio Prima: De Corpore*. Edited by K. Schuhmann. Paris: Vrin, 1999.

Holmes, Brooke. "Body, Soul, and the Medical Analogy in Plato." In *When Worlds Elide: Classics, Politics, Culture*, edited by J. Peter Euben and Karen Bassi, 345–85. Lanham, MD: Lexington, 2010.

Holmes, Brooke. *The Symptom and the Subject: The Emergence of the Physical Body in Ancient Greece*. Princeton, NJ: Princeton University Press, 2010.

Holmes, Brooke. "In Strange Lands: Disembodied Authority and the Role of the Physician in the Hippocratic Corpus and Beyond." In *Writing Science: Medical and Mathematical Authorship in Ancient Greece*, edited by Markus Asper, 431–72. Berlin: Walter de Gruyter, 2013.

Holmes, Brooke. "Galen on the Chances of Life." In *Probabilities, Hypotheticals, and Counterfactuals in Ancient Greek Thought*, edited by Victoria Wohl, 230–50. Cambridge, UK: Cambridge University Press, 2014.

Hölzel, B. K., et al. "Stress Reduction Correlates with Structural Changes in the Amygdala." *Social Cognitive and Affective Neuroscience* 5, no. 1 (2010): 11–17.

Hölzel, B. K., et al. "Mindfulness Practice Leads to Increases in Regional Brain Gray Matter Density." *Psychiatry Research: Neuroimaging* 191, no. 1 (2011): 36–43.

Huebner, B. "Do Emotions Play a Constitutive Role in Moral Cognition?" *Topoi* 34, no. 2 (2015): 427–40.

Huebner, B., S. Dwyer, and M. Hauser. "The Role of Emotion in Moral Psychology." *Trends in Cognitive Sciences* 13, no. 1 (2009): 1–6.

Hugh of St. Victor, II. *De unione: Spiritus et Corporis*. Edited by A. M. Piazzoni. Spoleto, Italy: Centro italiano di studi sull'alto medioevo, 1980.

Hursthouse, Rosalind. *On Virtue Ethics*. Oxford: Oxford University Press, 1999.

Ibn Daud, Abraham. *The Exalted Faith*. Edited and translated by N. M. Samuelson. London and Toronto: Associated University Presses, 1986.

Ibn Gabirol, Solomon. *The Improvement of Moral Qualities*. Translated by Stephen S. Wise. New York: Columbia University Press, 1901.

Ibn Pakuda, Bachya. *The Duties of the Heart*. Translated by Y. Feldman. Northvale & London: 1996.

Ibn Saddiq, Joseph. *The Microcosm of Joseph ibn Saddiq*. Edited and Translated by Jacob Haberman. Madison, NJ: Fairleigh Dickinson University Press, 2003.

Inwood, B., and L. P. Gerson, eds. *Hellenistic Philosophy: Introductory Readings*. 2nd. Ed. Indianapolis: Hackett, 1997.
Isen, Alice M., and Paula F. Levin. "Effect of Feeling Good on Helping: Cookies and Kindness." *Journal of Personality and Social Psychology* 21, no. 3 (1972): 384–8.
James, William. *The Principles of Psychology*. New York: Dover, 1918.
Johannsen, Wilhelm. *Elemente der exakten Erblichkeitslehre*. Jena: G. Fischer, 1909.
Johannsen, Wilhelm. "The Genotype Conception of Heredity." *The American Naturalist* 45, no. 531 (1911): 129–59.
Johnson, Mark. *Morality for Humans: Ethical Understanding from the Perspective of Cognitive Science*. Chicago: University of Chicago Press, 2015.
Jouanna, Jacques. *Hippocrates*. Translated by M. DeBevoise. Baltimore: The Johns Hopkins University Press, 1999.
Judah Halevi. *The Kuzari*. Translated by H. Hirschfeld. New York: Schocken, 1964.
Kepler, Johannes. *Gesammelte Werke*. Edited by Walther von Dyck et al. Munich: C.H. Beck, 1937–.
Kepler, Johannes. *Harmony of the World*. Translated by E. J. Aiton, A. M. Duncan, and J. V. Field. Philadelphia: American Philosophical Society, 1997.
Kepler, Johannes. *Optics: Paralipomena to Witelo, & Optical Part of Astronomy*. Translated by William H. Donahue. Sante Fe: Green Lion, 2000.
Kerr, Catherine E., et al. "Effects of Mindfulness Meditation Training on Anticipatory Alpha Modulation in Primary Somatosensory Cortex." *Brain Research Bulletin* 85, no. 3–4 (May 2011): 96–103.
Kerr, Catherine E., et al. "Mindfulness Starts with the Body: Somatosensory Attention and Top-down Modulation of Cortical Alpha Rhythms in Mindfulness Meditation." *Frontiers in Human Neuroscience* 7 (2013): http://www.frontiersin.org/Human_Neuroscience/10.3389/fnhum.2013.00012/abstract
Kirk, Ulrich, J. Downar, and P. R. Montangue. "Interoception Drives Increased Rational Decision-Making in Meditators Playing the Ultimatum Game." *Frontiers in Decision Neuroscience* 5 (2011): 49.
Knappett, C. "Beyond Skin: Layering and Networking in Art and Archaeology." *Cambridge Archaeological Journal* 16, no. 2 (2006): 232–59.
La Mettrie, Julien Offray de. *Œuvres philosophiques*. Edited by F. Markovits. 2 vols. Paris: Fayard, 1987.
La Mettrie, Julien Offray de, and Hermann Boerhaave. *Institutions de médecine de M. Hermann Boerhaave*. Vol. 5. Translated with commentary by La Mettrie. Paris: Huart & Cie, 1747.
Lambek, Michael. "Body and Mind in Mind, Body and Mind in Body: Some Anthropological Interventions in a Long Conversation." In *Bodies and*

Persons: Comparative Perspectives from Africa and Melanesia, edited by M. Lambek and A. Strathern, 103–23. Cambridge, UK: Cambridge University Press, 1998.

Lang, Helen. "Plato on Divine Art and the Production of Body." In *The Frontiers of Ancient Science: Essays in Honor of Heinrich von Staden*, edited by B. Holmes and K.-D. Fischer, 307–38. Berlin: Walter de Gruyter, 2015.

Lazar, S. W., et al. "Meditation Experience Is Associated with Increased Cortical Thickness." *Neuroreport* 16, no. 17 (2005): 1893–7.

Le Camus, Antoine. *Médecine de l'esprit, où l'on traite des dispositions et des causes physiques qui sont des conséquences de l'union de l'âme avec le corps, influant sur les opérations de l'esprit; et des moyens de maîtriser ses opérations dans un bon état ou de les corriger quand elles sont viciées*. Paris: Ganeau, 1753.

Leenhardt, Maurice. *Do kamo: La personne et le mythe dans le monde mélanésien*. Paris: Gallimard, 1947.

Leibniz, G. W. *Sämtliche Schriften und Briefe*. Berlin: Edition of the German Academy of Sciences, 1923.

Liebniz, G. W. *Opuscules et Fragments Inédits de Leibniz*. Edited by L. Couturat. Hildesheim, Germany: Olms, 1961.

Leibniz, G. W. *Gottfried Wilhelm Leibniz: Philosophical Papers and Letters*. Translated by L. E. Loemker, 2nd ed. Dordrecht, The Netherlands: Reidel, 1969.

Leibniz, G. W. *Die Philosophichen Schriften von Leibniz*. Edited by C. I. Gerhardt. 7 vols. Berlin: [Weidmann, 1875–1890] Olms, 1978.

Leibniz, G. W. *Philosophical Essays*. Edited and translated by R. Ariew and D. Garber. Indianapolis: Hackett, 1989.

Leibniz, G. W. *De Summa Rerum: Metaphysical Papers 1675–1676*. Edited and translated by G. H. R. Parkinson. New Haven, CT: Yale University Press, 1992.

Leibniz, G. W. *Leibniz's "New System" and Associated Contemporary Texts*. Translated by R. S. Woolhouse and R. Francks. Oxford: Oxford University Press, 1997.

Leibniz, G. W. *Recherches générales sur l'analyse des notions et des vérités*. Edited by J. B. Rauzy. Paris: Press Universitaires de France, 1998.

Leibniz, G. W. *The Labyrinth of the Continuum: Writings on the Continuum Problem, 1672–1686*. Translated by R. T. W. Arthur. New Haven, CT: Yale University Press, 2001.

Levin, Susan B. *Plato's Rivalry with Medicine: A Struggle and Its Dissolution*. Oxford: Oxford University Press, 2014.

Lévi-Strauss, Claude. "Race et histoire." In *Anthropologie structurale deux*, by Claude Lévi-Strauss. Paris: Plon, 1973 (1952).

Lipsius, J. *Physiologiae Stoicorum libre tres*. Antwerp, 1604.
Lloyd, G. E. R. "Plato as a Natural Scientist." *Journal of Hellenic Studies* 88 (1968): 78–92.
Long, Anthony, and David Sedley, ed. and trans. *The Hellenistic Philosophers*, Volumes 1–2. New York: Cambridge University Press, 1987.
Lutz, Antoine, et al. "Mental Training Enhances Attentional Stability: Neural and Behavioral Evidence." *The Journal of Neuroscience* 29, no. 42 (October 21, 2009): 13418–27.
Lydall, Emma S., Gary Gilmour, and Dominic M. Dwyer. "Rats Place Greater Value on Rewards Produced by High Effort: An Animal Analogue of the 'Effort Justification' Effect." *Journal of Experimental Social Psychology* 46, no. 6 (November 2010): 1134–7.
Mackay, Christopher S, trans. and ed. *Malleus Maleficarum*. Cambridge, UK: Cambridge University Press, 2006.
MacLean, K. A., et al. "Intensive Meditation Training Improves Perceptual Discrimination and Sustained Attention." *Psychological Science* 21, no. 6 (May 11, 2010): 829–39.
Magendie, François. *Précis élémentaire de physiologie*. 2nd revised ed. Paris: Méquignon-Marvis, [1816] 1825.
Maimonides, Moses. *The Guide of the Perplexed*. Translated by Shlomo Pines. 2 vols. Chicago: University of Chicago Press, 1963.
Matson, Wallace I. "Why Isn't the Mind-Body Problem Ancient?" In *Mind, Matter, and Method: Essays in Philosophy and Science in Honor of Herbert Feigl*, edited by Paul K. Feyerabend and Grover Maxwell, 92–102. Minneapolis: University of Minnesota Press, 1968.
Menn, Stephen. "Aristotle's Definition of the Soul and the Programme of the *De anima*." *Oxford Studies in Ancient Philosophy* 22 (2002): 82–139.
Ménuret de Chambaud, Jean-Joseph. "Mort." In *Encyclopédie ou Dictionnaire raisonné des sciences, des arts et des métiers*, edited by D. Diderot and J. D'Alembert, X, 718–27. Paris: Briasson, 1765.
Ménuret de Chambaud, Jean-Joseph. "Œconomie Animale (Médecine)." In *Encyclopédie ou Dictionnaire raisonné des sciences, des arts et des métiers*, edited by D. Diderot and J. D'Alembert, XI, 360–6. Paris: Briasson, 1765.
Ménuret de Chambaud, Jean-Joseph. "Spasme." In *Encyclopédie ou Dictionnaire raisonné des arts et des métiers*, edited by D. Diderot and J. D'Alembert, XV, 434–8. Paris: Briasson, 1765.
Merritt, Maria, John Doris, and Gilbert Harman. "Character." In *The Moral Psychology Handbook*, edited by John M. Doris, 355–401. Oxford: Oxford University Press, 2010.

Milgram, Stanley. *Obedience to Authority*. Harper & Row, 1974.

Miller, Thomas M. "Plato's Doctrine of the Immortality of the Soul," Ph.D. diss., Princeton University, 2015.

Mol, Annemarie. *The Body Multiple: Ontology in Medical Practice*. Durham, NC: Duke University Press, 2002.

Naddaf, Gerard. *The Greek Concept of Nature*. Albany: SUNY Press, 2005.

Newton, I. *The Principia: Mathematical Principles of Natural Philosophy*. Edited by I. B. Cohen. Berkeley: University of California Press, 1999.

Newton, I. *Philosophical Writings*. Edited by A. Janiak. Cambridge, UK: Cambridge University Press, 2004.

Nussbaum, Martha. *The Therapy of Desire*. Princeton, NJ: Princeton University Press, 1993.

Oresme, Nicolas. *Le livre du ciel et du monde*. Edited by Albert D. Menut and Alexander J. Denomy. Translated by Albert D. Menut. Madison: University of Wisconsin Press, 1968.

Origen, "On First Principles," In *An Exhortation to Martyrdom, Prayer, and Selected Works*, edited and translated by Rowan A. Greer. New York: Paulist Press, 1979.

Porter, J. I., and Mark Buchan. "Introduction." In *Special Issue: Before Subjectivity? Lacan and the Classics*, edited by J. I. Porter and M. Buchan, 1–19. *Helios* 31. Lubbock, TX: Texas Tech University Press, 2004.

Potter, P., and J. P. Wright, eds. *Psyche and Soma: Physicians and Metaphysicians on the Mind-Body Problem from Antiquity to Enlightenment*. Oxford: Oxford University Press, 2000.

Prinz, Jesse J. *The Emotional Construction of Morals*. New York: Oxford University Press, 2007.

Prinz, Jesse, and Shaun Nichols. "Moral Emotions." In *The Moral Psychology Handbook*, edited by John M. Doris, 111–47. Oxford: Oxford University Press, 2010.

Purves, Alex. "Ajax and Other Objects: Homer's Vibrant Materialism." In *Special Issue: New Essays in Homer: Language, Violence, Agency*. Edited by Helen Morales and Sara Lindheim. *Ramus* 44, no. 1–2 (2015): 75–94.

Raphson, J. *De Spatio Reali*. London: Johannem Taylor, 1702.

Rapp, Christof. "Interaction of Body and Soul: What the Hellenistic Philosophers Saw and Aristotle Avoided." In *Common to Body and Soul: Philosophical Approaches to Explaining Living Behaviour in Greco-Roman Antiquity*, edited by R. A. H. King, 187–208. Berlin: Walter de Gruyter, 2006.

Regius, Henricus. *Fundamenta physices*. Amsterdam: Elzevier, 1646.

Renehan, R. "The Meaning of ΣΩMA in Homer: A Study in Methodology." *California Studies in Classical Antiquity* 12 (1979): 269–82.

Richert, R. A., and P. L. Harris. "The Ghost in My Body: Children's Developing Concept of the Soul." *Journal of Cognition and Culture* 6, no. 3–4 (2006): 409–27.

Roberts, A., and J. Donaldson, eds. *The Anti-Nicene Fathers, Vol. 3: Tertullian.* Buffalo, NY: The Christian Literature Publishing Company, 1885.

Robinson, T. M. 2000. "The Defining Features of Mind-Body Dualism in the Writings of Plato." In *Psyche and Soma: Physicians and Metaphysicians on the Mind-Body Problem from Antiquity to Enlightenment*, edited by P. Potter, and J. P. Wright, 37–55. Oxford: Oxford University Press, 2000.

Saadia Gaon. *The Book of Beliefs and Opinions*. Translated by S. Rosenblatt. New Haven: Yale University Press, 1948.

Schroeder, Timothy, Adina Roskies, and Shaun Nichols. "Moral Motivation." In *The Moral Psychology Handbook*, edited by John M. Doris, 72–110. Oxford: Oxford University Press, 2010.

Schwitzgebel, Eric. "Do Ethicists Steal More Books?" *Philosophical Psychology* 22, no. 6 (2009): 711–25.

Schwitzgebel, Eric, and Fiery Cushman. "Expertise in Moral Reasoning? Order Effects on Moral Judgment in Professional Philosophers and Non-Philosophers." *Mind & Language* 27, no. 2 (2012): 135–53.

Schwitzgebel, Eric, and Joshua Rust. "The Moral Behaviour of Ethicists: Peer Opinion." *Mind* 118, no. 472 (2009): 1043–59.

Schwitzgebel, Eric, and Joshua Rust. "The Moral Behavior of Ethics Professors: Relationships among Self-Reported Behavior, Expressed Normative Attitude, and Directly Observed Behavior." *Philosophical Psychology* 27, no. 3 (2014): 293–327.

Seneca. *Natural Questions*. Translated by Harry M. Hine. Chicago: University of Chicago Press, 2010.

Slingerland, Edward. "The Situationist Critique and Early Confucian Virtue Ethics." *Ethics* 121, no. 2 (January 2011): 390–419.

Snell, Bruno. *The Discovery of the Mind*. Translated by T. Rosenmeyer. Oxford: Blackwell, 1953.

Solmsen, F. "The Vital Heat, the Inborn Pneuma and the Aether." In *Kleine Schriften*, 605–11. Hildesheim: Olms, 1968.

Spinoza, Baruch. *The Collected Works of Spinoza, Vol. 1*. Translated and edited by Edwin Curley. Princeton, NJ: Princeton University Press, 1985.

Stahl, Georg Ernst. *Negotium otiosum, seu Schiamaxia adversus positiones aliquas fundamentales theoriae verae medicaea Viro quodam celeberrimo intentata sed adversis armis conversis*. Halle: Impensis orphanotrophei, 1720.

Steel, Carlos. "The Moral Purpose of the Human Body: A Reading of *Timaeus* 69-72." *Phronesis* 46, no. 2 (2001): 105–28.

Suárez, Francisco. *Opera Omnia*. 28 vols. Paris: Ludovicum Vivès, 1856.
Suárez, Francisco. *Commentaria Una Cum Quaestionionibus in Libros Aristotelis "De Anima."* Edited by Salvador Castellote. Madrid: Labor, 1992.
Sze, Jocelyn A., et al. "Coherence between Emotional Experience and Physiology: Does Body Awareness Training Have an Impact?" *Emotion* 10, no. 6 (2010): 803–14.
Tenison, T. *The Creed of Mr. Hobbes Examined*. London: Francis Tyton, 1670.
Teske, Roland. *Letters* by Augustine. Volume 2. Hyde Park, NY: New City Press, 2002.
Todd, Robert C. *Alexander of Aphrodisias on Stoic Physics: A Study of the De Mixtione with Preliminary Essays, Text, Translation and Commentary*. Leiden, The Netherlands: Brill, 1976.
Toland, J. *Letters to Serena*. London: Bernard Lintot, 1704.
Toland, J. *Pantheisticon*. London: Cosmopoli, 1720.
Trivers, Robert. "The Evolution of Reciprocal Altruism." *The Quarterly Review of Biology* 46, no. 1 (1971): 35–57.
Vernant, Jean-Pierre. *Mortals and Immortals*. Edited and translated by F. I. Zeitlin. Princeton, NJ: Princeton University Press, 1991.
Virgil. *Eclogues, Georgics, Aeneid I-VI*. Translated by H. Rushton Fairclough. Loeb Classical Library. London: William Heinemann, 1916.
Viveiros de Castro, Eduardo. *Métaphysiques cannibales: Lignes d'anthropologie post-structurale*. Translated by Oiara Bonilla. Paris: Presses Universitaires de France, 2009.
Vlastos, Gregory. *Plato's Universe*. Seattle: University of Washington Press, 1975.
von Haller, Albrecht. *A Dissertation on the Sensible and Irritable Parts of Animals*. [London, J. Nourse: 1755]: Baltimore: John Hopkins, 1936.
von Staden, Heinrich. "The Discovery of the Body: Human Dissection and Its Cultural Contexts in Ancient Greece." *The Yale Journal of Biology and Medicine* 65, no. 3 (1992): 223–41.
Weismann, August. *The Germ-Plasm: A Theory of Heredity*. New York: Charles Scribner's Sons, 1893.
William of Ockham. *Opera philosophica et theological*. Edited by Gedeon Gál et al. 17 vols. St. Bonaventure, New York: The Franciscan Institute, 1967–1988.
Williams, Bernard. *Shame and Necessity*. Berkeley: University of California Press, 1993.
Willis, Thomas. "De anima brutorum quae hominis vitalis ac sensitiva est" (1672). In *Opera omnia, quorum posthac exstat Catalogus. Cum elenchis rerum & indicibus necessariis*. Geneva: Samuel de Tournes, 1676.

SECONDARY

Ablondi, Fred. "Automata, Living and Non-Living: Descartes' Mechanical Biology and His Criteria for Life." *Biology and Philosophy* 13, no. 2 (1998): 179–86.

Adams, Marilyn McCord. *William Ockham*. 2 vols. Notre Dame, Indiana: University of Notre Dame Press, 1987.

Adams, Robert Merrihew. *Leibniz: Determinist, Theist, Idealist*. New York: Oxford University Press, 1994.

Altmann, A., and S. M. Stern. *Isaac Israeli—A Neoplatonic Philosopher of the Early Tenth Century*. Oxford: Oxford University Press, 1958.

Arthur, Richard T. W. *Leibniz*. Cambridge, UK: Polity, 2014.

Arthur, Richard T. W. "Reply to Ohad Nachtomy." *The Leibniz Review* 24 (2014): 131–3.

Aucante, Vincent. *La philosophie médicale de Descartes*. Paris: PUF, 2006.

Bailey, Michael. *Battling Demons: Witchcraft, Heresy, and Reform in the Late Middle Ages*. University Park: Pennsylvania State University Press, 2003.

Baltzly, Dirk. "Stoic Pantheism." *Sophia* 42, no. 2 (2003): 3–33.

Barnes, Jonathan. "Roman Aristotle." In *Philosophia Togata II: Plato and Aristotle at Rome*, edited by Jonathan Barnes and Miriam Griffin, 1–69. New York: Oxford University Press, 1997.

Beeley, Philip. "Mathematics and Nature in Leibniz's Early Philosophy." In *The Young Leibniz and his Philosophy (1646–1676)*, edited by S. Brown, 123–45. Boston: Springer/Kluwer, 1999.

Bellis, Delphine. "Empiricism Without Metaphysics: Regius' Cartesian Natural Philosophy." In *Cartesian Empiricisms*, edited by M. Dobre and T. Nyden-Bullock, 151–83. Dordrecht: Springer, 2014.

Bennett, Jonathan. *A Study of Spinoza's Ethics*. Indianapolis: Hackett, 1984.

Bitbol-Hespériès, Annie. *Le principe de vie chez Descartes*. Paris: Vrin, 1990.

Bloch, Olivier. "Marx, Renouvier, et l'histoire du matérialisme." *La Pensée* 191 (1977): 3–42.

Boner, Patrick J. *Kepler's Cosmological Synthesis: Astrology, Mechanism and the Soul*. History of Science and Medicine Library 39. Leiden, The Netherlands: Brill, 2013.

Boureau, Alain. "Le Sabbat et la question scolastique de la personne." In *Le Sabbat des sorciers (XVᵉ-XVIIIe siècles)*, edited by Nicole Jacques Chapin, 33–46. Grenoble, France: Jérôme Million, 1993.

Brandom, Robert. "Adequacy and the Individuation of Ideas in Spinoza's Ethics." *Journal of the History of Philosophy* 14, no. 2 (1976): 147–62.

Brandt, Frithiof. *Thomas Hobbes' Mechanical Conception of Nature.* Copenhagen: Levin & Munksgaards, 1917.

Brittain, Charles. "Non-Rational Perception in the Stoics and Augustine." *Oxford Studies in Ancient Philosophy* 22 (2002): 253–308.

Broedel, Hans P. *The* Malleus Maleficarum *and the Construction of Witchcraft: Theology and Popular Belief.* Manchester, UK: Manchester University Press, 2003.

Brooke, J. *The Refiner's Fire: The Making of Mormon Cosmology: 1644–1844.* Cambridge, UK: Cambridge University Press, 1944.

Brown, Montague. "Augustine and Aristotle on Causality." In *Augustine: Presbyter Factus Sum,* edited by Joseph Leinhard, Earl Muller, and Roland Teske, 465–76. New York: P. Lang, 1993.

Brown, Stuart, ed. *The Young Leibniz and his Philosophy (1646–1676).* Boston: Springer/Kluwer, 1999.

Busson, Henri. *La religion des classiques.* Paris: PUF, 1948.

Byers, Sarah. *Perception, Sensibility, and Moral Motivation in Augustine.* New York: Cambridge University Press, 2013.

Byers, Sarah. "Augustine and the Philosophers." In *A Companion to Augustine,* edited by Mark Vessey, 175–87. Malden, MA: Wiley Blackwell, 2015.

Bynum, Caroline W. "Why All the Fuss about the Body? A Medievalist's Perspective." *Critical Inquiry* 22 (1995): 1–33

Canguilhem, Georges. *Études d'Histoire et de Philosophie des Sciences.* Paris: Vrin, 1968.

Canguilhem, Georges. "La théorie cellulaire." In *La Connaissance de la Vie,* by Georges Canguilhem, 53–101. Paris: Vrin, 2009.

Canguilhem, Georges. "Note sur les rapports de la théorie cellulaire et de la philosophie de Leibniz." In *La Connaissance de la Vie,* by Georges Canguilhem, 240–2. Paris, Vrin, 2009.

Chappell, Timothy. *Aristotle and Augustine on Freedom.* New York: St. Martin's Press, 1995.

Cottingham, John. "Cartesian Trialism." *Mind* 94, no. 374 (1985): 218–30.

Courcelle, Pierre. *Late Latin Writers and their Greek Sources.* Translated by Harry Wedeck. Cambridge, MA: Harvard University Press, 1969.

Cover, Jan A., and John O'Leary-Hawthorne. *Substance and Individuation in Leibniz* Cambridge, UK: Cambridge University Press, 1999.

Curley, Edwin. "'I Durst Not Write So Boldly' or How to Read Hobbes' Theological-Political Treatise." In *Hobbes e Spinoza,* edited by D. Bostrenghi, 497–593. Naples, Italy: Bibliopolis, 1992.

Curley, Edwin. "Hobbes versus Descartes." In *Descartes and His Contemporaries: Meditations, Objections and Replies,* edited by R. Ariew and M. Grene, 97–109. Chicago: University of Chicago Press, 1995.

Daniel, S. *John Toland: His Method, Manners and Mind*. Montreal: McGill-Queens University Press, 1984.

Davidson, Herbert. "Saadia's List of Theories of Soul." In *Jewish Medieval and Renaissance Studies*, edited by A. Altmann, 75–94. Harvard: Harvard University Press, 1967.

Deleuze, Gilles. *Le pli: Leibniz et le baroque*. Paris: Les Éditions de Minuit, 1988.

Della Rocca, Michael. *Representation and the Mind-Body Problem in Spinoza*. Oxford: Oxford University Press, 1996.

Della Rocca, Michael. "Points of View and the Two-fold Use of the Principle of Sufficient Reason in Spinoza." In *Uitgeverij Spinozahuis* 94 (2014).

Des Chene, Dennis. *Spirits and Clocks: Machine and Organism in Descartes*. Ithaca, NY: Cornell University Press, 2001.

Duchesneau, François. *La physiologie des Lumières. Empirisme, modèles et théories*. The Hague: Martinus Nijhoff/Kluwer, 1982.

Duchesneau, François. *Les modèles du vivant de Descartes à Leibniz*. Paris: Vrin, 1998.

Dumas, Marie-Noëlle. *La Pensée de la vie chez Leibniz*. Paris: Vrin, 1976.

Dyson, R. W. *Augustine: The City of God Against the Pagans*. Cambridge, UK: Cambridge University Press, 1998.

Eagleton, Terry. *After Theory*. London: Allen Lane, 2003.

Eilberg-Schwartz, Howard. "Introduction: People of the Body." In *People of the Body: Jews and Judaism from an Embodied Perspective*, edited by Howard Eilberg-Schwartz, 1–15. Albany: SUNY Press, 1992.

Eisenmann, Esti. "Body and Soul, Materiality and Spirituality in R. Sa'adia's Thought" (in Hebrew). *Mo'ed* 20 (2010): 135–52.

Engels, Friedrich. Ludwig Feuerbach und der Ausgang der klassischen deutschen Philosophie. Vol. 21, Werke. Berlin: Dietz Verlag, [1888] 1982.

Eran, Amira. *Me-Emunah Tamah Le-Emunah Ramah (From Simple Faith to Sublime Faith): Ibn Daud's Pre-Maimonidean Thought* (in Hebrew). Tel-Aviv, Israel: Hakibbutz Hameuchad, 1998.

Evans, D. *Tertullian's Adversus Praxean Liber*. London: S.P.C.K., 1948.

Fichant, Michel. "Leibniz et les machines de la nature." *Studia Leibnitiana* 35, no. 1 (2003): 1–28.

Foisneau, L. "Beyond the Air-Pump: Hobbes, Boyle and the Omnipotence of God." *Rivista di storia della filosofia* 59, no. 1 (2004): 33–49.

Foley, Henry. *Records of the English Province of the Society of Jesus, Vol. VI*. London: Burns and Oates, 1880.

Fontaine, T. A. M. *In Defence of Judaism: Abraham ibn Daud: Sources and Structures of Ha-Emunah Ha-Ramah*. Assen, The Netherlands: Van Gorcum, 1990.

Foucault, Michel. *Naissance de la clinique*. Paris: PUF, 1963.

Garber, Daniel. "Spinoza's Cartesian Dualism in the *Korte verhandling*." In *The Young Spinoza: A Metaphysician in the Making*, edited by Yitzhak Melamed, 68–82. Oxford: Oxford University Press, 2015.

Gaukroger, Stephen. "Pain and the Nature of Psychological Attributes." In *Brain Theory: Essays in Critical Neurophilosophy*, edited by Charles Wolfe, 35–44. Basingstoke, UK: Palgrave Macmillan, 2014.

Gayon, Jean. "Déterminisme génétique, déterminisme bernardien, déterminisme laplacien." In *Le hasard au cœur de la cellule. Probabilités, déterminisme, génétique*, edited by J.-J. Kupiec, 79–90. Paris: Editions Syllepse, 2009.

Gelfand, Toby. *Professionalizing Modern Medicine: Paris Surgeons and Medical Science and Institutions in the 18th Century*. Westport, CT: Greenwood, 1980.

Giglioni, Guido, "The Cosmoplastic System of the Universe: Ralph Cudworth on Stoic Naturalism." *Revue D'Histoires Des Sciences* 61, no. 2 (2008): 313–38.

Gilson, Etienne. *The Christian Philosophy of Saint Augustine*. New York: Random House, 1960.

Gorham, Geoffrey. "Causation and Similarity in Descartes." In *New Essays on the Rationalists*, edited by Rocco Gennaro and Charles Huenemann, 296–308. Oxford: Oxford University Press, 2002.

Gorham, Geoffrey. "Descartes on God's Relation to Time." *Religious Studies* 44, no. 4 (2008): 413–31.

Gorham, Geoffrey. "Newton on God's Relation to Space and Time: The Cartesian Framework." *Archiv für Geschichte der Philosophie* 93, no. 3 (2011): 281–320.

Gorham, Geoffrey. "The Theological Foundations of Hobbesian Physics: A Defense of Corporeal God." *British Journal for the History of Philosophy* 21 (2013): 240–61.

Gorham, Geoffrey. "Mixing Bodily Fluids: Hobbes's Stoic God." *Sophia: International Journal for the Philosophy of Religion* 53, no. 1 (2014): 33–49.

Gossett, Suzanne. "Drama in the English College, Rome, 1591-1660." *English Literary Renaissance* 3, no. 1 (1973): 60–93.

Gossett, Suzanne. "Introduction [to *Blame Not Our Author*]." In *Collections, Volume XII*, edited by Suzanne Gossett, 87– 93. Oxford: The Malone Society, 1983.

Granada, Miguel A. "New Visions of the Cosmos." In *The Cambridge Companion to Renaissance Philosophy*, edited by James Hankins, 270–86. Cambridge, UK: Cambridge University Press, 2007.

Grant, Edward. *Planets, Stars, & Orbs: The Medieval Cosmos, 1200–1687*. Cambridge, UK: Cambridge University Press, 1994.

Grmek, Mirko Drazen. *Raisonnement expérimental et recherches toxicologiques chez Claude Bernard*. Geneva: Droz, 1973.

Hacking, Ian. "The Cartesian Body." *BioSocieties* 1, no. 1 (2006): 13–15.

Hadot, Ilsetraut. *Arts libéraux et philosophie dans la pensée antique: contribution à l'histoire de l'éducation et de la culture dans l'Antiquité*. 2nd edn. Paris: Vrin, 2005.

Hamlyn, D. W. Introduction and Notes to Aristotle's *On the Soul: Books II and III (with Certain Passages from Book I)*. Oxford: Clarendon, 1968.

Hirai, Hiro. *Medical Humanism and Natural Philosophy: Renaissance Debates on Matter, Life and the Soul*. Medieval and Early Modern Science 17. Leiden, The Netherlands: Brill, 2011.

Hoffman, Paul. "The Unity of Descartes's Man." *Philosophical Review* 95 (1986): 339–70.

Hölscher, Ludger. *The Reality of the Mind: Augustine's Philosophical Arguments for the Human Soul as a Spiritual Substance*. New York: Routledge & Kegan Paul, 1986.

Huneman, Philippe. *Bichat : La vie et la mort*. Paris: PUF, 1998.

Huneman, Philippe. "'Animal Economy': Anthropology and the Rise of Psychiatry from the *Encyclopédie* to the Alienists." In *The Anthropology of the Enlightenment*, edited by Larry Wolff and Marco Cipolloni, 262–76. Stanford, CA: Stanford University Press, 2007.

Hutchins, Barnaby. "Descartes and the Dissolution of Life." *The Southern Journal of Philosophy* 54, no. 2 (2016): 155–73.

Ishiguro, Hide, "Unity Without Simplicity." *The Monist* 81, no. 4 (1998): 534–52.

Ishiguro, Hide, "Is There a Conflict between the Logical and the Metaphysical Notion of Unity in Leibniz?" In *Nihil sine ratione: Mensch, Natur und Technik im Wirken von G. W. Leibniz*, edited by H. Poser et al., VII. Internationaler Leibniz-Kongreß, 3 vols, 535–41. Hannover, Germany: Gottfried-Wilhelm-Leibniz-Gesellschaft [in Komm.], 2001.

Jacobs, Louis. "The Body in Jewish Worship: Three Rituals Examined." In *Religion and the Body*, edited by Sarah Coakley, 71–89. Cambridge, MA: Cambridge University Press, 1997.

Jesseph, Douglas. "Hobbes's Atheism." *Midwest Studies in Philosophy* 26, no. 1 (2002): 140–66.

Jesseph, Douglas. "Hobbesian Mechanics." In *Oxford Studies in Early Modern Philosophy*, Vol. 3, edited by Daniel Garber and Steven Nadler, 119–52. Oxford: Oxford University Press, 2006.

Kaitaro, Timo. "'Man is an admirable machine'—A Dangerous Idea?" *Mécanisme et vitalisme*, special issue of *La lettre de la Maison française d'Oxford*, edited by M. Saad, 14 (2001): 105–21

Kassler, Jamie C. "The Paradox of Power: Hobbes and Stoic Naturalism." In *The Uses of Antiquity: The Scientific Revolution and the Classical Tradition*, edited by Stephen Gaukroger. Dordrecht, The Netherlands: D. Reidel, 1991.

Kirkebøen, Geir. "Descartes' Embodied Psychology: Descartes or Damasios Error?" *Journal of the History of the Neurosciences* 10, no. 2 (2001): 173–91.

Klaniczay, Gábor. "Entre visions angéliques et transes chamaniques: le sabbat des sorcières dans le *Formicarius de Nider.*" *Médiévales* 44, 2003: 47–72. Accessed February 5 2016. Doi: http://medievales.revues.org/710

Leijenhorst, Cees. *The Mechanisation of Aristotelianism: The Late Aristotelian Setting of Thomas Hobbes' Natural Philosophy*. Leiden, The Netherlands: Brill, 2002.

Leijenhorst, Cees. "Hobbes's Corporeal Deity." *Rivista di storia della filosofia* 59, no. 1 (2004): 73–95.

Leijenhorst, Cees. "Suárez on Self-Awareness." In *The Philosophy of Francisco Suárez*, edited by Henrik Lagerlund and Benjamin Hill. Oxford: Oxford University Press, 2012.

Lenz, Martin. "Why Can't Angels Think Properly? Ockham against Chatton and Aquinas." In *Angels in Medieval Philosophical Inquiry: Their Function and Significance*, edited by Isabel Irribaren and Martin Lenz, 155–67. Farnham, UK: Ashgate, 2008.

Lesch, James E. *Science and Medicine in France: The Emergence of Experimental Physiology, 1790–1855*. Cambridge, MA: Harvard University Press, 1984.

Levey, Samuel. "On Unity: Leibniz-Arnauld Revisited." *Philosophical Topics* 31, no. 1–2 (2003): 245–75.

Lodge, Paul, ed. *Leibniz and His Correspondents*. Proceedings of a Conference Held 16–18 March, 2001 at Tulane University. New York: Cambridge University Press, 2004.

Look, Brandon. "On Monadic Domination in Leibniz's Metaphysics." *British Journal for the History of Philosophy* 10, no. 3 (2002): 379–99.

Lupoli, Agostino. "Fluidismo e Corporeal Deity nella filosofia naturale di Thomas Hobbes." *Rivista di storia della filosofia* 54, no. 4 (1999): 573–609.

Mann, William. "Immutability and Predication: What Aristotle Taught Philo and Augustine." *International Journal for Philosophy of Religion* 22, no. 1–2 (1987): 21–39.

Manning, Gideon. "Out on the Limb: The Place of Medicine in Descartes' Philosophy." *Early Science and Medicine* 12, no. 2 (2007): 214–22.

Marshall, Colin. "The Mind and the Body as 'One and the Same Thing' in Spinoza." *British Journal for the History of Philosophy* 17, no. 5 (2009): 897–919.

Marx, Karl and Friedrich Engels. *Basic Writings on Politics and Philosophy*, edited by L. S. Feuer. New York: Doubleday/Anchor, 1959.

Matthews, Gareth. "Augustine and Ibn Sina on Souls in the Afterlife." *Philosophy* 89, no. 3–4 (2014): 463–76.

Mazzio, Carla. "The Three-Dimensional Self: Geometry, Melancholy, Drama." In *Arts of Calculation: Quantifying Thought in Early Modern Europe*, edited by David Glimp and Michelle R. Warren, 39–65. New York: Palgrave Macmillan, 2004.

Melamed, Yitzhak. "Spinoza's Metaphysics of Thought: Parallelisms and the Multifaceted Structure of Ideas." *Philosophy and Phenomenological Research* 86, no. 3 (2013): 636–83.

Melzack, Ronald. "Phantom Limbs." *Scientific American*. Special Edition: *Secrets of the Senses* 16, no. 3 (2006): 52–9.

Mercer, Christia. *Leibniz's Metaphysics: Its Origin and Development*. Cambridge, UK: Cambridge University Press, 2001.

Mercer, Christia, and Robert C. Sleigh. "Metaphysics: The Early Period to the Discourse on Metaphysics." In *The Cambridge Companion to Leibniz*, edited by N. Jolley, 67–124. Cambridge, UK: Cambridge University Press, 1995.

Merchant, Carolyn. *The Death of Nature: Women, Ecology, and the Scientific Revolution*. San Francisco: Harper and Row, 1980.

Merleau-Ponty, Maurice. *Phenomenology of Perception*. Translated by C. Smith. London: Routledge & Kegan Paul, 1962.

Merleau-Ponty, Maurice. *The Structure of Behaviour*. Translated by A. L. Fisher. Boston: Beacon, 1963.

Miller, Jon and Brad Inwood, eds. *Hellenistic and Early Modern Philosophy*. Cambridge, UK: Cambridge University Press, 2003.

Mintz, Samuel I., *The Hunting of Leviathan*. Cambridge, UK: Cambridge University Press, 1962.

Nachtomy, Ohad. "The Individual's Place in the Logical Space: Leibniz on Possible Individuals and their Relations." *Studia Leibnitiana* 30, no. 2 (1998): 161–77.

Nachtomy, Ohad. "Leibniz on Possible Individuals." *Studia Leibnitiana* 34, no. 1 (2002): 31–58.

Nachtomy, Ohad. "Leibniz on Nested Individuals." *British Journal for the History of Philosophy* 15, no. 4 (2007): 709–28.

Nachtomy, Ohad. *Possibility, Agency, and Individuality in Leibniz's Metaphysics*. Dordrecht, The Netherlands: Springer, 2007.

Nachtomy, Ohad. "Leibniz's view of Living Beings: Embodied or Nested Individuals." (this volume)

Niederbaccher, Bruno. "The Human Soul: Augustine's Case for Soul-Body Dualism." In *The Cambridge Companion to Augustine*, 2nd ed., edited by David Meconi and Eleonore Stump, 125–41. Cambridge, UK: Cambridge University Press, 2014.

Normore, Calvin. "The Invention of Singular Thought." In *Forming the Mind: Essays on the Internal Senses and the Mind/Body Problem from Avicenna to the Medical Enlightenment*, edited by Henrik Lagerlund, 109–28. Dordrecht, The Netherlands: Springer, 2007.

O'Callaghan, John. "Imago Dei: A Test Case for St. Thomas's Augustinianism." In *Aquinas the Augustinian*, edited by Michael Dauphinais, Barry David, and Matthew Levering, 100–44. Washington, DC: Catholic University of America Press, 2007.

Oksenberg Rorty, Amélie. "Descartes on Thinking with the Body." In *The Cambridge Companion to Descartes*, edited by J. Cottingham, 371–92. Cambridge, UK: Cambridge University Press, 1992.

Pasnau, Robert. "Henry of Ghent and the Twilight of Divine Illumination." *The Review of Metaphysics* 49, no. 1 (September 1995): 49–75.

Pasnau, Robert. "Cognition." In *The Cambridge Companion to Duns Scotus*, edited by Thomas Williams, 285–311. Cambridge, UK: Cambridge University Press, 2002.

Pasnau, Robert. *Metaphysical Themes: 1274-1671*. Oxford: Oxford University Press, 2011.

Passmore, John Arthur. *Ralph Cudworth*. Cambridge, UK: Cambridge University Press, 1951.

Paster, Gail Kern. "Nervous Tension: Networks of Blood and Spirit in the Early Modern Body." In *The Body in Parts*, edited by D. Hillman and C. Mazzio, 107–25. London: Routledge, 1997.

Paul, Erich. *Science, Religion, and Mormon Cosmology*. Urbana: University of Illinois Press, 1992.

Pépin, François. *La Philosophie expérimentale de Diderot et la chimie*. Paris: Garnier, 2012.

Perler, Dominik. "Thought Experiments: The Methodological Function of Angels in Late Medieval Epistemology." In *Angels in Medieval Philosophical Inquiry: Their Function and Significance*, edited by Isabel Iribarren and Martin Lenz, 143–54. Aldershot, UK: Ashgate, 2008.

Phemister, Pauline. "Leibniz and the Elements of Compound Bodies." *British Journal for the History of Philosophy* 7, no. 1 (1999): 57–78.

Pichot, André. *Histoire de la notion de gène*. Paris: Flammarion, 1999.

Pickavé, Martin. "Human Knowledge." In *The Oxford Handbook of Aquinas*, edited by Brian Davies and Eleonore Stump, 311–26. Oxford: Oxford University Press, 2012.

Pigné, Christine. "Du *De malo* au *Malleus Maleficarum*: Les conséquences de la démonologie thomiste sur le corps de la sorcière." *Cahiers de recherches médiévales et humanistes* 13 (2006): 196–220.

Policante, Amedeo. "Foucault, Subjectivity and Flight. Witchcraft, Possession and the Resistance of the Flesh." *Materiali Foucaultiani* 1, no. 1 (2012): 235–59.

Pollock, Sheldon. *The Language of the Gods in the World of Men: Sanskrit, Culture, and Power in Premodern India*. Berkeley: University of Califoria Press, 2006.

Poser, Hans, et al., eds. *Nihil sine ratione: Mensch, Natur und Technik im Wirken von G. W. Leibniz*, VII. Internationaler Leibniz-Kongreß. 3 vols. Hannover: Germany: Gottfried-Wilhelm-Leibniz-Gesellschaft [in Komm.], 2001.

Pyle, Andrew. *Malebranche*. London and New York: Routledge, 2003.

Radner, Daisie. "Descartes's Notion of the Union of Mind and Body." *Journal of the History of Philosophy* 9, no. 2 (1971): 159–70.

Radner, Daisie. "Spinoza's Theory of Ideas." *The Philosophical Review* 80, no. 3 (1971): 338–59.

Rather, L. J. *Mind and Body in Eighteenth-Century Medicine. A Study Based on J. Gaub's* De regimine mentis. Berkeley: University of California Press, 1965.

Ravitzky, Aviezer, ed. *Crescas' Sermon on the Passover and Studies in his Philosophy*. Jerusalem: Magnes, 2005.

Reill, Peter Hanns. *Vitalizing Nature in the Enlightenment*. Berkeley: University of California Press, 2005.

Reiss, Timothy. "Denying the Body? Memory and the Dilemmas of History in Descartes." *Journal of the History of Ideas* 57, no. 4 (1996): 587–607.

Renz, Ursula. "Finite Subjects in the Ethics: Spinoza on Indexical Knowledge, the First Person and the Individuality of Human Minds." In *The Oxford Handbook of Spinoza*, edited by Michael Della Rocca. Oxford: Oxford University Press, 2013.

Riverso, E. "Denotation and Corporeity in Leviathan." *Metalogicon* 4, no. 1 (1991): 78–92.

Rosen, Edward. "The Dissolution of the Solid Celestial Spheres." *Journal of the History of Ideas* 46, no. 1 (March 1985): 13–31.

Rozemond, Marleen. *Descartes's Dualism*. Cambridge, MA: Harvard University Press, 2002.

Rublack, Ursula. "Fluxes: The Early Modern Body and the Emotions." *History Workshop Journal* 53 (2002): 1–16.

Sawday, Jonathan. *The Body Emblazoned: Dissection and the Human Body in Renaissance Culture*. London: Routledge, 1995.

Schwartz, D. "The Neutralization of the Messianic Idea in Medieval Jewish Rationalism" (in Hebrew). *Hebrew Union College Annual* 64 (1994): H1–H22.

Sellars, J. "Is God a Mindless Vegetable? Cudworth on Stoic Theology." *Intellectual History Review* 21, no. 2 (2011): 121–33.

Shapiro, Lawrence. *Embodied Cognition*. London: Routledge, 2011.

Shapiro, Lisa. "The Health of the Body-Machine? Or Seventeenth Century Mechanism and the Concept of Health." *Perspectives on Science* 11, no. 4 (2003): 421–42.

Simmons, Alison. "Mind-Body Union and the Limits of Cartesian Metaphysics." Unpublished draft.

Smith, Justin E. H. *Leibniz, Microscopy, and the Metaphysics of Composite Substance*. PhD diss., Columbia University, 2000.

Smith, Justin E. H. "On the Fate of Composite Substances After 1704." *Studia Leibnitiana* 31, no. 1 (1999): 1–7.

Sorabji, Richard, ed. *The Philosophy of the Commentators, 200–600 AD: A Sourcebook*. Vol. 2. London: Duckworth, 2004.

Sorabji, Richard. *Self: Ancient and Modern Insights about Individuality, Life, and Death*. Chicago: University of Chicago Press, 2006.

South, James B. "Suárez, Immortality, and the Soul's Dependence on the Body." In *The Philosophy of Francisco Suárez*, edited by Henrik Lagerlund and Benjamin Hill, 121–36. Oxford: Oxford University Press, 2012.

Springborg, Patricia. "Hobbes's Challenge to Descartes, Bramhall and Boyle: A Corporeal God." *British Journal for the History of Philosophy* 20, no. 5 (2012): 903–34.

Stewart, Matthew. *Nature's God: The Heretical Origins of the American Republic*. New York: W.W. Norton, 2014.

Stolberg, Michael. *Experiencing Illness and the Sick Body in Early Modern Europe*. Translated by Leonhard Unglaub and Logan Kennedy. New York: Palgrave Macmillan, 2011.

Strauss, Leo. *The Political Philosophy of Hobbes*. Chicago: University of Chicago Press, 1952.

Strawson, P. F. *Individuals*. London: Routledge, 1959.

Stroumsa, Sarah. *Dāwūd ibn Marwān al-Muqammiṣ's Twenty Chapters ('Ishrūn Maqāla)*. Leiden: Brill, 1989.

Stump, Eleonore. "The Mechanisms of Cognition: Ockham on Mediating Species." In *The Cambridge Companion to Ockham*, edited by Paul Vincent Spade, 168–203. Cambridge, UK: Cambridge University Press, 1999.

Stump, Eleonore. *Aquinas*. Arguments of the Philosophers. New York: Routledge, 2005.

Suarez-Nani, Tiziana. *Les anges et la philosophie*. Paris: Vrin, 2002.

Sullivan, R. *John Toland and the Deist Controversy*. Cambridge, MA: Harvard University Press, 1982.

Sutton, John. "The Body and the Brain." In *Descartes' Natural Philosophy*, edited by S. Gaukroger, J. A. Schuster, and J. Sutton, 697–722. London: Routledge, 2000.

Sutton, John. "Spongy Brains and Material Memories." In *Embodiment and Environment in Early Modern England*, edited by M. Floyd-Wilson and G. Sullivan, 14–34. London: Palgrave, 2007.

Sutton, John, and Evelyn B. Tribble. "Materialists Are Not Merchants of Vanishing: Commentary on David Hawkes, 'Against Materialism in Literary Theory.'" *Early Modern Culture* 9 (2011).

Teske, Roland. *Studies in the Philosophy of William of Auvergne, Bishop of Paris (1228–1249)*. Milwaukee, WI: Marquette University Press, 2006.

Thompson, Evan. *Mind in Life*. Cambridge, MA: Harvard University Press, 2007.

Thomson, A. *Bodies of Thought: Science, Religion and the Soul in the Early Enlightenment*. Oxford: Oxford University Press, 2008.

Thomson, Ann. "Mechanistic Materialism versus Vitalistic Materialism." *Mécanisme et vitalisme*, special issue of *La Lettre de la Maison française d'Oxford*, edited by M. Saad, 14 (2001): 21–36.

Toivanen, Juhana. "Perceptual Self-Awareness in Seneca, Augustine, and Olivi." *Journal of the History of Philosophy* 51, no. 3 (2013): 355–82.

Weber, D. *Hobbes et le corps de Dieu*. Paris: J. Vrin, 2009.

Weiss, R. L., and C. E. Butterworth. *Ethical Writings of Maimonides*. New York: New York University Press, 1975.

Williams, Elizabeth. "Sciences of Appetite in the Enlightenment, 1750–1800." *Studies in History and Philosophy of Science Part C: Studies in History and Philosophy of Biological and Biomedical Sciences* 43, no. 2 (2012): 392–404.

Williams, Michael E. *The Venerable English College, Rome: A History*. 2nd ed. Herefordshire, UK: Gracewing, 2008.

Williams, Richard L. "Ancient Bodies and Contested Identities in the English College Martyrdom Cycle, Rome." In *Roman Bodies: Antiquity to the Eighteenth Century*, edited by Andrew Hopkins and Maria Wyke, 185–200. London: The British School at Rome, 2005.

Wilson, Catherine. "*De Ipsa Natura*: Sources of Leibniz's Doctrines of Forces, Activity and Natural Law." *Studia Leibnitiana* 19, no. 2 (1987): 148–72.

Wilson, Catherine. *The Invisible World*. Princeton, NJ: Princeton University Press, 1995.

Wilson, Margaret. "Cartesian Dualism." In *Descartes: Critical and Interpretative Essays*, edited by Michael Hooker, 197–233. Baltimore: Johns Hopkins University Press, 1978.

Wilson, Margaret. "Objects, Ideas, and 'Minds': Comments on Spinoza's Theory of Mind." In *Ideas and Mechanism*, edited by Margaret Wilson, 126–40. Princeton, NJ: Princeton University Press, 1999.

Wolfe, Charles T. "A Happiness Fit for Organic Bodies: La Mettrie's Medical Epicureanism." In *Epicurus in the Enlightenment*, edited by N. Leddy and A. Lifschitz, 69–83. Oxford: Voltaire Foundation, 2009.

Wolfe, Charles T. "Vitalism and the Resistance to Experimentation on Life in the Eighteenth Century." *Journal of the History of Biology* 46, no. 2 (2013): 255–82.

Wolfe, Charles T. "Teleomechanism Redux? Functional Physiology and Hybrid Models of Life in Early Modern Natural Philosophy." *Gesnerus* 71, no. 2 (2014): 290–307.

Wolfe, Charles T. "Epigenesis as Spinozism in Diderot's Biological Project." In *The Life Sciences in Early Modern Philosophy*, edited by O. Nachtomy and J. E. H. Smith, 181–201. Oxford: Oxford University Press, 2014.

Wolfe, Charles T., and Ofer Gal, eds. *The Body as Object and Instrument of Knowledge: Embodied Empiricism in Early Modern Science.* Dordrecht, The Netherlands: Springer, 2010.

Wolfe, Charles T., and Motoichi Terada. "The 'Animal Economy' as Object and Program in Montpellier Vitalism." *Science in Context* 21, no. 4 (2008): 537–79.

Wright, John P. "Metaphysics and Physiology. Mind, Body, and the Animal Economy in Eighteenth-Century Scotland." In *Studies in the Philosophy of the Scottish Enlightenment*, edited by Michael A. Stewart, 251–302. Oxford: Clarendon, 1990.

Wright, John P. "Substance vs. Function Dualism in Eighteenth-Century Medicine." In *Psyche and Soma: Physicians and Metaphysicians on the Mind–Body Problem from Antiquity to the Enlightenment*, edited by J. P. Wright and P. Potter, 237–54. Oxford: Clarendon, 2003.

Young, Iris Marion. *On Female Body Experience: "Throwing Like a Girl" and Other Essays.* New York: Oxford University Press, 2005.

Zarka, Yves-Charles. "First Philosophy and the Foundations of Knowledge." In *Cambridge Companion to Hobbes*, edited by Tom Sorell. Cambridge, UK: Cambridge University Press, 2006.

Index

Ablondi, Fred 246 n. 13
Abu Ghraib 277
Actuality 51, 53–55, 57–58, 60–62, 64–65, 146–147, 149, 158, 161, 303
Adams, Marilyn McCord 156 n. 26, n. 28
Aesthetics 18, 70–71, 74, 81–85, 113
Al-Muqammitz, Dawud ibn Marwan 125 n. 33
Alexandrakis, Aphrodite 70 n. 3
Allen, Michael J. B. 70 n. 3
Altruism and Altruistic Behavior 287, 289, 297–295
Ammonius 83
Anatomy, 4, 28 n. 26, 30, 38, 243, 260, 262–265, 322
Anaxagoras 25
Angels and Angelology 3, 12–13, 15, 111, 143, 145, 148–150, 155–165, 168–170, 184, 317–318
Animality (in celestial physics) 318–323

Aquinas, Thomas 151–170
Archetype 80
Archilochus 27 n. 24
Archimedes 314
Aristotle and Aristotelianism, 15, 19, 19 n. 5, 23 n. 16, 25, 30, 33–34, 36, 70, 73, 76, 77–78, 77n, 78n, 83, 87–89, 92–96, 104–107, 144–148, 151–152, 154–155, 166–167, 169, 279, 290
Armstrong, A. H. 76 n. 22, 78
Arnauld, Antoine 234 n. 2, 192–193, 197 n. 22, n. 24
Art 70, 71, 74, 80, 84–85
Arthur, Richard T. W. 190–191, 192 n. 7, 196
Atheism 13, 173, 176 n. 24, 180 n. 44, 181
Atoms and Atomism 31 n. 32, 71–73, 93, 103, 177 n. 29, 192, 198 n. 28, 242, 327
Aucante, Vincent 247 n. 14
Augustine 12, 70 n. 5, 87–108, 144, 300
Automata 244, 274–275

Ayache, L. 36 n. 41
Averroes and Averroism 225, 317

Bahya ibn Paquda 120–121, 125–127, 132, 135–136, 137
Baird, Benjamin 286 n. 13
Baltzky, Dirk 180 n. 45
Banks, Curtis 277 n. 1
Bar Hayya, Abraham 126 n. 35
Barnes, Jonathan 88 n. 4
Barthez, Paul Joseph 269, 271
Batson, C. Daniel 280 n. 3, 291–293
Beauty 5, 70, 73, 74, 78–81, 82, 84–85, 86
Beeley, Philip 203 n. 40
Bellis, Delphine 247
Bennett, Jonathan 289–290
Bernard, Claude 11, 246, 262–263, 265, 267, 270–272, 274–276
Bichat, François-Xavier 245, 256, 260–267, 269–276
Bitbol-Hespériès, Annie 247 n. 14
Blame Not Our Author 311–316
Bloch, Olivier 247 n. 16
Bloom, Paul 18 n. 3
Boerhaave, Herman 248–251
Boesoou 8
Bolens, Guillemette 29 n. 29
Boner, Patrick 317 n. 1, 320 n. 13
Bordeu, Théophile 258, 271
Borelli, Giovanni Alfonso 246
Brady, Michael S. 286
Brahe, Tycho 319
Brain 4, 11, 38, 220, 246, 253, 255, 264–265, 279–280, 287, 307–310, 320 n. 12
Bramhall, John 172–174, 182
Brandom, Robert 238 n. 62
Brandt, Frithiof 174 n. 19
Brewer, Judson A. 286 n. 14
Brill, Sarah 45 n. 65
Brittain, Charles 87 n. 1
Broadie, Sarah 19 n. 5, 40 n. 53
Brooke, J. 186 n. 71
Brown, Montague 88 n. 1
Bruno, Giordano 319–320
Buchan, Mark 29 n. 27

Buddhism 15, 285–287, 290–291, 293–295
Burman, Frans 219
Busson, Henri 248 n. 18
Byers, Sarah Catherine 12, 90 n. 9
Bynum, Caroline W. 242 n. 4, 243 n. 5

Canguilhem, Georges 275 n. 74, 326
Cardano, Girolamo 319
Carone, G. R. 19 n. 5, 40 n. 53, 45 n. 65, 48 n. 75
Cartesians and Cartesianism 171, 178, 195, 226, 235, 241, 243, 245–248, 250–253, 275
Celestial bodies, souls of 319–323
Cell and Cell Theory 94, 209, 326–329
Chambaud, Ménuret de 250, 257, 258
Chamberlain, Colin 215 n. 1, 237 n. 57
Chanut, Pierre 237
Chapman, H. A. 288
Chappell, Timothy 88 n.1
Charles-Saget, Annick 82 n. 35
Christian and Christianity 6, 9, 12–13, 21, 69, 70 n. 5, 78 n. 29, 87, 103, 111, 121, 144, 148, 150, 165, 181–182, 300–301, 304, 315
Cicero, Marcus Tullius 103, 185, 320
Circignani, Niccolò 315
Clark, R. I. 75 n. 19
Clarke, Michael 30 n. 30, 30 n. 31
Clarke, Samuel 186
Claus, David B. 41 n. 56
Clavius, Christoph 313
Cognition 150–156, 168 n. 32, 162–164, 167, 169–170
Comte, Auguste 260 n. 51
Condon, P. 287
Confucius and Confucianism 15, 281–283, 285, 295
Consciousness and Conscious Experience 18, 26, 31–32, 36–37, 48, 90, 144 n. 1, 153, 180, 217, 223 n. 30, 304
Conway, Anne 3, 183
Corrigan, Kevin 70 n. 5
Corruption and Corruptibility 87, 100, 104, 123, 146, 166, 185–186, 236, 320 n. 12

INDEX

Courcelle, Pierre 88 n. 4
Copernicus and Copernicanism 320–321
Corpse 26–27, 95, 100 n. 43, 120, 140, 141 n. 74, 212, 302
Cottam, Thomas 315
Cottingham, John 218 n. 10
Counter-reformation 311, 313, 315
Coward, William 183–184, 186
Craik, Elizabeth 22 n. 12
Crescas, Hasdai 140–142
Crick, Francis 330
Csordas, T. 21 n. 8, 31 n. 33
Cudworth, Ralph 176 n. 24, 100 n. 44, 182–183
Cullen, William 250–251, 259
Curley, Edwin 173 n. 7, 174 n. 14, 182 n. 53, 252 n. 31
Cushman, Fiery 283 n. 8

Daley, John M. 280 n. 3
Daniel, Steven 185 n. 69
Dante 317–318
Darley, John M. 280 n. 3
Darwin, Charles 327–330
Davidson, Herbert 121 n. 20
Davies, Martin 70 n. 3
Davis, Jake 11, 14, 295 n. 35
De Certeau, Michel 304
De Hart, S. 22 n. 12, 23 n. 14, 33 n. 34, 35 n. 38
de la Forge, Louis 247
De Volder, Burchard 197 n. 26, 205
Dean-Jones, Lesley 23 n. 15, 39 n. 47
Death 26, 35, 45, 89, 92 n. 16, 94–96, 99 n. 37, 101–108, 139, 165–167, 169, 170 n. 70, 244 n. 8, 260, 264–265, 275, 301–303
Decaix, Véronique 15
Deism 172, 182–187
Deleuze, Gilles 323
Della Rocca, Michael 215 n. 1, 225 n. 34, 238 n. 62
Democritus and Democritean 41, 72
Des Chenes, Dennis 245

Descartes, René, 7, 14, 19–21, 70 n. 5, 171–174, 171–173, 174 n. 18, 178, 182, 194, 215–223, 225–226, 231, 233 n. 48, 235, 237, 239–244, 241, 244–249, 273, 307–310, *see also* Cartesianism
Descola, Philippe 17–18, 26
Desire 37, 43, 44 n 63, 45–46, 48–49, 58, 85, 99, 108, 119, 125–127, 132, 137–138, 169, 175, 218, 243, 259 n. 46, 293–294, 316
Determinism, 262–263, 270–272, 275
Devil 184, 300–304, *see also* Satan
D'Holbach, Baron 253
Diderot, Denis, 251, 253–256
Dillon, Brian 25 n. 18
Diogenes Laertius 179
Dodds, E. R. 69 n.1
Dombrowski, Daniel A. 69 n.1
Doris, John 280–282, 284
Drama 74–75
Dualism 18, 21, 28, 29 n. 27, 40–41, 44–45, 47, 73, 77 n. 24, 89–90, 92, 97, 99, 178, 181 n. 48, 247–248, 250–251
Duchesneau, François 191, 202 n. 39, 203, 204, 205 n. 47, 207
Duden, Barbara 23 n. 14
Dwyer, Dominic M. 290 n. 28
Dwyer, S. 289 n. 24
Dyer Williams, Lesley-Anne 12
Dyson, R. W. 101 n. 45

Eagleton, Terry 273
Egoism and Egoistic Behavior 291–292
Eilberg-Schwartz, Howard 110, 111 n. 4
Eisenmann, Esti 121 n. 20
Elisabeth of Bohemia 218–222, 235
Elizabeth I of England 320
Emanation 76, 79, 100–101, 107
Embodiment 241–244, 256, 260, 262, 265, 267, 273–275
Emotion 29–30, 46, 221, 277–279, 282–283, 285–286, 288–291, 293–294, 309–310
Empedocleanism 72
Engels, Friedrich 254–255
English College in Rome 311, 313, 315, 316

Entelechy 76–77, 192, 197–199, 201, 203, 205–206, 209
Epicurus and Epicureanism, 19 n. 5, 72, 78, 103, 248
Equiano, Olaudah (Gustavus Vassa) 5
Eran, Amira 114 n. 7, 131 n. 48
Erasistratus 38
Euclidean geometry 313, 314
Extension (Spatial) 20, 90 n. 7, 93, 95, 114, 148, 185, 217, 222, 226–228, 230–231, 235, 239

Fardella, Michaelangelo 192 n. 8, 198 n. 27, 205 n. 46
Fatalism 182
Fehr, Ernst 288 n. 22
Festinger, Leon 290
Fichant, Michel 197 n. 23
Ficino, Marsilio 319
Fields, Keota 215 n. 1
Flanagan, Owen J. 280 n. 4
Flesh 90–92, 94–100, 102
Fontaine, T. A. M. 131 n. 48
Form 54–60, 64–65, 81, 84, 86, 88 n. 3, 91–99, 107, 146–147, 149, 152–154, 158–159, 164, 166, 170
Foucault, Michel 24 n. 16, 40 n. 52, 260 n. 50, 304 n. 5, 304–305
Fox, Kieran C. R. 286 n. 15
Frede, Dorothea 40 n. 52, 48 n. 75

Gächter, Simon 288 n. 21
Gal, Ofer 243 n. 4
Galen 36, 41 n. 54, 248
Gallonio, Antonio 315–316
Ganeri, Jonardon 295 n. 35
Garfield, J. 295 n. 35
Gassendi, Pierre 219
Gaub, Hieronymus 248–250
Gaukroger, Stephen 15, 245
Gaultier, Abraham 253
Gavrylenko, Valeria 29 n. 28, 31 n. 32
Gawronski, Bertram 290
Gayon, Jean 270 n. 65
Gelfand, Toby 260 n. 50

Gell, Alfred 31 n. 33
Generation (Processes of) 56, 57 n. 29, 61, 92 n. 16, 97, 140, 146–147, 154 n. 20, 179, 256, 320–321, 326, 328
Gersh, Stephen 70 n. 3, n. 5
Gerson, Lloyd P. 76 n. 22, 77, 78 n. 27
Gersonides (Gershon, Levi ben) 119
Giglioni, Guido 176 n. 24
Gilbert, William 319–320
Gill, Christopher 29 n. 27, 47 n. 71
Gilmour, Gary 290 n. 28
Gilson, Etienne 89 n. 7
God and The Gods 2–3, 5, 9, 13, 31, 33, 35, 37, 65–67, 73, 76, 80, 88 n. 2, 99–100, 115–117, 121–126, 127 n. 37, 129, 133–135, 138–139, 144, 146–150, 155, 157–158, 161–163, 164 n. 57, 165, 171–187, 195, 197 n. 23, 226–230, 232–234, 236, 238–239, 251 n. 27, 300, 303, 312, 317–318
God (Stoic) 71, 179–180
Goldie, Peter 286
Gossett, Suzanne 311 n. 1, 312 n. 2
Gnosticism, 70, 78–81, 86
Gorham, Geoffrey 13, 171 n. 1, 172 n. 3, 173 n. 6, 174 n. 17, 178 n. 36, 182 n. 49, 219 n. 12
Granada, Miguel A. 319 n. 6
Grant, Edward 317 n. 2
Gravity (Newtonian) 318
Greene, J. 289 n. 24
Griswold, Charles L. 84 n. 36
Grmek, Mirko Drazen 263 n. 57, 270 n. 66
Gundert, Beate 39 n. 50
Gurtler, Gary M. 73 n. 13

Habit and Habitual 99, 279–280, 283–284, 286, 295, 309
Hacking, Ian 273
Hadot, Ilsetraut 88 n. 1
Hadot, Pierre 24 n. 16
Halevi, Judah 130 n. 45, 132, 133, 136–137
Haller, Albrecht von 248, 249 n. 21, 251, 259–260
Halliwell, Stephen 70 n. 3

INDEX

Hamlyn, D.W. 56 n. 28
Haney, Craig 277 n. 1
Hanson, A. E. 39 n. 47
Harman, Gilbert 280–282, 284
Harris, P. L. 18 n. 3
Hauser, M. 289 n. 24
Havelock, Eric 42
Health 34, 36, 39 n. 49, 43–44, 98, 100, 115, 133, 245–246, 257, 265, 320, 322
Hedley, Douglas 70 n. 3
Hegel, Georg Wilhelm Friedrich 70 n. 5, 261 n. 54
Heim, Maria 291 n. 29
Hemsterhuis, Franz 253
Hendrix, John 70 n. 3
Henry of Ghent 154 n. 23, 155 n. 25
Herophilus 38
Herring, Emily 15
Hesiod 27 n. 24
Hill, Edmund 98 n. 35, n. 37
Himmler, Heinrich 289–290
Hirai, Hiro 319 n. 9
Hippocrates and Hippocratic philosophy 19, 22, 24, 31 n. 32, 32, 35 n. 38, 36 n. 39, n. 40, n. 41, 38–39, 48, 266, 327
Hobbes, Thomas 13, 172–186, 252–253
Hoffman, Paul 216 n. 3, 218 n. 10
Holmes, Brooke 7, 12, 20 n. 6, 20 n. 7, 23 n. 16, 27 n. 24, 36 n. 42, 39 n. 51, 41 n. 55, 48 n. 75, 90 n. 7
Hölscher, Ludger 90 n. 8
Hölzel, B. K. 287 n. 18
Homer 7, 11, 21–22, 26–31
Horn, Christopher 77 n. 24
Huebner, Bryce 289 n. 24
Hugh of St. Victor 144–145
Huneman, Philippe 14, 252 n. 28, 260 n. 49, 264, n. 61
Hursthouse, Rosalind 279 n. 2
Hutchins, Barnaby 246, n. 13
Hylomorphism 12, 25, 70–71, 76–78, 81, 86, 191, 197, 201, 212, see also Entelechy
Hypnosis 326

Ibn Daud, Abraham 113–114, 119, 130–131
Ibn Gabirol, Solomon 113, 127–130
Ibn Tzaddiq, Yoseph 114–115
Imagination and Imaginary 52, 63, 90, 120, 141, 152–153, 167, 173–174, 183, 217, 221–222, 237, 239, 278, 304, 309, 321
Image 5, 23 n. 14, 64, 73, 79, 82–85, 100, 135, 207, 254–255, 273 n. 70, 294, 304, 310, 315
Imitation 84–85
Intellect 150, 153, 154–156, 160–161, 163–164, 166–170
Intellect (agent) 154, 160, 162
Intellect (potential) 146, 154, 160–162, 168
Intelligible World 74, 79–80, 83–85
Internal environment, see milieu intérieur
Isaac Israeli 112
Isen, Alice M. 280 n. 3
Ishiguro, Hidé 202 n. 37

Jacobs, Louis 110 n. 3
James, William 285, 286 n. 11
Jesseph, Douglas 173 n. 7, n. 14, 174 n. 19
Jesuits 313
Jewish 13, 78 n. 29, 109–112, 115, 117, 120, 126, 132, 133, 135 n. 57, 138–139, 142
Johannsen, Wilhelm 325, 329–330
Johnson, Mark 289 n. 24
Jouanna, Jacques 22 n. 11

Kaitaro, Timo 255 n. 39
Kalligas, Paul 76 n. 21
Kalogiratou, Androniki 74
Kassler, Jamie C. 182 n. 50
Kepler, Johannes 319–322
Kerr, Catherine E. 287 n. 17
Kersten, Felix 290
Kirk, Ulrich 287–289
Kirkebøen, Geir 273 n. 72
Knappett, C. 31 n. 32
Knowledge 18, 24, 38, 40, 60–65, 109, 111, 129, 131, 133–135, 139, 143–144, 150–151, 154–156, 159–163, 166, 169–170, 175–176, 193, 223 n. 32, 227, 236, 252, 263, 265, 267, 274–275, 318, 319 n. 7

La Mettrie, Julien Offray de, 247–249, 251, 253, 255, 274
Lambek, Michael 18 n. 2, 21 n. 8
Lang, Helen 12, 20 n. 6, 25 n. 19, 40 n. 53
Lazar, S. W. 287 n. 18
Le Camus, Antoine 251–252
Leenhardt, Maurice 8
Leeuwenhoek, Antony von 192, 199
Leibniz, Gottfried Wilhelm and Leibnizian 13–14, 183–184, 186, 189–194, 196–212, 244, 246, 258 n. 45, 326, 329
Leijenhorst, Cees 169, 172 n. 6, 173 n. 14, 174 n. 19
Lenz, Martin 163 n. 51
Lesch, James E. 260 n. 51
Lévi-Strauss, Claude 9
Levin, Paula F. 280 n. 3
Levin, Susan B. 43 n. 60
Life 52–53, 55–57, 65–66, 88 n. 2, 88 n. 3, 94, 101–106, 108
Lipsius, Justus 180, 182
Lloyd, G. E. R. 47 n. 70
Locke, John 174 n. 18, 184
Lowe, Jonathan E. 90 n. 8
Lucretius 103
Lupoli 172 n. 6
Lutz, Antoine 286 n. 13
Lydall, Emma S. 290 n. 28

Machine 189–190, 193–196, 197 n. 23, n. 25, 203, 206, 207 n. 50, 209, 211, 217, 243, 245–247, 253–259, 269, 273–274, 318, 319 n. 8
MacLean, K. A. 287 n. 13
Magendie, François, 266–269, 271, 275–276
Maimonides 117–119, 130 n. 45, 132, 133–134, 137–138
Malebranche, Nicholas 199, 219
Malpighi, Marcello 199, 202 n. 39
Manichaen and Manichaenism 88–90, 91 n. 10, 96
Mann, William 88 n. 1
Manning, Gideon 247
Marshall, Colin 224 n. 33

martyrology 315, 316
Marx, Karl 247, 254 n. 35
Matter 52–60, 64–67, 88 n. 3, 90–100, 104, 106–107, 144–149, 152, 154–155, 158–159, 164, 166, 170
Materialism, materialist, 6, 25, 28, 41, 71, 75–77, 78, 172–173, 178, 180–181, 183–184, 186–187, 244–245, 250–254, 273–274
Matson, Wallace I. 19 n. 4
Matthews, Gareth 99 n. 37
Matter 70, 71–74, 76–77, 83, 85–86
Maupertuis 255 n. 36, 326–327
Mazzio, Carla 312 n. 2
Mechanism (Functional) 261, 270–271, 276, 318
Mechanism (Mechanical Philosophy) 162, 194, 204, 241, 244–246, 248, 253, 258, 273–276, 304, 318
Meditation and Mindfulness 285–287
Meixner, Uwe 90 n. 8
Melamed, Yitzhak 227, 228 n. 43
Melzack, Ronald 309–310
Memory 141, 152
Mencius 282
Menn, Stephen 19 n. 5
Mercer, Christia 203 n. 40
Merchant, Carolyn 244 n. 8
Merleau-Ponty, Maurice 242, 243 n. 6
Merrit, Maria 284–285
Mersenne, Marin 173, 182
Meyrav, Yoav 13
Miles, Margaret 70 n. 4
Milgram, Stanley 280, 284–285, 292–293, *see also* Stanford Prison Experiment
Milieu intérieur 262–263, 269, 272, 274–276
Miller, Thomas M. 40 n. 53, 45 n. 65
Mimesis, *see* Imitation
Mind 13–14, 18–22, 24–28, 30, 35–37, 39, 62–64, 72, 80, 82, 90, 98–99, 106, 125–127, 136, 142, 150, 163, 176, 178–179, 194, 215, 216 n. 3, 217–227, 229 n. 44, 230–240, 242, 244 n. 7, 246–253, 273, 276, 286, 294–295, 308, 319 n. 7, *see also* Soul

INDEX

Mind-Body Problem 19 n. 4, 20, 25 n. 18, 215, 218, 220, 223 n. 32, 225 n. 35, 229 n. 44, 231, 236, 239, 247–249, 251–253
Mintz, Samuel 180 n. 44, 183 n. 55
Mol, Annemarie 22 n. 12
Monad 191, 196, 199, 204, 206, 207 n. 50, 326, 329
More, Henry 171 n. 2, 178, 179 n. 40, 184
Mormonism 186
Moutafakis, Nicholas J. 70 n. 3
Mover (First, Unmoved) 53 n. 10, 65, 67, *see also* God
Munro, Alexander 259

Nachtomy, Ohad 14, 202 n. 38, 210 n. 53, 258 n. 45
Naddaf, Gerard 33 n. 19
Nájera, Rafael 12
Narcotics 326
Nasifoglu, Yelda 15
Neo-Stoicism 180
Neuroscience 11–12, 287
Newton, Isaac and Newtonianism 171–172, 185, 267, 318, 326
Nicene Creed 173, 177
Nichols, Shaun 289 n. 24, n. 25
Niederbacher, Bruno 90 n. 8
Normore, Calvin 153 n. 17
Nussbaum, Martha 23 n. 16
Nutrition 55, 57, 60

O'Brien, Denis 72 n. 12
O'Callaghan, John 98 n. 37
Ockham, William of 153 n. 17, 154 n. 23, 155–156, 162–165
Oken, Lorenz 326
Opsomer, Jan 73 n. 15
Orbs, mechanical 317–318
Oresme, Nicole 318
Origen 3
Organs (Organic, Organism) 243–244, 254–255, 257–258, 260–263, 265–266, 272, 275
Organism 94–95, 102, 114, 116

Painting 84
Paracelsian 319
Pascal, Blaise 193
Pasnau, Robert 145 n. 3, 149 n. 7, 155 n. 25, 156 n. 26, 166 n. 62
Passmore, John Arthur 180 n. 44
Paster, G. K. 242 n. 4
Patrizi, Francesco 319
Paul, Erich 186 n. 71
Pépin, François 254 n. 36
Perceiving and Perception 7, 11, 14, 18, 21 n. 8, 31, 37, 45, 49, 52–53, 79–80, 124, 133–134, 144, 153, 155, 160, 162, 167–168, 218, 234–237, 242, 261, 273, 284, 286, 330, *see also* Sense and Sensation
Perler, Dominik 13
Person, Personhood and Personal Identity 17–22, 24, 26–32, 37, 40–41, 44 n. 63, 47, 49, 83, 85, 99, 101, 103, 106, 125, 130, 139–141, 157, 243, 280, 291–293, 300, 303, 305, 310, 329
Peterman, Alison 14
Peterson, Linda 170 n. 70
Phantom limbs 307–310
Philips, John F. 72 n. 12
Physiology 4, 15, 24, 244–245, 247, 248 n. 19, 253, 255–256, 259–267, 269–275
Pichot, André 328–329
Pickavé, Martin 150 n. 8, 151 n. 9, n. 11, 155 n. 24
Pino, Tikhon Alexander 77 n. 26
Pitcairne, Archibald 246
Plato and Platonism 3, 12, 19–21, 23 n. 16, 24–26, 39–49, 69 n. 1, 70 n. 5, 72, 73 n. 13, 77–79, 81, 83, 87, 88 n. 4, 105–106, 112–113, 144–145, 147–148, 186, 319
Plotinus 69–86, 88, 93 n. 18, 95 n. 25, 100, 103, 107
Poetry 84
Pollock, Sheldon 7
Pompanazzi, Pietro 167
Porphyry 69, 78n, 81–86, 100 n. 42, 106
Porter, J. I. 29 n. 27

INDEX

Potency and Potentiality 51, 57, 58, 60–61, 63–64, 73 n. 13, 88 n. 3, 94, 107, 146–147, 158, 243, *see also* Intellect (Potential)
Primus, Kristin 209–215 n. 1
Prinz, Jesse 289 n. 24
Pseudo-Dionysius 148, 161
Ptolemy 38
Purves, Alex 31 n. 32
Pyle, Andrew 199 n. 30, 203 n. 39

Radner, Daisie 218 n. 10, 238 n. 62
Raphson, Joseph 184–185
Rapp, Christof 19 n. 4
Rees, V. 70 n. 3
Regier, Jonathan 15, 321 n. 14
Regius, Henricus 247
Reiss, T. 242 n. 4
Renehan 29 n. 27
Renouvier, Charles 247
Renz, Ursula 225 n. 35, 232 n. 46
Ricard, Mathieu 294
Richert, R. A. 18 n. 3
Reverso, E. 181 n. 48
Robinson, T. M. 41 n. 56, 44 n. 63
Roest, Bert 70 n. 3
Rorty, Amelie Oksenberg 242 n. 1
Rosen, Edward 319 n. 8
Roskies, Adina 289 n. 25
Rouelle, Guillaume-François 254
Rozemond, Marleen 218 n. 10, 221 n. 25
Rublack, Ursula 242 n. 3
Rust, Joshua 283 n. 8

Saadya Gaon 115–117, 118, 119, 121–125, 139–140, 141, 142
Satan 300–304, *see also* Devil
Satlow, Michael L. 135 n. 57
Sawday, Jonathan 243, 244 n. 7
Scaliger, Julius Caesar 319
Schelling, Friedrich Wilhelm Joseph 326
Schopenhauer, Arthur 261 n. 54
Scotus, Duns 154 n. 23, 156 n. 26
Schroeder, Timothy 289 n. 25
Schwartz, Dov 135 n. 57

Sculpture 84
Schwitzgebel, Eric 283 n. 8
Self and Selfhood 6, 9, 11–12, 17–20, 25, 28, n. 26, 30–32, 36–37, 42–43, 49, 135–136, 169, 196, 244 n. 7, 246, 273 n. 71, 276, 278, 282, 291–292, 303, 305, 309, 315–316
Sellars, J. 176 n. 24, 180 n. 44, 183 n. 54
Seneca 320
Sense and Sensation 7, 18, 29, 31, 33, 45, 53, 58, 60–64, 66, 79–80, 102–103, 122, 124, 128–131, 143–144, 152–155, 160, 162, 167–168, 175–178, 216–217, 220–222, 223 n. 32, 229, 231, 234–235, 239–240, 242, 246, 250, 259 n. 46, 261, 267 n. 64, 307–309, 328, *see also* Perceiving and Perception
Sex and Sexuality 34, 110–111, 116, 126, 134 n. 56, 138, 243, 305, 321
Shapiro, Lisa 245
Shaw, L. L. 293 n. 33
Shoemaker, Sidney 90 n. 8
Simmons, Alison 215 n. 1, 223 n. 32
Singer, Tania 294
Slingerland, Edward 280–283, 285
Smith, Justin E. H. 190, 192, 203 n. 42, 204 n. 44, 317 n. 1
Snell, Bruno 7, 21–22, 26–29
Socrates 19, 24–26, 41–48
Solmsen, F. 36 n. 39
Sorabji, Richard 93 n. 18, 99 n. 37
Soul 18–28, 40–49, *see also* Mind
Soul, 70, 71, 73–78, 82, 85–86
    Individual Soul, 79, 83
    Universal Soul, 76, 79
    World Soul, 80
South, James B. 166 n. 62, 167, 168 n. 65
Space, Renaissance theories of 322–323
Species (Classificatory) 159
Species (Sensible and Intelligible) 152–156, 161–165, 168–169
Spinoza, Baruch 13–14, 172, 186, 215–216, 219, 224–240, 241, 253 n. 32
Spirit and Spirits 3, 7–8, 172–176, 179 n. 40, 180–181, 220, 235, 246, 318, 319 n. 7, 322
Spirit (Holy) 88

Spiritual and Spirituality 107, 110–111, 125, 135, 141, 144–145, 152, 159, 168, 191, 212
Spiritus (in celestial physics) 322
Springborg, Patricia 172 n. 6, 182 n. 53
squaring of the circle 314, 316
Stahl, Georg-Ernst 244–245, 246 n. 11, 254, 264
Stanford Prison Experiment (*see also* Milgram, Stanley) 277, 280, 282, 285, 293
Steel, Carlos 40 n. 53, 47 n. 71
Stern-Gillet, Suzanne 77 n. 25
Stewart, Matthew 186 n. 71
Stoicism 19 n. 5, 36, 38, 71, 72, 78, 87, 178–182
Stolberg, Michael 322
Strauss, Leo 173 n. 7
Stroumsa, Sarah 125 n. 33
Stump, Eleonore 153, 156 n. 26, n. 27
Suárez, Francisco 144, 151 n. 11, 155 n. 25, 156, 157 n. 29, 163–169
Suarez-Nani, Tiziana 148 n. 5, n. 6
Substance 3, 12, 14, 19 n. 5, 45 n. 65, 54–59, 64, 88 n. 3, n. 4, 89–90, 92–94, 96–99, 101, 107, 113, 121–123, 141, 145–149, 155, 157–161, 164, 167, 173–175, 178–181, 184, 190 n. 2, 191, 193, 196–209, 211–212, 217–219, 226–228, 231, 245, 247–248, 250–252, 256, 266, 275, 320 n. 12
Substrate 55–58, 92 n. 16, 147
Sullivan, R. 183 n. 55, 185 n. 69
Sutton, John 242 n. 4, 244 n. 8, 245
Swammerdam, Jan 192, 199 n. 30
Richard Swinburne 90 n. 8
Sze, Jocelyn A. 286 n. 16

Telesio, Bernardino 319
Tenison, Thomas 183
Terada, Motoichi 255 n. 40, 258
Tertullian 181, 182 n. 49
Teske, Roland 98 n. 36, 100 n. 41
Thomson, Anne 183 n. 55, 255 n. 38, n. 40

Thompson, Evan 244 n. 7, 295 n. 35
Thought and Thinking 52–53, 58, 60–67, 107
Tissue(s) 260–261, 265
Toivanen, Juhana 88 n. 4
Toland, John 172, 184–186
Torture 312, 315–316
Tribble, Evelyn B. 244 n. 8
Trivers, Robert 288–289
Turner, John Douglas 70 n. 5

Ultimatum Game 287–288
Unmoved Mover argument 84

Venel, Gabriel-François 254
Vernant, Jean-Pierre 28 n. 26
Victorinus 88
Virgil 319
Vitalism 14, 244–245, 255–259, 262–263, 266, 267, 269, 271, 274–276, 320
Viveiros de Castro, Eduardo 9
Vlastos, Gregory 33
Von Staden, Heinrich 38 n. 46

Wallis, John 181
Watson, James 330
Weber, D. 172 n. 6, 173 n. 14, 177 n. 31, 178 n. 39, 179 n. 40
Weisman, August 328–330
Williams, Bernard 17, 21, 29 n. 27
Williams, Elizabeth 258 n. 46
Willis, Thomas 4
Wilson, Catherine 197 n. 24, 203 n. 39
Wilson, Margaret 218 n. 10, 238 n. 62
Wolfe, Charles T. 14, 243 n. 4, 249 n. 20, 255 n. 40, 256 n. 42, 258, 259 n. 49
Wright, John P. 249 n. 21, 259 n. 47

Young, Iris Marion 242 n. 1, n. 4

Zarka, Yves-Charles 178 n. 38
Zimbardo, Philip 277